*Special Education
for a
New Century*

Special Education
for a
New Century

LAUREN I. KATZMAN

ALLISON GRUNER GANDHI

WENDY S. HARBOUR

and

J. D. LAROCK

Editors

Harvard Educational Review

Reprint Series No. 41

Library of Congress Control Number 2004116558

ISBN 0-916690-44-X

Published by the Harvard Educational Review,
an imprint of the Harvard Education Publishing Group

Harvard Educational Review
8 Story Street
Cambridge, MA 02138

Cover Design: Anne Carter
Typography: Sheila Walsh

The typefaces used in this book are Kuenstler 480 (Bitstream) for text
and Tiepolo (Adobe) for display.

Contents

Introduction

———— $\mathcal{S}$ ————

Special Education for a New Century is a wide-ranging, timely collection of essays on the complex and evolving special education field. It addresses and illuminates several issues of special interest to educators, policymakers, and scholars today: the need to confront assumptions about students with disabilities, to connect issues of disability and race in special education, and to deal with the complexities of implementing inclusive practices in a standards-based environment. Federal special education law is now thirty years old, and the education of students with disabilities has changed enormously in that time. The first edition of this book, *Special Education at the Century's End*, focused on the first twenty years of progress in federal special education law. The book presented a collection of seminal articles that helped to shape the context of special education as it is today, and it remains a sought-after text. This new edition, *Special Education for a New Century*, addresses the current context of special education policy and practice, which coincides with an era of standards-based reform. It is our intention to help set an agenda for the future of special education by providing policymakers, researchers, and practitioners with a collection of articles that draws on thirty years of experience to challenge us to further improve the educational experiences of students with disabilities.

The education of students with disabilities has advanced with dramatic speed over the last thirty years. Before 1975, states were not required to admit students with disabilities to public schools, and consequently, one million children were excluded from public education (U.S. Department of Education, 1995). With few options, many families turned to residential institutions, and close to 200,000 people with significant disabilities lived in these facilities, known predominantly for their dismal living conditions and lack of any educational services (Blatt, 1970). Thirty years later, in 2005, there are more than five million students with disabilities being educated in U.S. public schools, representing over 11 percent of the school-age population (U.S. Department of Education, 2002); fewer than 3,500 students remain institutionalized (Hehir & Gamm, 1999). Today, students with disabilities are arguably the most legally protected student group in our public schools; Section 504 of the Rehabilitation Act of 1973 prohibits discrimination against individuals with disabilities, and the Education for all Handicapped Children Act of 1975, renamed the Individuals with Disabilities Education Act (IDEA) in 1990, provides students who have disabilities with a "free appropriate public education" in the "least restrictive environment." Under IDEA, schools receive federal funds to provide special education or other services designed to support the unique educational needs of students with disabilities.

Special Education for a New Century focuses on the progress being made in the field of special education today, which is being driven largely by the 1997 and 2004 reauthorizations of IDEA and by the No Child Left Behind Act of 2001 (NCLB). While the original special education legislation ensured access to public schools, the 1997 reauthorization shifted IDEA's focus to ensure access to the general education curriculum and to further clarify that students with disabilities are to be educated in the least restrictive environment (U.S. Department of Education, 1995). Concurrently, NCLB requires that schools be held accountable for the educational attainment of all students, including those with disabilities. The 2004 reauthorization of IDEA further strengthens the accountability that schools have for ensuring that their students with disabilities reach high academic standards by aligning IDEA's accountability standards with NCLB requirements. Together, these laws work to bring the responsibility for the education of students with disabilities back into the realm of general education by reconnecting what has historically been two separate educational entities — for students with and for those without disabilities. The opportunity, and challenge, of this current period is to develop a more inclusive educational experience for students with disabilities, one that is based on high academic standards and on practices that bring the majority of special education services into general education classrooms.

Without diminishing the enormous progress made in the field of special education, it is important to recognize that there are a number of underlying issues that continue to plague the effective education of students with disabilities. *Special Education for a New Century* addresses three of these issues: assumptions surrounding the ability of students with disabilities to achieve to high standards; the difficulty of effectively connecting special education to issues of social justice, particularly as they relate to students of color; and the challenges of implementing special education reform within a standards-based policy context. As the book's editors, in an effort to reflect the tenets of inclusive education, we have joined articles from the field of special education with others not specifically focused on the field, such as Lisa Delpit's classic, "The Silenced Dialogue: Power and Pedagogy in Educating Other People's Children." We hope that this book can be a model for educators to use ideas in the field of education at large to broaden the dialogue about best practice in special education.

The three issues discussed in this book address some of the current realities in schools. For example, in schools today, negative assumptions persist concerning what students with disabilities can achieve. Disability is seen as pathological, a medical condition that prevents individuals from achieving to high academic standards. Such negative assumptions have led to a standard of low expectations for students with disabilities (Hebbeler, 1993) and at times even paternalism, with educators seeking to protect students from perceived frustration and not exposing them to challenging academic standards. Rarely is disability seen as an integral and positive part of a student's identity or as part of the overall diversity of a school. Furthermore, these attitudes are rarely examined within the wider framework of societal attitudes about disability and difference. This has influenced how special education services have been implemented: as a separate system within general education. Students with disabilities have had to earn their way out of this system and into general education classes by seeming as nondisabled as possible.

The fact that more and more students with disabilities are being educated in general education environments (U.S. Department of Education, 2002) does not necessarily mean that educators believe students with disabilities can succeed in general education classes, even with the supports and accommodations that many will undoubtedly receive. Changing beliefs is a tremendous task and will take a great deal of time. In Part One of this book, "Challenging Assumptions," we offer three articles meant to start conversations that help shift educators' paradigms toward more positive assumptions about the potential of students with disabilities. Our hope is that educators will reconceptualize their perceptions and describe disability as part of the overall diversity of the school, and thus begin to turn their attention to improving students' access to curricula, rather than to "fixing" students' disabilities.

Assumptions about students with disabilities often parallel assumptions held about the abilities of students of color, and students of color who are classified as having a disability often face double discrimination. The parallels between students with disabilities and students of color in their struggle for equal access date back at least as far as 1954, during the *Brown v. Board of Education* case. Basing their argument on the concept of desegregation, parents of children with mental retardation were the first in the disability community to organize and fight for equal access to public schools. In 1967, Judge D. Frank Wilkins ordered the state of Utah to admit to school two children with mental retardation who had previously been denied access. He wrote, "Segregation, even though perhaps well intentioned, under the apparent sanction of law and state authority, has a tendency to retard the educational, emotional, and mental development of the children" (Hehir & Gamm, 1999, p. 211). The content of Section 504 of the Rehabilitation Act of 1973, which prohibits discrimination against otherwise qualified individuals with disabilities in any program or activity receiving federal funds (Silverstein, 2000), is almost identical to that of Title VI of the Civil Rights Act of 1964, which prohibits discrimination based on race, color, or national origin (National Research Council [NRC], 1999).

Regardless of these intimate connections between struggles for access, issues concerning the education of students with disabilities and the education of students of color are most often seen as two distinct entities. For example, students of color, particularly African American males, are disproportionately represented in special education (Oswald, Coutinho, & Best, 2002). The overrepresentation of students of color has been an issue since the *Brown* decision. As desegregation became law, so began the practice of overidentifying students of color as disabled and segregating them from the general education mainstream. In 1965, just one year after the Civil Rights Act of 1964, there were allegations that schools in San Francisco used "special education classes as a cover for segregation" (Harry & Anderson, 1995, p. 603). Dunn (1968) found that, in the late 1960s, classes with mentally retarded children served a disproportionate number of minority students. Congress identified the disproportionate representation of students of color as such an important issue that they mandated a study in 1982, and again in 2002, both of which found that students of color remain disproportionately represented in special education (NRC, 1982, 2002). Additionally, African Americans and Hispanics are much more likely than their White counterparts to be educated in substantially separate classrooms (Fierros & Conroy, 2002). These two issues — disproportionate representation of students of color and segregative special education classes — are often raised as distinct issues. In this book we recognize that there is an opportunity for educators to connect such issues and to develop new paradigms for change. In Part Two of this book, "Critical Conversations about Disability and Race in Special Education," we offer three articles intended to spark dialogue about the connections between inclusive education and the education of students of color. We hope these articles will inspire readers to think about how these issues intersect in their own work and to move toward models that more comprehensively address the needs of all students.

Change, however, is difficult. Now that students with disabilities are being educated more and more in inclusive settings and federal requirements have mandated for the first time that all students achieve to high academic standards, educators are often at a loss as to how to meet these demands. How do we realize the ideals of individualization and access to the general education curriculum in an environment that calls for standardization of curriculum? How do we implement the federal legislation of IDEA and NCLB, which is inherently linear, within the inherently chaotic nature of schools? Such are the dilemmas of implementing effective educational services for students with disabilities.

We find such dilemmas instructive and see them as windows of opportunity. As educators work to meet these new demands, we see opportunities to enact radical changes in the structure and organization of schools. In fact, such changes will be necessary to support all students in meeting high academic standards. In order to effectively educate students with disabilities, schools will have to develop structures to support collaborative practices between special and general educators. Such practices bring diverse expertise and targeted resources into the general education class and, consequently, all students benefit. In Part Three, "Inclusive Practice in a Standards-Based World," we include three articles that ask educators to examine the implementation of practices that raise expectations for the academic achievement of students with disabilities. These articles raise both theoretical and practical questions and draw from examinations of special education and standards-based reforms. We hope that readers will use these articles to support changes and to develop more inclusive practices in schools.

The editors of this book encourage researchers, policymakers, and practitioners to use these articles to generate conversation and action that support a stronger education for students with disabilities. By changing assumptions, by participating in authentic discussions and actions that connect issues of disability and race, and by grappling with the dilemmas of implementing more inclusive special education services, students with disabilities, we believe, will benefit. Further, it is our experience and belief that when students with disabilities are educated more effectively in a school, all students in that school are educated more effectively. Therefore, we hope that researchers, policymakers, and practitioners who do not typically see special education as their realm will see how it can benefit schools. Ultimately, creating rigorous and meaningful educational experiences for our students with disabilities brings out the best in our educators, schools, and communities.

Lauren I. Katzman

REFERENCES

Blatt, B. (1970). *Exodus from pandemonium.* Boston: Allyn & Bacon.

Donovan, M. S., & Cross, C. T. (Eds.). (2002). *Minority students in special and gifted education.* Washington, DC: National Academy Press.

Dunn, L. M. (1968). Special education for the mildly retarded: Is it justifiable? *Exceptional Children, 23,* 5–21.

Fierros, E. G., & Conroy, J. W. (2002). Double jeopardy: An exploration of restrictiveness and race in special education In D. J. Losen & G. Orfield (Eds.), *Racial inequity in special education* (pp. 39–70). Cambridge, MA: Harvard Education Press.

Hebbeler, K. (1993). *Traversing the mainstream: Regular education and students with disabilities in secondary school.* Washington, DC: U.S. Department of Education.

Hehir, T., & Gamm, S. (1999). Special education: From legalism to collaboration. In J. P. Heubert (Ed.), *Law and school reform: Six strategies for promoting educational equity* (pp. 205–227). New Haven, CT: Yale University Press.

Heller, K. A., Holtzman, W. H., & Messick, S. (Eds.). (1982). *Placing children in special education: A strategy for equity.* Washington, DC: National Academy Press.

Heubert, J. P., & Hauser, R. M. (Eds.). (1999). *High stakes: Testing for tracking, promotion and graduation.* Washington, DC: National Academy Press.

No Child Left Behind Act of 2001, 20 U.S.C. § 6301 et seq.

Oswald, D. P., Coutinho, M. J., & Best, A. M. (2002). Community and school predictors of overrepresentation of minority children in special education). In D. J. Losen & G. Orfield (Eds.), *Racial inequity in special education* (pp. 1–13). Cambridge, MA: Harvard Education Press.

Silverstein, R. (2000). Emerging disability policy framework: A guidepost for analyzing public policy. *Iowa Law Review, 85,* 1691–1806.

U.S. Department of Education. (1995). *Individuals with Disabilities Education Act Amendments of 1995: Reauthorization of the Individuals with Disabilities Education Act (IDEA).* Washington, DC: Author.

U.S. Department of Education. (2002). *Twenty-fourth annual report to Congress on the implementation of the Individuals with Disabilities Education Act.* Washington, DC: Author.

Part One:
Challenging Assumptions

"There is more than one way to walk, talk, paint, read, and write. Assuming otherwise is the root of fundamental inequities."
— Thomas Hehir

At the beginning of a new century, despite decades of research on best practices in special education, debates continue about inclusion versus segregation, the impact of standards-based reform on children with disabilities, the roles of law and policy in driving practice, and best practices for teachers and administrators. The authors in this section focus on a different debate than the particulars of implementation and issue a call to reexamine fundamental attitudes and assumptions underlying not only special education, but also the education and learning of all students. They also demonstrate how philosophy and theory can have direct practical effects on the debates and issues facing educators, parents, and students with disabilities.

In "Eliminating Ableism in Education," Thomas Hehir notes that assumptions about disability lead not only to lowered expectations, but also to discrimination, exclusion, and an overall "devaluation and disregard of people with disabilities." After naming these societal attitudes "ableist," Hehir asks educators to refocus their efforts on improving access to curricula and on building the strengths of students with disabilities, instead of attempting to "fix" disabilities and making assumptions about perceived deficits. Hehir suggests that best practices can be informed not only by the narratives of adults with disabilities, parents of disabled students, and students with disabilities, but also through an understanding of evolving laws, policies, and disability history. Through examples involving deaf children, children who are blind and visually impaired, and children with learning disabilities, Hehir shows how inclusive education can redefine and build on understandings of what "communicating" and "learning" really mean, and how efforts to eliminate ableism may lead to universally designed schools and classrooms.

In "The Deaf as a Linguistic Minority: Educational Considerations," Timothy Reagan looks at ableism as applied to deaf learners. He explains how a pathological view of deafness solely as a medical condition has led researchers and educators to overlook cultural and linguistic aspects of being deaf and communicating through American Sign Language. Despite its having been published before the 1988 "Deaf President Now" revolt at Gallaudet University invigorated deaf culture and disability movements, Reagan's call for bilingual and bicultural models of education is still cutting edge. This philosophy of education remains a source of contention among educators of deaf children, who essentially remain split between oralists who believe deaf children should learn through spoken communication and manualists who believe sign language should be used for communication (for a more detailed discussion of current practices in deaf education, see Marcschark & Spencer, 2003). Reagan notes that deaf people not only live with the lowered expectations that typically come with a disability label, but also with limitations that prevent people from seeing other identities or descriptors that people with disabilities may embody (limitations that people of color or English-language learners who have disabilities also experience). This article is a powerful reminder that special education may function as a tool of "imperialism," as well as a call for interdisciplinary efforts among bilingual education, general education, and special education.

Showing that Hehir's and Reagan's ideas are not an elusive ideal, the third article in this section is an ethnographic study by Christopher Kliewer and his colleagues. It provides examples of classrooms where inclusive practices successfully created the holistic view of children and learning that Hehir and Reagan describe. In "Citizenship for All in the Literate Community: An Ethnography of Young Children with Significant Disabilities in Inclusive Early Childhood Settings," preschool and kindergarten teachers redefine meanings of literacy and disability, proving that traditional labels and professional expectations do not necessarily foretell what is possible for any child. As children in this study developed their ability to use semiotic systems (e.g., alphabets, word boards, drama, poetry, symbols), they not only became more literate, but also became literate members of a larger community of learners. Kliewer et al. echo Reagan's concerns about power and education, comparing imposed limitations of significantly disabled students to historically held attitudes about the potential of slaves or agrarian workers. As they observed definitions of literacy changing in classrooms, researchers also noted how students defied labels, teachers gained confidence with flexible individualized instruction, and all students, including those without disabilities, benefited from the increased opportunities available in a classroom designed to expand learning and literacy in multiple forms.

The overarching theme among the authors in this section is that as special education continues to evolve, paradigm shifts about disability will contribute, as Kliewer et al. write, to an "awareness of human possibility" that can invigorate future research, educational practices, and policy. As debates continue within the field of education, as new medical advances and research lead to new understandings of disability, and as increasing diversity among students with disabilities requires greater interdisciplinary efforts, universal design and inclusive practices hold great promise for all teachers and learners, but only to the extent that our own historical biases and ableism do not limit the potential of such promises.

REFERENCES

Lane, H., Hoffmeister, R., & Bahan, B. (1996). *A journey into the deaf-world.* San Diego: DawnSign Press.

Marschark, M., & Spencer, P. E. (Eds.). (2003). *Oxford handbook of deaf studies, language, and education.* New York: Oxford University Press.

Shapiro, J. P. (1993). *No pity: People with disabilities forging a new civil rights movement.* New York: Times Books.

Eliminating Ableism
in Education

THOMAS HEHIR

ABLEIST ASSUMPTIONS

When Joe Ford was born in 1983, it was clear to the doctors and to Joe's mom Penny that he would likely have disabilities. What wasn't clear to Penny at the time was that she was entering a new world, that of a parent of a child with disabilities, a world in which she would have to fight constantly for her child to have the most basic of rights, a world in which deeply held negative cultural assumptions concerning disability would influence every aspect of her son's life. She and Joe had entered the world of ableist assumptions.

Penny remembers an event that made it clear that she had entered a new world of lowered expectations. She recalls her first visit with a social worker from a preschool program for kids with disabilities. This person, though empathetic and supportive, made it clear to Penny that she could not have the same dreams and aspirations for Joe that she had for her seven nondisabled children. As Penny explains, "She was aghast that I expected that Joe would one day be employed" (Ford, 1993, p. 2). Another event added further clarification. At a workshop for parents of disabled kids, Penny was told that she had to go through a period of mourning the arrival of her disabled child. Deeply insulted, Penny's response was, "I have lost a child at birth and I have had a disabled child. I know the difference. My son is a gift not a tragedy" (p. 1). Penny was quickly developing the view, held by most disability advocates, that while disability is not a tragedy, society's response to disability can have tragic consequences for those who have disabilities.

Penny had yet to benefit from the narratives of disability activists such as former U.S. Assistant Secretary of Education Judy Heumann. Throughout her eight-year tenure during the Clinton administration, Heumann emphasized that "disability only becomes a tragedy for me when society fails to provide the things we need to lead our lives — job opportunities or barrier free buildings" (Shapiro, 1994, p. 20). But Penny

Harvard Educational Review   Vol. 72   No. 1   Spring 2002, 1–32

was beginning to write her own narrative, joining legions of other like-minded activists seeking to fundamentally change the world of ableist assumptions (Ford, 1993).

Penny's early instinctual reaction to the negative assumptions held by many of the service providers she encountered led her to seek the advice of adults with disabilities. She recalls becoming friendly with an employee of the U.S. Department of Education's Office of Civil Rights (OCR), a woman who had been disabled since childhood due to a form of muscular dystrophy. As a child, when it became apparent she was disabled, she was removed from the school she was attending and moved to a separate and, in her view, inferior school. She warned Penny against going along with prevailing practices based on low expectations. Penny recalls her counsel: "Don't assume he has the same educational rights as every other child. You're going to have to fight for that" (Ford, 1993, p. 3). This woman helped Penny understand that federal law, Section 504 of the Rehabilitation Act of 1973, prohibited discrimination against her son, and that this law, along with the Individuals with Disabilities Education Act (IDEA), supported Penny's desire for a quality education for Joe.[1] However, even though these laws were strong, existing practices were often difficult to change, due to deeply held negative cultural assumptions about disability. By the time Joe was four, Penny had filed a complaint against the Chicago Public Schools with OCR seeking Joe's placement in a regular school and not in the special school into which the school system wanted to place him. She had begun the journey to secure an appropriate education for her son.

In this article, I examine how ableist assumptions influence the education of children with disabilities and how these assumptions undermine the educational attainment of these children. I ground this discussion within the context of standards-based reform and the contemporary disability rights movement. This piece is based on the relevant research, the narratives of individuals with disabilities and their parents, and my thirty years of experience in the field of education.

ABLEISM AND SCHOOLING

The various definitions of ableism in the literature share common origins that are rooted in the discrimination and oppression that many disabled people experience in society (Overboe, 1999; Weeber, 1999). Laura Rauscher and Mary McClintock (1996) define ableism as "a pervasive system of discrimination and exclusion that oppresses people who have mental, emotional and physical disabilities. . . . Deeply rooted beliefs about health, productivity, beauty, and the value of human life, perpetuated by the public and private media, combine to create an environment that is often hostile to those whose physical, mental, cognitive, and sensory abilities . . . fall out of the scope of what is currently defined as socially acceptable" (p. 198). Black disability activist and talk-show host Greg Smith captures the essence of definitions of ableism in his article "The Brother in the Wheelchair." "I've faced unintentional discrimination, and it's just as damaging as racism. . . . It's called ableism, the devaluation and disregard of people with disabilities" (Smith, 2001, p. 162).

Applied to schooling and child development, ableist preferences become particularly apparent. From an ableist perspective, the devaluation of disability results in societal attitudes that uncritically assert that it is better for a child to walk than roll, speak than sign, read print than read Braille, spell independently than use a spell-check, and hang out with nondisabled kids as opposed to other disabled kids, etc. In short, in the eyes of many educators and society, it is preferable for disabled students to do things in the same manner as nondisabled kids.

Certainly, given a world that has not been designed with the disabled in mind, being able to perform in a manner that is similar to that of nondisabled children gives disabled children distinct advantages. If efficient ambulation is possible, a child who has received the help he needs to walk is at an advantage in a barrier-filled world. Similarly, a child with a mild hearing loss who has been given the amplification and speech therapy she needs may have little difficulty functioning in a regular classroom.

However, ableist assumptions become dysfunctional when the educational and developmental services provided to disabled children focus inordinately on the characteristics of their disability to the exclusion of all else, when changing disability becomes the overriding focus of service providers and, at times, parents. Narratives of disabled people and their parents are replete with examples of how changing disability became the focus of their young lives and how such a focus denied them the opportunities taken for granted by nondisabled people. These narratives speak to the deep cultural prejudices against disability that they had to endure from an early age — that disability was negative and tragic and that "overcoming" disability was the only valued result (Ferguson & Asch, 1989; Rousso, 1984).

In *No Pity,* his history of the disability civil rights movement, Joseph Shapiro (1994) chronicles the dominant cultural responses to disability. One model is exemplified by the poster children of the muscular dystrophy telethon, which he refers to as "Tiny Tims" — "the idea that disabled people are childlike, dependent, and in need of charity and pity" (p. 14). Cyndi Jones, a disability activist and former poster child, argues that "the poster child says it's not okay to be disabled . . . but it says if you just donate money the disabled child will go away" (p. 14). Marilynn Phillips, a professor at Morgan State University who has studied images of poster children, recalls that the image of the valiant "crippled" child on crutches learning to walk emerged in the mid-1950s. She argues that children like herself who had polio before a vaccine was developed were an affront to the postwar faith in medical technology. Disabled children were now "damaged goods" who had to try harder to deserve charity and respect (p. 15).

According to Shapiro (1994), the belief that disability could be overcome led to the rise of the other dominant image of disability: the inspirational disabled person, or the "supercrip." Shapiro argues that this image is deeply moving to many nondisabled people and the press, but is widely regarded as oppressive to most disabled people. The extensive press coverage of a blind man who recently climbed Mt. Everest is a good example of the supercrip image. Cyndi Jones argues that, like the image of the poster child, this image implies that a disabled person is presumed deserving of pity — instead of respect — until the person proves capable of overcoming disability through extraordinary feats (Shapiro, 1994). Both of these dominant stereotypes of disability, "Tiny Tims" and "supercrips," have at their core ableist perspectives, the failure to accept and value disabled people as they are.

I contend that negative cultural assumptions about disability continue to have a negative influence on the education of children with disabilities. The pervasiveness of ableist assumptions in the education of these children not only reinforces prevailing prejudices against disability but may very well contribute to low levels of educational attainment and employment. School time spent devoted to activities associated with changing disability may take away from the time needed to learn academic material. In addition, the ingrained prejudice against performing activities in ways that might be more efficient for disabled people but that are different from how nondisabled perform them, such as reading Braille or using sign language, may add to educational deficits. There is considerable emerging evidence that unquestioned ableist assumptions are handicapping disabled children and are a cause of educational inequities.

I will illustrate how ableist assumptions are having a profound and negative impact on the education of children with disabilities using issues around the education of three groups: the deaf, the blind, and students with the learning disability dyslexia. I will weave in Joe and Penny's experiences, as well as my own.

THE EDUCATION OF THE DEAF

The education of deaf children provides a compelling example of ableism in action. Unlike some disability populations, such as students with significant levels of cognitive disability, educational programs for deaf children have existed in the United States for over 150 years. Therefore, there is significant history and research to draw on that should guide our efforts to improve education for the deaf.[2]

Educators who were deaf themselves heavily influenced some of the earliest educational programs for deaf children. Thomas Gallaudet, an early advocate for educating the deaf, visited Europe in 1816 seeking educational models to bring back to the United States. While in Europe, he met a talented young deaf teacher, Laurent Clerc. Together they opened the American Asylum for the Deaf and Dumb in Hartford, Connecticut, in 1817. The teachers were fluent signers and most were deaf themselves. By using American Sign Language (ASL), the school demonstrated that literacy could be raised impressively among the deaf (Baynton, 1996). In her landmark study of the impact of a high percentage of deaf people living in a Martha's Vineyard community in the 1800s, Nora Groce (1985) found that graduates of the Hartford School had achieved higher levels of literacy than many of their hearing neighbors. Unlike the deaf, many hearing people had left school early to fish or farm. Some of the less educated hearing people would bring documents to their deaf neighbors to explain. Deafness was so common on the island that most hearing people learned to sign. As a result of their relatively high education levels, deaf people held many positions of leadership in the community.

Despite these promising early results, the education of deaf children was severely set back by oralism in the latter half of the nineteenth century. Spurred on by the establishment of the Clarke School for the Deaf and by the advocacy of Samuel Gridley

Howe, the founder of the Perkins Institute for the Blind, and of Horace Mann, the oralist methodology claimed success in educating deaf children by teaching them to lip-read and speak. This methodology prohibited the use of manual language, as proponents felt that signing decreased the motivation to learn to speak. Another prominent advocate of the methodology was Alexander Graham Bell, who was, ironically, married to a deaf woman. Bell was a staunch supporter of oralism and sought to have sign language banned from programs for the deaf. In a speech delivered to the National Academy of Sciences in 1883, he further advocated for the enactment of eugenics laws to forbid the "intermarriage of deaf mutes" (Baynton, 1996). As Shapiro (1994) points out:

> Oralism fit well with the conformist spirit of the times. The Victorian culture was unsparing toward minority culture. . . . If one did not have speech then one did not have language and, went the thinking that dated back to Aristotle, was presumably unable to reason. To remain silent then was to be prey to the devil. All this suggested that deafness was a sickness, something that needed to be cured. Oralism held out the hope of correction. (p. 90)

The influence of Bell and other oralist advocates would prove to be surprisingly enduring, even to this day. This remains true in the education of deaf children as an enduring legacy of ableism. For many, the deaf "supercrip" is the deaf person who can read lips and speak, despite the fact that few deaf people master oralism (Jacobs, 1989; Lane, 1995). Those who have done so tend to be postlingually deaf, people who became deaf after they had developed language (Jacobs, 1989). Leo Jacobs, a deaf educator, compares lip-reading with breaking eighty in golf or painting a masterpiece, since under the best of circumstances only 30 percent of speech can be read from lip movements (Jacobs, 1989).

The grip of oralism on the education of deaf children started to break in the 1960s, when research began to reveal the benefits of manual communication (Stuckless & Birch, 1966). Many educators of the deaf began experimenting with new communication methodologies, such as total communication, which involved a combination of speech and signed English. Another methodology, cued speech, employed handshapes formed near the mouth to aid lip-reading. Though many viewed these innovations as progress, neither of these methodologies involved ASL in the way that the Hartford School did a century before. Thus, oralism continues to have a negative impact on the education of deaf children as an enduring legacy of ableism.

In the 1970s, important research in linguistics confirmed what many deaf people already knew: that ASL was a language with its own syntax and grammar, and that manual language developed naturally in deaf children similarly to the way oral language developed in hearing children. Timothy Reagan (1985), in his landmark piece in the *Harvard Educational Review,* stated, "ASL's linguistic features are now understood, at least in fairly broad outline. It is a language in every sense of the word, relying on visual, rather than auditory, encoding and decoding. ASL has a complex, rule-governed phonology, syntax, and morphology" (p. 270).

Other important research has followed that further supports ASL as the foundation for language development and educational attainment for deaf children. A particularly important line of research involves deaf children whose parents are also deaf. These children, about one in nine deaf children, provide an ideal "natural experiment" to test assumptions about language development and to investigate the potential negative impact of ableist assumptions. Most deaf parents communicate with their infants and toddlers in their natural language, ASL. A number of studies have revealed that these children display superior language development and thus obtain higher scores on intelligence measures than deaf children of hearing parents (Courtin, 2000; Sisco & Anderson, 1980; Zwiebel, 1987). Similar findings have been reported in studies conducted on deaf children of deaf families in Denmark, Israel, and Greece (Lane, 1995).

Further, it is unlikely that deaf parents carry with them the negative cultural views of people who are deaf. The birth of a deaf baby to deaf parents is not a tragedy to be grieved, but rather a celebrated event. I have deaf friends who, upon learning they are about to become parents, have told me that they would prefer that their child be deaf.

Studies of deaf children whose parents are deaf are revealing. These children start school with vocabularies comparable to their hearing peers and have higher levels of educational and occupational success than most deaf children of hearing parents (Lane, 1995). Comparing students entering school with high levels of ASL ability with those who have lower levels, Michael Prinz and Philip Strong (1998) found that those with high ASL ability achieved higher levels of literacy, even when IQ is held constant. The evidence supporting the need to develop manual language in deaf children is so compelling that a National Academy of Sciences study concluded, "Parents and preschool teachers can enhance deaf children's communicative and reading ability growth by beginning early to communicate with these children through finger spelling and manual signing" (Snow, 1998, p. 164).

This research underscores the point that language is the fundamental cornerstone upon which educational achievement is built for all children. Unless children have well-developed language before learning to read, they are unlikely to achieve high levels of literacy (Snow, 1998). Deaf children are no different from their hearing counterparts in this regard. However, the optimal way for these children to learn language is different because they cannot hear. It seems clear that deaf children should be encouraged to learn ASL from infancy, and that educational programs should recognize that a well-developed ability in ASL is a strength in deaf children upon which their future progress rests. The continued adherence to the ableist assumption that it is better for deaf children to lip-read and speak than to learn sign language will surely guarantee poor educational results for this population.

Though history and recent research converge to provide clear evidence that recognizing the importance of developing manual language in deaf children is the foundation for literacy and for later educational and occupational success, educational practices often do not reflect these findings. Though deaf infants and toddlers and their families are entitled to early intervention and special education services from birth, many deaf children of hearing parents start school with vocabularies of fewer than fifty words (Shapiro, 1994). This is likely due to the lack of emphasis on the development of ASL skills in their preschool programs or at home. Further, many of the school programs these children attend do not recognize the importance of developing and using manual language. In short, many programs still reflect ableist assumptions about the deaf.

The ultimate institutionalization of ableist assumptions can be seen in a U.S. Supreme Court interpretation of IDEA in the case of *Rowley v. Board of Education of the Gloversville Enlarged City School* (1993). The Court decided that a deaf girl who was integrated into a regular class was not entitled to a sign language interpreter because she was "receiving benefit" — that is, she was passing. This decision in effect says that it was acceptable for this deaf child to understand only some of what the teacher was saying. Clearly, this child was not given the same access to educational opportunity afforded hearing children. Would parents of hearing children tolerate such a standard being applied to their children's education? School board meetings would be full of parents demanding change. However, deaf children are few in number and therefore unlikely to sway a school board. In my view, the Court failed to serve its role of protecting a minority, a deaf student, from the rule of the majority, the school board.

Though the deaf community may have lost in court under *Rowley*, it has been using its political power to advocate for significant changes in educational programs for deaf children. Deaf children's low level of educational attainment has been the rallying point, and federal intervention has been sought. It is noteworthy that, though there has been a significant deaf intellectual community in the United States since the founding of Gallaudet University in 1864, deaf people have not had a sufficiently powerful influence on policymaking involving their own education. This was brought into sharp relief during the naming of a new president for Gallaudet in 1988. When two deaf applicants were passed over for a hearing candidate, the campus erupted in protest and the university was closed down (Shapiro, 1994). The deaf student body could not accept the continuation of 124 years of hearing presidents at the premier institution for the deaf. After a well-organized protest with appeals to both the U.S. Congress and the president of the United States, a deaf individual, I. King Jordan, was named president.

Another example of the increased role of deaf adults in policymaking occurred in 1990 with the issuance of the Deaf Education Policy Guidance by the deaf Assistant Secretary of Education Robert Davilla. This document emphasizes the importance of language development and communication in the education of deaf children. When Judy Heumann became assistant secretary in 1993, she and I reissued the guidance at the urging of the deaf community. When IDEA was reauthorized in 1997, the deaf community sought and achieved some significant changes to IDEA that further supported the centrality of language development and communication in the education of deaf children. IDEA now requires that when an Individual Educational Plan (IEP) is developed for a deaf child, the child's communication needs must be addressed. Some have interpreted these changes in the law (and I would agree) as challenging the *Rowley* interpretation of IDEA and opening the way for a greater use of bilingual approaches to the education of deaf children (Pittman & Huefner, 2001).

The foundation for the improvement of educational results for deaf children therefore lies in the rejection of the ableist assumptions that surround their education. Deaf children can achieve at comparable levels to their hearing peers, not by ill-conceived attempts to minimize deafness but by recognizing that deaf children optimally develop language manually and that a high level of ASL ability can serve as a basis for future educational progress. This is not to say that lip-reading is not an important adaptive skill for deaf people in a hearing world; it is. However, as a method of language acquisition it is inefficient and ineffective for large numbers of deaf children. By allowing deaf children to be deaf and by building on their inherent strengths through the development of manual language, they will ultimately (and, some might think, paradoxically) be better able to compete in a hearing world.

THE EDUCATION OF BLIND AND VISUALLY IMPAIRED CHILDREN

The bias of schools against Braille and their failure to teach it to blind and visually impaired students is another example of how ableist assumptions influence educational programs. In 1829, Louis Braille invented Braille, a system of raised dots that enabled blind people to read. Yet, many blind and significantly visually impaired students are not benefiting from this old technology (Johnson, 1996). Though some attribute this to the rise of newer technologies such as taped books and voice synthesizers that may be making Braille obsolete (Shapiro, 1994), I believe the failure to teach blind children Braille is another example of ableism. Reading Braille is a disability-specific method of reading that many nondisabled people view as unacceptable, preferring that children with very low vision read print even if they are inefficient readers due to their vision disabilities, and that totally blind children listen to tapes. As one young person who has a significant vision disability said to me recently, "I was taught to read print, not Braille, because everyone felt it would make me more like sighted people." This, despite the fact that reading print is difficult and exhausting for her.

The National Federation of the Blind (NFB), an advocacy organization of blind people, has taken a strong position favoring the teaching of Braille to blind children and those with other vision impairments:

> There's no substitute for Braille in taking notes, reading a speech, looking up words in a dictionary, studying a complicated text, or just having the fun of reading for yourself. Talk of forcing blind children to learn Braille shows the prejudice. Nobody talks of forcing sighted children to learn print. It is taken for granted as a right, a necessary part of education; so it should be with Braille and blind children. (National Federation of the Blind, n.d.)

The NFB took action on this issue in the late 1980s by advocating for the passage of "Braille bills" by state legislatures throughout the country. These bills have sought to promote the teaching of Braille.

Though some totally blind students are not learning Braille, the controversy around Braille often revolves around students with limited vision. Some students with vision impairments can learn to read print or can read print with accommodations such as large print. If these students have stable, nonprogressive vision conditions and can learn to read print efficiently, they should. However, when educators and parents insist that vision-impaired children read print to the exclusion of reading Braille, many visually impaired children remain functionally illiterate.

Another controversy regarding the education of blind children centers on whether schools are required to provide orientation and mobility services (O&M) to blind students under related services provisions of IDEA. O&M teachers teach blind students how to get around using canes and other means. The goal of these services is to increase independence. It seems logical that, if the goal of public education is to prepare students to function in the world, O&M would be a required component of the educational program of blind children. Though this seems logical, advocates for the blind complained to me when I worked as the director of the Office of Special Education Programs for the U.S. Department of Education that they were having difficulty securing these services because the law at this time did not specifically name the service. Some have argued that school districts objected to providing these services due to cost, and this argument may have some merit. However, advocates pointed out that some of the same districts had hired full-time aides to assist blind students, an expensive and, in the eyes of many disability activists, potentially harmful practice (Ferguson & Asch, 1989). Many advocates believe the schools would have been better off teaching these kids to navigate on their own using O&M techniques.

In my view, the controversy around the provision of O&M raises broader questions about ableism in education. I am becoming increasingly concerned with the way I see school districts, and at times parents, respond to the needs of students with significant disability by assigning them a full-time aide. Adrienne Asch, a blind woman who teaches at Wellesley College, cautions, "An aide is not (or at least should not be) a chaperone, an administrative spy, a surrogate parent, or a personal servant. Any such role turns the aide into a shield or a barrier between the disabled student and his or her nondisabled peers" (Ferguson & Asch, 1989, p. 129).

These concerns are compounded when aides take the place of teachers and compromise the quality of instruction. One of my graduate students at the Harvard Graduate School of Education spent a semester observing a child with significant disabilities who was included in general education classes with the support of a full-time aide. As a highly experienced and skilled special educator, she was deeply concerned that the middle school student had not learned to read. After careful observation, she concluded that he had not been *taught* to read; instead, the aide viewed it as his job to read the material to the boy. Therefore, despite the fact that, according to her assessment, he had normal receptive language and could fully understand language, and was in a regular classroom where significant resources were being spent on his education, this boy was being deprived of the opportunity to learn to read.

Assigning full-time aides to children with disabilities rather than, as has been the case with blind children, teaching them to get around independently through O&M reflects, in my view, deep cultural prejudices about significant disabilities. That is, it suggests that people with significant disabilities are weak and incapable of doing things on their own. The reaction of many educators to the integration of significantly disabled students into typical schools and classrooms is to demand full-time aides. For example, when Penny Ford prevailed in her complaint with the OCR to have Joe attend a regular kindergarten, the "negotiated agreement" between the school and the Chicago Board of Education was to provide Joe with a full-time aide. Penny recalls her discomfort with the agreement: "I found it repugnant that my son's rights were a matter of negotiation. He didn't need an aide. All he needed was for someone to flip pages for him. Another kid could do that! He already knew how to read. He also needed some help in the bathroom. That's not a full-time job" (P. Ford, personal communication, October 2001). Penny's initial discomfort was prescient. When Joe showed up for school on the first day, he was denied entrance to the classroom because the aide had not cleared all the personnel hurdles. Already the object of two years of struggle over his entrance into the school attended by his sisters and friends, Joe Ford spent the first day of first grade in the school office, not in the classroom. It seemed the school could not conceive of approaching his education directly without the intermediary of a paraprofessional.

Like the deaf community, the blind community has sought action by the federal government to address the shortcomings of the educational system. When the Clinton administration took office in 1993, representatives of the blind community successfully sought the issuance of a guidance similar to that issued concerning the education of deaf children. This guidance emphasized the importance of specialized services such as O&M and supported Braille instruction. When IDEA was reauthorized in 1997, a requirement was added to mandate that when teams meet to develop IEPs for blind and visually impaired students, Braille must be considered. Further, the reauthorized law added O&M as related services.[3] Hopefully, these specific legal requirements will begin to change the ableist practices that have compromised the education of blind and visually impaired children.

THE EDUCATION OF STUDENTS WITH LEARNING DISABILITIES

Blindness, deafness, and significant physical disability are relatively rare; their combined incidence is less than 1 percent of the total population of school-aged children (U.S. Department of Education, 1996). On the other hand, students with learning disabilities (LD) are common, comprising about 5 percent of children. Although definitional arguments concerning the identification of these children abound (Lyon et al., 2001), educators have long recognized the phenomenon of children who seem intellectually able but experience marked difficulty learning to read. This condition, commonly known as dyslexia, is by far the most frequent form of learning disability, affecting about 80 percent of the learning disability population (Lyon et al., 2001). Given its prevalence, one might think that these children would be less likely to be subjected to inappropriate ableist practices. However, the available evidence shows that these children are subjected to inappropriate educational approaches at an alarming level.[4]

The National Longitudinal Transition Study (NLTS) investigated the educational results of a large sample of students with disabilities who attended high schools in the mid-1980s. This study, the largest and most thorough of its kind, paints a less than satisfactory picture (Wagner, Blackorby, Cameto, & Newman, 1993). The NLTS, along with other data such as the performance of students with disabilities on statewide assessments and more recent research, confirms that the educational attainment levels of students with learning disabilities is less than adequate. Students with learning disabilities drop out of school at relatively high rates — about twice that of nondisabled students (Wagner et al., 1993). These students also participate in higher education in relatively small numbers. NLTS also documents that relatively large numbers of these students are not taking challenging academic subjects. Given these findings, it might not be surprising that more recent data indicates that students with learning disabilities fail statewide assessments at alarming rates (Katzman, 2001).

I believe the reasons for the lack of acceptable educational outcomes for students with learning disabilities are complex. The fact that dyslexia has as its main symptomatology the failure of children to learn to read, a primary goal of education for all students, and that dyslexic children are not the only children who struggle with reading means that explanations for this failure go to the very structure of schooling. Therefore, using an ableist lens alone is inadequate. Some students' failure to learn to read may be due to poor instruction, thus compounding the impact of disability. However, there is evidence that ableist assumptions may have a particularly negative influence on the education of those children who struggle the most with learning to read — dyslexic children.

The failure of students to learn to read has been of concern to educators and the general public for some time; therefore, significant resources have been directed to the study of reading failure. In fact, early reading may be the most researched area of education. As schools implement standards-based reforms, educators are increasingly looking to research to help guide schools in improving their performance. To meet this need, the U.S. Department of Education (DOE) contracted with the National Research Council (NRC) of the National Academy of Science to conduct a research synthesis in the area of early reading. The resulting book, *Preventing Reading Difficulties in Young Children* (Snow, 1998), has become the biggest seller at the NRC. As one party involved in the initial study design, the DOE insisted that the synthesis employ an inclusive design. The DOE considered this important because any inquiry into disabled children's failure to learn to read must be viewed in the overall context of how children learn to read. Conversely, given the relatively large number of students who have disabilities, the failure to address the needs of disabled students in a study of this magnitude would render the study noncomprehensive.[5] This study, therefore, contains a wealth of information about those students who have the most difficulty learning to read, including those likely to be dyslexic. Along with this study, more recent work published by researchers funded by the National Institutes of Health (NIH) provides a converging picture of how schools handle young students with dyslexia. Adding the data from NLTS and other sources, the view through the ableist lens is most revealing.

One example of how ableist assumptions may be impeding the effective education of children with disabilities has to do with the reluctance to intervene on behalf of children experiencing marked difficulty with learning to read. Some of this reluctance may be due to a lack of appropriate options or inadequate teacher preparation (Lyon et al., 2001). However, some of the inaction may be due to the desire of schools not to label children, which undoubtedly reflects the deep stigma associated with disability in our culture. The mere label of disability carries such negative connotations that many educators and some parents seek to avoid it. Another reason that some may seek to avoid labeling is the fact that labeling may result in inferior special education placements. These placements often reflect the ableist notion that disabled children should not be challenged. Thus, some educators and parents justifiably avoid such placements. Finally, the federal definition of learning disability, which requires that a child exhibit a discrepancy between intelligence (IQ) and performance, may also inhibit early intervention. That is, the child must first fail to learn the material that his intelligence would indicate he should be able to learn before he can establish eligibility for special education services. From my perspective, the ethics of allowing young children to fail at learning to read without providing intensive help is questionable for all children — disabled and nondisabled.

The dilemma parents and educators face around the issue of labeling need not exist if schools employ research-based practices and improve their special education programs. The NIH has conducted an extensive set of studies using large data sets that examine the nature of early reading failure. These studies have documented that relatively large numbers of students experience significant difficulty with initial reading. There is evidence that of the 12 to 18 percent of the K–1 student population that has the most difficulty learning to read, research-based interventions are effective with 70 percent (Lyon et al., 2001). Though not all students fully benefited from these interventions, they can serve to identify those students who are highly likely to need more extensive help — that is, those who may have a disability that will require accommodations and support throughout their schooling. Once it is clear that a child has not responded to powerful interventions and is still struggling with reading, that child should get the protections of the IDEA.

Though early intervention for students experiencing reading difficulty will help identify students who may have LD, educators need to ensure that once children are identified they receive the types of services and supports that will maximize their educational attainment. We must seek to remove the stigma associated with disability labels. Further, as with their peers who have other disabilities, ableist practices are evident in current practices with students with learning disabilities. The education of these children tends to be inordinately oriented toward the presenting characteristics of the disability and suffers from low expectations.

Most of these children are placed for part of the day in special education resource rooms and part of the day in regular classes. Some are placed in regular classes all day. For large numbers of these students, neither regular nor special class placements seems to be meeting their needs. Research looking at the type of instruction LD students experience in special classes raises serious issues. Sharon Vaughn and her colleagues (2000) studied elementary schoolchildren with LD assigned to special classes and found that their instruction was characterized by large multi-aged groups and was largely non-differentiated. Other studies have found that special education placement results in students reading less (Allington & McGill-Franzen, 1989).

Some have responded to the failure of certain special education placements with a call for full inclusion in general education classes. However, research has raised questions concerning mainstream placements as well. NLTS documented that a large number of students with LD who were placed in general education classrooms did not receive accommodations or support. Such students were more likely to fail and drop out of school. Another more recent study documented that 80 percent of the poorest readers placed in regular classrooms made no progress over an entire academic year (Klinger et al., cited in Lyon et al., 2001).

Students with dyslexia *can* learn to read. However, they need more intensive help to do so, and even with the best approaches they are likely to experience significant difficulty with reading, writing, and spelling throughout their schooling. Torgesen (2000) and his colleagues have demonstrated impressive results with intensive intervention for severely disabled readers in grades three through five over an eight-week period. However, even though these students experienced gains in certain reading skills, they remained very slow readers. The picture that emerges from the research on remediation after grade two shows that reading improvement can continue but that those who have the most difficulty reading are likely to continue to have these problems and that their problems compound. Children with poor reading skills avoid reading and thus build up enormous educational deficits (Lyon et al., 2001). Given the centrality of reading to most instruction, severe reading problems can affect all areas of students' curricular attainment.

The research discussed thus far indicates several clear implications for educational practice. First, there is a population of children who are likely to experience significant difficulty with reading even with the best interventions. *Dyslexia is clearly a disabling condition*. Second, reading improvement for these students can continue to occur throughout their schooling *if that intervention is sufficiently intensive and appropriate*. Third, those with the most severe problems in reading print are likely to experience increasing difficulty in school as the cumulative effects of reading deficiency become apparent. Fourth, significant numbers of these students are receiving inappropriate educational assistance in terms of both the interventions they receive and their access to the curriculum.

Though research strongly indicates that students with LD need more intensive services in reading than their nondisabled peers and that they should receive this assistance throughout their schooling, focusing their special education program solely on learning to read is not appropriate. For students with LD, this reflects the ableist assumption that special education's role should be to change disabilities even if that is not fully possible. These children must also have access to the rest of the curriculum with appropriate accommodations and supports. Therefore, educators planning programs for students with LD must strategize around how these students will most efficiently access the curriculum, given that they are typically laborious readers. Though this seems like common sense, there is significant evidence that large numbers of students with LD are not getting sufficient accommodations, services, and supports to give them equal opportunity to benefit from the curriculum.

As previously cited, NLTS documented that many students with LD receive relatively low levels of service and do not receive accommodations and supports in general education classes. Other research on IEPs has shown that these documents typically focus on discrete skills and are not connected to the overall curriculum (U.S. Department of Education, 1995). Should it be a surprise to anyone that so many of these children are achieving at such low levels?

Again, I believe that ableism at least partially explains our failure to better educate those with LD. First, as is the case with other disabilities, the programs for these students often focus on the characteristics of their disability, their reading deficiencies, to the exclusion of their total educational needs. Like the deaf who must learn to lip-read and speak before they can access the curriculum, it appears that many believe that those with LD must learn to read at grade level before they can access other subjects. This approach clearly magnifies the negative educational impact of the disability. This situation was brought home to me when I was associate superintendent of schools in Chicago in 1992. A general education teacher asked to meet with me concerning students with LD in her class. She told me that she was also a parent of a child with LD and that she knew a good deal about the disability. She went on to say that she had a number of students in her classes with LD who were failing and that she had not been seen by anyone from the special education department in her school. Later a staff member met with special education staff in the school who informed her that it was not their job to meet with the general education teachers. They viewed their responsibility as only working on the goals and objectives in the IEPs, which were largely discreet skills centered on reading and writing. Therefore, these students were being expected to handle text four and five grade levels above their reading level without accommodation. No wonder they were failing.

Can students with LD access curriculum above their reading level? Of course they can. However, for many of these students, that access cannot be dependent on their ability to read print or write at grade level. Fortunately, there are accommodations available that can help students with LD to access text written above their reading level. Taped books have been available to blind students for many years and are increasingly used by people with dyslexia. Recordings for the Blind recently changed its name to Recordings for the Blind and Dyslexic to reflect the changing demand for their services. Also, as more text is digitized, computers will be able to read text using screen readers. Other techniques such as increasing the ability of students to handle text through pre-teaching multisyllabic and technical words can greatly increase students' ability to handle difficult texts. Word processing and spell-checks can greatly increase the ability of students with LD to produce writing assignments.

Though there are effective ways by which students with LD can access the general education curriculum, schools may have to modify some deeply held beliefs about what constitutes acceptable student performance in order for students with LD to benefit from these technologies. In many places, students are required to handle grade-level or higher text in order to be mainstreamed into regular classes. Taped books are not available or are not allowed. Still other schools do not allow students to use computers when taking exams, thus greatly diminishing some students' ability to produce acceptable written work. Though some may defend this rigidity as a means to maintain standards, for students with LD this posture will likely lead to lower educational attainment.

The late disabilities advocate Ed Roberts had polio as a child, which left him with significant physical disabilities, including the need for an iron lung. He attended school from home in the 1960s with the assistance of a telephone link. When it was time for graduation, the school board was going to deny him a diploma because he had failed to meet the physical education requirement. His parents protested and Ed eventually graduated (Shapiro, 1994). It would be difficult to imagine that happening today, given disability law and improved societal attitudes toward disability. Yet, reflecting widespread ableist assumptions, students with LD are routinely required to read print at grade level to access educational opportunities. As the disability movement has demonstrated over and over, there is more than one way to walk, talk, paint, read, and write. Assuming otherwise is the root of fundamental inequities.

STUDENTS WITH DISABILITIES AND STANDARDS-BASED REFORM

A disability advocate recently sought my advice on the placement of an eight-year-old student with disabilities. The boy has various communication and motor disabilities due to brain damage at birth. He has received excellent early intervention and preschool services. His speech, though labored, is easily understood and his vocabulary approximates that of peers his age. He has some difficulties in coordination, fine motor skills, and behavior, but is not significantly cognitively impaired. Unfortunately, his current school placement is woefully inadequate. At his most recent IEP meeting, his mother asked what he was learning in science. She wanted to make sure he was being prepared to take the statewide assessment in grade four. The special education teacher responded, "We're not doing science. We're concentrating on fine motor development." Again, like too many children with disabilities, his educational program concentrates inordinately on the characteristics of his disability at the expense of access to the curriculum.

This example illustrates why many disability advocates view standards-based educational reforms as holding great promise to help eradicate the most insidious ableist assumption: that people with disabilities are not intellectually capable. The education of students with disabilities has been plagued by low expectations, which is why many in the disability community have sought to have students included in state and national accountability systems (Thurlow, 2000). The hope is that by including students in statewide assessments, more attention will be paid to assuring that these students receive quality programs (McDonnell, McLaughlin, & Morrison, 1997). In 1997, advocates were successful in getting IDEA amended to require students with disabilities to be included in statewide assessments.

It is noteworthy that, before this federal requirement, most states excluded most students with disabilities from these important accountability systems (Thurlow, 2000) — this at a time when most states were implementing various forms of standards-based reform. A number of explanations may address this exclusion. It is possible that disabled students were viewed as not capable of achieving standards. Another explanation might be that the performance of disabled students was not important to track. Both of these explanations clearly reflect ableist attitudes, that disabled students are either incapable or unimportant. Another explanation is that in high-stakes environments school districts may actually be placing more students in special education to avoid accountability (Allington & McGill-Franzen, 1989). A more positive view might be that states simply did not know how to accommodate students with disabilities in assessments. There are many technical issues involved in the inclusion of students with disabilities, especially those who receive accommodations (Koretz & Hamilton, 2000). Though the truth probably lies somewhere among these views, the exclusion of students with disabilities from state and local assessment systems may result in their exclusion from the curriculum and thus reinforce the status quo of low expectations, leaving students with disabilities seriously undereducated. Fortunately, this exclusion is now illegal.

Though there was widespread exclusion of students with disabilities from state-wide accountability systems before the passage of the 1997 amendments to IDEA, some states had begun to implement inclusive policies prior to the federal requirement. These states provide an interesting window on the impact of these policies. There is some emerging evidence that indicates that inclusion in statewide assessment may be improving the educational opportunities of students with disabilities.

In New York State, where an emphasis on including students with disabilities in the Regents Exam began in 1998, the number of students passing this high-level test has greatly increased. Comparing data from 1997 and 2000 shows dramatic change. In 1997, only 4,419 students with disabilities took the Regents English Exam, with 3,414 passing. Three years later, over twice as many disabled students *passed* the test as had taken it in 1997. In 2000, 13,528 took the test and 9,514 passed (New York State Department of Education, 2001). Prior to this inclusionary push, some school districts in the state did not have *one* student with disabilities taking the test. It appears that in these school districts, the view was indeed ableist; no child with disabilities was viewed as capable of passing this test. The impact of the exclusion of students with disabilities from the Regents over the years was undoubtedly significant. Important benefits can result from passing the Regents, from scholarships to college admissions. Further, the widespread exclusion from the Regents prior to 1997 probably meant that thousands of students with disabilities did not take higher level high school courses.

In Maryland, where students with disabilities have been included in the state's basic-skills test, many districts have shown steady progress to the point where the vast majority of students with disabilities are passing the test. Maryland has years of disaggregated performance data. These data were used to help negotiate an agreement to end a longstanding class action suit concerning students with disabilities in Baltimore City. This agreement broke new ground in that it focused on educational outcomes (*Vaughn, G. et al.*, 2000). The previous agreement, like many special education class action suits, had focused largely on processes (Hehir & Gamm, 1999). The previous agreement made no mention of academic performance in any area. Though the agreement went into effect in the 2000–2001 school year and thus it is too soon to evaluate its impact, the city's special education director speaks positively of how the agreement is focusing staff on teaching and learning (G. Amos, personal communication, 2001).

Though the inclusion of students with disabilities in statewide assessments shows great promise, the imposition of high-stakes consequences for students who do not perform well on these tests gives rise to serious concerns. This is particularly the case when state policy requires the passage of high-level tests in order to receive a diploma or to move from grade to grade. Concerns range from technical issues involving construct validity to the impact of failure on students' persistence in school.

Given the nature of disability and the type of assessments most states employ, the inclusion of disabled students in statewide assessments is complicated. Many disabled students require accommodations specific to their disability, and issues of construct validity may arise out of the accommodations students receive (Fuchs & Fuchs, 1999; Koretz & Hamilton, 2000). For instance, a test that seeks to determine if a child can read print is invalidated if a test is read to the child. On the other hand, a math test may be invalid if it is not read to a child who is print-disabled because the child has no way to demonstrate the math she knows if she has to read print to do so. The issues of construct validity are complex and, given the relative lack of experience in including disabled students in large-scale assessments, significant research will be required before we can be confident that these assessments are accurately measuring what students know and are able to do (Koretz & Hamilton, 2000).

Though there are numerous unresolved technical issues involved in including students with disabilities in assessments, high-stakes decisions are being made that have the potential to deny students important opportunities such as promotion or graduation. Further, beyond the technical issues is the nature of the constructs themselves. A major concern is whether the constructs are sufficiently broad to enable disabled students to demonstrate what they know and are able to do. A case that came to my attention when I was working at the DOE illustrates this point. The case involved a student who had become blind during high school. Although he was beginning to learn Braille, he was using taped books as his main means of learning from print. The state policies required all students to pass a test to graduate. The issue was whether he could participate in the language arts test through a taped administration. One of the constructs to be evaluated by this test was the ability to read print. He could not read print because he could not see print. Of course he was not the only blind child in the state, and state policy allowed the state test to be administered in Braille. This boy, however, was not a proficient Braille reader because he was newly blind. The state decided to waive its policy that prohibited reading the language arts aloud as an allowable accommodation for this student.

This example goes to the heart of the issues of construct validity, accommodations, and ableist assumptions regarding acceptable performance modes. The fundamental question here is this: What is reading? The state had previously answered the question that reading was reading print or reading Braille. Extracting meaning from recorded text was not considered reading. Therefore, the statewide test was designed to measure these two modes of reading. Answering comprehension questions based on listening to recorded text would thus violate the construct validity of the test. However, significant numbers of disabled people use recorded text as their reading mode. These include people with a range of disabilities beyond blindness, including people who have dyslexia and people with certain types of cerebral palsy that make focusing and reading print exhausting and inefficient. Joe Ford, for example, uses taped books for this reason. Even though the use of recorded text is widespread, some states refuse to allow taped administration of language arts tests, thereby refusing to recognize the mode that many disabled people use to read. Applying this narrow definition of reading to high-stakes decisions may mean that large numbers of disabled students will be denied diplomas and thus future educational opportunity. Further, such a decision is likely to discourage the use of taped texts in schools, even though they may represent the most efficient means by which some students with disabilities gain access to the curriculum.

Even if states broadly define modes of performance and successfully deal with measurement issues around construct validity, another issue is arising in states that have high-level content/high-stakes assessment programs — that is, the problem of students who are incapable of passing the high-stakes tests due to the nature of their disability. This is particularly true of students with cognitive disabilities or mental retardation. Though it is important to have high expectations for all students, if states or local districts have diploma or promotion policies that assume the mastery of high levels of skill and knowledge, students with mental retardation, due to the pervasive nature of their significantly subaverage intellectual functioning, may be subject to inappropriate retention and will unlikely receive diplomas. Most in the field of special education would agree that keeping kids with mental retardation back because they have not achieved grade-level work is absurd and serves no useful purpose. Indeed, such a practice is likely to be detrimental if these children lose contact with their age-appropriate peers. The larger issue is whether these children will "graduate" and receive some form of diploma that recognizes their accomplishment in school, or drop out of school because they do not see the possibility of graduation. This is not an insignificant societal issue in that as many as 2 percent of children have some form of cognitive disability (U.S. Department of Education, 1996). Further, if these children receive high-quality services in school, they have a higher likelihood of being employed upon leaving school. Dropping out is associated with significantly poorer outcomes for all disabled kids (Wagner et al., 1993). Therefore, setting standards policies without these children in mind may have a devastating impact on a relatively large number of students.

A final point about high-stakes policy is that some aspects of the impact of these policies on students with disabilities are relevant for nondisabled students as well. There is relatively little support in the research for the use of high-stakes promotion policies as a vehicle for promoting higher achievement. In *High Stakes: Testing for Tracking, Promotion and Graduation*, Jay Heubert and Robert Hauser (1999) conclude, "The negative consequences, as grade retention is currently practiced, are that retained students persist in low achievement levels and are more likely to drop out of school" (p. 285). This finding also is consistent with the finding in NLTS that failing high school subjects is associated with kids with disabilities dropping out.

TOWARD ENDING ABLEISM IN EDUCATION

There is much that educators, parents, and advocates can do toward ending ableism in education. As is the case with racism and sexism, progress toward equity is dependent first and foremost on the acknowledgment that ableism exists in schools. The examples given here have centered around three disability groups: the deaf, the blind and visually impaired, and the learning disabled. However, I believe that de-constructing dominant educational practices applied to other disability groups can yield similar results. Ableist assumptions and practices are deeply embedded in schooling. Further, the absence of discussion and dearth of scholarly inquiry within mainstream educational circles concerning the effects of ableism is stunning.

Though the lack of attention to ableism in schooling is unfortunate, activists within the disability community have long recognized its impact (Rauscher & McClintock, 1997). Therefore, as more adults with disabilities take on more powerful roles in society and seek to influence schooling, the attention to these issues will hopefully increase (Shapiro, 1994). In addition to this political force, the lack of ac-ceptable educational outcomes for large numbers of children with disabilities in an era of standards-based reform should force a reexamination of current practices. For-tunately, there is a foundation in both research and practice upon which to build a better future. Schools can take action now. I offer the following suggestions:

Include disability as part of schools' overall diversity efforts. Schools are increasingly recognizing the need to explicitly address diversity issues as the country becomes more racially and ethnically diverse. Some schools are expanding diversity efforts to include disability. Recently, a local high school student with Down's syndrome, whom I had met at a school assembly devoted to issues of disability rights, addressed one of my classes. She stated, "There are all kinds of kids at my school: Black kids, Puerto Rican kids, gay and lesbian kids. Meagan uses a wheel chair. Matt's deaf, and I have Down's syndrome. It's all diversity." Her high school has done a great job of in-cluding disabled kids and has incorporated discussions about disability in its efforts to address diversity issues. Adults with disabilities address student groups and dis-ability is presented in a natural way. Students learn about people with disabilities who have achieved great things as well as those who live ordinary lives. People with dis-abilities are not presented in a patronizing or stereotypical manner. Deaf people are not "hearing challenged" nor are people with mental retardation "very special." Ableism is not the norm; disability is dealt with in a straightforward manner. In schools like this, students with disabilities learn about their disabilities and learn how to be self-advocates (Jorgensen, 1997).

Encourage disabled students to develop and use skills and modes of expression that are most effective and efficient for them. This article has sought to demonstrate that the strong preference within society, reflected in school practice, to have disabled stu-dents perform in the same way that nondisabled children perform can ultimately be handicapping for some students. This is not to say that it is not desirable for disabled kids to be able to perform in the way nondisabled kids perform. For instance, deaf stu-dents who can read lips have a competitive advantage in a hearing world. However, assuming that most deaf children can develop elaborate language through oral meth-ods has been proven false, and employing these methods without allowing for the nat-ural development of language almost assures poor language development. What may appear to be a paradox to some is that a deaf child who has well-developed language through learning ASL from birth may actually have a higher likelihood of reading lips because he simply has a larger vocabulary. The problem is not, therefore, in the natural desire of parents and educators to have children be able to perform in a typical manner, but rather the missed educational opportunities many disabled kids experience because of a lack of regard for what are often disability-specific modes of learning and expression.

Special education should be specialized. There has been a persistent debate in the special education literature over the degree of specialization needed by special educators (Biklen, 1992; Jorgensen, 1997; Milofsky, 1974; Skrtic, 1991; Will, 1986). In 1970, Burton Blatt quoted Alice Metzner's feelings about special education that continue to be echoed by others: "The problem with special education is that it is neither special nor education" (Metzner, quoted in Blatt, 1970, p. 21). This critique reflects the well-documented history of inferior education experienced by many in special classes at the time (Kirp, 1974). This critique of special education persists to this day with considerable support from research (Gartner & Lipsky, 1996; Wagner et al., 1993).

The notion that once children are placed in special education they receive a different education should be rejected. This is yet another example of ableism. Though students with disabilities may have individual needs, by and large their education should be based on the same curriculum as that of nondisabled students. This is why advocates worked so hard to amend IDEA in 1997 to specifically require IEP teams to address issues of curricular access. Deafness does not mean students should not be taking physics and dyslexia should not preclude access to great literature. Viewed in this light, special education should not mean a different curriculum, but rather the vehicle by which students with disabilities access the curriculum and the means by which the unique needs that arise out of the child's disability are addressed. This role requires a good deal of specialized knowledge and skill.

Unfortunately, one by-product of the well-justified critique of special education practice has been the minimization of the need for specialization (Biklen, 1992; Jorgensen, 1997; Will, 1986). Motivated by the desire for greater inclusion, particularly for those with cognitive disabilities, personnel preparation programs have minimized the need for specialization. In many states, specialized preparation of special education personnel is minimal and requires preparation as a general educator first. Though this is desirable in the ideal, this emphasis on general education may take away from the need to learn specialized skills and also may inadvertently be contributing to the increasing shortage of special education and related services personnel (U.S. Department of Education, 1996).

If one accepts that the role of special educators and related services personnel is to help disabled children access the curriculum and meet the unique needs that arise out of their disability, the need for specialization should be obvious. Teaching Braille, knowing how to help students with significant communication disorders to use communication devices, developing positive behavioral interventions for a student with autism, and providing a comprehensive approach to accommodating the curriculum while continuing to assist a dyslexic student in learning to read are but a few of the specialized competencies required to assure full access to education for students with disabilities. Though it is important to increase the skills of regular educators in accommodating and modifying instruction for students with disabilities, it is unrealistic to assume that all regular educators can possess these skills. The lack of availability of specialized support has been cited in recent research as a reason some students were placed in segregated settings though they otherwise may have been served in inclusive settings (Hanson et al., 2001). Well-trained special educators are needed to assist general educators and the students they teach in inclusive settings and, at times, to provide intensive instruction outside those settings.

The need to assure that special educators learn specialized skills is not an argument for traditional categorical (by disability) special education teacher-training programs. Such programs often reinforce existing approaches that focus on the characteristics of disability to the exclusion of access to the general curriculum. Further, some traditional programs are not teaching the specialized skills required by students' IEPs. For instance, when I worked at the Office of Special Education Services, advocates for the blind complained that many "vision teachers" could not teach Braille. A review of existing teacher-training programs for the vision impaired by the U.S. Department of Education revealed that many programs did not teach this skill. This lack of disability-specific skill focus is not confined to the field of blindness. Examples of such deficiencies exist in virtually all areas of special education teacher preparation. A number of deaf advocates have complained that many teachers of the deaf are not proficient signers, a complaint that reflects the controversies about oralism in the field. LD advocates have been so concerned about the lack of appropriate skills on the part of both regular and special educational personnel that the National Center on Learning Disabilities sponsored a summit on teacher preparation in 1996. A major concern emerged over the lack of appropriate training in the area of teaching reading to dyslexic students.

We need to develop clear standards for special education teacher-preparation programs that recognize the specific needs of disabled students and ensure that teachers have the skills necessary to develop the individualized programs that these children need. These programs must explicitly challenge the ableist assumption that the manner in which nondisabled children perform school-related tasks is always the preferred goal for disabled students. Teachers must be able to give these kids the skills that will enable them to perform at their maximum level and provide their regular education teachers with the help they need to assure maximum access to the curriculum. Without special education teachers with disability-specific skills, children with disabilities will continue to lack the skills they need to most efficiently and effectively deal with the demands of school and life.

Move away from the current obsession with placement toward an obsession with results. The movement to include greater numbers of students with disabilities, particularly those with significant cognitive disabilities, in regular education classes has had a profound effect on the education of students with disabilities. Over the past decade, more and more students with disabilities are educated for more of the day in regular education classrooms (U.S. Department of Education, 2000).

The inclusion movement in education has supported the overall disability movement's goal of promoting societal integration, using integration in schooling as a means to achieve this result. In 1977, disability activists took over federal offices in San Francisco for twenty-five days, demanding that regulations for implementing Section 504 of the Rehabilitation Act, the first federal act to broadly ban discrimination based on disability, be released. Of particular concern to the protesters were leaked draft regulations that provided for separate segregated education for disabled students. Judy Heumann, one of these protesters, stated, "We will accept no more segregation" (Shapiro, 1994). The final rules were revised to encourage integration in schooling, and the newly passed P.L. 94-142 (later renamed IDEA) incorporated the current requirement that children be educated in the least restrictive environment (i.e., in regular classes as much as is appropriate for the child).

The strong legal preference for placement in regular classes, coupled with the political movement of disability activists and parents, has resulted in significant positive change for students with disabilities, who are moving on to jobs and accessing higher education at unprecedented levels (Hehir & Gamm, 1999). Virtually every school has had to confront the issue of inclusion as parents seek integration for their children with disabilities. However, like all change movements, inclusion has encountered opposition. Some opposition has reflected deeply held negative attitudes toward people with disabilities similar to that experienced by Joe and Penny Ford when he sought enrollment in first grade. I can recall a principal challenging me in a large public meeting concerning our efforts to promote inclusion in Chicago: "You don't really mean kids who drool in regular classes?" The reaction against the integration of students with significant disabilities into regular schools and classrooms has been so strong that TASH, an advocacy group promoting integration, adopted the slogan, "All means all," which reflects the group's efforts to clarify its goal to promote integration for students with significant disabilities.

Another source of criticism has come from within the disability community (Kauffman & Hallahan, 1995).[6] Deaf advocates have expressed concerns over the lack of language development and communication access many deaf children experience in regular classes (Lane, cited in Kauffman & Hallahan, 1995). Supported by some of the research cited above, advocates for the learning disabled have questioned the ability of regular education classrooms to provide the intensive help these students need for skill development (Fuchs & Fuchs, 1994, 1995). These criticisms receive support from research. The NLTS documented that many students integrated into regular education classrooms did not receive much in the way of accommodation or support, and that many who were integrated into regular classes failed, thus increasing their likelihood of dropping out. The issue is so controversial within the community that virtually every disability group has developed a position. A review of websites reveals, for example, TASH's strong support for full inclusion and deep reservation on the part of the Learning Disabilities Association of America (see www.tash.org and www.ldanatl.org).

The controversy over inclusion within the disability community is ultimately dysfunctional and allows those who would limit the rights of students with disabilities to use this as a wedge issue. Fortunately, the community united during the reauthorization of IDEA in 1997 to help prevent a weakening of the act. However, threats to

IDEA's fundamental protections remain. In 2001, Congress considered amendments to the Elementary and Secondary Education Act that would enable schools to fully exclude some students with disabilities. In order to fight these regressive provisions, the community must be united.

I believe the lens of ableism provides a useful perspective through which the inclusion issue can be resolved within the disability community. First, there needs to be a recognition that education plays a central role in the integration of disabled people in all aspects of society both by giving children the education they need to compete and by demonstrating to nondisabled children that disability is a natural aspect of life. Central to this role is the need for students with disabilities to have access to the same curriculum provided to nondisabled children. Further, education plays a vital role in building communities in which disabled children should be included. Therefore, for most children with disabilities, integration into regular classes with appropriate accommodations and support should be the norm.

However, the lens of ableism should lead to the recognition that for some students certain disability-related skills might need attention outside the regular classroom. Learning Braille or ASL or how to use a communication device are typically not in the curriculum and might be more efficiently taught outside the mainstream classroom. The dyslexic high school student who needs intensive help in reading may feel deeply self-conscious if such instruction is conducted in front of his nondisabled friends. The 19-year-old student with a significant cognitive disability may need to spend a good deal of time learning to take public transportation, a skill that will ultimately increase her ability to integrate into the community as an adult. Nondisabled students do not spend time in school learning this skill because they learn this easily on their own. The nature of mental retardation is such that this type of learning does not typically happen incidentally; it must be taught over time and within the context in which the skill will be used (Brown et al., 1991). Uniting around the goal of societal integration and recognizing that the difference inherent in disability is a positive one that at times gives rise to disability-specific educational needs may help advocates move away from the fight over placement to one that focuses on educational results.

Promote high standards, not high stakes. An important point to reiterate here is that the most damaging ableist assumption is the belief that disabled people are incapable. Therefore, the movement to include students with disabilities in standards-based reforms holds promise. However, high-stakes testing that prevents students from being promoted or from receiving a diploma based on performance on standardized tests is problematic, given the concerns previously cited about basic access to the curricula and those surrounding the construct validity of the tests. In a very real sense, some students with disabilities will have to become nondisabled in order to be promoted or graduate. This is ableism in the extreme. Thus, a promising movement, standards-based reform, may ultimately reinforce current inequities if performance on high-stakes tests becomes the only means by which disabled students can demonstrate what they know and are able to do. As such, disability advocates should oppose high-stakes testing. It is important to note that disabled students are not the only group for whom high-stakes testing is being questioned (Heubert & Hauser, 1999). Other groups that have been poorly served by our educational systems, such as children from high-poverty backgrounds and children with limited English proficiency, may be equally harmed by these policies.

Employ concepts of universal design to schooling. A principle of disability policy that has evolved is the concept of universal design. First applied to architecture, this principle called for the design of buildings with the assumption that people with disabilities would be using them. With the legal backing of the Americans with Disabilities Act, these principles are applied increasingly to new construction and renovation of public buildings. Ramps, automatic door opening devices, accessible toilets, and fire alarm systems with lights activated for the deaf are examples of universal design features incorporated into contemporary buildings. Other examples extend to technologies. Captioning devices are required features on all televisions and digital text can be read from computers with screen readers. Universal design allows for access without extraordinary means and is based on the assumption that disabled people are numerous and should be able to lead regular lives.

However, the concept of universal design has yet to become widespread in schooling. For instance, even though learning disabilities are common in students, we have yet to design our reading programs with these children in mind (Lyon et al., 2001). We tend to have "one size fits all" reading programs in the primary grades. This is true of other areas as well, such as how schools handle students with disabilities that affect behavior. Using the analogy of architecture, we often attempt to retrofit the child with inappropriate interventions after they have failed in school, rather than design the instructional program from the beginning to allow for access and success. And, as is the case with architecture, the failure to design universally is inefficient and ineffective.

An interesting by-product of universal design is the benefit it brings to nondisabled people as well. People pushing baby carriages appreciate curb-cuts. Hearing people trying to keep up with the Super Bowl in a noisy bar can do so via captioning. The same can be said for education. Reading programs that are successful with dyslexic students will be better able to reach those who may be struggling for other reasons. A school that includes a child with autism who has difficulty with school behavior requirements is likely to be a school that can serve others with behavior problems more effectively (Sugai, Sprague, Horner, & Walker, 2000). However, I do not believe that disability services should be justified on the basis of their impact on the nondisabled. Universal design is a matter of simple justice. I mention these examples here simply to increase the force of the argument that universal design is truly universal in its impact.

EPILOGUE

I would like to conclude this piece with an update on Joe Ford. He is currently a senior in high school and has applied to college. His Scholastic Aptitude Tests scores place him within the top 5 percent of his peers, so competitive schools have been vying for his attendance. I am pleased that Harvard College will be benefiting from Joe's presence in September 2002. This success, however, has required the constant advocacy of both Joe and his mother. Although universal design has not been a feature of his schooling, he has clearly benefited from inclusive education, and at times he has benefited from specialized services. At other times, however, the lack of specialized services has put a great burden on both Joe and Penny to find the most efficient means for him to access education. They have found that the most efficient way for him to read is through taped books, though other accommodations, particularly in certain areas of math instruction, have been lacking. He has no trouble moving about his city in his motorized chair, aided by an accessible public transportation system. One of his favorite pastimes is going downtown to challenge all comers to chess matches. He usually wins. Deeply interested in politics, he does not miss an opportunity to challenge the liberal views of this writer. Penny's intuitive challenge to ableism is paying off, and she looks forward to the day when Joe will not only support himself, but help support her.

NOTES

1. Section 504 of the Rehabilitation Act of 1973 was the first federal law that guaranteed education to all disabled children by prohibiting discrimination against the disabled by any institution that received federal funds. Therefore, given the fact that public schools accepted federal money, they were covered under the act. IDEA, originally P.L. 94-142, the Education for all Handicapped Children Act (EHA), passed shortly after Section 504 in 1975. P.L. 94-142 provided funds to states to assist in the education of the disabled, along with significant regulatory requirements. All states eventually chose to accept this money and therefore are subject to IDEA's regulatory requirements.
2. I have chosen not to address the issue of cochlear implants in this article due to the complexity of the issue and the relative newness and rapidly changing nature of these devices. Though there is much controversy surrounding these devices, there is evidence that they can increase language development in deaf children. However, more research is needed to determine whether these devices can, by themselves, substitute for the development of language that can occur when deaf children are given access to American Sign Language (ASL) from birth. For this reason, some cochlear implant advocates recommend that ASL be taught to these children as well (Zwiebel, 1987).
3. The IDEA mandates that educational decisions regarding disabled children be made by an appropriate team of educators and the parent. This meeting results in an IEP that delineates the child's program and services.
4. For the purpose of this article, I use the terms *learning disability* (LD) and *dyslexia* interchangeably for the following reasons. First, though the population of students with learning disabilities is diverse, a high percentage of children with learning disabilities have marked reading problems. Second, much of the research on LD is not categorized by type of LD. Finally, the way schools respond to dyslexia, in my view, is similar to the way they respond to other types of LD.
5. More than 11 percent of students age six to seventeen received special education services during the 1998–1999 school year (U.S. Department of Education, 2000).
6. The term *community* is used loosely here to include those who have disabilities, parents of children with disabilities, and their advocates.

REFERENCES

Allington, R. L., & McGill-Franzen, A. (1989). School response to reading failure: Instruction for chapter one and special education students grade two, four, and eight. *Elementary School Journal, 89,* 529–542.

Baynton, D. C. (1996). *Forbidden signs: American culture and the campaign against sign language.* Chicago: University of Chicago Press.

Biklen, D. (1992). *Schooling without labels: Parents, educators, and inclusive education.* Philadelphia: Temple University Press.

Blatt, B. (1970). *Exodus from pandemonium.* Boston: Allyn & Bacon.

Brown, L., Schwarz, P., Udvari-Solner, A., Kampschroer, E. F, Johnson, F., Jorgenson, J., & Gruenewald, L. (1991). How much time should students with severe intellectual disabilities spend in regular education classrooms and elsewhere? In J. Rogers (Ed.), *Inclusion: Moving beyond our fears* (pp. 111–122). Bloomington, IN: Phi Delta Kappa Center for Evaluation, Development, and Research.

Courtin, C. (2000). The impact of sign language on the cognitive development of deaf children: The case of theories of the mind. *Journal of Deaf Studies and Deaf Education, 5,* 266–276.

Ferguson, P. M., & Asch A. (1989). Lessons from life: Personal and parental perspectives on school, childhood and disability. In D. Biklen, D. Ferguson, & A. Ford (Eds.), *Schooling and disability: Eighty-eighth yearbook of the national society for the study of education: Part II* (pp. 108–141). Chicago: University of Chicago Press.

Ford, P. (1993). *Something to be gained: A family's long road to inclusive schooling.* In J. Rogers (Ed.), *Inclusion: Moving beyond our fears* (pp. 101–111). Bloomington, IN: Phi Delta Kappa Center for Evaluation, Development, and Research.

Fuchs, D., & Fuchs, L. S. (1994). Inclusive schools movement and the radicalization of special education reform. *Exceptional Children, 60,* 294–309.

Fuchs, D., & Fuchs, L. S. (1995). What's "special" about special education? *Phi Delta Kappan, 76,* 522–530.

Fuchs, L. S., & Fuchs, D. (1999). *Accountability and assessment in the 21st century for students with learning disabilities.* Nashville, TN: Peabody College of Vanderbilt University.

Gartner, A., & Lipsky, D. K. (1996). Inclusion, school restructuring, and the remaking of American society. *Harvard Educational Review, 66,* 762–796.

Groce, N. E. (1985). *Everyone here spoke sign language: Hereditary deafness on Martha's Vineyard.* Cambridge, MA: Harvard University Press.

Hanson, M. J., Horn, E., Sandall, S., Beckman, P. Morgan, M., Marquart, J., Barnwell, D., & Chou, H. (2001). After preschool inclusion: Children's educational pathways over the early school years. *Exceptional Children 68*(1), 65–83.

Hehir, T., & Gamm, S. (1999). Special education: From legalism to collaboration. In J. Heubert (Ed.), *Law and school reform* (pp. 205–227). New Haven, CT: Yale University Press.

Heubert, J. P., & Hauser, R. M. (Eds.). (1999). *High stakes: Testing for tracking, promotion and graduation.* Washington, DC: National Academy Press.

The Individuals with Disabilities Education Act Amendments of 1997, Pub L. No. 105-17, §1400, 37 Stat. 111 (1997).

Jacobs, L. (1989). *A deaf adult speaks out.* Washington, DC: Gallaudet University Press.

Johnson, L. (1996). The Braille literacy crisis for children. *Journal of Visual Impairment and Blindness, 90,* 276–278.

Jorgensen, C. (1997). *Restructuring high schools for all students: Taking inclusion to the next level.* Baltimore: Paul Brooks.

Katzman, L. I. (2001). *The effects of high-stakes testing on students with disabilities: What do we know?* Unpublished qualifying paper, Harvard Graduate School of Education, Cambridge, MA.

Kauffman, J. M., & Hallahan, D. P. (Eds.). (1995). *The illusion of full-inclusion: A comprehensive critique of a current special education bandwagon.* Austin, TX: Pro-Ed.

Kirp, D. L. (1974). The great sorting machine: Special education trends and issues. *Phi Delta Kappan, 55*, 521–525.

Koretz, D. M., & Hamilton, L. S. (2000). Assessment of students with disabilities in Kentucky: Inclusion, student performance, and validity. *Education Evaluation and Policy Analysis, 22*, 255–272.

Lane, H. (1995). The education of deaf children: Drowning in the mainstream and the sidestream. In J. M. Kauffman & D. P. Hallahan (Eds.), *The illusion of full inclusion: A comprehensive critique of a current special education bandwagon* (pp. 275–287). Austin, TX: Pro-Ed.

Lyon, G. R., Fletcher, J. M., Shaywitz, S. E., Shaywitz, B. A., Torgenson, J. K., Wood, F. B., Shulte, A., & Olson, R. (2001). Rethinking learning disabilities. In C. E. Finn, A. J. Rotherman, & C. R. Hokanson (Eds.), *Rethinking special education for a new century* (pp. 259–287). Washington, DC: Thomas B. Fordham Foundation and the Progressive Policy Institute.

McDonnell, L. M., McLaughlin, M. J., & Morison, P. (1997). Educating one and all: Students with disabilities and standards-based reform. Washington, DC: National Academy Press.

Milofsky, C. D. (1974). Why special education isn't special. *Harvard Educational Review, 44*, 437–458.

National Federation of the Blind (n.d.). *What is Braille and what does it mean to the blind?* [On-line]. Available: http://www.nfb.org/books/books1/ifblnd03.htm.

New York State Department of Education. (2001). *Reforming education for students with disabilities.* Albany: New York State Education Department Office of Vocational and Educational Services for Individuals with Disabilities.

Overboe, J. (1999). "Difference in itself": Validating disabled people's lived experience. *Body and Society, 5*(4), 17–29.

Pittman, P., & Huefner, D. S. (2001). Will the courts go bi-bi? IDEA 1997, the courts and deaf education. *Exceptional Children, 67*, 187–198.

Prinz, P. M., & Strong, M. (1998). ASL proficiency and English literacy within a bilingual deaf education model of instruction. *Topics in Language Disorders, 18*(4), 47–60.

Rauscher, L., & McClintock, J. (1996). Ableism curriculum design. In M. Adams, L. A. Bell, & P. Griffen (Eds.), *Teaching for diversity and social justice* (pp. 198–231). New York: Routledge.

Reagan, T. (1985). The deaf as a linguistic minority: Educational considerations. *Harvard Educational Review, 55*, 265–277.

Rehabilitation Act of 1973, 504, 29 U.S.C. § 794.

Rousso, H. (1984). Fostering healthy self esteem: Part one. *Exceptional Parent, 14*(8), 9–14.

Rowley v. Board of Education of the Gloversville Enlarged City School. 192 A.D.2d 814; 596 N.Y.S.2d 561 (N.Y. App. Div. 1993)

Sisco, F. H., & Anderson, R. J. (1980). Deaf children's performance of the WISC-R relative to hearing status of parents and child-rearing experiences. *American Annals of the Deaf, 125*, 923–930.

Shapiro, J. P. (1994). *No pity: People with disabilities forging a new civil rights movement.* New York: Random House.

Skrtic, T. M. (1991). The special education paradox: Equity as the way to excellence. *Harvard Educational Review, 61*, 148–206.

Smith, G. (2001, July 20). Backtalk: The brother in the wheelchair. *Essence*, p. 162.

Snow, C. (Ed.). (1998). *Preventing reading difficulties in young children.* Washington, DC: National Research Council.

Stuckless, R. E., & Birch, J. W. (1966). The influence of early manual communication on the linguistic development of deaf children. *American Annals of the Deaf, 111*(2/3), 71–79.

Sugai, G., Sprague, J. R., Horner, R. H., & Walker, H. M. (2000). Preventing school violence: The use of office discipline referrals to assess and monitor school-wide discipline interventions. *Journal of Emotional and Behavioral Disorder, 8*, 94–101.

Thurlow, M. L. (2000). Standards-based reform and students with disabilities: Reflections on a decade of change. *Focus on Exceptional Children, 33*(3), 1–16.

Torgesen, J. K. (2000). Individual differences in response to early intervention in reading: The lingering problem of treatment resisters. *Learning Disabilities Research and Practice, 15*(1), 55–64.

U.S. Department of Education. (1995). *Individuals with Disabilities Education Act amendments of 1995: Reauthorization of the Individuals with Disabilities Education Act*. Washington, DC: Author.

U.S. Department of Education. (1996). To assure the free and appropriate public education of all children with disabilities. *Eighteenth annual report to Congress on implementation of the Individuals with Disabilities Education Act*. Washington, DC: Author.

U.S. Department of Education. (2000). To assure the free and appropriate public education of all children with disabilities. *Twenty-second annual report to congress on implementation of the Individuals with Disabilities Education Act*. Washington, DC: Author.

Vaughn, G., et al. v. Mayor and City Council of Baltimore, et al. Consent Order, 2000.

Wagner, M., Blackorby, J., Cameto, R., & Newman, L. (1993). *What makes a difference? Influences of postschool outcomes of youth with disabilities* (Report from the National Longitudinal Transition Study of Special Education Students). Washington, DC: U.S. Department of Education.

Weeber, J. E. (1999). What could I know of racism? *Journal of Counseling and Development, 77*(1), 20–23.

Will, M. (1986). Educating children with learning problems: A shared responsibility. *Exceptional Children, 52*, 411–415.

Zwiebel, A. (1987). More on the effects of early manual communication on the cognitive development of deaf children. *American Annals of the Deaf, 132*, 16–20.

The Deaf as a Linguistic Minority
Educational Considerations

———⸹———

TIMOTHY REAGAN

What is it like to "hear" a hand?
You have to be deaf to understand.

....

What is it like to comprehend
Some nimble fingers that paint the scene,
And make you smile and feel serene
With the "spoken word" of the moving hand
That makes you part of the world at large?
You have to be deaf to understand.
            — Wilard J. Madsen, "You Have to Be Deaf to Understand"[1]

T he last thirty years have seen remarkable changes in the educational system of the United States, not the least of which have been those affecting social and linguistic minorities. The 1954 *Brown v. Board of Education*[2] Supreme Court decision provided the legal basis for widespread desegregation in the schools and an end to the long tradition of separate and unequal education for blacks and whites in U. S. society.[3] Nevertheless, some twenty years later, meaningful racial integration is still an unrealized ideal in many parts of the nation.

In 1974, the *Lau* v. *Nichols*[4] decision expanded the coverage of the doctrine of "equal educational opportunity" to include the provision of "affirmative steps" for minority-language children unable to function in school in English.[5] While the Court did not specify that bilingual programs were the only acceptable way school districts might meet the educational needs of non-English-speaking students, the "*Lau* remedies," initially issued by the Department of Health, Education and Welfare (HEW) in the summer of 1975, clearly favored the implementation of bilingual education programs.[6]

Harvard Educational Review   Vol. 55   No. 3   August 1985, 256–277

In a 1979 decision in Ann Arbor, Michigan, the educational problems faced by speakers of Black English were addressed for the first time by a court of law.[7] The *King*[8] decision recognized Black English as a viable and legitimate variety of English and acknowledged that the learning problems of many poor blacks may be partly linguistic in nature. The decision, however, was far from radical.[9] Indeed, it recommended such approaches as in-service sociolinguistic training for teachers rather than the development of bilingual or bidialectical programs for speakers of Black English.[10] Still, the rights of those whose native language is a specific nonstandard variety of English were recognized in *King*, and future judicial challenges may conceivably apply similar criteria to other nonstandard varieties of English.[11] We see, then, an expansion of concern with and sensitivity to the special educational needs and problems of minority students, especially linguistic minorities. The rights of one sizable linguistic minority group, however, have been overlooked throughout this period, probably through a combination of ignorance, bias, and a generally unrecognized history of oppression. I am referring to the deaf.[12]

Commonly identified as simply "handicapped," little attention has been given to the deaf as a cultural and linguistic minority group with distinctive educational needs. The federal law that defined special education in the United States, P. L. 94–142, has been used rather than *Lau* to provide the legal basis for contemporary developments in the education of the deaf. This has resulted in widespread misunderstanding of the deaf in educational circles, as well as to pedagogical approaches in deaf education which, were they to be directed toward any other minority language population in the United States, would be condemned by educators and policymakers alike. This paper provides an analysis of the cultural and linguistic aspects of the deaf community, of the education of the deaf as a cultural and linguistic minority, and of alternative approaches in the education of the deaf. It also offers arguments for the provision of bilingual education programs for the deaf.

LINGUISTIC SITUATION

Although small numbers of the deaf use speech and lipreading as their primary means of communication, the vast majority rely on a variety or combination of varieties of sign language and manual "codes."[13] In general, three major types of signing are used by the deaf in the United States: American Sign Language (ASL), Pidgin Sign English (PSE), and different kinds of Manually Coded English (MCE). The distinctions among them have important educational consequences.

ASL is the language used by the deaf and is, in fact, the single "most effective signal of membership in the deaf community."[14] It has been the focus of a great deal of linguistic study since the 1960 publication of William Stokoe's landmark work, "Sign Language Structure."[15] ASL's linguistic features are now understood, at least in fairly broad outline. It is a language in every sense of the word, relying on visual, rather than auditory, encoding and decoding. ASL has a complex, rule-governed phonology, syntax, and morphology.[16] For example, each sign contains at least five distinct pa-

FIGURE 1

Changes in the Parameters That Result in a Different Sign

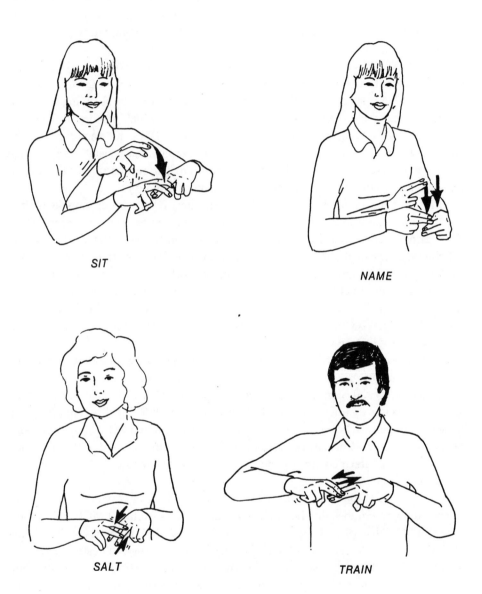

SIT

NAME

SALT

TRAIN

rameters which delimit its meaning. These parameters are handshape(s), movement of hand, position/location of hand, palm orientation, and facial expression and other body movement(s).[17] These parameters, which also affect meaning in most other sign languages, function in ASL roughly as phonological distinctions do in oral languages.[18] Figure 1 shows how a change in one or more of the parameters can result in the formation of a different sign.[19]

Although ASL has traditionally been considered the low-status variety of signing (as contrasted with those varieties which more closely approximate English) by both the deaf and hearing worlds,[20] this negative attitude appears to be changing.[21] Undoubtedly, "deaf pride" has played a role in this change, which has been further encouraged by the preparation of new instructional materials for the teaching of ASL to hearing individuals.[22] As ASL becomes increasingly accepted as a "legitimate" foreign language in colleges and universities, and continues to gain recognition by hearing individuals, this change is likely to become even more profound.

An interesting sociological feature of ASL is that, unlike other languages, it is passed on more commonly from child to child — usually in residential schools for the deaf — rather than from parent to child. Indeed, since only an estimated 12 percent of deaf children have deaf parents, it can be argued that "for close to 90 percent of the deaf population, the group language [ASL] and sociocultural patterns are not transmitted from parent to child."[23] Further, ASL provides a language of "group solidarity" not generally shared with hearing individuals.[24] Its use is almost never allowed in formal or educational settings, a fact which has important social and pedagogical implications and to which we will return.[25]

Pidgin Sign English refers to a range of different types of signing that incorporate varying amounts of ASL and English in a pidgin system. In general, PSE can be defined as the use of ASL signs in English word order.[26] Words which have no ASL equivalents (such as *the, a,* and so on) may be fingerspelled in PSE, but this is not required. PSE serves as a bridge between the deaf and hearing individuals who know some sign language but who may or may not know ASL.[27] It is commonly used in the education of the deaf at the intermediate, secondary, and postsecondary levels,[28] for example at Gallaudet College.[29]

Manually Coded English (MCE) encompasses a number of very different systems designed to represent visually the English language. The systems of MCE include Seeing Essential English (SEE I), Signing Exact English (SEE II), Linguistics of Visual English (LOVE), Cued Speech, and Fingerspelling (including the Rochester Method).[30] The key is that MCE is a manual *code* used to transmit English, rather than a language in and of itself.[31] This is no doubt one of the principal arguments in favor of its use, as Gustason notes: "The most important principle of Manual English systems is that English should be signed as it is spoken for the deaf child to have linguistic input that would result in his mastery of English."[32] This aspect of MCE, together with its ease of acquisition for hearing individuals, helps to explain its popularity in both preschool and primary education.[33] Nevertheless, the use of MCE in early childhood education, while pedagogically superior to an oral (that is, nonmanual) approach, has not been particularly effective in providing an adequate education for the deaf.

FIGURE 2

Overlapping Continua of the Three Major Types of Signing

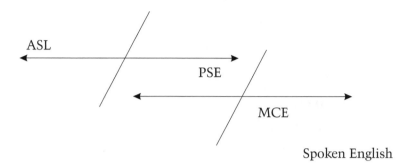

These three major types of signing can be conceptualized as falling along two over-lapping continua.[34] If viewed as a continuum ranging from the most private, exclusive to the deaf, to the most public, common to most of U.S. society, the types of signing can be envisioned as shown in Figure 2.

Since ASL and English are not historically related languages — in the way that English and German are, for example — we must use two overlapping lines, rather than a single line, to represent the range of sign systems. As a pidgin, PSE incorpo-rates enough syntactic, semantic, and morphological variation to fall along both con-tinua, and hence can be seen as mediating between the two distinct linguistic com-munities. Figure 3 provides an illustration of how the continua between ASL and MCE function for the English sentence, "I have eaten."

The result of this range of signing systems has been what Stokoe has called "sign language diglossia."[35] The term *diglossia*, coined by Ferguson in the late 1950s,[36] is normally used to describe a situation in which "two varieties of a single language exist side by side throughout the community, with each having a definite role to play."[37] Commonly, the two varieties of the language are the literary and colloquial, as in the differential usage in Greece of *katharevusa* (the *H*, or high-status, variety) and *dhimotiki* (the *L*, or low-status, variety).[38] Fishman has expanded this definition of diglossia, suggesting that diglossia may also refer to a situation in which two different languages are used for different functions in a community.[39]

Within Fishman's broader definition, the situation for the deaf community in the United States is diglossic.[40] Sign varieties approximating English are the *H* varieties, while ASL serves as the *L* variety.[41] Woodward clearly explicates the situation: "As in other diglossic situations, the literary variety (English) is used in formal conversa-tions in church, in classrooms, for lectures, and so on. The colloquial variety (ASL) is used in smaller, less formal, more intimate conversations. English is considered supe-rior to ASL, and ASL is regarded as ungrammatical or non-existent."[42] The diglossic situation of the deaf community is likely to remain, but the relative status of English to ASL, as noted earlier, appears to be changing. Few today would consider English in-

FIGURE 3

Lexical and Syntactic Variations in Sign Varieties of the English Sentence

FINISH ME	(right hand)	ASL
EAT	(left hand)	
EAT FINISH ME		
I FINISH EAT		PSE
I END EAT		
I HAVE EAT		
I HAVE(V) EAT		
I HAVE(V) EAT FINISH		MCE

From James Woodward, "Sociolinguistic Research on American Sign Language: A Historical Perspective," in *Sign Language and the Deaf Community: Essays in Honor of William C. Stokoe*, ed. Charlotte Baker and Robbin Battison (Silver Springs, MD: National Association of the Deaf, 1980), p. 123. Printed by permission of the publisher.

nately superior to ASL, and no one could now justifiably maintain a belief in the supposed "ungrammaticality" of ASL.

CULTURAL SITUATION

The deaf constitute a unique subculture in American society. Although many of the characteristic features of the deaf subculture are linguistic, or at least partially linguistic, in nature, other important cultural values, attitudes, and traditions are present as well. One of the more significant features of deaf life has been the role played by residential schools for the deaf in the maintenance and transmission of deaf culture.[43] As we noted earlier, this is one of the principal ways in which the deaf differ from other minority groups, because it means that the culture is, in most instances, passed on from child to child. Four general features demarcate the deaf subculture.

Language

Language generally plays a key role in cultural and ethnic identification, and this is especially true for the deaf. Membership in the deaf community is contingent upon communicative competence in ASL, which thus serves a dual function as both the community's vernacular language and its principal identifying characteristic.[44] Given the diglossic nature of language use in the deaf community, ASL serves in many instances as an effective barrier to hearing people's access to the deaf subculture.[45] As Meadow has noted about language in general, "It can serve as a cohesive, defining source of pride and positive identification and simultaneously as a focus for stigma and ridicule from members of the majority culture."[46] This is clearly the case with respect to ASL, though, again, the hearing world's resistance to ASL appears to be changing.

Group Identification

The deaf community in the United States perceives itself as a distinctive group, in both social and linguistic terms, and is generally recognized as a distinctive population by the dominant society, though perhaps not a culturally distinct one. Interestingly, there are significant differences in how the parameters of the group are established and how that grouphood is evaluated.

In the hearing world, distinctions based on the extent to which an individual can hear (for example, hearing vs. hard-of-hearing vs. deaf) are seen as reasonably significant. Further, hearing-impaired individuals are commonly "valued" based on the extent to which they can hear. In the deaf community this is not the case. Rather, the degree or extent of hearing loss is simply not regarded as a criterion for membership in the deaf community so long as there is some degree of hearing loss.[47] Indeed, Padden notes that "there is one name for all members of the cultural group, regardless of the degree of hearing loss: Deaf. In fact, the sign DEAF can be used in an ASL sentence to mean 'my friends,' which conveys the cultural meaning of 'Deaf'."[48]

Endogamy

The maintenance of endogamous marriages is often seen by cultural and ethnic groups as a key to their survival. Among the deaf, intermarriage appears to be the most typical pattern. Estimates for the rate of endogamous marriage in the deaf community range from 86 percent to well over 90 percent.[49] By these estimates the deaf are significantly more endogamous than most other contemporary U.S. cultural and ethnic groups.

Organizational Network

Lastly, the network of voluntary organizations that serves the deaf community is comparable to that serving any other cultural or ethnic group in U.S. society.[50] In addition to the National Association of the Deaf (NAD) and the various state associations of the deaf, there are social clubs, sports teams, the "Deaf Olympics," the National Theatre of the Deaf, and a host of others. This is especially significant given Padden's observation that "Deaf people consider social activities an important way of maintaining contact with other deaf people."[51] In short, such organizational networks help both to maintain the cohesiveness of the group and to serve the companionship needs of group members.

The deaf, then, do indeed appear to constitute a subcultural community in contemporary U.S. society. Figure 4 shows the classifications and significant features of the deaf community. This same diagram, with only minor modifications, has been used to describe the deaf community in Great Britain and could presumably be applied to a number of other nations as well.[52]

FIGURE 4

Classifications and Significant Features of the Deal

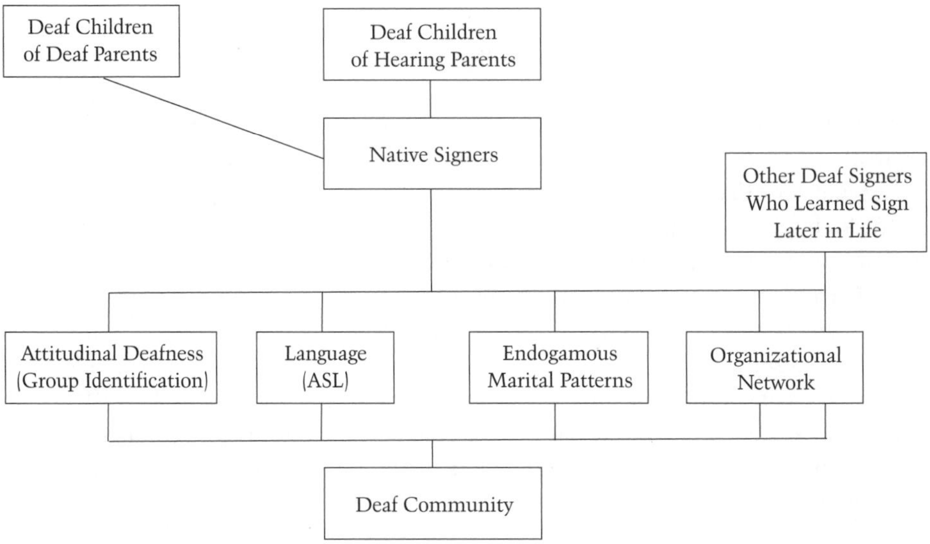

This figure is adapted from Lilian Lawson, "The Role of Sign in the Structure of the Deaf Community," in *Perspectives on British Sign Language and Deafness*, ed. Bernice Woll, James Kyle, and Margaret Deuchar (London: Croom Helm, 1981), p. 168. Printed by permission of the publisher.

COMPETING APPROACHES IN THE EDUCATION OF THE DEAF

Historically, the major controversy in the education of the deaf in the United States has been the debate between the oralists and the manualists.[53] The oralists, working in the tradition of Alexander Graham Bell,[54] have emphasized the need for deaf children to acquire competence in English, as manifested in lipreading and the ability to produce speech. Signing is discouraged and generally not allowed in schools.[55] At the present time, approximately one-third of the educational programs for the deaf in the United States use the oral approach.[56] Such programs are ideologically similar to traditional, pre-*Lau* approaches to non-English speaking minority groups whereby children were commonly punished for using their native language.

Manualists, on the other hand, have advocated a combination of speech and signing (in English word order) in the classroom. The role and extent of signing, however, even in the manual approach, has tended to be limited. Rather than using ASL, the manualists favor sign systems which approach English syntactically, so that speech and signs can be used together.[57] As Woodward has noted, "Until recently, there has never been any question that the language code in the classrooms should approach English; the question has been through what channel could English be best represented and understood."[58]

A new wrinkle appeared in the oral-manual controversy in the late 1960s, however, as total communication gained popularity in deaf education.[59] Like so many other educational slogans,[60] "total communication" gained widespread support because it could mean so many different things to so many different people. Commonly, total communication meant that "no change in philosophy took place; to all other methods, techniques, training, and curricula, signs were merely added."[61] This is especially interesting in view of the fact that NAD has specifically defined the term as "a philosophy of communication which implies acceptance, understanding, and use of all methods of communication to assist the deaf child in acquiring language and the deaf adult in understanding."[62] In short, while there may have been greater acceptance of sign language in the education of the deaf, there was hardly a revolution in deaf education. Total communication has been used to mean nothing more than the "simultaneous method" in many programs.[63] In schools it has not engendered the acceptance, understanding, or use of sign languages in general, or of ASL in particular.

BILINGUAL EDUCATION AND THE DEAF

Despite widespread international support for initial mother-tongue approaches in education,[64] bilingual education programs in the United States have been far from popular. Empirical evidence for the effectiveness of such programs is often ambiguous.[65] The successes of early immersion programs for Anglophone students in Canada are commonly used to support calls for similar English as a Second Language programs for minority language students in this country.[66] There is some agreement that initial mother-tongue programs are most likely to be effective where children come from lower socioeconomic status (SES) backgrounds, where they may not be proficient in their native language, where their native language has low social status, and where teachers in regular classrooms are of a different ethnicity or language background.[67]

These criteria suggest that the deaf might be an ideal population for bilingual education programs. While the social class background of the deaf population is quite varied, an increasing percentage of the school-age deaf population is coming from minority and lower SES backgrounds.[68] More significant, though, is the generally low SES that the deaf as a community continue to face in U.S. society as a result of social and economic discrimination. The question of the deaf child's native language is difficult because, for the deaf child, "home language" and "native language" are not necessarily synonymous, except in the rare cases where a deaf child is born to deaf, ASL-using parents. In any event, visual rather than auditory languages are the natural communicative approach for the deaf child. Taking this into account, and recognizing both the role of ASL in the deaf community and the artificial nature of MCEs, it is reasonable to treat the deaf child *as if* his/her native language were ASL. This means, of course, that in the vast majority of cases the child will not be proficient in the native language. We have already discussed the traditionally low social status accorded ASL in both the deaf and hearing worlds. With respect to the ethnicity and language backgrounds of the teachers, there is a classic colonial model in the education of the deaf in which great resistance to the hiring of deaf professionals persists. Further, the control of deaf education, at all levels, is firmly in the hands of hearing individuals.

The need for the deaf child to learn to cope with and function in both the hearing and deaf cultures would make a bicultural — as well as a bilingual — approach especially desirable. Indeed, the deaf have a uniquely powerful argument for such programs. Nevertheless, despite the strong arguments in favor of a bilingual-bicultural approach in the education of the deaf, only a few individuals have proposed such programs, and their audience has been limited for the most part to those already immersed in and sympathetic to studies of deaf culture and the linguistics of ASL.[69] Furthermore, few of their proposals have been published, and even these have reached a narrow audience.[70] Educators involved with bilingual education, minority studies, and multicultural education, on the other hand, have generally tended to ignore the deaf, save in discussions about blacks, Latinos, and so forth, who happen also to be deaf. The notion that being deaf in and of itself might have important cultural and linguistic implications appears to have been overlooked. Woodward correctly claims that "the Deaf community has had a more difficult time overcoming inferiority stereotyping by the majority culture than other minority groups, since deaf people are viewed as a *medical* pathology."[71]

In the development and implementation of a bilingual-bicultural program for the deaf, two conditions would have to be met.[72] First, ASL — *not* PSE or some form of MCE — would have to be not only allowed but encouraged in the classroom. This would require reeducating teachers of the deaf as well as others, but the rewards would almost certainly be worth the effort. Second, members of the deaf community would need to be active and, ideally, coequal partners in the control, administration, and teaching of the programs.[73] Given the resistance even to the hiring of deaf teachers in many schools, this would require significant amounts of time, effort, and pressure.[74] To do otherwise, however, would be to allow an essentially imperialistic approach to the education of a sizable minority group in the United States to continue unabated. Such a path cannot, I believe, be condoned.

This approach does not mean that the acquisition of English skills should be eliminated or minimized in the education of the deaf. English remains the written language of the deaf community and is an indispensible key to the hearing world. The question, instead, has to do with the best way for the deaf student to acquire English and, with the educational role of ASL, the language of the deaf community. It is time to recognize the deaf as a cultural and linguistic community and to reject the view of deafness as an exclusively physiological condition. Perhaps, in time, hearing people may even come to realize how much they have to learn from the deaf. Perhaps, someday, we will understand what it means to "'hear' a hand."

NOTES

1. Original poem printed by permission of the author.
2. 347 U.S. 483 (1954).

3. See Richard Kluger, *Simple Justice: The History of Brown* v. *Board of Education and Black America's Struggle for Equality* (New York: Vintage Books, 1975). Also of interest is Meyer Weinberg, *A Chance to Learn: A History of Race and Education in the United States* (Cambridge, Eng.: Cambridge University Press, 1977).

4. 414 U.S. 563 (1973).

5. See Hebert Teitelbaum and Richard J. Hiller, "Bilingual Education: The Legal Mandate," *Harvard Educational Review*, *47* (1977), 138–170.

6. The "*Lau* Remedies" originally appeared as "H.E.W. Memorandum on 'Task Force' Findings Specifying Remedies Available for Eliminating Past Educational Practices Ruled Unlawful Under Lau v. Nichols, Summer, 1975."

7. See Center for Applied Linguistics, *The Ann Arbor Decision: Memorandum Opinion and Order & The Educational Plan* (Arlington, VA: Center for Applied Linguistics, 1979); and *The Ann Arbor Black English Case*, ed. Arthur Brown (Gainesville, FL: John Dewey Society, 1980).

8. Martin Luther King Junior Elementary School Children v. Ann Arbor School District Board. Civil Action No. 7-71861 (E.D. Mich. 12 July 1979).

9. See Geneva Smitherman, "'What Go Round Come Round': *King* in Perspective," *Harvard Educational Review*, *51* (1981), 40–56.

10. Smitherman, "'What Go Round Come Round'"; Walt Wolfram, "Landmark Decision Affects Black English Speakers," *The Linguistic Reporter*, *22* (1979), pp. 1, 6–7.

11. See Walt Wolfram, "Beyond Black English: Implications of the Ann Arbor Decision for Other Non-Mainstream Varieties," in *Reactions to Ann Arbor: Vernacular Black English and Education*, ed. Marcia Farr Whiteman (Arlington, VA: Center for Applied Linguistics, 1980), pp. 10–23.

12. See Harlan Lane, "A Chronology of the Oppression of Sign Language in France and the United States," in *Recent Perspectives on American Sign Language*, ed. Harlan Lane and Francois Grosjean (Hillsdale, NJ: Eribaum, 1980), pp. 119–161; Edward L. Scouten, *Turning Points in the Education of Deaf People* (Danville, IL: Interstate, 1984); and Donald F. Moores, *Educating the Deaf: Psychology, Principles, and Practices* (Boston: Houghton Mifflin, 1978), pp. 27–64.

13. Barbara M. Kannapell and Paul E. Adams, *Orientation to Deafness: A Handbook and Resource Guide* (Washington, DC: Gallaudet College Press, 1984), ch. 4, pp. 9–10.

14. Carol Erting, "Language Policy and Deaf Ethnicity in the United States," *Sign Language Studies*, *19* (1978), 139.

15. Stokoe, "Sign Language Structure: An Outline of the Visual Communication Systems of the American Deaf," *Studies in Linguistics: Occasional Papers*, *8* (1960); also of interest in Stokoe, Dorothy Casterline, and Carl G. Croneberg, *A Dictionary of American Sign Language* (Washington, DC: Gallaudet College Press, 1965).

16. Stokeo, "Sign Language Structure"; Charlotte Baker and Carol Padden, *American Sign Language: A Look at Its History, Structure, and Community* (Silver Spring, MD: T. J. Publishers, 1978); and Ronnie Wilbur, "The Linguistic Description of American Sign Language," in *Recent Perspectives on American Sign Language*, pp.7–31.

17. Based on Kannapell and Adams, *Orientation to Deafness*, ch. 4, p. 3. See also Robbin Battison, "Signs Have Parts: A Simple Idea," in *Sign Language and the Deaf Community: Essays in Honor of William C. Stokoe*, ed. Charlotte Baker and Robbin Battison (Silver Spring, MD: National Association of the Deaf, 1980), pp. 35–51.

18. See, for example, Margaret Deuchar, *British Sign Language* (London: Routledge & Kegan Paul, 1984), ch. 3.

19. See also Martin L. A. Sternberg, *American Sign Language: A Comprehensive Dictionary* (New York: Harper & Row, 1981).

20. See Kathryn P. Meadow, "Sociolingustics, Sign Language, and the Deaf Sub-Culture," in *Psycholinguistics and Total Communication: The State of the Art*, ed. T. J. O'Rourke (Washington, DC: American Annals of the Deaf, 1972), pp. 19–33; Stokoe, "Sign Language Diglossia," *Studies in Linguistics*, *21* (1970); 27–41; and James Woodward, "Some Sociolinguistic Aspects

of French and American Sign Languages," in *Recent Perspectives in American Sign Language*, pp. 103–118.

21. See Kannapell and Adams, *Orientation to Deafness*, ch. 4, p. 3.

22. Kannapell and Adams, *Orientation to Deafness*. Good examples of such materials are Charlotte Baker and Dennis Cokely, *American Sign Language: A Teacher's Resource Text on Grammar and Culture* (Silver Spring, MD: T. J. Publishers, 1980); Elaine Costello, *Signing* (Toronto: Bantam, 1983); Louie J. Fant, Jr., *Ameslan: An Introduction to American Sign Language* (Northridge, CA: Joyce Media, 1972); and Tom Humphries, Carol Padden and T. J. O'Rourke, *A Basic Course in American Sign Language* (Silver Spring, MD: T. J. Publishers, 1980).

23. Erting, "Language Policy and Deaf Ethnicity," p. 140.

24. James Woodward, *How You Gonna Get to Heaven If You Can't Talk With Jesus: On Depathologizing Deafness* (Silver Spring, MD: T. J. Publishers, 1982), p. 33.

25. See Kannapell and Adams, *Orientation to Deafness*, ch. 4, p. 3.

26. See Judy Reilly and Marina L. McIntire, "American Sign Language and Pidgin Sign English: What's the Difference?" *Sign Language Studies*, 27 (1980), 151–192; and James C. Woodward, Jr. "Some Characteristics of Pidgin Sign English," *Sign Language Studies*, 3 (1973), 39–60.

27. James Woodward, "Some Characteristics of Pidgin Sign English."

28. Kannapell and Adams, *Orientation to Deafness*, ch. 4, p. 4.

29. Gallaudet College is significant here because it is the only liberal arts college for the deaf in the world.

30. For SEE I, see David Anthony, ed., *Seeing Essential English* (Greeley: University of Northern Colorado, 1971); see also Paul W. Ogden and Suzanne Lipsett, *The Silent Garden: Understanding the Hearing Impaired Child* (New York: St. Martin's Press, 1982), pp. 109–118; and Jerome D. Schein, *Speaking the Language of Sign: The Art and Science of Signing* (Garden City, NY: Doubleday, 1984), pp. 64–77. For SEE II, see Gerilee Gustason, D. Pfetzing, and E. Zawalkow, *Signing Exact English: Seeing Instead of Hearing* (Rossmoor, CA: Modern Sign Press, 1972); see also Anthony, *Seeing Essential English*. For LOVE, see Dennis Wampler, *Linguistics of Visual English* (Santa Rosa, CA: Santa Rosa City Schools, 1971); see also Gustason, Pfetzing, and Zawalkow, *Signing Exact English*. For Cued Speech, see R. O. Cornett, *Cued Speech: A New Aid in the Education of Hearing Impaired Children* (Washington, DC: Gallaudet College, 1966); see also, Wampler, *Linguistics of Visual English*.

31. See Baker and Cokely, *American Sign Language*, pp. 65–71; Ogden and Lipsett, *The Silent Garden*, pp. 110–111; and Schein, *Speaking the Language of Sign*, pp. 64–66.

32. Gustason as quoted in Kannapell and Adams, *Orientation to Deafness*, ch. 4, p. 5.

33. Kannapell and Adams, *Orientation to Deafness*, ch. 4, p. 5.

34. This is not the way the ASL-English continuum is commonly presented. Normally, the two languages are shown as two extremes of a single continuum. This is problematic, as explained in the text. For examples of the more general usage, see Baker and Cokely, *American Sign Language*, p. 77; Ogden and Lipsett, *The Silent Garden*, pp. 110–111; Carol Padden and Harry Markowicz, "Cultural Conflicts Between Hearing and Deaf Communities," in *Proceedings of the Seventh World Congress of the World Federation of the Deaf* (Silver Spring, MD: National Association of the Deaf, 1976), pp. 407–411; and Woodward, "Some Sociolinguistic Aspects of French and American Sign Languages."

35. See Stokoe, "Sign Language Diglossia," p. 1.

36. See Charles A. Ferguson, "Diglossia," *Word*, 15 (1959), 325–340; see also James Woodward, "Sociolinguistic Research on American Sign Language: A Historical Perspective," in *Sign Language and the Deaf Community*, pp. 119–122.

37. Ferguson, "Diglossia," p. 1.

38. Ferguson, "Diglossia," pp. 2–5.

39. See Joshua Fishman, "Bilingualism With and Without Diglossia: Diglossia With and Without Bilingualism," *Journal of Social Issues*, 23 (1967), 29–38.

40. See Woodward, "Sociolinguistic Research," p. 120.

41. Woodward, "Sociolinguistic Research," p. 120.

42. Woodward, "Sociolinguistic Research," p. 120.

43. See Kathryn P. Meadow, "The Deaf Subculture," *Hearing and Speech Action, 43* (1975), 16–18; and Arden Neisser, *The Other Side of Silence: Sign Language and the Deaf Community in America* (New York: Knopf, 1983), pp. 281–282.

44. See Erting, "Language Policy and Deaf Ethnicity," pp. 139–140; Harry Markowicz and James Woodward, "Language and the Maintenance of Ethnic Boundaries in the Deaf Community," *Communication and Cognition, 11* (1978), 29–37; Meadow, "The Deaf Subculture"; Meadow, "Sociolinguistics, Sign Language, and the Deaf Sub-Culture"; and Padden, "The Deaf Community and the Culture of Deaf People," in *Sign Language and the Deaf Community*, pp. 89–103; and Padden and Markowicz, "Cultural Conflicts Between Hearing and Deaf Communities."

45. See Meadow, "The Deaf Subculture," p. 17; Woodward, *How You Gonna Get to Heaven*, pp. 32–33.

46. Meadow, "The Deaf Subculture," p. 17.

47. See Erting, "Language Policy and Deaf Ethnicity," p. 140; and Padden, "The Deaf Community and the Culture of Deaf People," pp. 95, 99–100.

48. Padden, "The Deaf Community and the Culture of Deaf People," p. 100.

49. See, for example, *Family and Mental Health Problems in a Deaf Population*, ed. John D. Rainer, Kenneth Z. Altshuler, and Franz J. Kallmann (New York: New York State Psychiatric Institute, Columbia, 1963); and Jerome D. Schein and Marcus Delk, *The Deaf Population of the U.S.* (Washington, DC: Gallaudet College Press, 1974).

50. Erting, "Language Policy and Deaf Ethnicity," p. 140; Kannapell and Adams, *Orientation to Deafness*, ch. 2, pp. 48–49; and Meadow, "The Deaf Subculture," p. 16.

51. Padden, "The Deaf Community and the Culture of Deaf People," p. 97.

52. See Lilian Lawson, "The Role of Sign in the Structure of the Deaf Community," in *Perspectives on British Sign Language and Deafness*, ed. Bencie Woll, James Kyle, and Margaret Deuchar (London: Croom Helm, 1981), pp. 166–177.

53. Woodward, *How You Gonna Get to Heaven*, p. 15.

54. See Scouten, *Turning Points in the Education of Deaf People*, pp. 152–166, 383–384.

55. Kannapell and Adams, *Orientation to Deafness*, ch. 4, p. 7.

56. Kannapell and Adams, *Orientation to Deafness*, ch. 4, p. 7.

57. Woodward, *How You Gonna Get to Heaven*, p. 15.

58. Woodward, *How You Gonna Get to Heaven*, p. 15.

59. See Scouten, *Turning Points in the Education of Deaf People*, pp. 326–330.

60. For an excellent discussion of educational "slogans," see B. Paul Komisar and James E. McClellan, "The Logic of Slogans," in *Language and Concepts in Education*, ed. B. Othanel Smith and Robert H. Ennis (Chicago: Rand McNally, 1961), pp. 195–214.

61. Neisser, *The Other Side of Silence*, p. 4.

62. Quoted in Kannapell and Adams, *Orientation to Deafness*, ch. 4, p. 8.

63. See Kannapell and Adams, *Orientation to Deafness*, ch. 4, p. 6; Moores, *Educating the Deaf*, p. 16.

64. See, for example, *Mother Tongue Education: The West African Experience*, ed. Ayo Bamgbose, (Paris: UNESCO, 1976); *Issues in International Bilingual Education: The Role of the Vernacular*, ed. Beverly Hartford, Albert Valdman, and Charles R. Foster (New York: Plenum, 1982); and UNESCO, *The Use of Vernacular Languages in Education* (Paris: UNESCO, 1953).

65. See, however, Timothy Reagan, "Bilingual Education in the United States: Arguments and Evidence," *Education and Society, 2* (1984), 131–135; and Rudolph C. Troike, *Research Evidence for the Effectiveness of Bilingual Education* (Rosslyn, VA: National Clearinghouse for Bilingual Education, 1978).

66. Of interest here is Merrill Swain and Sharon Lapkin, *Evaluating Bilingual Education: A Canadian Case Study* (Clevedon, Avon: Multilingual Matters, 1982).

67. See Christina Bratt Paulston, "Ethnic Relations and Bilingual Education," *Working Papers in Bilingualism*, No. 6 (Toronto: Ontario Institute for Studies in Education, 1975); G. Richard Tucker, "The Linguistic Perspective," in *Bilingual Education: Current Perspectives*, Vol. II (Arlington, VA: Center for Applied Linguistics, 1977), pp. 1–40. Also of interest is Iris C. Rotberg's "Some Legal and Research Considerations in Establishing Federal Policy in Bilingual Education," *Harvard Educational Review*, 52 (1982), 149–168.

68. See *The Hispanic Deaf: Issues and Challenges in Bilingual Special Education*, ed. Gilbert L. Delgado (Washington, DC: Gallaudet College Press, 1984), p. 28

69. See Kannapell, "Bilingualism: A New Direction in the Education of the Deaf," *The Deaf American, 26* (1974), 9–15; Kannapell, "Personal Awareness and Advocacy in the Deaf Community," in *Sign Language and the Deaf Community*, pp. 105–116; Barbara Luetke-Stahlman, "Using Bilingual Instructional Models in Teaching Hearing-Impaired Students," *American Annals of the Deaf, 128* (1983), 873–877; Raymond Stevens, "Education in Schools for Deaf Children," in *Sign Language and the Deaf Community*, pp. 177–191; William C. Stokoe, Gallaudet College, "An Untried Experiment: Bicultural Education of Deaf Children," unpublished manuscript, 1975; and James Woodward, "Some Sociolinguistic Problems in the Implementation of Bilingual Education for Deaf Students," in *Second National Symposium on Sign Language Research and Teaching*, ed. Frank Caccamise and Doin Hicks (Silver Spring, MD: National Association of the Deaf, 1980).

70. Woodward, "Some Sociolinguistic Problems."

71. Woodward, *How You Gonna Get to Heaven*, p. 11.

72. Woodward, *How You Gonna Get to Heaven*, p. 22.

73. Woodward, *How You Gonna Get to Heaven*, p. 33.

74. See also Hugh T. Prickett and J. T. Hunt, "Education of the Deaf — The Next Ten Years," *American Annals of the Deaf, 122* (1977), 365–381.

Citizenship for All
in the Literate Community

An Ethnography of Young Children with Significant Disabilities in Inclusive Early Childhood Settings[1]

CHRISTOPHER KLIEWER
LINDA MAY FITZGERALD
JODI MEYER-MORK
PATRESA HARTMAN
PAT ENGLISH-SAND
DONNA RASCHKE

You can have no fun at school! There is to be no fun at school!" were the playfully stated phrases that greeted us as we opened the door to the Corner Nook, the given name of a dynamic combined preschool/kindergarten classroom within the Shoshone School, an early childhood education center located in an urban industrial community we refer to as Empire City.[2] While the building that housed Shoshone was old and crumbling, a reflection of the surrounding neighborhood, its interior was colorful and filled with life.

This vibrancy was one of several factors that led us to include the Corner Nook as the first of what would become nine school settings that served as research sites in our ethnography of literacy development in young children with significant disabilities — children often entirely excluded from school-based literacy opportunities. Other factors common among our classroom settings included (a) a focus on preschool- to kindergarten-aged children; (b) educational environments where children with significant disabilities and those without disabilities were taught together;[3] (c) educational environments in which faculty generally viewed literacy development as integral to all aspects of the early childhood curriculum; (d) an established research relationship between the ethnographers and the school; and (e) educational environments with widespread reputations of excellence among their respective communities.

Harvard Educational Review   Vol. 74   No. 4   Winter 2004, 373–403

THE LITERATE COMMUNITY OF AN INCLUSIVE
EARLY CHILDHOOD CLASSROOM

Shayne Robbins, lead teacher to seventeen preschool- and kindergarten-aged children in the Corner Nook classroom, repeated, "I said, 'There's to be no fun at school!'" Shayne was on her knees, forehead-to-forehead with Steven, a four-year-old who stood his ground. With finger jabbing toward Shayne, he made a series of enunciations that ran together like the sounds of a spoken sentence, but without discernible words. Shayne, however, appeared to understand perfectly. "You say you're going to have fun?" she asked. "I say, 'No way!'" Steven threw his head back and shook with laughter. Labeled with autism spectrum disorder, Steven had only two recognizable spoken words and thus was considered to have significant communication disabilities. In the class, he was one of five children labeled with disabilities.

Steven had arrived at school that morning in an extremely angry mood. He had scowled at peers, and during the first few minutes of the initial period of play, a time he generally enjoyed, Steven sat in a corner with his back to the classroom. Steven's closest friend, a nondisabled child named Soo-Nei, approached him with a toy car in hand, but Steven had swatted at his pal, and Soo-Nei retreated. Shayne Robbins, keeping one eye on the situation, approached Steven and said, "We have a new rule, and that new rule is that there will be no fun at school!"

While Steven argued with Shayne, Soo-Nei shouted, "Yes, fun at school!" Shayne said, "No fun at school! I am going to write the new rule on this strip [of paper] and I will hang it on the wall with the class rules, and then it will be our new official rule." The class rules were hung at the front of the room. Certain rules changed on an almost weekly basis, as children and adults gathered to discuss emerging issues and concerns. Implicit in these interactions were both the power and dynamic nature of the written word. Rules were not static but evolving, and authority could be captured and conveyed through graphic (i.e., recorded and observable) symbols. During this particular observation, a number of children now gathered near Shayne and watched intently as she wrote in large letters: "No fun at school." Two giggling students attempted to grab the strip away from Shayne.

A classroom teaching assistant, Aaron, approached Steven, Soo-Nei, and the rest of the children. He said to them, "If you're going to protest a rule you have to do it right. You need to have an official protest with signs saying what you're against." Steven watched with intensity as Aaron got out a piece of poster board and asked, "What should our protest sign say?" Soo-Nei shouted, "Yes, fun at school!" Another child called out in response to Aaron, "No Shayne at school!" Children were gathering, laughing, and chattering with excitement. Aaron wrote out the words, "Yes fun at school." Soo-Nei got his own piece of paper and followed Aaron's lead, writing out, "Yes fun at scool." With his own crayon in hand, Steven sat next to Soo-Nei and made several line marks on the same poster board.

By this point other students had gotten their own posterboard, and with the support of various adults in the class had created a variety of protest signs. One read, "No Shayne at school." Another read, "Yes fun at school." One child drew a quick picture of the school building then added a circle with a slash through it, apparently meaning something akin to "No school" at all. Lori, a four-year-old child with severe physical disabilities, was sitting with an associate teacher, Margaret, watching the excitement grow. Margaret said to her, "Do you want to make a sign?" Lori had a DynaVox positioned beside her. The DynaVox is a computerized communication device with voice output that Lori used to communicate. However, in this interaction, Lori chose the more efficient communication mode of smiling and bending forward — her sign for "yes."

Margaret carried Lori to a table where other children were making their signs. She asked Lori, "What do you want your sign to say?" Lori reached out to the DynaVox and touched an icon. The device stated in an automated fashion, "Yes" — the same word she had just indicated through body movement and facial signs. Lori was more apt to use the DynaVox when her language was directing another to write, draw, or otherwise symbolize her thoughts, combining expressive modalities. She followed up the "yes," however, with an uttered, "Muh-huh," her manner for orally articulating Margaret's name. Margaret said in a voice loud enough for Shayne to hear, "You want your sign to say 'Yes Margaret'? Does that mean 'No Shayne'?" Lori doubled forward, laughing with mouth wide open. Shayne called out, "Hey, why am I always the bad guy?" With Margaret's hand guiding Lori's, the two wrote in big letters across the poster board, "Yes Margaret." Any indication that surrounding adults did not believe Lori was capable of this level of sophisticated humor was entirely absent from the interaction.

Aaron announced to all the participating children, "Okay, if this is going to be a real protest, we need to march with our signs and chant. Where should we march to?" One child yelled out, "The office." "To the office it is!" Aaron cried, "Let's chant, 'Yes fun at school.'" Thirteen children filed out the door, led by Aaron, with Soo-Nei close behind and Steven holding onto a corner of Soo-Nei's sign. Margaret carried Lori and Lori's sign. Several children joined the chant, "Yes fun at school. Yes fun at school." When the protest ended, Shayne called all the children to a carpeted area of the room where class meetings were held. She said, "Okay, so this is a democracy, and we'll vote on whether 'No fun at school' becomes a rule." The vote against the rule was unanimous. Shayne said to a beaming Steven, "I guess you win this one."

In this hectic scene of preschool/kindergarten "hallway-level" democracy, a vibrant, literate community is clearly discernible. Shared graphic (i.e., observable, recorded) symbols (including alphabetic text) are used by children and adults of the Corner Nook as social tools for formulating, conveying, interpreting, debating, and reformulating ideas into personal and collective narratives. An intriguing aspect of this literate community, and the ethnographic focus of our research, was the seemingly natural and full citizenship of children with significant disabilities, children often excluded by tradition and convention from oral literacy-learning opportunities (Erickson & Koppenhaver, 1995; Koppenhaver & Erickson, 2003; Mirenda, 2003).

Three of the five students labeled with disabilities in the Corner Nook classroom (including Steven and Lori) were considered to have moderate to severe disabilities. Testing on developmental assessments for all three had only months earlier generated cognitive scores more usually associated with infant and toddler levels of development. Shayne Robbins and her classroom colleagues, however, perceived capacity and possibility for these children where prevalent professional disability discourses focused primarily on presumed defect and limitation (see also Mirenda, 2003). This fundamental presumption of human competence, including literate potential, translated into the described classroom-based actions such that the children with significant disabilities were seamlessly understood and supported as full citizens of the literate community. These actions included (a) Shayne converting her argument with Steven into a written phrase to be hung on the wall with other written rules, (b) Steven participating on his own initiative with Soo-Nei to construct a protest sign, and (c) Lori making use of icons on a screen to communicate direction and ideas.

With our ethnographic gaze affixed on the literate citizenship of children whose disability label commonly precludes community participation due to cultural assumptions, we sought to both continue and build on our previous interpretive studies of early childhood literacy with a particular interest in young children with significant developmental disabilities (Kliewer, 1998a, 1998b; Kliewer & Biklen, 2001; Kliewer & Landis, 1999). We were guided in our research by two questions: In the nine inclusive classrooms involved in this study, how are preschool and kindergarten students labeled with moderate to significant disabilities supported as full, competent citizens of the dynamic literate community? What obstacles hinder this full acceptance?

In exploring how each classroom approached the substance of our guiding questions, we developed an increasingly holistic sense of the nature of the literate community itself. Our effort here is designed to be both directly pragmatic and paradigmatic: We believe the rich descriptions of children with significant disabilities participating in the literate dynamics of general preschool and kindergarten classrooms can serve as a model for establishing particular forms of literate communities and supporting the active participation of other children who, based on cultural assumptions, are often and without question excluded. We also believe that our findings ultimately raise serious concerns about the current direction of research and policy in early literacy in general.

CULTURAL CONSTRUCTIONS OF LITERACY AND SIGNIFICANT DEVELOPMENTAL DISABILITY

Perceptions of literacy development in early childhood schooling have historically been influenced by shifting discourses about what literacy is and how acts of literacy occur (see Crawford, 1995, for an excellent discussion). In the mid-twentieth century, educators primarily viewed young children as passive recipients of texts read to them. This prepared them for a later stage when they might begin to learn the skills and subskills of decoding and then encoding printed language (Crawford, 1995). Over the past three decades, the discourse of passive preparation has been slowly subverted, first by an active developmental model described as emergent literacy, and more recently by one of systematic, direct phonics instruction along linear trajectories of phonemic, alphabetic, oral language, and orthographic skill development (Barratt-Pugh, 2000; Crawford, 1995).[4] Previously, direct drill was most prominent beginning in the primary years of elementary school, but it is now being used with ever-younger children (Richgels, 2001).

Clearly, no single, absolute, all-encompassing, or timeless sense of literacy development exists. Indeed, while the lead or predominant discourse of the moment always takes on the appearance of objective or scientific truth (Kliewer & Drake, 1998), in actuality the meaning of the term *literacy* and the inferences cast by the term *literate citizen* shift across time and place. For instance, into the nineteenth century, a distinction of literate citizenship was made between those who could and could not sign their own names — a skill that fewer than half the adult populations of even the most industrialized Western European countries possessed (Fernandez, 2001; Resnick & Resnick, 1977).

Within the first author's own family, old documents demonstrate that into the twentieth century in the United States many of his Mennonite ancestors had to place an "X" where a name was required.[5] How could these skilled farmers, parents, builders, craftspeople, and artisans (most often rolled into one) have been unable to perform this seemingly basic literate act expected today of five-year-old children? The answer, of course, lies in the social nature of literacy. What seemed so objectively real just a century ago now seems objectionably bizarre and unreal. The seemingly natural reality of whole classes of people necessarily living in an illiterate state was, in fact, an entirely unnecessary, unnatural — and at times vicious — social creation that was then reified through a myriad of collective informal and formal social means.[6]

Though the shifting nature of literacy is evident, the current predominant discourse on the development of literacy in young children has largely taken on an essential, objective, and fixed mechanistic aura. Within this paradigmatic view, literacy is considered a point reached along a trajectory of sequenced, mechanized skills adhering solely to abilities with alphabetic texts (Whitehurst & Lonigan, 2001). The literate citizen, according to this framework, is ultimately one who has — through formal instruction and drill — mastered and combined sets of phonemic subskills in linear fashion at a normative pace associated with efficient movement through the educational grades (see Adams, 2001; Adams, Foorman, Lunberg, & Beeler, 1997).

The Ladder to Literacy as Predominant Discourse

Elsewhere we have associated this linear, subskill model with a metaphoric ladder to literacy (Kliewer & Biklen, 2001). Each rung of the ladder constitutes increasingly complex, normative subskills, with the first or earliest rungs primarily associated with letter and phonemic abilities, as identified in school-based reading programs. Only later are the rungs associated with understanding and meaning of text. Adams (2001), for example, likens learning to read to an individual child's bodily kinesthetic maturation. "In any complex endeavor," she writes, "children must learn to walk [i.e., decipher phonemes] before they run [i.e., understand text]. Learning [to read] must start somewhere: if not with letters and phonemes, then where?" (p. 68).

It follows that instructional systems currently laying claim to the coveted title of scientifically based reading programs are entirely focused on detached, decontextualized phonics instruction.[7] These published reading methods craft a generic blueprint of literacy development for all children with no consideration given to the backgrounds (natured or nurtured) with which they arrive at school (Shannon, 1995). All children, according to these phonics-based plans, must first be made phonemic decoders in the exact manner of all other children. Only after achieving phonic mastery is there any systematic consideration given to a child's understanding of a text's message or meaning. In effect, the literate construction of meaning is reserved only for those children who have survived the early skill-and-drill efforts around phoneme awareness.

Lacking Literacy: Young Children with Significant Disabilities

Nearly absent from discussions of early literacy development and instruction is an interest in young children with what we refer to as *significant* developmental disabilities, including presumed moderate to severe intellectual disabilities (Kliewer & Biklen, 2001). For these children, eventual citizenship in the literate community following the ladder-to-literacy model is considered to be, at best, an intellectual improbability. Mirenda (2003) explained that "despite the fact that many individuals [with developmental disabilities] are able to demonstrate skills directly related to literacy, they are often seen as 'too cognitively impaired' or 'not ready for instruction' in this area" (p. 271). As Erickson and Koppenhaver (1995) write:

> It's not easy trying to learn to read and write if you're a child with severe disabilities in U.S. public schools today. . . . Your preschool teachers are unlikely to be aware of emergent literacy research or to include written language activities in your early intervention program. Many of the teachers you encounter across your public school career do not view you as capable of learning to read and write and consequently provide you with few opportunities to learn written language. (p. 676)

Erickson and Koppenhaver concluded that, for the few children with significant disabilities who do find themselves in settings that provide some literacy opportunities, instruction tends to reflect the ladder model, with these children decidedly stuck at the lower rungs. "You [the student] are likely," the researchers write, "to engage largely in word-level skill-and-drill activities, seldom reading or listening to text and even more rarely composing text" (p. 676).

As was the case with particular social classes from previous centuries, children with construed significant developmental disabilities are today primarily considered to be naturally illiterate — cerebrally unable to master the sequenced subskills thought to precede literate citizenship. While the assumed natural literacy limitations ascribed in previous eras to slaves or agrarian workers have come to be understood as the cultural imposition of subliteracy on one class by another more powerful group, the severely limited literacy skills associated today with children labeled developmentally disabled are considered to be organic and innate. So-called manifestations of global cortical defects are thought to be beyond sociohistorical creation, construction, or ideology; they are, in effect, thought to be objectively real (Kliewer & Fitzgerald, 2001).

In contrast to disability doctrine, however, there is a relatively small but accumulating body of work that documents the development of literacy skills on the part of individuals generally considered to be hopelessly illiterate due to presumed intellectual deficits.[8] In several of our own ethnographies of literacy (Kliewer, 1998a; Kliewer & Landis, 1999; Kliewer & Biklen, 2001), it became apparent that this awareness of human possibility arose in environments where the adults, both parents and teachers, had challenged the paradigm of historic segregation of children with disabilities and the model of a singular ladder to citizenship in the literate community. By emphasizing a holistic vision of the literate community over rigid adherence to sequenced phonemic subskill mastery, teachers appeared to open up citizenship to young children who were traditionally excluded.

ON METHODS

In this study we have used ethnographic research methods to study literacy and young children with significant disabilities. Several important principles of ethnography guided our efforts. First, we studied real-world settings. We were interested in the literate citizenship of young children with significant disabilities, so we purposefully (Bogdan & Biklen, 2003) entered inclusive settings where preschool and kindergarten students with significant disabilities were actively participating in literacy opportunities. The study originated in the Corner Nook classroom at the Shoshone School, where Shayne Robbins was lead teacher. As coding schemes developed out of themes from our Shoshone data, we turned to other inclusive early childhood settings to confirm, deepen, and refine our tentative findings. Ultimately, this study is based on data gathered in nine classrooms across five separate schools and education programs.

Second, our data were primarily narrative and were collected using multiple methods historically associated with ethnography and phenomenology. We conducted participant observations in the classrooms, as well as interviews with participating adults. We also systematically collected documents associated with the contexts under study. Our team composed field notes following observations that resulted in interpretive memos. We have more than twenty hours of transcribed/described video footage from the classrooms, in addition to interview transcriptions.

Third, our analysis was interpretive and grounded in the narrative data (Strauss & Corbin, 1994). The research team met biweekly and shared field notes, observational anecdotes, emergent themes, and coding categories. Our analysis was primarily inductive. For instance, we initially focused on observing children's use of alphabetic text and how children with significant disabilities struggled in this regard (thus acknowledging certain of our preconceived notions and biases). As the findings of this study will illustrate, our perceptions of literacy changed through the process of this research. Discussions with the teachers and participant observation taught us to look for a broadened understanding of the meaning of literacy in young children's experiences.

Finally, we are concerned that the theory presented herein accurately reflects the social settings and observations from which it is derived. To this end, this research effort included:

- field observations conducted in nine classrooms across five programs over two years
- observation of 213 children, sixty-two of whom had disabilities, and forty-five of whom were labeled with moderate to severe (i.e., significant) disabilities[9]
- 226 observations and interviews, detailed in field notes conducted by five researchers
- biweekly research meetings attended by four of the five researchers to discuss ongoing data analysis
- participating teachers' intimate involvement in data analysis through member checks, and their participation in presentations of the data at international, regional, and local conferences, as well as in graduate classes

The thoroughness of the study combined with the open-door policy that was provided the participating teachers suggests that the data analysis is reflective of the classrooms under study.

FINDINGS: LITERACY AS MAKING SENSE AND CHILDREN WITH SIGNIFICANT DISABILITIES AS SENSE-MAKERS

In the introduction to this article, we described the children in Shayne Robbins' Corner Nook classroom at the Shoshone School as they protested their lead teacher's initiation of the new rule, "There will be no fun at school." Our interest in the literacy development of young children, including those with significant disabilities, clearly focused our attention on the various printed language aspects that were such a natural part of the scene. In a number of research interviews, however, Shayne Robbins emphasized that, in order to understand early literacy, our attention should be equally directed toward children's play, imagination, interests, stories, experiences, interactions, and actions that underlie and ultimately may be expressed through the social tools of printed language and symbols.

In one interview, Shayne said, "I think the most important literacy we do in here is . . . the way they pretend. [It] is their way into [literacy]." In another interview she expressed a similar sentiment: "It's really all about literacy. There's very little we do that's not literacy related, even when it doesn't look like reading the way you and I look when we sit down and read a book." Shayne later clarified her view of literacy, saying, "It's about making sense. It's about meaning. . . . It's kids being able to have something to tell, and to be able to tell it and hear it in a lot of ways so that it's understood."

Children's sense-making and meaning take shape in multiple symbolic forms of what we refer to as narrative: ideas, thoughts, concerns, interests, desires, and stories that may be told, made sense of, understood, retold, or altered in such a way that a symbolic connectedness — in essence, a literate community — is crafted in the class-room.[10] For Shayne, narrative is the story to be told, whether that is arguing against a new rule such as "No fun at school!" or drafting a protest sign. Narrative is the orga-nizing principle, the central core of the literate community.

Shirley Kehoe, co-teacher at the inclusive St. John Nursery School located in the basement of a Lutheran church on the far west side of Empire City, echoed Shayne Robbins' assertion of early literacy as children's narrative:

> Literacy is taking the kids seriously at every level — their experiences they come with, their emotions, their interests. You put them in a setting where all those things are acknowledged and built on, and they all realize they have something to say, and they say it in so many ways. Sometimes with their voice, but just as often in a lot of other ways. And their expressiveness just grows and they start to read — each other, books, art.

Like Shayne Robbins, when considering literacy development, Kehoe focused her at-tention less on traditional text and more on the multiple modalities children used to express and understand stories emerging from their experiences.

The Teacher's Imagination and the Participation of Children with Significant Disabilities

Fostering the idea of a literate community crafted on children's narrative does not au-tomatically support the citizenship of young children with significant disabilities who are conventionally excluded from literate opportunities. Our observations and inter-views suggested that teachers must also shed conventional disability orthodoxy if they are to see in all children the capacity to generate and interpret narrative. Dianna Lowell, lead teacher of a preschool classroom of seventeen students that included two children with severe developmental disabilities, insisted, "It's very difficult to predict what a child — any child — is ever going to be capable of. Especially regarding [disabil-ity] labels. You assume the child is able and you start from there."

Lowell's sense that a teacher needs to assume the competence of children with dis-abilities and open narrative opportunities based on that assumption was echoed by other teachers in this study. At the Shoshone School, Shayne Robbins took a sip of coffee during an interview and said, "You know, after all these years, I really, really see it as about my imagination for a kid. Like Elijah, his only limitations were how I imagined he could do things." Elijah was a former student of Robbins' who had Down's syndrome.

When Elijah entered Shayne's classroom, his speech was extremely limited and highly irregular for a three-year-old. His only consistently understandable word was "No!" Elijah was also labeled cognitively impaired. Developmental assessments sug-gested that he was functioning cognitively in the ninth- to eleventh-month age range. Yet, Shayne Robbins suggested that Elijah's possibilities were as expansive as her own imagination allowed. This is a radical reconfiguration of convention, influenced by the medical model that places limitations and impairments within the body of the person labeled and not in the minds of others.

Demonstrating Belief in the Narrative Lives of Children with Significant Disabilities

The presumption that children's limitations are limitations in the imaginations of surrounding adults resulted in the participating teachers opening narrative forms to all children in their classrooms. Active opportunities to pretend, imagine, dramatize, role play, and tell and interpret stories are considered fundamental to contemporary conceptualizations of healthy early childhood development — unless the discussion is focused on young children with significant developmental disabilities.

Classrooms segregated for children with moderate to severe disabilities commonly have no child-oriented books or pretend-play opportunities, based on the assumption that such opportunities lack function in the lives of children so labeled (Kliewer, Fitzgerald, & Raschke, 2001; Kliewer & Landis, 1999; Mirenda, 2003). In a previous ethnography, Kliewer and Biklen (2001) identified one stark theme: that for many children with significant disabilities, any participation in a literate community was commonly limited to extremely brief, adult-designed expressions of physical demands. A child with limited spoken language might, for example, have a communication board with "Bathroom" and "Eat" symbolized, and little else. The expectation was that a child with significant disabilities had nothing to say beyond what might be termed *immediate need* narratives. Consequently, when that did in fact become the only narrative form engaged in by the child, professional assumptions about the child's impaired capacity appeared to be confirmed.

In the classrooms involved in this study, however, teachers actively sought to support students with significant disabilities alongside their nondisabled peers in the full range of narrative forms comprising the early childhood literate community. Thus, the participating teachers demonstrated a fundamental belief in the capacity of children with significant developmental disabilities to engage in narratives of transcendence, in which the imaginations and interests of young children prodded their focus from the here and now, and shifted it to the abstractions of play and stories.

An example of supporting a child with significant disabilities as a part of the imaginative life of a classroom occurred during an observation conducted at Corner Nook. On this particular day, a pretend-play restaurant scene unfolded. In the center of the room, teachers had arranged a few tables with salt shakers, plastic utensils, and various menus borrowed from local establishments. Several children sat at the tables, poring over the menus, shouting out orders to a "waiter," who scribbled on a pad and exhibited tremendous control over his customers. "I want the hamburger," one student yelled. "You get the pizza," the waiter explained, scribbling furiously on his pad. "How much is my supper?" a student asked the waiter, grabbing a stack of fake money. "Eight hundred dollars," the waiter responded. "I don't have eight hundred dollars," the patron retorted. "Then you're out of the restaurant!" the waiter yelled. "I don't have eight hundred dollars either," another customer said. "Then you're kicked out too," the waiter responded.

As the drama unfolded, we watched Jamie sit on the periphery of the play, piecing together a jigsaw puzzle but taking numerous quick glances toward the children involved in the restaurant scene. Jamie, who was labeled with autism, was considered moderately to severely developmentally disabled. He had only recently begun to use any spoken language. Children with such a high degree of autistic behavior are commonly considered to reside at a pre-symbolic stage. As such, pretend play is thought to be an impossibility (Maurice, 1993). In obvious contradiction to this characterization, Jamie appeared extremely intrigued by the restaurant play.

Eventually one of the patrons kicked out of the restaurant by the dictatorial waiter stumbled over Jamie, and the two rolled on the floor, giggling, until a teacher cut short the roughhousing. The boy continued on, and Jamie stood and walked to one of the restaurant tables. In discussing this vignette, Margaret, one of Shayne Robbins' associate teachers, explained that Jamie often appeared "stuck" until the touch of another seemed to allow him to initiate actions of participation. "It's not that he can't do the things," Margaret explained. "It's more like he's stuck until someone can give him that little nudge." Rather than cloaking this apparent need for physical facilitation in clinical descriptions of impairment, Margaret chose to instead normalize Jamie's behavior: "We all need different kinds of nudges," she said.

On entering the restaurant scene, Jamie sat and picked up a menu, holding it upside down. A passing teacher noticed and paused to further support Jamie's participation. The teacher turned the menu over in Jamie's hand and said, "What are you going to order? What're the choices?" With the teacher's hand over his, Jamie pointed to the word hamburger (which had a picture of a hamburger next to it). He quietly voiced, "Hamburger." They repeated this with several choices.

After reviewing the menu, the teacher said, "Okay, what're you going to order?" Then she cried out, "Oh waiter, we're ready to make an order." The waiter appeared, pad and pen poised, and waited while the teacher quietly voiced in Jamie's ear, "I want to order the —." Jamie paused, then finished the sentence, "hamburger." "Hamburger," the waiter said, scribbling into his pad, "That'll be eight hundred dollars please." The matter-of-fact manner in which the waiter stood by while Jamie hesitated in his order, and the way the waiter responded to Jamie and not to the teacher, demonstrated the general acceptance of Jamie in this classroom, despite certain unusual behaviors. In short order, Jamie, like every other patron, had been kicked out of the restaurant for lack of money.

From the above scene, elements that appeared helpful to Jamie's increasingly sophisticated social participation included other children serving as models and understanding Jamie's behavioral uniqueness, an intervening teacher who understood how to foster Jamie's independent participation, and various props, including the photo- and text-based menu. Underlying each of these, however, and making Jamie's competent participation possible, was the fundamental belief in his capacity to engage in narrative as a rightful member of the classroom's literate community.

In Tammy Wolcott's class at the Lincoln Early Childhood Center, located in a midwestern city, we noticed through systematic observation that, in contrast to Shayne Robbins' Corner Nook class, her six students with significant disabilities rarely engaged in dramatic or pretend play. This seemed to be the result of the degree of disability segregation built into the instructional model of this classroom. Tammy Wolcott's six students, all labeled with significant disabilities, joined ten children without disabilities from a day-care center for a part of each day. Otherwise the two groups were separated, with Wolcott's students in a segregated special education classroom and the children without disabilities returning to their day-care classroom.

Tammy Wolcott expressed a desire to increase the children's interaction in pretend-play situations, but had also found other paths to narrative engagement for her students with developmental disabilities. Importantly, she used storytelling narratives to bring the children, disabled and nondisabled, together. This required Tammy's fundamental belief in the capacity of her students with significant disabilities to understand and make meaning of story narratives. It appeared that this belief held tremendous developmental opportunities for Tammy's students. For instance, during one particular observation, three-year-old Paulie approached a researcher copying down a poem from an easel. The poem had been the centerpiece of the morning meeting, with children reciting and acting out the rhyme under adult guidance. Paulie was one of Tammy's six students with significant disabilities. He was considered to have global developmental delays, including cognitive and communication disabilities.

Paulie faced the researcher and patted his stomach with both hands. In a telling misinterpretation of his communication, the researcher asked, "Are you hungry, Paulie?" In actuality, Paulie was attempting to join her in discussing the poem, but the researcher's immediate reaction was to assume Paulie was conveying an immediate physical need, hunger. Paulie, recognizing the misinterpretation, attempted to correct the researcher by pointing to the easel. The eight-line poem she had been copying was a fictional account of the meeting between a snowman and rabbit. A picture icon appeared after each line representing the key idea contained in that line. The first icon was of the snowman. Paulie pointed to it. Patting the stomach was the sign used in the class to represent the word "snowman."

On Paulie's clarification, the researcher said, "Oh, the snowman. Do you want to read the poem?" Paulie affirmed this by moving closer to the easel. The researcher read out loud, "A pudgy little snowman." Paulie repeated his sign for snowman. The researcher read, "Had a carrot nose." Paulie gestured with his right hand, signing a representation of a growing nose. As the researcher continued reading, Paulie — with clear delight — continued adding symbolic gestures representing the picture icons. It was a very interactive recitation that demonstrated Paulie's ability to focus on the poem during the morning meeting, his adeptness at translating his thoughts into sign systems, and a general sophistication with literacy that confounded assessment descriptions of Paulie that suggested a severe cognitive impairment.

After the poem was completed, Paulie immediately went to a shelf filled with children's storybooks. He looked across the shelf and, with definite intent, pulled down a particular book. He carried it to the researcher and the two adjusted themselves, with Paulie sitting on the researcher's lap. Paulie continued signing key words, this time related to the saga of a lost mitten, in spite of the fact that there were no picture icons as cues.

Storybooks as well as poetry are narrative opportunities of the imagination, allowing children to get lost in the fables and imagery presented. At the time of this observation, the students with disabilities in Tammy Wolcott's classroom struggled to join the play of their nondisabled counterparts. However, while concerned about expanding pretend-play skills, Tammy also worked to consistently bring literature into her students' lives. As such, she was demonstrating a fundamental belief in their capacity to understand and engage in narratives. It was here, in story texts, that Paulie clearly demonstrated sophisticated emergent skills and interest in symbolically making sense of the larger world.

Multiple Literacies in the Inclusive Early Childhood Classroom

In the data vignettes of Jamie at the Shoshone School and Paulie at the Lincoln Early Childhood Center, both boys were described as using a variety of representational social tools for participation. Despite his limited spoken language, Jamie made use of recognizable (albeit teacher-supported), interactive pretend-play behaviors, meaningful gestures toward a text- and photo-based menu, and some use of pretend money. Paulie effectively used picture icons, systematically gestured using the classroom version of signed English, and interpreted printed language in the form of a written poem and storybooks.

In an interview, Shirley Kehoe, a research participant and coteacher at the St. John Nursery School, rattled off a list of symbolic social tools used by children in her classroom to both organize and convey meaning and understanding across the literate community. "It's all the signing we do," she explained, "the art, music, pictures, the symbols, all the symbols and tools we use in play, and of course the stories we write and read and perform, like the skits we put on, books we act out. It's everywhere."

Our data ultimately contained descriptions of multiple sign, movement, pictorial, numerical, graphic, and printed-language systems that citizens of the early childhood literate community made use of as social tools to interpret, understand, and express narratives. Narrative gives shape to the literate community, and these multiple semiotic systems are the social tools that give shape to the various narrative forms.

Our borrowing the term *semiotic systems* (Barton & Hamilton, 1998, p. 9) suggests a range of coherent bodies of meaningful and at least semiformalized symbols, signs, sounds, and gestures conceived as a means of communicating or interpreting thought, emotion, or experience, and the systems or rules for their common usage. Spoken language is an example. However, our use of the term *literacies* reflects observable, tactile, or otherwise graphically knowable semiotic systems used as social tools to bring forth and give literate shape to narrative. Certainly, the graphic nature of the final "text" ranged dramatically from highly fleeting (e.g., observing one another's body language during pretend play) to relatively permanent written products (e.g., a painted protest sign or a story book). Ultimately, literacy is the development of increasing sophistication and competence in children's use of graphic semiotic systems to meaningfully participate in, generate, and sustain narrative.

Providing a Range of Literate Opportunities

A teacher's sense of students as capable sense-makers in the construction and interpretation of narrative forms appeared to be fundamental to literate citizenship for children with significant disabilities. Our data suggest that this presumption of competence was fostered by giving the children with disabilities thoughtful opportunities across a range of literacies (i.e., multiple semiotic systems contextualized in, and lending shape to, a variety of narrative forms). This finding contradicts a deeply ensconced professional belief that children with disabilities require more restrictive programs and activities than do their nondisabled counterparts, and that as the so-called severity of the disability increases, the degree of options and opportunities must be narrowed (for a critique of this historic truthism, see Kluth, Straut, & Biklen, 2003).

The importance of giving young children with significant disabilities opportunities with multiple literacies was exemplified in an observation of Damian, a nearly five-year-old child in Diana Lowell's inclusive preschool classroom. Damian was defined as having intellectual and communication disabilities.

This particular observation of Damian occurred over a regularly scheduled 45-minute period of the day called Centers Time, during which children could choose to spend time in a variety of teacher-created activities generally independent of direct teacher supervision. As the vignette suggests, had Damian not been provided with a range of opportunities, a sense of his literate presence might have been severely restricted.

Damian began Centers Time in the classroom's cooking area. He and a nondisabled friend, Paula, followed a large, laminated set of directions that led to making blueberry muffins in paper cups. Damian stood next to Paula and ran his finger, left to right, across one line of the directions. His words approximated the sentence, "Gots to four spoons." The actual line of the directions read, "Add four teaspoons of muffin mix." The sentence was followed by the outline of four teaspoons and a line drawing of the muffin mix box.

Diana Lowell, the lead teacher, had set up this particular center with a number of objectives in mind. With little direct teacher support but in cooperation with one another, she wanted children to decipher alphabetic, numeric, and picture-symbol text in order to come away with a completed product. In so doing, students were experiencing a number of semiotic systems within the familiar narrative forms of baking/cooking and cooperating with peers toward a shared goal. The center was also linked to a previous field trip the students had taken to a bakery, so there was a wider community orientation as well. Damian's relatively sophisticated ability to interpret and make sense of the text appeared to be fostered by the drawn icons, the active involvement of peers, and the meaningful context, both in the immediate sense that Damian understood he was to create a muffin and in the sense of the familiarity he had with cooking as a daily, relatively independent activity in the class.

Paula, Damian's friend, also counted the teaspoon outlines, "One, two, three, four, five, six." Two of the outlines she counted twice, pounding with her index finger. "Nuh-huh," Damian responded with some distress. Shoving her hand away, he recounted, touching each spoon outline only once. The two pushed and shoved against one another, and their focus seemed to stray from the recipe to a larger struggle over the chair. Eventually an adult noticed the altercation and intervened. The two returned to the recipe, with each scooping far more mix into their cups than four or six full spoons.

Several more lines of the laminated directions eventually led to the command, "Place in microwave for forty-five seconds." Again there was a line drawing, this one depicting a muffin cup in a microwave oven. Paula and Damian raced to the microwave, with Paula arriving first. She positioned her body to block Damian, put her cup in the oven, slammed the door, and — demonstrating an expert's familiarity — typed in the desired number of seconds, which for her was ninety-three. Damian watched with growing agitation. He ran back to the directions and pounded on the indicated "forty-five seconds." "Four-five," he said several times. Paula smiled at him, confirmed that none of the teachers was paying attention, then pushed the "Start" button, thus establishing a new narrative of rule-breaking around microwave muffin experimentation.

Damian moved to a small "computer area" of the classroom that was secluded by shelves. Damian sat at one of the two old Apple computers and gestured for an observing researcher to sit beside him. A nondisabled student quickly followed and sat down at the open computer. Damian played a matching game, narrating as he proceeded for the observer, "One, two, three, . . . eight" (as he counted, his finger touched the screen). "Find eight," he said, clicking on various animated pictures to see if the numeral eight appeared. When he matched the correct numeral to the number of dots, the picture on the computer screen exploded with sound and lights. Damian stood each time this happened, with hands over head, awaiting applause from the researcher.

Next to him, the other student opened a game in which a picture of an object appeared with space to label it. The required letters were scrambled below the space. The object was to click on the letters in correct sequence to spell the name of the object. If a child chose letters out of sequence, the computer simply "waited" until the correct one was chosen. The child appeared to click on letters randomly until the correct word was spelled.

This appeared to annoy Damian, who began to monitor both his own game and the game next to him. A picture of a bed appeared on the second computer screen. The child clicked on the letter that appeared first in the mixed-up sequence, letter "E." Damian cried out, "Bed, bed, bed. B! B, b, b!" His hand shot over to maneuver the mouse, and the other student slammed her fist down on his fingers. Damian, with one eye on his own screen, formed a fist and whacked his neighbor's shoulder with an overhand punch. With surprising immediacy, each then refocused on his or her own computer screen.

Damian next moved to an area labeled "Dramatic Play." Much noise and activity had been emanating from here throughout Centers Time, as one of the students, Alyssa, had used dress-up clothing and other props to organize her own wedding. Damian rarely entered the pretend play of other children, and during this observation he stood quietly on the periphery. He watched as children created ever-shifting scenes and dialogue with one another, but he did not join in. While he had been actively engaged in the multiple literacies involved in the various narratives at the other two stops, in Dramatic Play he took on the role of observer. Eventually Damian left the Dramatic Play area and drifted back to the muffin-making area.

Evident in the observation of Damian was the importance of not reducing all of early literacy to a set of teacher-directed drills. Although nothing in our data suggested that drill-and-skill opportunities should not be provided, it was precisely in the vast, active, engaging range of choices that we were able to see literate abilities emerge. For instance, with both the muffin recipe and the computer games, Damian demonstrated the capacity to recognize and make use of numerals, alphabetic text, and pictorial representations. He demonstrated spelling skills, letter recognition, and left-to-right orientations within meaningful narrative forms. All of these were aspects of the formal, constructivist classroom curricula, but here Damian was demonstrating his abilities without teacher direction. He did so in an active, self-directed manner, and at his own thoughtful pace. Diana Lowell explained: "Damian shines when he's allowed to be independent. That's when you really see some of his skills that you really didn't see at the beginning of the year. Of course he had never really been a part of an inclusion situation before."

In contrast to his active cooking and computer use, however, Damian's participation in the narratives of dramatic play appeared to be limited to the role of observer. "Pretending is not really his strong suit," Diana Lowell mentioned in a brief discussion with a researcher. "It's something we need to work on." Again, had this preschool classroom been primarily organized around dramatic play, Damian's literate abilities may not have been fully realized. His skills were found in the active use of text across other narrative forms.

Providing Teacher-Guided Literate Opportunities

Damian's experience at Centers Time demonstrated that a teacher's presumption of potential literate citizenship in children, including those with significant disabilities, allowed literate opportunities to be presented across a range of play and activities performed independent of direct adult oversight. However, some children with significant disabilities struggled to keep pace with these seemingly natural, often spontaneous, highly fluid literacy opportunities.

Lori, the four-year-old mentioned earlier as she communicated with a DynaVox, experienced this struggle with the hectic pace of her preschool/kindergarten class. Lori's serious physical disabilities meant that her movement around the classroom required adult support or supervision. Her speech was limited to a few easily articulated sounds and was primarily discernible only to adults. Thus, the DynaVox, an alternative to speech, was theoretically liberating but had its limitations. For instance, stretching to touch the screen icons required patience from both Lori and those around her, who awaited the voice-output message. Certain adapted switches had been tested, but the required physical manipulation remained difficult and awkward.

Supporting Lori's participation in spontaneous literate exchanges appeared to require extensive adult intervention. Such intervention, of course, altered the spontaneity of the event, and it often took on a much more work-like (as opposed to play-like) appearance. Because of this struggle, Lori's teachers commonly made use of other more structured, teacher-guided opportunities to foster and support Lori's full communicative and literate classroom participation. For instance, several classrooms in this research, including Corner Nook, had a *Child of the Week* activity, a show-and-tell opportunity where a particular child was selected to bring in photographs, mementos, and other objects to share with peers.

When Lori was named child of the week, she brought in a bulletin board with several photographs showing her on vacations or at home with her family. The pictures were all neatly labeled with sentences describing the scene (one read, "Lori goes horse-back riding"). Lori sat with Shayne at the front of the class, the photographs facing her peers. Shayne said, "Which picture do you want to show first?" With a wide smile, Lori slowly stretched toward a preprogrammed icon on her DynaVox. The device responded with a female child's voice, "I am go-ing horseback riding in Ver-mont."

The other students, many on their knees trying to get a better look, scanned Lori's photographs. Some began shouting about their own horseback riding experiences. Shayne interrupted, saying, "Stop and remember. Who has a . . ." She paused, pointing to a board that read, "Wh Questions: Who? What? When? Where? Why?" Several students shouted "W-h question!" and hands shot up with students calling, "I have a question!"

The teacher-guided *Child of the Week* period provided a format and pace that allowed Lori to skillfully use the DynaVox, one of her most effective symbolic modes of participation. The logo- and text-based icons of the DynaVox, the photos with text explanations, the "W-h" question board, and teacher support all played a role in Lori's literate ability to provide her peers with a deeper sense of her experiences, tastes, likes, and dislikes. The children appeared completely at ease with the technology when it fit so seamlessly into the structured meeting.

Pertinent to Lori's moments of success with the DynaVox, however, was the role her mother played in programming the device. For *Child of the Week*, Lori's mother had entered and recorded a separate icon for each photograph, as well as some related messages. In one research interview, Shayne expressed a sentiment she often repeated in conversations about Lori. "I don't know what we would do without her mom," Shayne said. "We just don't have all the time we need to program the DynaVox and we really rely on her. It's like a full-time job for her." Shayne's acknowledgment of the essential role Lori's mother played in supporting her daughter's classroom participation, even in a setting like the Shoshone School, filled with professional educators and language therapists, illustrated the complexity of active citizenship for young children with significant disabilities.

Alternative Goals within Multiple Literacies

Our participating teachers' presumption of the literate citizenship of all their children did not translate into a general belief that each child would participate in the literate community in exactly the same fashion. Our teachers appeared instead to direct their attention to creating communal opportunities for all children to engage in a variety of semiotic systems across narrative forms, but would often emphasize literate goals considered specific to a particular child's determined ability, need, or interest.[11] An example of this curricular individualization occurred during a lesson on graphing data in lead teacher Sheila Oswald's preschool class, which included sixteen three- and four-year-old children, three of whom had disability labels.

During one observation, Sheila Oswald had her children graph the frequency of classroom birthdays across the twelve months. This provided the children with a new representational and symbolic manner for organizing information about their class. The semiotic systems at play included alphabetic text, numbers, three-dimensional bodies in movement, and two-dimensional graphs. Jordan, a child labeled with communication and intellectual disabilities, sat among his peers holding a printed number line. Sheila called out, "Everyone with birthdays in January, stand up."

Sheila scanned the children standing and compared the result to a birthday chart. She pointed to a written name on the chart and said, "One more of you should be up. Who's not up?" Several students, reading the name, called out, "Joey." Joey was startled out of his apparent day-dream and leapt to his feet. Shelia Oswald then called to Jordan, "How many January birthdays, Jordan?" An associate teacher seated behind Jordan peeked over his head as he started jabbing at the number line with his index finger. She reached around and put her hand over his, slowing down what appeared to be impulsive pointing. He pointed to the four. The associate said, "No, count again. How many kids?" With her hand over his, they arrived at the three on the number line. "Three," she called out. Sheila said, "Good. Come up here, Jordan, and we'll put three down for January." Jordan was immediately on his feet, moving to Sheila, who helped him stick three circles above the word "January" on what would become a birthday bar graph. The lesson continued like this for each of the twelve months.

Sheila Oswald's motivation for Jordan's participation in this activity did not necessarily stem from a firm belief in his ability to grasp the abstract nature of graphing information. Oswald later explained in a research interview, "Is [Jordan] getting everything? Probably not. We're not sure what he grasps and what he doesn't, but he's working on things like responding on cue, being part of conversations, being aware." He also had goals of developing one-to-one correspondence and numeral recognition. Sheila Oswald believed these objectives neatly fit into an activity where it was thought most of the other students were engaged in a more abstract manner. Still, though Sheila expressed skepticism about Jordan's ability to understand, she acknowledged the possibility that he was cognizant, and she did not deny him the opportunity to engage in and perhaps develop graphing skills.

Turning Children's Strengths into Literate Opportunities

Jamie, a child introduced earlier who took part in the pretend-play restaurant scenario in Shayne Robbins's classroom, was fascinated with the maps and globes Shayne made available and often used in the classroom. Conventional interpretations of severe autism, Jamie's label, might dismiss his keen interest as nothing more than a bizarre mode of self-stimulation or compulsive, perseverative behavior that lacked intellectual meaning (see Mirenda, 2003, for a critique of this still-common approach to explaining the performance of people labeled autistic). In the classrooms involved in this study, children with significant disabilities were considered to be sense-makers in the flow of narrative forms. A child's intense focus or interest was never dismissed in such patronizing fashion. Thus, Jamie's curiosity with maps was considered just that — a healthy interest that could further support his citizenship in the literate community.

In one observation, we watched Mushi, Shayne Robbins's graduate-level student teacher, lead a class circle time discussing how she missed and remained in contact with her family in South Korea. She had the classroom globe beside her. Mushi called Jamie to the front of the room. Shayne and Mushi had decided earlier that Jamie should be Mushi's helper for the circle time because he was the child most adept at using and understanding maps. Mushi later explained in an informal interview on the activity: "Jamie can do things with maps like no one else in here, and it's nice for his friends to see. He's still not talking so much at all so sometimes I think the other ones think he's younger [and] forget how smart he is."

Once called forward, Jamie received a gentle nudge from a nearby adult and he stood and tentatively approached Mushi. He clapped quickly several times and let out a "Yee-ah" sound he often made when excited. She pointed to the globe and said, "Show the kids where we are located — where we are now. Show them [our state]." Jamie excitedly dropped to his knees. He spun the globe. Other children moved in. Shayne called out, "Everyone needs to stay on their spot so that everyone can see." Jamie pointed to the correct state, but only Mushi could see. She said, "Show all the kids." He moved awkwardly in an effort to stop blocking the view of the globe. She then said, "Okay, now show my home, Korea." Again, Jamie spun the globe and seemed to become transfixed. Finally, Mushi and Shayne asked, "Can you find Korea?" He quickly landed his finger on Korea. Mushi emphasized how Jamie's finger had to "cross the ocean," just as she had done, in order to find Korea.

Mushi continued with the lesson, weaving multiple literacies throughout. She discussed maintaining contact with her parents through letters, email, and phone calls. She showed the students postcards she received from Korea, written, of course, in Korean. Jamie, still beside her, studied the postcards with tremendous intensity. In discussing the lesson later, Mushi said, "Jamie and I have looked at the globe together a lot. I have shown him Korea, Seoul, many times. I talk about home a lot. I think of all the kids, he really understands."

Shayne and Mushi were uncertain how much Jamie understood the abstract nature of crossing oceans, missing family far away, and sending postcards. However, the same uncertainty exists for any young child, and exposure to constructs of worlds separated by time and distance is considered healthy and important in developing a sense of self, others, and community. Shayne Robbins believed the same importance applied to Jamie's experience as it did to the experiences of nondisabled students. In turning that belief into a literate experience for Jamie, she enabled him to demonstrate and further his literate capacities.

Turning Experience into Text

The emergence of phonemic awareness as the beginning of literate citizenship in early childhood has had the unfortunate effect of skill-and-drill phonics activities largely displacing activities in which young children represent stories through text, symbol, and drawing as a route to reading (Adams, 1990; McGuinness, 1997). In our participating classrooms, however, where multiple literacies appeared to be valued, writing was considered an integral part of full citizenship, and children were supported in turning their experiences into written or otherwise graphically represented texts. For instance, one classroom had a daily "journaling" period during which children "wrote" to their parents, describing events they had participated in over the course of a school day.

Jessica, a child with Down's syndrome and significant motor and communication disabilities, worked daily with an adult, using multiple options to complete her journal. For instance, one line of a mimeographed sheet read, "I played in the ____ area." Jessica usually filled in the blank by pointing to a symbol reflecting an area of the room in which she had spent time. With the adult's assistance, the symbol was then glued over the blank in the sentence. However, Jessica was always given a choice of how she wanted to journal, and some days she chose to manipulate a marker or pencil, scribbling lines in the blank. A teacher then wrote next to Jessica's form of writing where Jessica had spent time.

Jessica's teacher, Cheryl Bigelow, noted the development of a number of skills related to Jessica's expressive communication. In a research interview, Cheryl told us:

> [Jessica] has really developed a sense of her own place in this classroom. Just lately it seems . . . she's pointing to symbols and some written words to really say things, and she's making demands and letting her voice be heard. If you don't make sure she has options, there's hell to pay! She really is into making decisions.

Previous developmental assessments measured Jessica's cognitive level as topping out at approximately what was expected of a child aged one year, six months — far below her chronological age of four years, five months. Cheryl, however, pointed out that Jessica's symbol and text use, apparently just beginning to flower, was influencing perceptions of her competence and abilities.

A notebook children maintained at the St. John nursery school was similar to Jessica's experience, but related to the early childhood narrative in the domain of science. Teacher Janet Vaughn had ordered a package of live butterfly eggs that, if properly cared for, could be hatched in order to study the metamorphosis process. Janet had the children observe and record the transformation of the butterflies from eggs, through larva, pupa, and finally into butterflies. One student in the class, Marty, was nonverbal, with a label of pervasive developmental disorder (PPD). He participated in the activity daily by choosing from a series the picture he felt most closely resembled the current life- cycle. The picture he pointed to was then pasted in his butterfly notebook.

Turning Text into Experience

Studying butterflies at St. John also served to illustrate the importance that the participating teachers placed on turning text and symbols into visible, active experience when promoting the literate citizenship of all children. Teachers at St. John, as in each classroom under study, regularly made use of both formal and informal role-play opportunities to bring storybooks and tales into three dimensions.

In addition to traditional role play, the St. John faculty had incorporated the physical therapy the children with disabilities received into its general community. The visiting therapist led the children both with and without disabilities through an early childhood version of yoga. For instance, during the unit on butterflies, the therapist organized a twenty-minute yoga session following the life-cycle theme. She used a chart made by a teacher depicting the four stages of a butterfly's life, complete with drawings and written labels. In silence, the therapist pointed to the chart's depiction of a larva emerging from its egg. The classroom staff and the children, including those with disabilities, followed the therapist's lead in silently and symbolically moving through the four stages.

Including Basic Phonemic Skills

As described earlier, the current predominant discourse on literacy skills development is focused on fluencies surrounding phonemic awareness and certain other skills (e.g., Good & Kaminski, 2002). Participating faculty in this study were generally resistant to the rigidity of this narrow focus in defining and fostering literate citizenship, but did view instruction in and exposure to the idea of basic literacy skills as one useful dimension of a multidimensional approach to literacy.

In the Corner Nook classroom at Shoshone School, Shayne Robbins had begun a "weird word book" when one child had noticed the nonphonetic nature of many spelled words. "Why is *phone* spelled like that?" he had asked. Soon after, another child asked, "Why is there an 'R' in Feb-*U*-ary?" Initially with Shayne's involvement, strangely spelled and nonphonetic words were added to the book daily, but within a matter of just a few weeks, a number of students became the primary instigators of using the weird word book. This, of course, required their understanding of and involvement in analyzing the graphemes of written language — a discourse many had been unaware of before the weird word book creation.

In one class meeting that involved the weird word book, Shayne announced, "Sean, tell us where you're just back from. Where did you go to see your grandma?" Sean was a child with physical disabilities and very limited speech. The teaching team had prepared for this meeting by making up a word board with relevant words that he could point to in response to questions. Sean leaned forward and pointed to "Ottawa." An adult seated next to him called out, "Ottawa." A friend without disabilities immediately burst out, "Sean oughta went to Ottawa!" What ensued then, making use of a white board and marker, was a lengthy discussion of the spelling and pronunciation of the words "Ottawa," "Ought [with emphasis on the 'gh']," "Ought to," and the slangy "Oughta," all of which were dutifully entered into the weird word book. While Sean's attention appeared riveted, his participation in the weird word discussion was limited because the spontaneous conversation had, of course, been unplanned. However, his ability to use written words for communication purposes demonstrated an emergent reading capacity beyond that of many of his nondisabled peers.

Historically, the semiotic system of most value in terms of citizenship in the literate community has been alphabetic text. The focus in the participating classrooms on multiple symbolic modes of narrative participation (i.e., citizenship), not just alphabetic text, may be construed by some as a devaluation of the skills and subskills currently thought to underlie literacy development. In fact, there was no devaluation of printed alphabetic language abilities. We determined from our data that valuing multiple symbolic modes of narrative participation both indirectly and directly affected children's development of printed-language skills. First, such a values framework opened opportunities for children with significant disabilities to participate in classrooms with a rich, literate curriculum. A rigid requirement that only nondisabled children with conventional, normative participation skills belong in regular preschool and kindergarten programs obviously cuts out students with moderate to severe disabilities and sends them into segregated programs that quite commonly offer very little in the way of literacy experiences of any kind (Kliewer & Landis, 1999; Kliewer & Raschke, 2002; Mirenda, 2003).

Second, fostering a degree of participation in the literate community for children who are commonly segregated from such participation opened opportunities to weave further and more sophisticated symbolic modes into the children's experiences. For instance, some children with significant communication disabilities pointed to picture symbols to communicate immediate needs and desires. In some classrooms, as the children's facility with pictures appeared to increase, teachers added written labels. In time, some of these children were actually constructing their own words and sentences out of letter options.

Third, as children's competencies were recognized with multiple semiotic systems, teachers appeared to grow increasingly comfortable shifting their instructional support between children's general skills with sense-making to specific skills associated with the narrative form of basic literacy skill instruction. Our participating teachers generally agreed that creative instruction associated with phonemes, graphemes, or orthography might benefit the printed-language skills of any child, including those with significant disabilities. Teacher Cheryl Bigelow noted, "I am very interested in our children understanding that words can be taken apart, put back together, read from left-to-right, sounded out, turned upside down, whatever. It's a part of the whole picture."

Literacy and the Subterranean Culture of Children

Supporting students with significant disabilities as sense-makers and as full participants in the classroom's literate community created certain ambiguities related to child behavior for participating teachers in this study. For instance, the question emerged, "How do you support a child to misbehave?" In early childhood, subterranean youth cultures already emerge with profound implications for what might be termed normal socialization (Paley, 1988, 1992). Indeed, children's "misbehavior" may in fact be part of normal socialization. Those concerned with children's full participation recognized the importance of a child fitting into social patterns separate from adult oversight and control.

In early childhood, subterranean cultures stereotypically involve such things as "potty talk," inane riddles, cliquish ganging up, or teasing. Graphic semiotic systems giving shape to youth culture are most commonly associated with adolescence, from note passing in class to symbols used to associate with a particular teenage clique. However, using multiple literacies as a way to connect certain children while excluding adults and other students who do not fit in clearly begins in the preschool and kindergarten classrooms.

By its very definition, the subterranean culture, with its many narrative forms, is child-initiated and quite separate from adult influence — factors that appear to make participation difficult for children with significant disabilities who often rely on high levels of adult support. Once adults actively begin to assist a child, any ongoing narratives are no longer subterranean. Still, in our observations we noted children with disabilities at times finding their way into subterranean discourses, with multiple literacies playing a role. For instance, in the Corner Nook classroom, we observed several girls take over a corner of the room where both boys and girls tended to play. Led by Kassie, a nondisabled child, the girls engaged in the literate act of producing two signs with markers and crayons. One read, "No boys," and the other had a bright red circle with a slash mark over the word "Boys," meaning, again, "No boys allowed." Lori, the girl with severe disabilities, was included in the group. While she was not directly involved in the fast-paced action of creating the signs, she was a part of the giggling conspiracy.

Some of the classroom boys began to take notice of the signs being posted and attempted to enter the area — only to be greeted by girls who would not allow them in. "No boys allowed," was the mantra. The boys' primary focus was to wrench down the signs. This central effort demonstrated the power of the written form. It was as if the signs were the key to the girls' authority; remove them and order would be restored.

Jamie, the child with autism introduced earlier, moved about skittishly at the edge of the group trying to break into the area. He was largely ignored by both the boys and girls, suggesting perhaps that in this struggle his presence was considered nonthreatening. At times he found himself in the middle of a shoving match, and he would giggle and clap his hands and go running. Suddenly, in a flash, Jamie reached out and grabbed one sign. He ran from the scene shrieking with laughter, several girls after him and several boys shouting support. The commotion brought the classroom adults to the scene to end the play, but not until after Jamie had taken on the rare role of hero.

While teachers primarily remained outside the subterranean narratives, other than to shut them down, there was ambivalent recognition that such participation was healthy for the children with significant disabilities. Shayne Robbins, later discussing Jamie's role in the narrative just described, said, "It's so much what inclusion is about. . . . [Jamie] came in this year, he was so clueless in the beginning about all the social stuff — reaching out to other kids, asserting himself, standing up to others and for his rights." Shayne said she had noticed dramatic growth in terms of Jamie's ability to fit in with groups of children: "It's amazing to watch him now. Sometimes I'll just stand back and watch, and he's a leader. He gets kids doing things. He's just so important in this class." Shayne continued, "That's the important stuff. Sometimes you kind of have to look the other direction, let him break a rule or two, because he's learning how to fit in, how to just be a normal part."

CONCLUSIONS:
CONSTRUCTING CONTEXTS OF SUPPORT FOR LITERACY

Inclusive education appeared to be fundamental to the literate citizenship of children with significant disabilities. In its rejection of the status quo of segregated schooling, inclusion immersed students in the wonderfully chaotic patterns, semiotic systems, and narrative forms of the early childhood literate community. Beyond mere presence, however, was the teachers' active belief that literacy was many things and that all students, including those with the most complex disabilities, were capable sense-makers. Through a teacher's educational imagination, children were supported in the literate engagement of a variety of narrative forms made available in their hectic classrooms.

We are not the first researchers to have explored young children's narratives as fundamental to literacy. Most notably, Kieran Egan and colleagues have systematically examined the varied stories of children and their relationship to a literate culture (Egan, 1999; McEwan & Egan, 1995; see endnote 11). Narrative, in McEwan and Egan's (1995) definition, is the language-based story that grows around, gives shape to, and symbolically extends the experience. They note, "What distinguishes narrative is that it takes shape, in however attenuated a form, as a rhythm that ultimately springs from patterns implicit in human life and interaction" (McEwan & Egan, 1995, p. vii). In relation to our own research, "human life and interaction" corresponds to the meaning, understanding, and sense-making that emerged as a motivating force in the lives of all young children.

The rhythm of which McEwan and Egan (1995) write is also described as a "pattern" out of which "more developed [e.g., less attenuated, increasingly sophisticated] patterns may emerge" (p. vii). In an insightful essay exploring the origins of literacy in preschool narratives, Egan (1999) cautiously noted certain links between the community young children create in early childhood classrooms and the sophisticated oral cultures out of which literacy itself once emerged thousands of years ago. He noted that, as with oral cultures, young children and surrounding adults build messages of importance into "developing narratives" or spoken stories. These stories provide the first "firm structures" for the abstractions of childhood ideas and understanding; they, in effect, "catch and fix meaning" (p. 16).

According to Egan (1999), as preschoolers grow in sophistication, so too do their stories and the manner in which those stories are caught and fixed. Young children's oral narratives engage the tools of rhyme, rhythm, meter, repetition of formulae, redundancy, and visual imagery (i.e., figures of speech) to expand and deepen messages of importance. These same tools, Egan asserted, are important in written texts aimed at a preschool audience (e.g., nursery rhymes and Dr. Seuss books), and in the early textual-representational efforts on the part of young children themselves.

Kieran Egan's descriptions of children's oral-based communities eventually merging with the literate, text-sated realities of the formal school agenda added depth to our own observations of narratives. However, his descriptive efforts, focused as they are on oral culture, could not capture the complexities of literate citizenship in inclusive early childhood classrooms where many of the children labeled with significant disabilities exhibited extreme problems with spoken language and were, in fact, at the margins of oral language participation.

Yet, teachers in the classrooms where our participant observations played out were firmly committed to the notion that all children, including those with the most complex disabilities, could be citizens of the literate community. Hence, while Egan and colleagues may argue that oral narrative is the origin of literacy, the efforts of our participating teachers and students suggested that narrative expressed through any of a variety of semiotic systems served as the basis for and developing sophistication in literacy for all children.

NOTES

1. The contents of this research were developed under a grant from the U.S. Department of Education (No. H324D010031). However, the contents do not necessarily represent the policy of the DOE, and no endorsement by the federal government should be assumed.
2. All proper names, including those of classrooms, schools, cities, adults, and children, have been altered, and identifying information has been obscured in order to maintain confidentiality.
3. Referred to in the disability education literature as inclusive education (see Biklen, 1992; Kliewer, 1998b).
4. Currently, the most visible proponents of direct subskill instruction for literacy development in early childhood (e.g., Adams, 1990, 2001; Adams, Foorman, Lundberg, & Beeler, 1997; McGuiness, 1997) conclude that teaching must directly focus, through drill, on three components. The first, considered most important to literacy, is referred to as phonemic awareness and is composed of a myriad of subcomponents. It is the conscious awareness on the part of young children that words are made up of phonemes. The second is commonly referred to as the alphabetic principle, and is a general description of knowledge about the alphabet, including awareness that phonemes can be graphically represented by letters and letter combinations. The third, oral language, is associated with vocabulary development and correct English usage. A fourth component that may be included in descriptions of the need for direct instruction is orthography, or direct instruction in spelling and the rules associated with spelling.
5. Based on records maintained in the archives of the Mennonite Heritage Museum, Mountain Lake, Minnesota.
6. One type of source among many vividly documenting the viciousness of imposed illiteracy is the autobiographical genre described as slave narrative, which emerged from the stories of freed and escaped American slaves prior to the Civil War (see Gates, 1987).
7. *Scientific-based* and *evidence-based* are current, synonymous educational catch-phrases related to particular forms of what is termed in psychology to be experimental research and the practices that are formulated therein. In reading research, it appears that only phonics-based instruction and assessment is currently branded as scientifically based. An example of qualifying research and derivative practice is the reading assessment referred to by its trade-marked title, *Dynamic Indicators of Basic Early Literacy Skills* (DIBELS; Good & Kaminski, 2002). DIBELS materials state that the *big ideas* of early literacy include phonological awareness, the alphabetic principle, and accuracy and fluency with connected text. In preschool, DIBELS' focus is placed

on assessing initial sound fluency and word-use fluency (which refers to using apparently ran-dom words correctly in random sentences). In kindergarten, letter-naming fluency, phoneme-segmentation fluency, and nonsense-word fluency are added to the assessed literacy skills. Not until first grade do we see an expectation around understanding and meaning (referred to in DIBELS lexicon as retell fluency).

8. An extremely narrow selection of this body of work includes, for example, biographical, autobio-graphical, clinical, and ethnographic accounts of the development of highly sophisticated literacies on the part of people with Down's syndrome (Andrews, 1995; Buck, 1955; Buckley, 1995; Burke & McDaniel, 1991; Goode, 1992; Hunt, 1966; Seagoe, 1964), autism (Biklen, 1992; Grandin & Scariano, 1986), and severe physical disabilities (Brown, 1989; Crossley & McDonald, 1984).

9. Different states, and even different Local Education Agencies (e.g., school districts) within a sin-gle state, vary in how children are labeled. All children defined here as having a significant dis-ability are students who qualify for special education services under the Individuals with Dis-abilities Education Act (IDEA). In addition, they are children who qualify for a significant level of resources because of the presumed degree of disability. Many but not all of the children had specific disability labels or diagnoses (e.g., autism, Down's syndrome, cerebral palsy, etc.). Pre-school children (and now older students), however, may receive services with a generic label (e.g., developmental disability [D.D.], entitled individual [E.I.], etc.).

10. Narrative is, of course, a broad construct. Our use of the term reflects McEwan and Egan's (1995) sense that "narrative is basically extended language configured in such a way that its ear-lier embodiment in life becomes revealed" (p. vii). The earlier embodiment may be a thought, idea, emotion, or experience, and its revelation may take on the configuration of, among other expressive or receptive communication forms, literacy.

11. Emphasizing a specific child's unique or idiosyncratic needs within a general curriculum is tra-ditionally associated with inclusive education and is commonly considered a process of making curricular adaptations or modifications. Initially it was termed the Principle of Partial Participa-tion (Baumgart et al., 1982), and has more recently been referred to as multilevel learning (Falvey, Givner, & Kimm, 1996) and differentiated instruction (Tomlinson, 1999).

REFERENCES

Adams, M. J. (1990). *Beginning to read: Thinking and learning about print.* Cambridge, MA: MIT Press.

Adams, M. J. (2001). Alphabetic anxiety and explicit, systematic phonics instruction: A cognitive science perspective. In S. B. Neuman & D. K. Dickinson (Eds.), *Handbook of early literacy research* (pp. 66–80). New York: Guilford Press.

Adams, M. J., Foorman, B. R., Lundberg, I., & Beeler, T. (1997). *Phonemic awareness in young chil-dren: A classroom curriculum.* Baltimore: Brookes.

Andrews, S. S. (1995). Life in Mendocino: A young man with Down syndrome in a Northern Califor-nia town. In S. J. Taylor, R. Bogdan, & Z. M. Lutfiyya (Eds.), *The variety of community experi-ence: Qualitative studies of family and community life* (pp. 101–116). Baltimore: Brookes.

Barratt-Pugh, C. (2000). The socio-cultural context of literacy learning. In C. Barratt-Pugh & M. Rohl (Eds.), *Literacy learning in the early years* (pp. 1–26). Buckingham, Eng.: Open Univer-sity Press.

Barton, D., & Hamilton, M. (1998). *Local literacies: Reading and writing in one community.* New York: Routledge.

Baumgart, D., Brown, L., Pumpian, I., Nisbet, J., Ford, A., Sweet, M., Messina, R., & Schroeder, J. (1982). Principle of partial participation and individualized adaptations in educational pro-grams for severely handicapped students. *Journal of the Association for the Severely Handi-capped, 7,* 17–27.

Biklen, D. (1992). *Schooling without labels: Parents, educators, and inclusive education.* Philadelphia: Temple University Press.

Bogdan, R., & Biklen, S. K. (2003). *Qualitative research for education: An introduction to theory and methods* (4th ed.). Boston: Allyn & Bacon.

Brown, C. (1989). *My left foot.* New York: Simon & Schuster.

Buck, J. N. (1955). The sage: An unusual mongoloid. In A. Burton & R. Harris (Eds.), *Clinical studies of personality* (vol. 3, pp. 455–481). New York: Harper & Row.

Buckley, S. (1995). Teaching children with Down syndrome to read and write. In L. Nadel & D. Rosenthal (Eds.), *Down syndrome: Living and learning in the community* (pp. 158–169). New York: Wiley-Liss.

Burke, C., & McDaniel, J. B. (1991). *A special kind of hero.* New York: Dell.

Crawford, P. A. (1995). Early literacy: Emerging perspectives. *Journal of Research in Childhood Education, 10,* 71–86.

Crossley, R., & McDonald, A. (1984). *Annie's coming out.* New York: Penguin.

Egan, K. (1999). *Children's minds, talking rabbits, and clockwork oranges.* New York: Teachers College Press.

Erickson, K. A., & Koppenhaver, D. A. (1995). Developing a literacy program for children with severe disabilities. *Reading Teacher, 48,* 676–684.

Falvey, M., Givner, C. C., & Kimm, C. (1996). What do I do Monday morning? In S. Stainback & W. Stainback (Eds.), *Inclusion: A guide for educators* (pp. 117–140). Baltimore: Paul Brookes.

Fernandez, R. (2001). *Imagining literacy: Rhizomes of knowledge in American culture and literature.* Austin: University of Texas Press.

Gates, H. L., Jr. (1987). *The classic slave narratives.* New York: Mentor.

Good, R. H., & Kaminski, R. A. (2002). *Dynamic indicators of basic early literacy skills* (6th ed.). Eugene, OR: Institute for the Development of Educational Achievement.

Goode, D. A. (1992). Who is Bobby? Ideology and method in the discovery of a Down syndrome person's competence. In P. M. Ferguson, D. L. Ferguson, & S. J. Taylor (Eds.), *Interpreting disability: A qualitative reader* (pp. 197–212). New York: Teachers College Press.

Grandin, T., & Scariano, M. M. (1986). *Emergence: Labeled autistic.* Novato, CA: Arena Press.

Hunt, N. (1966). *The world of Nigel Hunt: The diary of a mongoloid youth.* New York: Garrett.

Kliewer, C. (1998a). Citizenship in the literate community: An ethnography of children with Down syndrome and the written word. *Exceptional Children, 64,* 167–180.

Kliewer, C. (1998b). *Schooling children with Down syndrome: Toward an understanding of possibility.* New York: Teachers College Press.

Kliewer, C. & Biklen, D. (2001). "School's not really a place for reading": A research analysis of the literate lives of people with severe disabilities. *Journal of the Association for Persons with Severe Disabilities, 26,* 1–12.

Kliewer, C., & Drake, S. (1998). Disability, eugenics, and the current ideology of segregation: A modern moral tale. *Disability and Society, 13,* 95–111.

Kliewer, C., & Fitzgerald, L. M. (2001). Disability, schooling, and the artifacts of colonialism. *Teachers College Record, 103,* 450–470.

Kliewer, C., Fitzgerald, L. M., & Raschke, D. (2001). Young children's citizenship in the literate community: Significant disability and the power of early childhood inclusion. *TASH Connections, 27*(11/12), 8–11.

Kliewer, C., & Landis, D. (1999). Individualizing literacy instruction for young children with moderate to severe disabilities. *Exceptional Children, 66,* 85–100.

Kliewer, C., & Raschke, D. (2002). Beyond the metaphor of merger: Confronting the moral quagmire of segregation in early childhood special education. *Disability, Culture, and Education, 1,* 41–62.

Kluth, P., Straut, D. M., & Biklen, D. P. (Eds.). (2003). *Access to academics for all students: Critical approaches to inclusive curriculum, instruction, and policy.* Mahwah, NJ: Lawrence Erlbaum Associates.

Koppenhaver, D. A., & Erickson, K. A. (2003). Natural emergent literacy supports for preschoolers with autism and severe communication impairments. *Topics in Language Disorders, 23,* 283–292.

Maurice, C. (1993). *Let me hear your voice: A family's triumph over autism.* New York: Knopf.

McEwan, H., & Egan, K. (Eds.). (1995). *Narrative in teaching, learning, and research.* New York: Teachers College Press.

McGuiness, D. (1997). *Why our children can't read.* New York: Free Press.

Mirenda, P. (2003). "He's not really a reader": Perspectives on supporting literacy development in individuals with autism. *Topics in Language Disorders, 23,* 271–282.

Paley, V. G. (1988). *Bad guys don't have birthdays: Fantasy play at four.* Chicago: University of Chicago Press.

Paley, V. G. (1992). *You can't say you can't play.* Cambridge, MA: Harvard University Press.

Resnick, D. P., & Resnick, L. B. (1977). The nature of literacy: An historical exploration. *Harvard Educational Review, 47,* 370–385.

Richgels, D. J. (2001). Invented spelling, phonemic awareness, and reading and writing instruction. In S. B. Neuman & D. K. Dickinson (Eds.), *Handbook of early literacy research* (pp. 142–155). New York: Guilford Press.

Seagoe, M. V. (1964). *Yesterday was Tuesday, all day and all night: The story of a unique education.* Boston: Little, Brown.

Shannon, P. (1995). *Text, lies, and videotape: Stories about life, literacy, and learning.* Portsmouth, NH: Heinemann.

Strauss, A., & Corbin, J. (1994). Grounded theory methodology: An overview. In N. K. Denzin & Y. S. Lincoln (Eds.), *Handbook of qualitative research* (pp. 273–285). Thousand Oaks, CA: Sage.

Tomlinson, C. (1999). *The differentiated classroom: Responding to the needs of all learners.* Alexandria, VA: Association for Supervision and Curriculum Development.

Whitehurst, G. J., & Lonigan, C. J. (2001). Emergent literacy: Development from prereaders to readers. In S. B. Neuman & D. K. Dickinson (Eds.), *Handbook of early literacy research* (pp. 11–29). New York: Guilford Press.

Part Two:
Critical Conversations
about Disability and Race
in Special Education

———— *8* ————

"It is paradoxical that, as the inclusive education movement represents the emergence of empowered voices about disability rights and better educational services for this population, it has been painfully silent about the plight of minority students. Scholars working on overrepresentation (including myself) are guilty of a silence on the implications of the realization of inclusion for minority students."

—Alfredo Artiles

According to the U.S. Office of Special Education Programs, during the 2000–2001 school year, 18.5 percent of students classified for special education services were Black, even though their representation in the overall student population was only 15 percent. White students, on the other hand, comprised 58 percent of the population of students with disabilities, while their representation in the overall student population was 63 percent (U.S. Department of Education, 2002). Even more profound, Black students are more than three times as likely as White students to be classified as having mental retardation (Oswald, Coutinho, & Best, 2002). These figures demonstrate an overrepresentation of Black students and underrepresentation of White students in special education. Similar disproportion in representation exists to different degrees among other racial groups, within certain disability types, and in different areas of the country (see Donovan & Cross, 2002, and Losen & Orfield, 2002, for a more thorough description of this issue). Even since before the inception of federal special education law in 1975, scholars have written about this problem, hypothesized about its causes, and proposed solutions, and yet it persists, revealing deep inequities in education for children with and without disabilities.

At the same time, students with disabilities continue to move from segregated to integrated settings. In the 1999–2000 school year, 47 percent of students with disabilities were spending the majority of their school day in regular classrooms alongside nondisabled peers, 20 percent were being educated in a separate classroom, and 4 percent were being educated in a separate facility. These figures show considerable improvement since only ten years ago, when 33 percent were spending the majority of their school day in the regular classroom, 25 percent in self-contained classrooms, and 6 percent in separate schools (U.S. Department of Education, 2002). Scholars within the "inclusive education" movement advocate for increased access to educational opportunity and to the general education curriculum for students with disabilities. They argue that a restructuring of schools is necessary not only to ensure full access for students with disabilities, but also to meet the diverse needs of all students most effectively.

In "Special Education's Changing Identity: Paradoxes and Dilemmas in Views of Culture and Space," Alfredo Artiles refers to the convergence of these two trends — disproportionate representation and inclusive education — as a defining moment in the identity of special education. While others may see these two trends as distinct arms of the scholarship in special education, Artiles argues that they are intimately connected and criticizes scholars in the field for failing to recognize and comment on their interconnectedness. He calls on scholars of inclusive education to acknowledge and examine the diversity of the student population that is entering integrated classrooms, and on scholars of disproportionate representation to expand their notions of culture and space and to imagine new possibilities for change.

In this book, we present Artiles's article in order to set the tone for a new conversation around the intersection between disability and race. We seek to break the silence that Artiles claims is weakening the two areas and preventing them from realizing a new paradigm for change. As a step in this direction, we include two articles that do not explicitly address special education but effectively address issues of difference that lie at the intersection of the literature on inclusive education and on disproportionate representation. The inclusive education literature imagines possibilities for accommodating diverse learners in one system; the disproportionate representation literature points out the consequences of a system that currently does not deal with these differences.

Lisa Delpit and Jim Cummins propose strategies for dealing with difference, thus potentially forming a bridge between these two strands of scholarship. In her seminal article "The Silenced Dialogue: Power and Pedagogy in Educating Other People's Children," Delpit astutely demonstrates the dangers inherent in assuming that all children need and will learn from the same type of pedagogy. In so doing, she gets to the heart of the inclusive education movement — the belief that all children can learn, albeit in different ways, and that effective pedagogy takes into account an understanding of those differences. Delpit also demonstrates how power plays out in the classroom to "silence" the dialogue about learning differences. We ask readers of this book to consider how difference affects the classroom teacher and how the teacher should most effectively deal with difference in her day-to-day work. We ask them to think about how diversity related to race and culture is similar to or different from diversity related to disability and learning style. Furthermore, we hope readers will think about how these types of diversity are connected and how teachers can incorporate an understanding of all types of difference into their pedagogy.

Finally, in "Empowering Minority Students: A Framework for Intervention," Cummins presents a theoretical framework for addressing the achievement gap between minority and nonminority students. He posits that the empowering or "disabling" of minority students is largely a result of the ways in which educators define their roles vis-à-vis the students and communities they serve. Cummins identifies four dimensions of school organization — the incorporation of minority students' language and culture into the school program, minority community participation, pedagogy, and assessment — that have the potential to empower minority students to succeed in school. He cites the overrepresentation of minority students in special education as evidence of the failure to empower students of color appropriately, and encourages researchers and educators seeking to understand and address this problem to use his framework as a guide. We encourage readers to use this framework as well, and to think about ways in which educators can create inclusive classrooms that empower all of the students within them.

REFERENCES

Donovan, M. S., & Cross, C. T. (Eds.). (2002). *Minority students in special and gifted education*. Washington, DC: National Academy Press.

Losen, D. J., & Orfield, G. (Eds.). (2002). *Racial inequity in special education*. Cambridge, MA: Harvard Education Press.

Oswald, D. P., Coutinho, M. J., & Best, A. M. (2002). Community and school predictors of overrepresentation of minority children in special education. In D. L. Losen & G. Orfield (Eds.), *Racial inequity in special education* (pp. 1–13.) Cambridge, MA: Harvard Education Press.

U.S. Department of Education. (2002). *Twenty-fourth annual report to Congress on the implementation of the Individuals with Disabilities Education Act*. Washington, DC: Author.

Special Education's Changing Identity

Paradoxes and Dilemmas in Views of Culture and Space

———— *8* ————

ALFREDO J. ARTILES

U.S. classrooms today look dramatically different than they did thirty years ago, before the federal government passed its first comprehensive special education legislation — the Education for All Handicapped Children Act — in 1975. This law was reauthorized as the Individuals with Disabilities Education Act (IDEA) in 1990. Although educators now have theoretically more sophisticated and effective interventions at their disposal for serving students with disabilities, their work also is far more complex and challenging. For instance, as the population of students with disabilities and the proportion of minority students grow rapidly, we are witnessing the inexorable convergence of two of the most important developments in special education's contemporary history, namely, the inclusive education movement[1] and the overrepresentation of racial minority students in special education.[2] The increasing complexity of diversity in terms of racial background and ability level poses significant challenges to the refinement of special education services, the improvement of policies, and the development of a knowledge base, particularly when we acknowledge that the research literature on racial and linguistic minority students is rather thin (Donovan & Cross, 2002; Gersten, Baker, & Pugach, 2001). Moreover, minority overrepresentation and inclusion pose important challenges to special educators' understandings of culture, the role of culture in visions of disability, and the creation of a research ethos that is mindful of cultural differences.

Inclusion and overrepresentation will undoubtedly influence the transformation of special education's identity. Let us remember that a cornerstone of special education's original identity was grounded in a civil rights discourse for people with disabilities. As a result, IDEA was passed to ensure free and appropriate public education, parents' rights to be informed of evaluation and placement decisions (including the right

Harvard Educational Review   Vol. 73   No. 2   Summer 2003, 164–202

to due process hearings), individualized and nondiscriminatory assessment, individualized educational and related services, education in the least restrictive environment, and federal assistance to support states' and school districts' efforts to educate students with disabilities (Smith, 2001).

The passage and refinement of IDEA was a major accomplishment in the history of special education that has made a difference in the lives of millions of people with disabilities. However, given ongoing societal and professional transformations, the special education field must still address the following questions:

- How will special education's identity change as this system serves more racially diverse students with disabilities in general education contexts?
- How will understandings of culture be infused in special education's identity?
- How will this field acknowledge race and language background in research practices and how will researchers place these constructs in dynamic grids of cultural influence?
- As understandings of inclusion shift from a spatial location (the general education classroom) to the alignment of educational philosophies with visions of organizational arrangements, how will the new identity of the field account for racial differences, culture, and space?

It is imperative that the discourse communities working on inclusion and overrepresentation begin to craft a dialogue across their respective discourse boundaries to reflect on the implications of their labor for a new, emerging systemic identity.[3] Unfortunately, these discourse communities rarely reflect on their growing overlapping foci or on the implications of such convergence. Hence, in this article I discuss the intersection of inclusion and overrepresentation as it affects school-age individuals with high-incidence disabilities (particularly learning disabilities). I focus on this group because it comprises the United States' largest segment of the school population with disabilities.[4]

I build my analysis of the literatures on inclusion and overrepresentation on two ideas. First, current special education developments ought to be examined in the context of larger cultural and political processes located in educational reforms and society at large. This examination must include an analysis of the power differentials and struggles that shape the educational outcomes of racial minorities and students with disabilities. Second, the convergence of the inclusion movement and the overrepresentation of minorities in special education create paradoxes and dilemmas that can interfere with the development of socially just educational systems in a democratic society.

In this article, I present the preliminary findings of an analysis of the inclusion and overrepresentation literatures, namely: 1) silence about racial diversity in the implementation of inclusive models, 2) lack of vision for a culturally responsive educational system, 3) inadequate attention to sociohistorical context and the complexity of culture, 4) limited definitions of space, and 5) problematic views of difference. I conclude with a discussion of the implications of this analysis for a new generation of inclusion and overrepresentation research. Before developing these ideas, I situate overrepresentation and inclusion in the current cultural politics of educational reform.

THE CULTURAL POLITICS OF CURRENT EDUCATIONAL REFORMS

As I witness the ongoing debates about inclusive education and minority representation in special education, I cannot ignore the contexts in which these conversations are taking place. The most immediate is the sociopolitical context of general education reform. For example, the recent neoconservative tide of reforms largely assumes that schools should produce human capital (Apple, 1996). Neoconservative reformers reason that, in an era of increasing global competition and unprecedented economic progress, schools must produce a skilled and competitive labor force. Apple argues that this premise is ingrained in a larger and more complex cultural agenda that values individualism and competition. Implied in this premise is the idea that the educational system will have winners and losers (see also Varenne & McDermott, 1999).

Policymakers and the general public have generally concluded that in order for the United States to be competitive in this era of globalization, schools must produce the human capital necessary to meet the demands of the new economy. This commitment has generated a number of popular reform ideas, including the incorporation of national standards, curricula, and testing and privatized choice plans (see Apple, 1996, and McLaughlin & Tilstone, 1999, for analytic overviews of these reforms). Due in part to concerns over poor outcomes and low expectations for students with disabilities, the most recent reauthorization of IDEA has incorporated several accountability provisions that align with general education reforms. Examples of such provisions include performance goals and indicators, school-based improvement plans, participation in large-scale assessments, access to the general education curriculum, and greater collaboration between general and special education personnel (McLaughlin & Tilstone, 1999). It is feasible that general and special educators' potentially divergent views of effective instruction might create contradictions in the implementation of these policies (McDonnell, McLaughlin, & Morison, 1997). For example, it is not clear whether the new emphasis on standards-based reform for all students will shortchange students with disabilities as teachers feel compelled to cover content and promote more sophisticated forms of learning, thus leaving less time for teachers to support students who lag behind. Confused about when to modify curriculum versus when to provide instructional accommodations in order to access the curriculum, teachers often feel unprepared to apply this new accountability framework to special education populations (McLaughlin, Henderson, & Rhim, 1998; McLaughlin & Tilstone, 1999).

Apple (1996) argues that neoconservative reforms help to maintain economic and political security for the dominant group, preserve the dominant group's traditional values, and legitimize dominant definitions of knowledge and competence. These reforms ratify a politics of difference that favors neoconservatives because such reforms afford them the privilege to construct and impose exclusionary insider and outsider identities (i.e., "we" and "them"). "We" are homogeneous, hard working, and English speaking, and "we" do better in all labor, educational, and health outcome measures. In contrast, "they" are lazy, dirty, heterogeneous, misuse English, and take advantage of the government and the "we" (Apple, 1996). The consolidation of deficit views about "them" has drawn attention to issues of difference in education and beyond at a time when the nation is experiencing unprecedented cultural diversification.

Areas in which we observe the interplay between conservative educational reforms and their implicit pursuit of a cultural agenda that privileges dominant groups are language and literacy reform, particularly in the debates over bilingual education and the English-only movement. As these debates polarized, we witnessed the abolition of bilingual education programs in states including California, Arizona, and Massachusetts. These policies have had dreadful consequences as they became embodied in what some call "backlash pedagogies" (Gutierrez, Asato, Santos, & Gotanda, 2002), which aim to maintain the status quo that assumes inequality is a natural state of affairs in educational practice and reform. Backlash pedagogies disregard the history of oppression and marginalization suffered by minority populations (Gutierrez et al., 2002) and are ultimately grounded in colonialist views of literacy and learning.

As we witness the initial implementation of standards, accountability reforms, and English-only initiatives, we must consider the consequences for historically marginalized racial and linguistically diverse groups. For instance, will referrals of English language learners (ELLs) to special education increase? (Artiles, Rueda, Salazar, & Higareda, 2002). How will special education placement for ELLs influence access to the general education curriculum and affect dropout, graduation, or special education exit rates? How will the principles of the inclusive education movement be operationalized when placing ELLs in special education, considering that (a) ELLs are likely to be taught by teachers without credentials (Gándara et al., 2000), (b) there is a dramatic shortage of special education and bilingual teachers (García 1996; Reynolds & York, 1996), (c) most teachers receive poor training on the influence of language and culture in children's learning (Zeichner & Hoeft, 1996), and (d) teachers have limited experience with collaborative and/or team-teaching arrangements (Smith, 2001)?

These are the cultural politics enclosing the special education field in which an emphasis on individualism and competition, views of competence and literacy that privilege certain groups, and a troubling politics of difference intermingle. We must not lose sight of these cultural politics as we move toward a more inclusive special educational system and grapple with the overrepresentation of minority students in disability programs. An exhaustive analysis of inclusion and overrepresentation is beyond the scope of this manuscript. Therefore, in the next section, my goal is to sketch their boundaries and highlight key issues as a means to identify paradoxes and dilemmas that exist within and between these literatures.

OUTLINE OF THE INCLUSIVE EDUCATION MOVEMENT

Special education legislation requires that students with disabilities be educated in the least restrictive environment (LRE). Although this notion is a fundamental and identifying principle of contemporary special education, it is also one of the most controversial constructs in the field (Smith, 2001). In its early years, special education was provided in self-contained classrooms and separate schools. During the 1970s and 1980s, the LRE requirement allowed schools to mainstream students with disabilities in general education classrooms for a portion of the day, though this practice was done on a voluntary basis (Brantlinger, 1997). In the mid 1980s, Madeline Will, then director of the federal Office of Special Education Programs, challenged the field to transform traditional practices so that more students with disabilities would be integrated into general education classrooms (Will, 1984). These efforts were called the Regular Education Initiative. Although the law requires that LRE be individually determined and that services be available across a continuum of options from most to least integrated, debates ensued between parents, practitioners, policymakers, and researchers about best practices for implementation (Smith, 2001). These debates evolved from discussions about integration (as embodied in the REI) to the development of proposals based on the concept of inclusive education.

The inclusive education movement aims to change a school's ethos and practices to promote truly inclusive models and ultimately to promote student academic learning, social competence, social skills, attitude change, and positive peer relations. In its early years, the movement stressed full inclusion and focused primarily on students with severe disabilities; however, it has steadily expanded to include students with high-incidence disabilities (Fuchs & Fuchs, 1994). The inclusive education movement embodies several important characteristics and beliefs focusing on the student, the teacher, and the system. For example, the movement argues that all children can learn, that learning is supported by a strong sense of community, and that services are based on need rather than limited by location. Also, the movement promotes schoolwide approaches, such as teacher collaboration, enhanced instructional strategies, curriculum accommodations and modifications, and additional supports in general education settings. Finally, the movement focuses on the system, asserting that neighborhood schools enroll natural proportions of students with disabilities and demonstrate a concern for standards and outcomes for all students (Lipsky & Gartner, 1999).

Despite these common characteristics and beliefs, unclear goals and multiple definitions of inclusion seem to permeate the movement's discourse and research practices (Dyson, 1999; Fuchs & Fuchs, 1994). For instance, definitions can range from students' with disabilities part- or full-time placement in a general education classroom to the transformation of a school ethos or the construction of entire educational systems based on an inclusive education philosophy (Dyson, 1999). The diversity of definitions and goals of the movement contribute to the creation of multiple discourses. Dyson argues that discourses about inclusion can be organized along two dimensions: (a) the *rationale* for inclusion and (b) the *realization* of inclusion.

Rationale for Inclusion

With regard to the rationale dimension, Dyson (1999) identifies two discourses: 1) the rights-and-ethics discourse and 2) the efficacy discourse. The rights-and-ethics discourse uses a civil rights discourse to argue that individuals with disabilities have the fundamental human right to be educated, ideally alongside nondisabled peers

(Brantlinger, 1997). This basic right is grounded in ethical principles of fairness and social justice (Lipsky & Gartner, 1999; Skrtic, 1991). According to Dyson (1999), the rights-and-ethics discourse derives from structuralist analyses that suggest that societal inequalities are reproduced in educational systems. Individuals and groups who possess cultural capital have advantages over marginalized or oppressed people with educational and labor opportunities, since educational systems are built on the knowledge and values of dominant groups. When applied to people with disabilities, this critique asserts that special education, a historically segregated system parallel to general education, further privileges certain groups by separating and marginalizing students deemed problematic or difficult. The existence of this system in turn establishes general education as the norm and special education as deviant, and conceals the underlying need to restructure societal conditions. Therefore, the argument follows, special education placement decisions are inextricably linked to issues of equity and social justice. According to the rights-and-ethics discourse, the maintenance of a segregated special education system is incongruous with socially just educational systems, and ultimately with democratic ideals.

Despite the clear logic of this critique, particularly with regard to equity issues, we must acknowledge that competing definitions of social justice that permeate this discourse and the special education field add confusion to an already complex process (Christensen & Rizvi, 1996). For instance, current reforms based on notions of free market and choice, which in turn are grounded in individualistic meritocratic principles, define social justice as fairness of opportunity for individuals. As such, "social justice is no longer 'seen as linked to past group oppression and disadvantage' judged historically, but represented simply as a matter of guaranteeing individual choice under the conditions of a 'free market'" (Rizvi & Lingard, 1996, p. 15).

Conversely, within the rights-and-ethics discourse, social justice is defined as the access to and the redistribution of general education resources for students with disabilities. Unfortunately, as Rizvi and Lingard (1996) argue, even this distributive view is limited, for it does not "account adequately for either contemporary politics of difference, or the various complex ways in which exclusion and discrimination are now practiced, in both their individual and institutional forms" (p. 21). This is indeed a major shortcoming of this discourse in light of the growing overrepresentation of minorities in special education, which I take up in more detail in the following section.

The rationale based on the efficacy discourse is closely aligned with the rights-and-ethics thesis. This rationale cites evidence that suggests that students with disabilities who are placed in segregated programs do not exhibit greater educational gains than comparable peers educated in integrated contexts. Evidence is also cited about the lack of differentiation between the instructional practices observed in programs for various disabilities and general education classrooms (Lipsky & Gartner, 1996). This discourse's underlying view of social justice is also based on the aforementioned arguments of access and equity. Unfortunately, access does not guarantee meaningful participation, full membership, or more comparable outcomes (Rizvi & Lingard, 1996).

Realization of Inclusion

In addition to the discourses advanced to justify the creation of an inclusive educational system, visions of how such a system ought to be realized have been proposed. Dyson (1999) labels these discourses political and pragmatic. The political discourse is concerned with developing forms of resistance against the interest groups that uphold the traditional special education system. For example, the inclusion movement has faced strong resistance from segments of the special education professional community and it has spurred heated debates in professional journals and conferences. Some of these discussions revolve around technical issues, such as empirical bases of arguments or lack of specificity in proposed models (Fuchs & Fuchs, 1994; Kauffman & Hallahan, 1995; Wang & Walberg, 1988). Others are ideological or rhetorical, focusing on values and beliefs about learning, teaching, disability, research, and meanings of expressions such as "all children" (Brantlinger, 1997; Gartner & Lipsky, 1987; Pugach & Lilly, 1984; Stainback & Stainback, 1991).[5]

The pragmatic discourse has received by far the most attention from researchers. This discourse addresses what inclusive education programs and schools do and should look like. Some scholars have developed profiles of inclusive schools related to the ethos, structures, and processes in such contexts, while others have offered conceptual analyses of the fundamental differences between inclusive and non-inclusive schools (Skrtic, 1991; Villa & Thousand, 1995). It is common to find within this discourse practical materials and guides for teachers and administrators interested in developing inclusive programs and schools (Dyson, 1999). A potentially damaging consequence of the pragmatic discourse is that educators might become overly concerned with how to allocate human and material resources, carry out procedures, or create regulatory stipulations aimed at compensating for or avoiding discriminatory practices (Slee, 1996).

A review of research based on the pragmatic discourse reflects the following findings about the inclusion of students with disabilities in general education contexts (U.S. Department of Education, 1999): (a) higher frequency of interactions with nondisabled peers; (b) larger and more enduring nondisabled peer networks; (c) improved social and communication skills (e.g., initiation, self-regulation, choice, contact termination); (d) variations in relationships and status similar to friendships observed among nondisabled students; (e) contingent upon the types of assistance provided, adults as positive mediators of friendships between students with and without disabilities; (f) gains in some academic areas; and (g) success with cooperative learning and peer tutoring, although the impact of mixed-ability grouping on disabled student learning is inconclusive. Some studies that focus on students with learning disabilities find that these students do not always participate meaningfully in general education classrooms. They also show that instruction for this group is undifferentiated. Overall, the results of research "to improve the quality of instruction provided to students with disabilities in general education classrooms . . . have been mixed" (Gersten et al., 2001, p. 699). A few studies suggest that the presence of students with disabilities in inclusive contexts does not have a negative effect on nondisabled students' developmental or academic outcomes (e.g., Staub, 2000). Some argue that gains for nondisabled students is the most consistent finding in this line of inquiry (Manset & Semmel, 1997).

OVERVIEW OF MINORITY REPRESENTATION
IN SPECIAL EDUCATION

The special education population is increasingly segregated along racial lines, as reflected in the disproportionate representation of these minorities in such programs (Donovan & Cross, 2002; Dunn, 1968). While both over- and underrepresentation patterns are associated with disproportionality (Artiles & Trent, 2000), overrepresentation has by far received the most attention in the literature. African Americans and American Indians are most affected by overrepresentation, mostly in the high-incidence disability categories such as LD, MMR, and ED (see note 4).

Considerable efforts and resources have been spent to understand and address this problem, perhaps with more intensity in recent years. Over the last three decades, insights and alternative solutions to this problem have come about through litigation, new legal requirements, active lobbying and advocacy from professional, state, and civil rights groups, two National Research Council (NRC) reports (Donovan & Cross, 2002; Heller, Holtzman, & Messick, 1982), and increasing attention and support from the federal government (e.g., funding of research, technical assistance, and training projects,[6] coverage in recent annual reports to Congress, and attention from high-level administrators in official speeches, reports, and statements) (Hehir, 2002). Unfortunately, the problem is still reflected in current enrollment statistics (Losen & Orfield, 2002).

Although few question whether overrepresentation exists, there is some disagreement about the causes and magnitude of the problem, and some have even asked why overrepresentation is a problem (see Artiles, Trent, & Palmer, in press). Proposed causes cover a wide range; at opposite extremes of this range we find institutional racism and child poverty. The institutional racism thesis is based on social reproduction theory and argues that minority groups' overrepresentation in special education reflects their oppressed and marginalized status in society. Child poverty has also been offered as the cause of this predicament. The latest NRC report (Donovan & Cross, 2002) devoted a great deal of attention to this issue and summarized an extensive literature on the association between poverty and risk for disability. Unfortunately, to our dismay, "we know precious little about the intervening dynamics that connect socioeconomic status to disability" (Fujiura & Yamaki, 2000, p. 196). Sociological and cultural analyses about the connection between child poverty and disability are rarely conducted in the special education field, and thus we rarely consider the historical, cultural, and structural antecedents of the systematic link between poverty, race, and disability (Slee, 1996). A result of this is the implementation of deficit-based studies that overlook the forces that can protect children's development even when they live in dreadful conditions (McLoyd, 1998). Research that aims to document children's deficits also ignores the structural correlates of poverty — for example, schools that serve poor minority students have significantly fewer material and financial resources, lower teacher and instructional quality, and bleak school climates. The existing literature in this field generally falls into two categories: research on placement patterns and research on the precursors to placement, both of which I discuss next.

Racial Minority Overrepresentation: Placement Patterns

The bulk of the overrepresentation literature focuses on special education placement patterns in various disability categories. Findings suggest that overrepresentation patterns vary, depending on whether the data are disaggregated by geographic location, ethnicity, or disability program. Overrepresentation trends can also vary according to ethnic representation in the school population, year, and indicator used (Artiles et al., 2002; Donovan & Cross, 2002; Finn, 1982; Reschly, 1997).

Based on 1998 data, the latest NRC report (Donovan & Cross, 2002) indicates that at the national level 12 percent of all students are served in special education, whereas the risk indices by ethnic group are as follows: 13.1 percent for American Indians, 14.3 percent for African Americans, 11.3 percent for Latinos/as, 5.3 percent for Asian Americans, and 12.1 percent for Whites. When racial minorities' placement rates are compared with White students (using odds ratios)[7] across all disabilities, only African Americans (1.18) and American Indians (1.08) are overrepresented (Donovan & Cross, 2002). There is some variability when the data are disaggregated by disability category. African Americans are overrepresented in mental retardation (MR) (2.35), LD (1.08), ED (1.59), and developmental delay (2.06). These patterns reiterate a consistent finding over the history of this problem regarding African Americans. American Indians are also overrepresented in MR (1.07) and LD (1.2) programs. Latinos are slightly overrepresented in LD (1.12), and Asian Americans are underrepresented in all high-incidence categories.[8]

Several caveats relate to the analysis of placement patterns such as problems with the procedures used to collect data for national datasets, variability in the definition and eligibility criteria for disability across states, and lack of data on factors that could deepen understanding of the contexts of overrepresentation (e.g., teachers' and administrators' beliefs, school climate, quality of instruction, and quality of prereferral interventions). For example, based on data gathered in New York's urban schools, Gottlieb, Alter, Gottlieb, and Wishner (1994) concluded that the fact that "1 in 6 students with LD have IQ scores that could render them eligible for classification as mentally retarded calls into question the definition of learning disabilities that is being applied" (p. 455). Thus, it seems that the LD category, which used to be reserved mostly for White middle-class students, may be becoming a repository for poor ethnic minorities, many of whom come from immigrant or migrant families (Gottlieb et al., 1994). Sometimes these placement decisions may be made to avoid accusations of bias due to the greater stigma of the MMR category or out of fear of litigation; other times, as Gottlieb et al. suggest, decisions are based on the need to use scarce resources for low-achieving students.

Racial Minority Overrepresentation: Precursors to Placement

An alternative strand of overrepresentation research is concerned with the precursors to special education placement. Thus, studies have examined referral, assessment, and decisionmaking processes (Artiles & Pak, 2000; Harry, Klingner, Sturges, & Moore, 2002; Mehan, Hartwick, & Meihls, 1986; Varenne & McDermott, 1999). Some studies have examined bias in referral and placement decisions as associated with teacher gender, race, classroom management ability, and beliefs, whereas other work has assessed the influence of examiner and test (content and development) biases in disability diagnoses (see Donovan & Cross, 2002, for a review of this literature).

Overrepresentation has received closer scrutiny in recent years and a new wave of evidence on the potential antecedents of placement is emerging (e.g., Losen & Orfield, 2002). For instance, funding seems to be associated with minority placement patterns. Parrish (2002) concluded that

> variation in the type of special education funding system suggests that funding systems based on category of disability are particularly prone to troubling patterns of minority overrepresentation and resource distribution. These systems appear much more likely to show overrepresentation of minority students into the disability category mental retardation, while at the same time providing greater special education funding to districts enrolling the lowest percentages of minority students. (p. 33)

Studies have also begun to document the complex interactions between school location, disability category, ethnic group, poverty, and proportion of minority school enrollment. For instance, Oswald, Coutinho, Best, and Singh (1999) documented interactions between demographic variables and overrepresentation patterns and found that Black overrepresentation in MR programs is associated with an increase in poverty, while overrepresentation in the ED category is associated with a decrease in poverty (Oswald et al., 1999). More recently, Oswald, Coutinho, and Best (2002) reported that American Indians were overrepresented in predominantly minority communities, most visibly in ED. Furthermore, "as communities become increasingly Nonwhite, however, white students are substantially less likely to be identified as LD. For Black students, particularly Black male students, living in a community with few Nonwhite students is a substantial risk factor for MR and SED [serious emotional disturbance] identification" (p. 9).

Another factor that could shape placement patterns is the availability of alternative programs (e.g., bilingual education), proportional representation in the district population, and district size. There is evidence, for instance, that Latino overrepresentation as MR was sizable in small districts with high Latino enrollment (i.e., over 70%) (Finn, 1982). Finn reported that overrepresentation was negatively related to the proportion of students placed in bilingual programs. A significant gap in the recent NRC report (Donovan & Cross, 2002) was the discussion of ELL placement in special education; there is indeed an urgent need to conduct more research with this population (Artiles et al., 2002; Ortiz, 1997).

Several important reforms are being implemented in general and special education that may ultimately influence placement in special education. Three such reforms include standards, high-stakes testing, and zero tolerance policies. Minority students are predicted to be most affected by these initiatives, but we are only beginning to study the impact of these reforms (Advancement Project & Civil Rights Project, 2000). For instance, we need more research to understand the impact of high-stakes tests on minority students and on the referral rates to special education. The results of these tests should be examined in conjunction with other indicators such as drop-out rates (paying attention to who was included/excluded in this index) and grade retention rates (Heubert, 2002). Impact assessments of these tests should also verify who was included or excluded in the tests, the procedures used to give the tests (particularly with minority students), and the potential impact of inappropriate accommodations (Heubert, 2002). Although increasing numbers of students with disabilities are passing high-stakes tests in recent years, these students continue to lag behind their nondisabled peers.

The specter of bias is always (tacitly or explicitly) present in discussions and analyses of this problem. Unfortunately, little unequivocal evidence is available. In this vein, the latest NRC report concluded that "the evidence available is insufficient to support a claim that *either* discrimination does or does not play a significant role" (Donovan & Cross, 2002, p. 78, emphasis in original). Nevertheless, given the historical legacies of discrimination and racism in our society, we cannot afford to ignore the potential mediating effect of bias on overrepresentation. Two key tasks for future efforts include addressing bias explicitly in research efforts and broadening the conceptualization of bias. As we suggested recently, "bias is not restricted to the actions and decisions of individuals. Bias can also take the form of historical residue and can be found in the social structures of educational settings and institutional regulations and practices that shape institutional discrimination" (Artiles et al., in press).

Overrepresentation is a multidimensional predicament with deep historical and systemic roots, and there are many areas and factors that need to be studied and initiatives that need to be pursued. Perhaps the two most urgent areas of action are the production of more and better data to understand this problem and the need to enforce IDEA's mandates to monitor and prevent it.[9] However, it is beyond the scope of this manuscript to discuss future directions (see Artiles et al., in press; Donovan & Cross, 2002; Losen & Orfield, 2002).

To conclude, it is important to ask, what is at the heart of the overrepresentation problem? Would the problem be solved with quotas so that racial minority students are proportionally represented in general and special education? Is overrepresentation a symptom of massive bias toward racial minorities? Is racial minority overrepresentation justified, given the higher poverty rate in these populations? Why is special education placement deemed negative if it embodies desirable features (e.g., individualized education, higher per-pupil expenditures, smaller teacher-student ratio) (Reschly, 1997)? Answers to these questions are not straightforward. The problem will not be solved with quotas, and it is an oversimplification to blame it on either massive bias or child poverty. Part of the problem is whether we are adequately addressing students' educational potential and needs; from this perspective, false positives and negatives are equally problematic. Let us remember that special education placement is a highly consequential decision, as disability labels carry visible stigma and have other high-cost repercussions. It adds another layer of difference to racial minorities, restricts their access to high-currency educational programs and opportunities, and further limits their long-term educational outcomes, as special education populations have lower graduation, higher dropout, and lower academic achievement rates than their general education counterparts. We should be aware, however, that the overrepresentation debate affords us the opportunity to shift our gaze inward and examine our assumptions about culture. We need to ask tough questions about the role of culture and power in learning and dis/ability and the visions that inform the work we do with students who have historically faced great adversity because of their skin color or the language they speak. My expectation is that such introspection will contribute to the creation of a pluralistic educational system that informs its research knowledge base with a historical and cultural consciousness. The analyses presented in this manuscript represent one step in this direction.

SILENCE IN THE INCLUSION
AND OVERREPRESENTATION DISCOURSES

A troubling fact evident in the preceding review of the overrepresentation and inclusion scholarship is the silence in and between these literatures. Special education is indeed engaged in an active process of identity transformation as it strives to make services and policies more inclusive. However, such efforts seem to portray educators and students as devoid of sociohistorical identities, even though a sizable segment of the special education population comes from nonmainstream racial, social-class, and linguistic backgrounds. Furthermore, the majority of students entering the special education system in the largest U.S. school districts are ethnic and linguistic minorities. The scholarship on minority placement in special education is silent about the implications of the inclusive education movement. The fact that there is silence in both the overrepresentation and inclusion literatures suggests that it is socially shared. But how can we interpret these silences? And what can we learn from theorizing silence?

The silence on issues of race in the implementation discourse of inclusive education is a major oversight, considering that the history and status of minority groups in our society play major roles in minority students' educational experiences and outcomes. Historically, minority students have been perceived as lacking the skills, experiences, and dispositions to be successful in general education, and, indeed, we know academic achievement is correlated with ethnicity, language background, and social class (Valencia, 1997). Thus, minority students exit general education and move into special education with a deficit identity that foregrounds the aforementioned markers of difference. When diversity is summoned in the inclusion literature (mainly in the rationale scholarship), it is generally associated with diversity of ability levels — indeed an important aspect of diversity — but the plight of minority students is tangentially recognized in the implementation discourse. It is paradoxical that, as the inclusive education movement represents the emergence of empowered voices about disability rights and better educational services for this population, it has been painfully silent about the plight of minority students.

It is also paradoxical that, due to the inclusion movement, minority students might be returning to general education, but with an identity that adds an additional layer of difference — that is, a label adding ability to the composite of racial, linguistic, and social-class markers.[10] This new identity dispensed by the special education system legitimizes the surveillance of these students through legal and technical means (Erickson, 1996). It can also help to perpetuate the poor school outcomes of minorities, since disability status (particularly MR) is correlated with high dropout rates, low school completion rates, low special education exit rates, and poor employment outcomes (Gottlieb et al., 1994; U.S. Department of Education, 1997; Wagner et al., 1993).

Moreover, let us remember that minority students with disabilities are returning to a general education system that is fraught with paradoxical policies and reform pressures, as reflected in the tensions between the push for individual entitlement to the same treatment (same standards and curriculum access) and entitlement to differential treatments (individualized education) (McLaughlin, Fuchs, & Hardman, 1999). It is not clear how this paradoxical situation will be resolved, and it will be interesting to trace whether these reforms are enforced differentially with various segments of the population with disabilities (e.g., minority v. nonminority students) or whether these reforms will benefit certain groups (e.g., nonminority students).

Scholars working on overrepresentation (including myself) are guilty of a silence on the implications of the realization of inclusion for minority students. Although culture (as a way of life) is acknowledged, the dominant overrepresentation discourse seems to favor a deficit view of traditionally silent groups — that is, racial minority groups (Donovan & Cross, 2002). There is a conspicuous silence about the oppressive weight of structural discrimination and about the cultural power, legitimacy, and competence of minority groups; furthermore, this scholarship is painfully devoid of the voices of minority families and students. However, as Sheriff (2000) warns, silence should not be interpreted as oppressed groups' "acceptance of dominant ideology" (p. 118). I argue that we will enhance our understanding of overrepresentation as we scrutinize the contradictory explanations of this predicament and face the silences that emerge from such analyses.

The discourse on the realization of inclusion, on the other hand, assumes White middle-class student experience as the norm, because race and student cultural practices are rarely mentioned. If we consider that the history of a field is built in part through the production of scholarship, we cannot deny that inclusion will be regarded in the future as a critical era in the history of special education. But how will we explain to the future generation of educators and the families they serve that those who benefited from inclusion had no race, class, or culture? We must contest this approach to the production of collective memory.

One potentially fruitful path is to analyze these silences as forms of cultural censorship. Sider explains that "the creation of culture is also, simultaneously and necessarily, the creation of silence. . . . We can have no significant understanding of any culture unless we also know the silences that were *institutionally* created and guaranteed along with it" (cited in Sheriff, 2000, p. 118, emphasis in original). Historically, the research community has created a silence about ethnic, racial, class, gender, and linguistic differences, as evidenced in a major analysis of contemporary special education research. Less than 3 percent of the empirical research published in four peer-reviewed special education journals over a 22-year period (1975–1994) examined data across ethnic and social class lines (Artiles et al., 1997).[11]

An important implication of this finding is that we must strive to understand the goals and functions of the institutionalization of silences about difference in the culture of special education scholarship. Walker (1999) explains that questions about culture are kept on the periphery of educational researchers' socialization. Future researchers are taught that culture should be controlled, that it amounts to variance that ought to be held constant, or worse, it is ignored because the lessons learned from White middle-class samples are assumed to be universal. Similar to the process of historical production (Trouillot, 1995), silences enter research processes at various crucial points: the moment of question formulation or problem statement, the moment of source identification or participant recruitment, the moment of fact creation or assembly (design of data collection tools and actual data collection), or the moment of fact retrieval and retrospective significance (data analysis and final writing).

As I acknowledged at the beginning of this manuscript, special education researchers have made important advances in the development of a scientific knowledge base. However, as this analysis suggests, researchers need to make visible the object of analysis, the language of analysis, and the position of the analyst (Geertz, 1983) to interrogate the identified silences and begin the critique and transformation of the existing knowledge base, the curricula, and the apprenticeship systems of doctoral and teacher education programs. Critiques and analyses of past research efforts should be mindful of the fact that there is always a presence in the past; as Trouillot (1995) reminds us, "It could not just be The Past. It had to be someone's past" (p. 142). Whose past is represented in the special education scholarship? What is the presence that authored the special education scholarship? To conclude, we find ourselves in a situation in which culture or "culturally different" students are "overlooked" (Bhabha, 1994) in the double sense of social surveillance, as in the overrepresentation literature and of invisibility as in the inclusion scholarship. We must end these silences so that we better inform future analysis of inclusion and overrepresentation and deepen our understanding of the processes that lead to and the consequences of overrepresentation patterns in inclusive contexts.

VISIONS OF CULTURE

The inclusion and overrepresentation discourse communities are concerned with issues of culture; the former in terms of issues of professional and organizational cultures, the latter of cultural issues related to student characteristics. Culture, however, is not easily defined, as is reflected in its multiple definitions. In fact, Williams (1983) states that culture is one of the most complicated notions in the English language. In his review of the concept, Brightman (1995) concludes, "Unstable in meaning and reference both synchronically and over time, the culture construct has exhibited exceptional lability" (p. 539). Space constraints prevent me from presenting an exhaustive analysis of this construct (see reviews in Brightman, 1995; Eagleton, 2000; Eisenhart, 2001; Erickson, 2001; Gallego et al., 2001; Rogoff & Angelillo, 2002; Varenne, 1984). Instead, I discuss the most common views of culture that permeate scholarship on inclusion and overrepresentation. I frame this discussion in the context of a description of culture's five primary underlying dimensions: cohesion, stability, location, temporality, and power.[12]

The Cohesion and Stability of Culture

Culture's underlying dimensions of cohesion and stability embody dialectical tensions between culture as homogeneous v. variable, ahistorical v. ever-changing, and reproductive v. improvisational (Brightman, 1995; Rogoff & Angelillo, 2002; Varenne, 1984). The scholarship on overrepresentation and inclusion favors distinct poles in each of these dialectical tensions.

Culture is assumed to be cohesive, to embody characteristics that are distinctive and clearly differentiate cultural groups. Group patterning serves a critical function, for it provides a sense of identity; it allows members of a group to recognize who is and who is not a member of their group (Erickson, 2001). It is also important to recognize that within-group diversity exists in every culture, as individuals are not mere replicas of their cultural histories. Individuals use their agency as they cope with life circumstances to create unique life histories, and such a process contributes to the creation of within-group and within-individual diversity (Anzaldúa, 1999). Culture is also assumed to be stable and can be regarded as fossilized. In such cases, culture is both cohesive and stable, since it is conceptualized as if there is a bounded culture that never changes. Although culture must be transmitted across generations so that newcomers can build on their ancestors' legacies, it is equally critical that cultures evolve and change in order to survive (Erickson, 2001).

An important insight is that cohesion and stability of culture embody dialectical tensions between group traits and within group diversity and between enduring legacies and cultural change. Disparate conceptions of culture emerge, depending on whether scholars privilege certain elements of these dialectical tensions over others. For instance, a common conception of culture in special education scholarship is "culture as a way of life." According to this view, the work of researchers is to document the cohesion and stability of a group's culture. A key assumption is that culture has effects that are independent from other potentially salient variables, which "warrants reification and essentialization" (Handwerker, 2002, p. 108); moreover, culture represents a successful adaptation to relatively constant external conditions. It is further assumed that such a cohesive "way of life" (culture) is transmitted to the next generation through socialization processes (e.g., child rearing). Thus, unless external conditions vary, culture remains stable over time; culture is seen as cohesive and stable.

The overrepresentation scholarship tends to stress two distinct analyses of the problem that ultimately rest on the view of culture as a way of life. One argument is that minorities are disproportionately placed in special education because these groups have distinctive cultures that are incongruent with the school culture.[13] This thesis assumes that misunderstandings and conflict arise when groups that have developed different ways of life come into contact (see Heath, 1983; Vogt, Jordan, & Tharp, 1993, for discussions of this theory in general education contexts). Prescriptions, interventions, and models have been advanced (and often succeeded) to bridge these discontinuities and improve minority students' experiences and outcomes in school (Eisenhart, 2001). The second argument is that racial minority students are disproportionately exposed to the culture of poverty that hinders their development and may put them in a situation that merits special education interventions (Donovan & Cross, 2002).

In turn, the inclusion discourse community uses various perspectives on culture. Let us remember that this literature focuses on the rationale and implementation of inclusion (Dyson, 1999). The work on the rationale tends to focus on the culture of institutions (e.g., schools, classrooms, groups), particularly their histories, assumptions, and traits, and bases its arguments on a view of culture as cohesive and stable over time. Schools organize activities, define roles for teachers and students, and create rules to privilege nondisabled middle-class students. Procedures and other institutional processes are orchestrated to instill in students particular (affective, cognitive) dispositions that reproduce their status in society. A critique of this view is that it is deterministic; the agent is stripped of strategy and improvisation (Brightman, 1995).

Although not always articulated explicitly, this literature relies on a social reproduction thesis. Social reproduction theory is grounded in Marxist precepts of the role of social class in society. Individuals relate to the means of production in routine activities and by assuming particular occupations. Over time, constellations of groups and families develop a shared history of relations to these means of production, which in turn produces a collective cosmovision, "a set of symbolic and conceptual forms by which a group's social class circumstances are made to seem reasonable and 'natural' " (Eisenhart, 2001, p. 212). This view of culture privileges a sociological imagination and foregrounds how cultures are reproduced across generations so that groups maintain their status; school is regarded as a primary site where reproductive processes take place (Anyon, 1997; Bowles & Gintis, 1976; Willis, 1977). This strand of the inclusion literature does not do justice to the perennial tension between cultural reproduction and cultural transformation. Instead, the rationale discourse privileges the reproduction thesis to justify inclusion.

In contrast, the implementation discourse is concerned primarily with cultural change as inclusionists strive to transform the culture of traditional schools. Because there is hardly any acknowledgement of the presence of minorities in special education in the inclusion implementation literature, and considering the history of marginalization of racial minorities in our society, I argue that attention to cultural reproduction processes is imperative. The implementation of inclusion must take into account the reproduction of the historical circumstances that marginalize minority students in the general education system and society at large. This means inclusion scholarship ought to transcend notions of difference based on ability and acknowledge more structural forces that shape minority students' experiences in general and special education alike.

Interestingly, the implementation-of-inclusion literature is grounded in two perspectives of culture, namely, a way-of-life and an interpretivist view. The former is reflected in descriptions of the cohesive and stable cultures of inclusive schools or in comparisons between inclusive and non-inclusive schools. This perspective highlights distinctive structures and processes, with prescriptions for practitioners for the engineering of cogent school cultures that are mindful of inclusion. The interpretivist perspective holds that individuals can actively transform the meanings brought from home as they negotiate their place and roles in the groups they encounter in schools and other contexts (Erickson, 1996); as a result, new meanings, ways to interpret the world, and practices (i.e., idiocultures) can be created. The inclusion work in this tradition either describes inclusive conditions/experiences or assesses the impact of interventions by looking at the meaning-making processes between disabled and nondisabled students in general education instructional (e.g., peer tutoring, cooperative learning groups) or social contexts (e.g., peer networks, communication skills, status, friendships, types of assistance to mediate interactional processes and outcomes). A vision of culture as a meaning-making process privileges the situatedness of social events and implicitly honors the within-group diversity embodied in the individual-in-action (though it does not disregard cohesion). Culture as a meaning-making process opens a space for cultural transformation since it concentrates on the unpredictable construction of local processes.

The Location of Culture

Depending on its definition, culture can be located internally and externally.[14] The former locates culture in the values, beliefs, worldviews, schemas, and knowledge that people develop locally to navigate the world, solve problems, and attain goals. When located internally, culture is ideational; it is inside the mind of individuals. The work on overrepresentation relies heavily on the internal location of culture. This "subjective knowledge" view assumes that membership in a given ethnic, racial, gender, social-class, ability, or linguistic group will produce distinctive patterns of beliefs, behaviors, customs, values, and so forth. It follows that such groups posses distinctive and homogeneous cognitive, communication, and relational patterns (Cole, 1996); a popular example is the idea of minorities' unique learning styles (see a critical review of the learning styles literature in Irvine & York, 1995). The interactions between markers of difference (e.g., race, ability, gender, language background, social class) are not explored. The scholarship on overrepresentation either argues that educators must be mindful of the distinctive traits of racial groups to avoid misunderstandings that lead to special education placement, or that the distinguishing cognitive and social deficits that characterize poor racial minorities explain their greater need for special education.

Culture can also be located externally, in the historical residues of institutional rules and practices, in the routines and expected ways of using language and nonverbal behavior, and in the social rituals, practices, and predictable means to coordinate actions. Note that these "external" aspects are typically invisible to members of a cultural group, for they have grown accustomed to them (Cole, 1996). The external or "material practices" view is applied to any group that interacts over time; studies of the dominant discourse in U.S. classrooms along with its concomitant social and cognitive consequences illustrate this perspective. The inclusion literature has used an external view of culture as the characteristics, values, and practices of either traditional or inclusive school organizations are identified. The internal/external dichotomy oversimplifies the complex locations of culture.

The Temporality of Culture

Culture has temporal properties. Researchers study the cohesion, stability, and location of culture across time. To illustrate, we know that changes in a group's culture (cultural history) occur at a faster speed than changes in the history of a species (phylogeny), while cultural historical change proceeds at a slower pace than changes in the life history of an individual (ontogeny) (Cole, 1996). Moving down one level in this hierarchy of temporal scales to the microgenesis of events (moment-to-moment history), one could ask, "How do moments add up to lives? How do our shared moments together add up to social life as such?" (Lemke, 2000, p. 273). Lemke uses the term *temporal heterarchy* to describe the "interdependence of processes at very different timescales . . . of an organizational hierarchy in a complex self-organizing system" (p. 280). These levels of history unfold simultaneously and are interdependent (Scribner, 1985).[15]

The integration of these scales enables us to depict the temporality of culture (see Figure 1). The vertical axis represents the time scales that correspond to phylogenetic (the history of a species), cultural historical (the history of a group, institution, or society), ontogenetic (history of an individual over his or her lifespan), and microgenetic (the history of moment-to-moment lived experience) levels. The vertical axis also suggests that there is a hierarchy of embedded temporal scales that vary according to the level of temporal aggregation at which we examine culture. The horizontal axis depicts the temporality of culture with respect to the past, present, and future, which allows us to conduct synchronic (at a given point in time) and diachronic (across time) analyses; in this vein, Cole and Engestrom (1993) remind us that "only a culture-using human being can 'reach into' the cultural past, project it into the future, and then 'carry' that (purely conceptual) future 'back' into the present in the shape of beliefs that then constrain and organize the present sociocultural environment" (p. 21).[16]

This differentiation of time scales contributes to explanations of cultural reproduction and cultural change. The cultural historical level represents the cultural patterning of a group, community, institution, or society that is reproduced from one generation to the next via apprenticeship processes (e.g., child-rearing practices).[17] When culture is studied at the cultural historical level, we find an emphasis on aspects such as ethnic groups' distinctive traits (e.g., learning or cognitive styles), or the distinctive features of "school cultures," "classroom cultures," or even "the culture of a reading group" (Jacob, 1995). The microgenetic level enables us to understand how

FIGURE 1

Distribution of Culture across Time Scales (adapted from Cole & Engestrom, 1993)

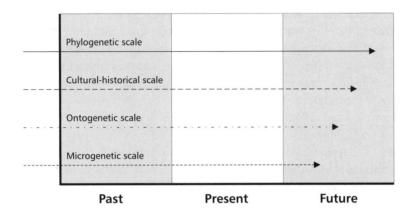

Past   Present   Future

an individual both acquires and reproduces such patterns. Individuals also have the potential to contribute to the transformation of cultural history as they exert their agency, though as we know, cultural change is a slower and more complex process. Depending on how one deals with the tensions between reproducing culture and crafting one's own life trajectory, individuals end up composing unique ontogenetic pathways and, ultimately, contribute to within-group diversity. In other words, inherent in ontogenetic development is the tension between normative views of developmental trajectories (i.e., what members of the cultural group are expected to achieve at different life stages) versus the hybridity of individuals (i.e., the within-individual diversity of a person).

The scholarship on overrepresentation tends to emphasize the cultural historical level. For example, recommendations from this discourse community exhort sensitivity toward the cultural historical characteristics of minority groups (e.g., dialect and language preferences, learning styles). It is paradoxical that, in their attempt to affirm cultural diversity, these suggestions end up advocating for essentialist and more static views of culture and cultural history. Furthermore, the risk of stressing a cultural historical view of minorities is that it might implicitly suggest that group traits are immutable features with no previous histories — that is, cultural reproduction is stressed.

Let us contrast the overrepresentation discourse community's traditional views of cultural history with a more dynamic perspective (Cole, 1996). In the case of Latinos/as, for example, we often ignore the fact that Latin America's evolution is fraught with political instability, oppression, ethnic, political, and religious conflict, and fragmented identities (Comas-Díaz, Lykes, & Alarcón, 1998). As a result, generations of Latinos/as, particularly in nations with sizable indigenous or Black populations, have been raised under savage economic, social, and educational inequalities and brutal repression; thus many of them (particularly members of racial minorities) have learned to live with fear, distrust, and/or despair (Galeano, 1989; Seed, 2001). However, these communities have not been merely passive recipients. They have developed and maintained incredible resiliency and perseverance to survive in such adverse circumstances (Comas-Díaz et al. 1998; Poniatowska, 1985).

When Latinos/as who have lived for generations under these conditions migrate to the United States, they engage in a complex process of coping and adapting to the host society that is inextricably intertwined with the cultural histories crafted in their homelands. Meanwhile, let us not forget that the cultural history of the dominant U.S. society has also influenced the evolving cultural histories of Latinos/as. In this process, recent immigrants begin to compose new cultural histories. As these immigrants weave new hybrid cultural histories in the context of U.S. society, generational differences emerge between themselves and their fellow ethnic peers who have lived in the United States for generations. Generational differences also arise between the recent immigrants and their own children as they are raised in the United States (Delgado-Gaitán, 1994; Suárez-Orozco & Suárez-Orozco, 1995). The result is that we find different combinations of stances (e.g., submission, resistance, assimilation, accommodation) among Latinos/as toward the values, institutions, and demands of the U.S. mainstream society, depending on their previous cultural histories, generation in the country, and the nature of experiences and contacts with dominant and subjugated communities (Suárez-Orozco & Suárez-Orozco, 1995).

This more complex perspective on the cultural histories of Latinos/as differs dramatically from the static view that permeates the overrepresentation discourse. It is indeed imperative that this discourse community take into account the interplay between historical legacies of domination and oppression in the U.S. society and the role of coping strategies, resilience mechanisms, and social and cultural capital in the construction of hybrid cultural histories in Latino and other minority communities. More importantly, researchers need to ask how these insights can inform research on placement patterns and the precursors of overrepresentation.

The inclusion literature, in turn, tends to focus on two time scales, namely, the cultural historical and ontogenetic levels. As explained above, inclusion has concentrated on the culture of traditional or inclusive schools (cultural history of institutions) or on the impact of inclusion on individuals' development or adaptation at certain ages and/or grade levels (ontogenesis); this work has examined one scale at a time (either cultural history or ontogenesis), and most investigators have preferred cross-sectional analyses. This is not surprising, given that special education research relies heavily on developmental psychology, which is inherently organized around chronological age as the primary index of the passage of time (i.e., ontogenetic development). Inclusion scholars face at least two major challenges. The first is to avoid an exclusive focus on single time scales so that the multiple developmental trajectories of students (ontogenetic level) that emerge within the cultural history of a given inclusive school can be documented. The second is to add complexity by acknowledging the racial, ability, language, gender, and class dimensions of students' and teachers' identities. Both challenges call for more complex research designs, as investigators will need to maintain a focus on both time scales throughout data collection and analysis activities while simultaneously considering multiple dimensions of identity.

Power in Culture

Even as we complicate the notion of culture around the dimensions identified thus far, we run the risk of grasping only a partial understanding of the construct if we do not include the role of power and its link to historicity. Gallego et al. (2001) define culture as "the socially inherited body of past human accomplishments that serves as the resources for the current life of a social group ordinarily thought of as the inhabitants of a country or region" (p. 362). From this perspective, culture is constituted in the sedimentation of historical experience and it is at the intersection of history and social processes that the political nature of culture emerges. As Erickson (2001) explains:

> We live in webs of meaning, caring, and desire that we create and that create us, but those webs also hang in social gravity. Within the webs all our activity is vested in the weight of history; that is, in a social world of inequality all movement is up or down" (p. 38).

Note that this view of culture embodies visible and invisible elements, and its production and reproduction are achieved in social interactions "from the partial and mutually dependent knowledge of each person caught in the process. It is constituted, in the long run, by the work they do together" (Varenne & McDermott, 1999, p. 137).

Let us remember, though, that the maintenance of domination (i.e., hegemony) by a segment of society is achieved by "supplying the symbols, representations, and practices of social life in such a way that the basis of social authority and the unequal relations of power and privilege remain hidden" (McLaren, 1989, p. 174). Thus, the dominant culture is naturalized and used as a reference point against which all other cultural practices are compared and evaluated. This explains why groups' cultural practices have differential status and prestige in a given society and opportunities to learn valued practices are restricted and controlled. Various groups learn disparate portions or sets of culture and occupy dissimilar power positions. The processes by which culture is unequally distributed across individuals, groups, and generations is the result of profoundly political processes (Erickson, 2001).

Research and scholarship on racial minority placement in special education has overlooked issues of power and history. The bulk of this literature is concerned with placement patterns of discretely defined groups in disability categories or programs. Although some work is mindful of the political dimension of special education placement, we have a long way to go in this area. This oversight is even more intriguing if we consider that work in this area involves cultural groups that have a long history of oppression in U.S. society. Although reviews of the literature and the research base continue to report mixed evidence about bias and discrimination, I argue that overrepresentation scholarship must be mindful of the legacy of deficit thinking about racial minorities in U.S. history that continue to inform policy and scholarly writings (Artiles, 1998). We must acknowledge that unidimensional and deficit-based views of racial minorities permeate societal perceptions and thus mediate educators' and schools' ideologies. The challenge becomes how to develop research approaches that enable us to disentangle and examine the role of power in the construction of minority overrepresentation in special education.

Inclusion, on the other hand, features power to support the rationale for inclusive educational systems. Critiques of the traditional educational system grounded in a disability rights perspective are exemplary in this regard, as they denounce the power differentials and discriminatory assumptions and practices that curtail people with disabilities' access and outcomes in mainstream society. Research on the implementation of inclusion, however, has ignored power issues. Although some work on the social dimension of inclusion (e.g., social status in classrooms, friendships) has the potential to shed light on power issues, most studies neither theorize nor problematize the compelling force of power issues in inclusive classroom and school cultures.

SPACE: DISCONTINUITIES IN UNDERSTANDING AND USES

A limited conception of space plays a critical role in the discourses on overrepresentation and inclusion. One central concern in the inclusion movement is access to general education spaces. Placement data suggest that, despite important variations across states, the nation's students with disabilities are increasingly educated in general education schools and classrooms, particularly students with LD (McLeskey, Henry, & Axelrod, 1999). We also know that discussions and investigations about minority overrepresentation are concerned with placement in various programs and the level of integration of such programs. It is important, therefore, to discuss the theoretical underpinnings of the concept of "space" and examine the inclusion and overrepresentation scholarships from this notion.

Systematic theorizing about space has intensified in recent years, particularly within the study of social life (Daniels & Lee, 1996; Foucault, 1986; Keith & Pile, 1993; Soja, 1996). I use the notion of space from the perspective of social geography to transcend the idea of space as simply physical location or destination. This perspective calls for "the study of physical space and human constructions, perceptions, and representations of spatiality as contexts for and consequences of human interaction" (Hargreaves, 1995, p. 7). Lefebvre (1991) argues for the creation of a "science of space," a unitary theory that aims to bridge the separation between the conception and analysis of space as physical/perceived space and the conception of space as conceived/mental space. Soja (1996) refers to the former as "FirstSpace" and to the latter as "SecondSpace." In this view, space is simultaneously physical, ideal, and the product of social translation and transformation (Lefebvre, 1991; Soja, 1989). The notion of space I am working from, therefore, transcends the traditional view of an a priori fixed entity and is conceived as "an achievement and an ongoing practice" (Shields, 2000, p. 155).

FirstSpace in the Inclusion and Overrepresentation Literatures

FirstSpace refers to physical space that is perceived; it entails the processes and forms of social "spatiality." The social or spatial practice of a society "is thus presented as both medium and outcome of human activity, behavior, and experience" (Soja, 1996, p. 66). Space structures and is structured by people's actions; that is, there is a dialectical tension between the deterministic force of space and people's agency to counter its reproductive weight. As Soja (1989) explains, "We make our own history and geography, but not just as we please; we do not make them under circumstances chosen by ourselves, but under circumstances directly encountered, given and transmitted from the historical geographies produced in the past" (p. 129).

FirstSpace represents our commonsense understanding of space in which physical/perceived space (or what is readily visible) plays a significant role. FirstSpace analysis thus "concentrates on the accurate description of surface appearances . . . [or] searches for spatial explanation in primarily exogenous social, psychological, and biophysical processes" (Soja, 1996, p. 75). Inclusion research has assumed that placement of special education students in the physical spaces of general education classrooms has an effect on disabled and nondisabled students' learning and development. Studies that are concerned with the description of practices in inclusive classrooms or that test the impact of instructional approaches on student learning (e.g., Baker & Zigmond, 1995; Mortweet et al., 1999), focusing on human activity, behavior, and/or experience, are examples of research that conceptualizes the space of inclusive classrooms simply in terms of FirstSpace. It is not uncommon that researchers assess such practices using data from published research or address process variables (e.g., participation in cooperative groups) indirectly through statistical analysis (Elbaum, Vaughn, Hughes, & Watson-Moody, 1999). Researchers have also examined parents', teachers', administrators', and students' understandings (cognitive/social skills, perceptions) of the physical spaces of inclusive classrooms. These studies have been conducted in an attempt to assess the viability of inclusive models, anticipate potential constraints, and inform inclusion approaches (e.g., Cook et al., 1999; Soodak, Podell, & Lehman, 1998).

Although it is important to address parents' and students' understandings of physical/perceived spaces of inclusion, it is also necessary to obtain detailed or moment-to-moment accounts of the construction processes of academic and social outcomes in those spaces. Evidence of the need for this line of research is apparent in studies reporting mixed results. In such instances the authors allude to contextual aspects. For example, in the case of the outcomes of mixed-ability groups, it was reported that "factors such as partner selection, teacher monitoring, and the establishment of a cooperative ethic appeared to influence the outcomes. Clearly, the structure and support are essential to the success of these arrangements" (U.S. Department of Education, 1999, p. III-29). Another example of studies that conceptualizes classrooms simply in terms of physical space is found in the research on the mixed impact of program models on students with disabilities; the reviewers conclude that such findings underscore "the need to pay greater attention to specific organizational and instructional practices in heterogeneous classrooms" (p. III-22).

The bulk of the overrepresentation literature is equally concerned with FirstSpace analyses as reflected in the almost exclusive attention to placement patterns for various ethnic groups in disability programs. Outcomes (i.e., placement patterns) are foregrounded in these analyses, and static markers of difference (e.g., ethnic labels) are included in studies to discern their association with various physical spaces (e.g., school location, type of special education program). For example, researchers have studied whether placement patterns are differentially shaped by student race, poverty level, academic achievement level, and school location (urban v. suburban) (Artiles et al., 1998; Oswald et al., 1999). With a few exceptions, the social practices that precede placement decisions are ignored. The understandings of physical/perceived spaces by teachers and other school personnel are also assessed (generally via surveys and questionnaires), typically to test a bias hypothesis (Donovan & Cross, 2002). Given the strong social desirability associated with measures of cultural bias, it is not surprising, that this evidence is mixed.

SecondSpace in the Inclusion and Overrepresentation Scholarship

SecondSpace refers to space as conceptualized by people; it encompasses conceived spaces and includes "representations of power and ideology, of control and surveillance. . . . It is the primary source of utopian thought and vision" (Soja, 1996, p. 67). SecondSpace is "the ideological content of codes, theories, and the conceptual depictions of space linked to production relations" (Shields, 2000, p. 163). Lefebvre (1991) referred to it as "conceptualized space, the space of scientists" (p. 38). There are far-reaching conceptualizations (conceived space) of inclusive education that situate the meaning and place of special education in larger societal and historical contexts (e.g., Ferguson, 1995; Lipsky & Gartner, 1996). These conceptualizations emphasize complexity, are comprehensive and ambitious, and generally suggest a revamping of the educational system's premises, values, and practices (Ferguson & Ferguson, 1997). Interestingly, these frameworks contrast with the more outcome-oriented focus of the inclusion research literature. In other words, there seems to be a discontinuity between the representations of inclusive education (the SecondSpace dimensions of space) and the actual examination of inclusion processes and outcomes (FirstSpace).

Unlike inclusion, the overrepresentation discourse has devoted hardly any effort to developing conceptualizations and visions of the types of spaces needed by students in inclusive classrooms. Given that SecondSpace is "entirely ideational, made up of projections into the empirical world from conceived or imagined geographies" (Soja, 1996, p. 79), the lack of utopian thinking or imagination in the overrepresentation discourse has potentially devastating consequences. This scholarship runs the risk of merely accumulating descriptions of spatial practices that are not guided by a theoretical imagination about the role of cultural differences in education or a vision of an ideal state of affairs in a pluralistic society. Unlike the inclusion discourse, the scholarship devoted to address solutions to this problem tends to lack a transformative bent.

There are gaps in the spaces examined by the inclusion and overrepresentation discourse communities. Although both communities tend to concentrate on the production of spatial practices (on space as FirstSpace), the inclusion community seems to be guided by visions of an inclusive education system (space conceptualized as SecondSpace). In contrast, overrepresentation lacks such conceived space. Without finding a way to bring the two literatures together, special educators risk reconstructing the educational system based on visions that ignore the history and implications of racial, ethnic, class, and linguistic differences in the social organization of learning in culturally and politically charged contexts. Likewise, we cannot afford to reconstruct the system without a vision of what we want to achieve in a heterogeneous educational system to consolidate a socially just society.

CHALLENGES FOR A NEW GENERATION OF INCLUSION AND OVERREPRESENTATION RESEARCH: THE PRODUCTIONS OF CULTURE, LIVED SPACES, AND DIFFERENCE

The convergence of inclusion and overrepresentation exposes the fact that the educational system may be educating more students with disabilities in general education contexts, but many of those being included are poor racial and linguistic minorities that have additional ability deficits superimposed onto their identities. It seems that both phenomena have stressed a technical perspective. The inclusion movement has focused on a redistribution of resources so that students with disabilities are educated in a presumed new breed of general education, whereas overrepresentation has been largely reduced to the study of placement proportions. These discourses have also emphasized legalistic issues. Inclusion has focused on new requirements for placement in general education, access to the curriculum, and accountability, while overrepresentation has pushed for the creation of antidiscriminatory regulations generally enforced by the Office for Civil Rights (Losen & Orfield, 2002). However, I argue that the overrepresentation and inclusion literatures have used partial perspectives on culture, have not adequately theorized space, and have been silent about difference. Future research cannot afford to ignore these aspects as we live in an increasingly pluralistic society.

Beyond "Ways of Life" and Places: The Productions of Culture and Lived Spaces

Both inclusion and overrepresentation scholarship need to adopt more complex and dynamic conceptions of culture and multiple time scales (cultural, historical, ontogenetic, microgenetic) in order to obtain a deeper understanding of human development as situated in cultural, historical, and social contexts. Traditional views of culture have faced mounting criticism due to the limits of their assumptions and premises. Scholars have criticized traditional views because they project an image of culture that (a) privileges group patterns at the expense of within-group diversity, (b) portrays culture as stagnant in time with clearly demarcated boundaries between groups, (c) ignores individual agency, and (d) overlooks the role of power in cultural processes (Eisenhart, 2001). Researchers face the challenge of incorporating "the fact of constant individual creativity into a theory of culture" (Varenne, 1984, p. 282). At the same time, we must avoid dichotomizing the individual and the society. As Rosaldo (1984) warns us, the "view of the repeated struggle between sacred individualism and sociological wisdom reduces complex historical processes to timeless conflicts" (p. 294).

One of the most ambitious projects that aims to transcend the limits of traditional views of culture is represented in the so-called cultural productions turn (Eisenhart,

2001). This view accounts for individual (e.g., beliefs, values) and societal (e.g., structures) cultural forces, and it argues that the convergence of such forces must be examined as situated in and shaped by the local social conditions of everyday practice. From this perspective, culture not only constrains but also enables individual performance. It constrains in the sense that a person enters a context where a culture is represented in the structural and historical legacies embedded in the artifacts, rules for interaction, and prescribed roles available in the setting. The subject, therefore, is constrained to operate with those elements and pressured to reproduce cultural tradition. At the same time, the individual's agency enables her to use artifacts in novel ways, challenge prescribed roles, and modify established rules. In this sense, culture can also enable the individual to disrupt tradition and promote change (see examples of this research in Engestrom, Miettinen, & Punamaki, 1999; Nespor, 1994).

The cultural productions view uses a unit of analysis that requires researchers to study classroom cultures "as a hybrid of the local and the social historical levels of analysis" (Gallego et al., 2001, p. 957). That is, it uses a unit of analysis that accounts for cultural acquisition, use, reproduction, and change. The recent work on cultural productions enhances our understanding of "how local practices of cultural production become meaningful and consequential to participants; differentiate otherwise similar individuals; make similar otherwise different people; are connected to wider processes of nationalism, stratification, globalization, and professionalism; and sometimes motivate change" (Eisenhart, 2001, p. 218). This perspective on culture, therefore, can help researchers generate knowledge that honors the complexities of the spaces, histories, and cultural practices of both overrepresentation and inclusion.

Similarly, inclusion and overrepresentation scholarship can benefit from a new science of space, building on knowledge of how First- and SecondSpaces interact and influence one another in the lived spaces of inclusive classrooms. Within the interactions between FirstSpace and SecondSpace, a ThirdSpace is created, capturing lived space, or spaces of representation (Soja, 1996). Lived space both encompasses and is distinct from the other two spaces. ThirdSpace is the "habitus of social practices, a constantly shifting and changing milieu of ideas, events, appearances, and meanings" (Kahn, 2000, p. 7). According to Soja (1996), counterspaces or spaces of resistance can be created in ThirdSpace because it is filled with ideology and politics, with relations of dominance and subordination, with the intricate interdependency of the real and the imagined. ThirdSpace is a powerful tool because it enables us to question simplifications of space as "site" or "destination" and to transcend dichotomies of representations such as insiders and outsiders. At the same time, ThirdSpace is a dynamic construct that surfaces as a result of the dialectic of the physical and the mental, the concrete and the abstract; it contains the perceived and conceived spaces simultaneously (Soja, 1996, Tejeda, 2000).

At a time when politically and ideologically charged reforms will likely have devastating consequences for poor and racial minority students, future research ought to focus on the genesis and transformation of ThirdSpaces — the site where attention to ideology and politics is prominent and where resistance is created. Attention to ThirdSpaces will inevitably compel us to be mindful of social justice as issues of power, subordination, and dominance are central. Researchers must conduct participatory research with teachers, families, and students and focus explicitly on the role of institutional forces in their lived experiences in schools, households, and communities.

Beyond Diversity: Toward an Understanding of Difference and Perspective

Ultimately, inclusion and overrepresentation researchers face dilemmas related to underlying assumptions about difference. Both discourse communities tend to use the notion of cultural "diversity," which is typically defined as "the recognition of pre-given cultural contents and customs" (Bhabha, 1994, p. 34). Two problems exist with this notion. First, the notion of diversity embodies a "transparent norm" (Alsayyad, 2001, p. 7) that essentializes culture and "turns the other into something monolithic, partly out of not only ignorance but also fear" (Viswanathan, 2001, p. 238). Second, racism is very much alive in *all* societies precisely because "the universalism that paradoxically permits diversity masks ethnocentric norms, values, and interests" (Bhabha, cited in Alsayyad, 2001, p. 7).

Cultural difference in turn questions binary distinctions (diverse, nondiverse) and foregrounds "the problem of the ambivalence of cultural authority" (Bhabha, 1994, p. 34). Minow (1990) stated that difference has been equated with deviance or stigma, and thus sameness is a prerequisite of equality. Therefore, it is not surprising that traditional treatments of difference ultimately reaffirm difference and offer options that signal the deficits or disadvantages typically associated with difference — it is paradoxical then that to recognize "difference reinforces hierarchy" (Abu-Lughod, cited in Brightman, 1995, p. 532). Special education has historically faced the dilemma of affirming or ignoring difference. On the one hand, it was argued that equal instructional treatment was unfair, institutionalizing an individualized educational system. On the other hand, the inclusion movement has argued that equal access to general education spaces, curriculum, and accountability standards are just. The former strategy recognizes difference while the latter diffuses it; ultimately, both are organized around it. In the case of minorities we observe a similar ambivalence in the solutions offered to the dilemma of difference — again, the underlying question has been whether we should ignore or affirm it. Indeed, access to the same (integrated) educational contexts was a major achievement for racial minorities in the civil rights era while linguistic minorities have fought for differential treatment in the form of bilingual education programs.

The inclusion and overrepresentation discourses have offered ambivalent and even conflicting responses to the question of how to handle difference due to their underlying assumptions. A first step is to make explicit the underlying assumptions of difference and counter them with alternative assumptions. As we use more complex views of culture in the discourses of inclusion and overrepresentation to address issues ultimately concerned with difference, we must ask, When does a difference count, under what conditions, in what ways, and for what reasons? (Varenne & McDermott, 1999).

Attention to culture and space as a way to understand notions of difference demands that we acknowledge the role of power in the creation of borders. It particularly calls our attention to the perspective of the observer, an issue that has been historically invisible and unquestioned in research practices. Implications of the role of perspective are twofold. First, the perspective of the observer or analyst (e.g., teacher, researcher) must be recognized. Second, we can gain greater insight from examining how people use notions of difference to create borders during social interactions in particular institutional contexts rather than studying the distinctive features of a group's cultural history (Barth, 1969). This is a particularly important theoretical insight, as overrepresentation and inclusion focus on borders, such as race, that possess great historical currency in U.S. society. As Rosaldo (1984) explains, "Race relations in North America involve a blend of assimilationist efforts, raw prejudice, and cultural containment that revolves around a concerted effort to keep each culture pure and in its place" (p. 212).

In turn, systematic attention to culture in research practices will force us to be aware of and disclose our assumptions about difference (e.g., researchers' understandings of development, time, space, and culture). Such heightened awareness will compel us to envision difference as produced in relationships and rooted in comparisons between a person and culturally based norms that can be unveiled, evaluated, and contested (Minow, 1990). Minow also challenges us to enable those who have been dispensed identities of difference, such as disability, to share alternative perspectives that are not always aligned with culturally based norms and expectations. This practice will allow us to reflect on the culturally based assumptions that underlie the design and implementation of school rules, curricula, and assessment practices. The practice of honoring multiple perspectives on inclusion and overrepresentation will also enable us to read these knowledge bases (borrowing from Said) "contrapuntally, to use the metaphor from music. [This practice would enable us to go] over the same history but from a different point of view" (Viswanathan, 2001, p. 245). This way, we could transcend the traditional dilemmas of difference (e.g., to provide equal or preferential treatment). Instead, analysis of culture-based notions of difference should focus on "the ways in which institutions construct and utilize differences to justify and enforce exclusions — and the ways in which such institutional practices can be changed" (Minow, 1990, p. 86). The potential role of institutional histories and contexts must be taken into account in such analyses; this is why it is critical to situate overrepresentation and inclusion analyses in the larger cultural politics of special education reforms.

Overrepresentation and inclusion are ultimately about how educators and educational systems deal with "difference" in politically and culturally charged contexts. I argue that we must examine these phenomena beyond special education placement issues, using more sophisticated views of culture and space. The present emphasis on reporting only the number of students with disabilities being educated in general education classrooms and schools is creating the illusion that the inclusive education movement is consolidating. This emphasis also disregards both the historicity and sociality of who is being identified as disabled and the sociocultural roots of disability constructions. As the complexity of the cultural politics of educational reform surfaces and as its influence on special education transformations intensifies, we must concern ourselves with the study of disability, inclusion, and overrepresentation in an elaborate cultural medium, mediated by multiple scales and planes of space and time.

In this manner, disability and special education scholarship will transcend the traditional individualistic perspective and infuse a social justice dimension so that the improvement of educational experiences and life opportunities for historically marginalized students are of central concern.

NOTES

1. "The term inclusion has been used so widely that it has almost lost its meaning" (Skrtic, Sailor, & Gee, 1996, p. 149). Some definitions stress physical placement — for example, "placement (full or partial) of students with mild disabilities in general education classrooms" (Cook, Semmel, & Gerber, 1999, p. 207). Others stress the notion of inclusive schools, which, according to Skrtic, Sailor, and Gee (1996), "are those designed to meet the educational needs of all their members within common, yet fluid, environments and activities" (p. 149). Inclusion is also seen as a process of developing a unified educational system that serves students with disabilities and their nondisabled peers "as active, fully participating members of the school community; that views diversity as the norm; and that ensures a high-quality education for students by providing meaningful curriculum, effective teaching, and necessary supports for each student" (Ferguson, 1995, p. 286).

2. Overrepresentation is defined as "unequal proportions of culturally diverse students in [special education] programs" (Artiles & Trent, 2000, p. 514); typically, this phenomenon is calculated in relation to a group's representation in general education or in reference to the representation of a comparison group (e.g., White students).

3. I use the notion of "discourse community" to describe groups (e.g., researchers, practitioners) that coalesce around a common interest or an object of study or labor. A discourse community devotes efforts and resources to produce knowledge about its object "and establishes conditions for who speaks and what gets heard. . . . Because it is institutionally sanctioned, their discourse is powerful . . . its 'regime' or 'politics of truth' sets standards for the field" (Brantlinger, 1997, p. 432). Although the notion of discourse community emphasizes cohesion, note that there are diverse perspectives within the overrepresentation and inclusion discourse communities.

4. Special education relies on a categorical model of disabilities. High-incidence disabilities include learning disabilities (LD), emotional disturbance (ED), mild mental retardation (MMR), and speech or language impairments; students with LD comprise about half of the special education population (Smith, 2001). Low-incidence disabilities include autism, deafness/hearing impairments, multiple disabilities, visual impairments, other health impairments, deaf-blindness, orthopedic impairments, and traumatic brain injury.

5. To the dismay of debate participants, general education hardly pays attention to these deliberations. To this day, large-scale efforts to monitor the implementation of major general education reforms "have generally ignored the issue of disability and . . . the information that is available has been collected in a piecemeal fashion" (Vanderwood, McGrew, & Ysseldyke, 1998, p. 366).

6. For instance, the federal government in recent years has funded the National Longitudinal Transition Study (Wagner et al., 1993), the COMRISE and LASER Projects, the National Institute for Urban School Improvement, and the National Center for Culturally Responsive Educational Systems (among others) to support research and technical assistance activities with an explicit attention to race and minority special education placement and urban education issues.

7. The risk index offers a measure of the proportion of students from a group that is placed in a disability category. It is calculated "by dividing the number of students in a given racial or ethnic category served in a given disability category by the total enrollment for that racial or ethnic group in the school population" (Donovan & Cross, 2002, pp. 42–43). The odds ratio divides the risk index of one racial/ethnic group by the risk index of another racial/ethnic group in order to provide a comparison. If the risk indices are identical for two groups, the odds ratio will

equal 1.0. Odds ratios greater than 1.0 indicate that the minority group students are at greater risk for identification, while odds of less than 1.0 indicate that they are less at risk (Donovan & Cross, 2002). To illustrate, let us assume that a comparison of Latino and White student LD identification in a given district results in an odds ratio of 1.36. This means Latino students would be 36 percent more likely than White students to be given the LD label in that school district.

8. Based on OSEP data, the NRC report concluded there is no "evidence that minority children are systematically represented in low-incidence disability categories in numbers that are disproportionate to their representation in the population" (Donovan & Cross, 2002, p. 61).

9. The reauthorization of IDEA in 1997 strengthened the nondiscriminatory requirements of the law, which include using nondiscriminatory assessment, collecting and monitoring placement data by race and class, providing educational services for expelled students or for school-age youngsters in correctional facilities, providing procedural safeguards for parents, and documenting the quality of instruction and opportunity to learn prior to special education referrals (Hehir, 2002; Smith, 2001).

10. As stated above, data are scarce on the types of placement contexts (segregated v. integrated) in which minority students with disabilities are being placed.

11. Artiles et al. acknowledged that "although we are not advocating the use of ethnicity or race as the most important proxies of culture in LD research, we chose to examine the research using these proxies to obtain baseline information about this knowledge base" (p. 83).

12. The five dimensions of culture are intricately interrelated, and I discuss them separately for heuristic purposes.

13. Several objections have been made to the cultural discontinuity hypothesis (Gallego et al., 2001; Varenne & McDermott, 1999). One criticism is that cultural discontinuities do not always result in miscommunications and school failure for minorities. Ogbu (1992), for instance, argues that groups create cultural frames of reference based on their unique histories (e.g., immigration, societal power status), which explains why various groups sometimes exhibit distinct responses to similar external conditions. This explains why a minority group that experiences a discontinuity between its own culture and the school's culture still exhibits educational success. Another criticism of the way-of-life view is that it is overly deterministic, as it assumes that home or group culture defines what people do when they enter new contexts.

14. Scholars have taken issue with the internal-external dualism and have advanced more complex views (Erickson 2001; Gallego et al., 2001). I differentiate these locations to explain that many definitions of culture artificially create this dichotomy and tend to privilege one location over the other.

15. Researchers are only beginning to investigate the embededdness of multiple historical domains and their mutual influences to understand the temporal distribution of culture in human development (Cole, 1996; Dien, 2000). For examples of this emergent scholarship, see Cole and Engestrom (1993), Cole (1996), Lemke (2000), and Dien (2000).

16. See Artiles, Gutierrez, and Rueda (2002), Cole (1996), and Stone (1993) for discussions of prolepsis and other processes that can help us understand how culture mediates learning.

17. Note that cultural history also embodies the transformed elements of cultural legacies that result from cultural change processes.

REFERENCES

Advancement Project & Civil Rights Project. (2000). *Opportunities suspended: The devastating consequences of zero tolerance and school discipline policies*. Cambridge, MA: Civil Rights Project at Harvard University. Retrieved on December 10, 2000, from http://www.law.Harvard.edu/groups/civilrights/conferences/zero/zt_report2.html

Alsayyad, N. (2001). Hybrid culture/hybrid urbanism: Pandora's box of the "third place." In N. Alsayyad (Ed.), *Hybrid urbanism: On the identity discourse and the built environment* (pp. 1–18). Westport, CT: Praeger.

Anyon, J. (1997). *Ghetto schooling: A political economy of urban educational reform.* New York: Teachers College Press.

Anzaldúa, G. (1999). *Borderlands/La frontera: The new mestiza* (2nd ed.). San Francisco: Aunt Lute Books.

Apple, M. W. (1996). *Cultural politics and education.* New York: Teachers College Press.

Artiles, A. J. (1998). The dilemma of difference: Enriching the disproportionality discourse with theory and context. *Journal of Special Education, 32,* 32–36.

Artiles, A. J., Aguirre-Muñoz, Z., & Abedi, J. (1998). Predicting placement in learning disabilities programs: Do predictors vary by ethnic group? *Exceptional Children, 64,* 543–559.

Artiles, A. J., Gutierrez, K., & Rueda, R. (2002, April). *Teacher education in a culturally diverse inclusive era: Implications of a cultural historical vision for teacher learning research.* Paper presented at the annual meeting of the American Educational Research Association, New Orleans.

Artiles, A. J., & Pak, M. (2000, July). *Becoming an inclusive education teacher in an urban multicultural school: Tensions, contradictions, and implications for inclusion research.* Paper presented at the International Special Education Conference, Manchester, England.

Artiles, A. J., Rueda, R., Salazar, J., & Higareda, I. (2002). English-language learner representation in special education in California urban school districts. In D. J. Losen & G. Orfield (Eds.), *Racial inequity in special education* (pp. 117–136). Cambridge, MA: Harvard Education Press.

Artiles, A. J., & Trent, S. C. (2000). Representation of culturally/linguistically diverse students. In C. R. Reynolds & E. Fletcher-Jantzen (Eds.), *Encyclopedia of special education, Vol. 1* (2nd ed., pp. 513–517). New York: John Wiley.

Artiles, A. J., Trent, S. C., & Kuan, L. A. (1997). Learning disabilities research on ethnic minority students: An analysis of 22 years of studies published in selected refereed journals. *Learning Disabilities Research and Practice, 12,* 82–91.

Artiles, A. J., Trent, S. C., & Palmer, J. (in press). Culturally diverse students in special education: Legacies and prospects. In J. A. Banks & C. M. Banks (Eds.), *Handbook of research on multicultural education* (2nd ed.). San Francisco: Jossey-Bass.

Baker, J., & Zigmond, N. (1995). The meaning and practice of inclusion for students with learning disabilities: Themes and implications from the five case studies. *Journal of Special Education, 29,* 163–180.

Barth, F. (1969). *Ethnic groups and boundaries: The social organization of culture difference.* Boston: Little Brown.

Bhabha, H. K. (1994). *The location of culture.* London: Routledge.

Bowles, S., & Gintis, H. (1976). *Schooling in capitalist America: Educational reform and the contradictions of economic life.* New York: Basic Books.

Brantlinger, E. (1997). Using ideology: Cases of nonrecognition of the politics of research and practice in special education. *Review of Educational Research, 67,* 425–459.

Brightman, R. (1995). Forget culture: Replacement, transcendence, relexification. *Cultural Anthropology, 10,* 509–546.

Christensen, C., & Rizvi, F. (Eds.). (1996). *Disability and the dilemmas of education and justice.* Buckingham, Eng.: Open University Press.

Cole, M. (1996). *Cultural psychology: A once and future discipline.* Cambridge, MA: Harvard University Press.

Cole, M., & Engestrom, Y. (1993). A cultural-historical approach to distributed cognition. In G. Salomon (Ed.), *Distributed cognitions: Psychological and educational considerations* (pp. 1–46). New York: Cambridge University Press.

Comas-Díaz, L., Lykes, M. B., & Alarcón, R. D. (1998). Ethnic conflict and the psychology of liberation in Guatemala, Peru, and Puerto Rico. *American Psychologist, 53,* 778–792.

Cook, B. G., Semmel, M. I., & Gerber, M. M. (1999). Attitudes of principals and special education teachers toward the inclusion of students with mild disabilities. *Remedial and Special Education, 20,* 199–207.

Daniels, S., & Lee, R. (Eds.). (1996). *Exploring human geography: A reader.* New York: Halstead Press.

Delgado-Gaitán, C. (1994). Socializing young children in Mexican-American families: An intergenerational perspective. In P. Greenfield & R. Cocking (Eds.), *Cross-cultural roots of minority child development* (pp. 55–86). Hillsdale, NJ: Lawrence Erlbaum.

Dien, D. S. (2000). The evolving nature of self-identity across four levels of history. *Human Development, 43,* 1–18.

Donovan, S., & Cross, C. (Eds.). (2002). *Minority students in special and gifted education.* Washington, DC: National Academy Press.

Dunn, L. M. (1968). Special education for the mildly retarded: Is much of it justifiable? *Exceptional Children, 35,* 5–22.

Dyson, A. (1999). Inclusion and inclusions: Theories and discourses in inclusive education. In H. Daniels & P. Garner (Eds.), *World yearbook of education 1999: Inclusive education* (pp. 36–53). London: Kogan Page.

Eagleton, T. (2000). *The idea of culture.* Oxford, Eng.: Blackwell.

Eisenhart, M. (2001). Changing conceptions of culture and ethnographic methodology: Recent thematic shifts and their implications for research on teaching. In V. Richardson (Ed.), *Handbook of research on teaching* (4th ed., pp. 209–225). Washington, DC: American Educational Research Association.

Elbaum, B., Vaughn, S., Hughes, M., & Watson-Moody, S. (1999). Grouping practices and reading outcomes for students with disabilities. *Exceptional Children, 65,* 399–415.

Engestrom, Y., Miettinen, R.,& Punamaki, R. (Eds.). (1999). *Perspectives on activity theory.* New York: Cambridge University Press.

Erickson, F. (1996). Inclusion into what? Thoughts on the construction of learning, identity, and affiliation in the general education classroom. In D. L. Speece & B. K. Keogh (Eds.), *Research on classroom ecologies* (pp. 91–105). Mahwah, NJ: Lawrence Erlbaum.

Erickson, F. (2001). Culture in society and in educational practices. In J. Banks & C. M. Banks (Eds.), *Multicultural education: Issues and perspectives* (pp. 31–58). New York: Wiley.

Ferguson, D. L. (1995). The real challenge of inclusion: Confessions of a rabid inclusionist. *Phi Delta Kappan, 77,* 281–287.

Ferguson, D. L., & Ferguson, P. M. (1997). Debating inclusion in Synecdoche, New York: A response to Gresham and MacMillan. *Review of Educational Research, 67,* 416–420.

Finn, J. D. (1982). Patterns in special education placement as revealed by the OCR surveys. In K. A. Heller, W. H. Holtzman, & S. Messick (Eds.), *Placing children in special education: A strategy for equity* (pp. 322–381). Washington, DC: National Academy Press.

Foucault, M. (1986). Of other spaces. *Diacritics, 16,* 22–27.

Fuchs, D., & Fuchs, L. S. (1994). Inclusive schools movement and the radicalization of special education reform. *Exceptional Children, 60,* 294–309.

Fujiura, G. T., & Yamaki, K. (2000). Trends in demography of childhood poverty and disability. *Exceptional Children, 66,* 187–199.

Galeano, E. (1989). *Las venas abiertas de América Latina.* Mexico DF: Siglo Veintiuno Editores.

Gallego, M. A., Cole, M., & Laboratory of Comparative Human Cognition. (2001). Classroom cultures and cultures in the classroom. In V. Richardson (Ed.), *Handbook of research on teaching* (4th ed., pp. 951–997). Washington, DC: American Educational Research Association.

Gándara, P., Maxwell-Jolly, J., García, E., Asato, J., Gutiérrez, K., Stritikus, T., & Curry, J. (2000, April). *The initial impact of Proposition 227 on the instruction of English learners.* Santa Barbara: University of California Linguistic Minority Research Institute.

García, E. (1996). Preparing instructional professionals for linguistically and culturally diverse students. In J. Sikula (Ed.), *Handbook of research on teacher education* (pp. 802–812). New York: Macmillan.

Gartner, A., & Lipsky, D. K. (1987). Beyond special education: Toward a quality system for all students. *Harvard Educational Review, 57*, 367–395.

Geertz, C. (1983). *Local knowledge: Further essays in interpretive anthropology*. New York: Basic Books.

Gersten, R., Baker, S., Pugach, M., with Scanlon, D., & Chard, D. (2001). Contemporary research on special education teaching. In V. Richardson (Ed.), *Handbook of research on teaching* (4th ed., pp. 695–722). Washington, DC: American Educational Research Association.

Gottlieb, J., Alter, M., Gottlieb, B. W., & Wishner, J. (1994). Special education in urban America: It's not justifiable for many. *Journal of Special Education, 27*, 453–465.

Gutiérrez, K., Asato, J., Santos, M., & Gotanda, N. (2002). Backlash pedagogy: Language and culture and the politics of reform. *Review of Education, Pedagogy, and Cultural Studies, 24*, 335–351.

Handwerker, W. P. (2002). The construct validity of cultures: Cultural diversity, culture theory, and a method for ethnography. *American Anthropologist, 104*, 106–122.

Hargreaves, A. (1995). Toward a social geography of teacher education. In N. K. Shimahara & I. Z. Holowinsky (Eds.), *Teacher education in industrialized nations* (pp. 3–40). New York: Garland.

Harry, B., Klingner, J., Sturges, K. M., & Moore, R. F. (2002). Of rocks and soft places: Using qualitative methods to investigate disproportionality. In D. J. Losen & G. Orfield (Eds.), *Racial inequity in special education* (pp. 71–92). Cambridge, MA: Harvard Education Press.

Heath, S. B. (1983). *Ways with words: Language, life and work in communities and classrooms*. Cambridge, Eng.: Cambridge University Press.

Hehir, T. (2002). IDEA and disproportionality: Federal enforcement, effective advocacy, and strategies for change. In D. J. Losen & G. Orfield (Eds.), *Racial inequity in special education* (pp. 219–238). Cambridge, MA: Harvard Education Press.

Heller, K. A., Holtzman, W. H., & Messick, S. (Eds.). (1982). *Placing children in special education: A strategy for equity*. Washington, DC: National Academy Press.

Heubert, J. P. (2002). Disability, race, and high-stakes testing of students. In D. J. Losen & G. Orfield (Eds.), *Racial inequity in special education* (pp. 137–165). Cambridge, MA: Harvard Education Press.

Individuals with Disabilities Education Act Amendments of 1997 (IDEA), 20 U.S.C. § 1400-87 (1997) (1994 & Supp. V 1999) (originally enacted as the Education for All Handicapped Children Act of 1975, Pub. L. No. 94-142, 89 Stat. 773).

Irvine, J. J., & York, D. E. (1995). Learning styles and culturally diverse students: A literature review. In J. A. Banks & C. A. McGee Banks (Eds.), *Handbook of research on multicultural education* (pp. 484–497). New York: Macmillan.

Jacob, E. (1995). Reflective practice and anthropology in culturally diverse classrooms. *Elementary School Journal, 95*, 451–463.

Kahn, M. (2000). Thaiti intertwined: Ancestral land, tourist postcard, and nuclear test site. *American Anthropologist, 102*, 7–26.

Kauffman, J. M., & Hallahan, D. P. (Eds.). (1995). *The illusion of full inclusion*. Austin, TX: Pro-Ed.

Keith, M., & Pile, S. (Eds.). (1993). *Place and the politics of identity*. New York: Routledge.

Lefebvre, H. (1991). *The production of space*. Oxford, Eng.: Blackwell.

Lemke, J. L. (2000). Across the scales of time: Artifacts, activities, and meanings in ecosocial systems. *Mind, Culture, and Activity, 7*, 273–290.

Lipsky, D. K., & Gartner, A. (1996). Inclusion, school restructuring, and the remaking of American society. *Harvard Educational Review, 66*, 762–796.

Lipsky, D. K., & Gartner, A. (1999). Inclusive education: A requirement of a democratic society. In H. Daniels & P. Garner (Eds.), *World yearbook of education 1999: Inclusive education* (pp. 12–23). London: Kogan Page.

Losen, D. J., & Orfield, G. (Eds.). (2002). *Racial inequity in special education*. Cambridge, MA: Harvard Education Press.

Manset, G., & Semmel, M. I. (1997). Are inclusive programs for students with mild disabilities effective? A comparative review of model programs. *Journal of Special Education, 31*, 155–180.

McDonnell, L., McLaughlin, M. J., & Morison, P. (Eds.). (1997). *Educating one and all: Students with disabilities and standards-based reform*. Washington, DC: National Academy Press.

McLaren, P. (1989). *Life in schools*. New York: Longman.

McLaughlin, M. J., & Tilstone, C. (1999). Standards and curriculum: The core of educational reform. In M. J. McLaughlin & M. Rouse (Eds.), *Special education and school reform in the United States and Britain* (pp. 38–65). London: Routledge.

McLaughlin, M. J., Fuchs, L., & Hardman, M. (1999). Individual rights to education and students with disabilities: Some lessons from U.S. policy. In H. Daniels & P. Garner (Eds.), *World yearbook of education 1999: Inclusive education* (pp. 24–35). London: Kogan Page.

McLaughlin, M. J., Henderson, K., & Rhim, L. M. (1998, September). *Snapshots of reform: How five local districts are interpreting standards-based reform for students with disabilities*. Alexandria, VA: Center for Policy Research.

McLeskey, J., Henry, D., & Axelrod, M. I. (1999). Inclusion of students with learning disabilities: An examination of data from reports to Congress. *Exceptional Children, 66*, 55–66.

McLoyd, V. C. (1998). Socioeconomic disadvantage and child development. *American Psychologist, 53*, 185–204.

Mehan, H., Hartwick, A., & Meihls, J. L. (1986). *Handicapping the handicapped: Decision-making in students' educational careers*. Stanford, CA: Stanford University Press.

Minow, M. (1990). *Making all the difference: Inclusion, exclusion, and American law*. Ithaca, NY: Cornell University Press.

Mortweet, S. L., Utley, C. A., Walker, D., Dawson, H. L., Delquadri, J. C., Reddy, S. S., Greenwood, C. R., Hamilton, S., & Ledford, D. (1999). Classwide peer tutoring: Teaching students with mild mental retardation in inclusive classrooms. *Exceptional Children, 65*, 524–536.

Nespor, J. (1994). *Knowledge in motion: Space, time, and curriculum in undergraduate physics and management*. London: Falmer Press.

Ogbu, J. U. (1992). Understanding cultural diversity and learning. *Educational Researcher, 21*(8), 5–14.

Ortiz, A. A. (1997). Learning disabilities occurring concomitantly with linguistic differences. *Journal of Learning Disabilities, 30*, 321–332.

Oswald, D. P., Coutinho, M. J., & Best, A. M. (2002). Community and school predictors of overrepresentation of minority children in special education. In D. J. Losen & G. Orfield (Eds.), *Racial inequity in special education* (pp. 1–13). Cambridge, MA: Harvard Education Press.

Oswald, D. P., Coutinho, M. J., Best, A. M., & Singh, N. N. (1999). Ethnic representation in special education: The influence of school-related economic and demographic variables. *Journal of Special Education, 32*, 194–206.

Parrish, T. (2002). Racial disparities in the identification, funding, and provision of special education. In D. J. Losen & G. Orfield (Eds.), *Racial inequity in special education* (pp. 15–37). Cambridge, MA: Harvard Education Press.

Poniatowska, E. (1985). *Fuerte es el silencio*. Mexico DF: Ediciones ERA.

Pugach, M., & Lilly, S. (1984). Reconceptualizing support services for classroom teachers: Implications for teacher education. *Journal of Teacher Education, 35*, 48–55.

Reschly, D. J. (1997). *Disproportionate minority representation in general and special education: Patterns, issues, and alternatives*. Des Moines: Iowa Department of Education.

Reynolds, M. C., & York, J. L. (1996). Special education and inclusion. In J. Sikula (Ed.), *Handbook of research on teacher education* (pp. 820–836). New York: Macmillan.

Rizvi, F., & Lingard, B. (1996). Disability, education and the discourses of justice. In C. Christensen & F. Rizvi (Eds.), *Disability and the dilemmas of education and justice* (pp. 9–26). Buckingham, Eng.: Open University Press.

Rogoff, B., & Angelillo, C. (2002). Investigating the coordinated functioning of multifaceted cultural practices in human development. *Human Development, 45*, 211–225.

Rosaldo, R. (1984). Comments. *Current Anthropology, 25*, 293–294.

Rueda, R., Artiles, A. J., Salazar, J., & Higareda, I. (2002). An analysis of special education as a response to the diminished academic achievement of Chicano/Latino students: An update. In R.

R. Valencia (Ed.), *Chicano school failure and success: Past, present, and future* (2nd ed., pp. 310–332). London: Routledge/Falmer.

Scribner, S. (1985). Vygotsky's uses of history. In J. V. Wertsch (Ed.), *Culture, communication, and cognition* (pp. 119–145). New York: Cambridge University Press.

Seed, P. (2001). *American pentimiento*. Minneapolis: University of Minnesota Press.

Sheriff, R. E. (2000). Exposing silence as cultural censorship: A Brazilian case. *American Anthropologist, 102*, 114–132.

Shields, R. (2000). *Lefebvre, love and struggle: Spatial dialectics*. London: Routledge.

Skrtic, T. M. (1991). The special education paradox: Equity as the way to excellence. *Harvard Educational Review, 61*, 148–206.

Skrtic, T. M., Sailor, W., & Gee, K. (1996). Voice, collaboration, and inclusion: Democratic themes in educational and social reform initiatives. *Remedial and Special Education, 17*, 142–157.

Slee, R. (1996). Disability, social class and poverty: School structures and policing identities. In C. Christensen & F. Rizvi (Eds.), *Disability and the dilemmas of education and justice* (pp. 96–118). Buckingham, Eng.: Open University Press.

Smith, D. D. (2001). *Introduction to special education: Teaching in an age of opportunity* (4th ed.). Boston: Allyn & Bacon.

Soja, E. (1989). *Postmodern geographies: The reassertion of space in critical social theory*. New York: Verso.

Soja, E. W. (1996). *Thirdspace: Journeys to Los Angeles and other real-and-imagined places*. Oxford, Eng.: Blackwell.

Soodak, L. C., Podell, D. M., & Lehman, L. R. (1998). Teacher, student, and school attributes as predictors of teachers' responses to inclusion. *Journal of Special Education, 31*, 480–497.

Stainback, W., & Stainback, S. (1991). Rationale for integration and restructuring: A synopsis. In J. W. Lloyd, A. C. Repp, & N. N. Singh (Eds.), *The Regular Education Initiative: Alternative perspectives on concepts, issues, and models* (pp. 225–239). Sycamore, IL: Sycamore.

Staub, N. (2000). *On inclusion and the other kids: Here's what research shows so far about inclusion's effect on nondisabled students*. Retrieved on March 1, 2001, from http://www.edc. org/urban

Stone, C. A. (1993). What's missing in the metaphor of scaffolding? In E. A. Forman, N. Minick, & C. A. Stone (Eds.), *Contexts for learning: Sociocultural dynamics in children's development* (pp. 169–183). New York: Oxford University Press.

Suárez-Orozco, C., & Suárez-Orozco, M. (1995). *Transformations: Migration, family life, and achievement motivation among Latino adolescents*. Stanford, CA: Stanford University Press.

Tejeda, C. (2000). *Mapping social space: A study of spatial production in an elementary classroom*. (Doctoral dissertation, University of California, Los Angeles, 2000). Ann Arbor: UMI 2001, Microform 9993008.

Trouillot, M. (1995). *Silencing the past: Power and the production of history*. Boston: Beacon Press.

U.S. Department of Education. (1997). *Nineteenth annual report to Congress on the implementation of the IDEA*. Washington, DC: Author.

U.S. Department of Education. (1999). *Twenty-first report to Congress on the implementation of the IDEA*. Washington, DC: Author.

Valencia, R. (Ed.). (1997). *The evolution of deficit thinking*. London: Falmer.

Vanderwood, M., McGrew, K. S., & Ysseldyke, J. E. (1998). Why we can't say much about students with disabilities during education reform. *Exceptional Children, 64*, 359–370.

Varenne, H. (1984). Collective representation in American anthropological conversations: Individual and culture. *Current Anthropology, 25*, 281–291.

Varenne, H., & McDermott, R. (Eds.). (1999). *Successful failure: The school America builds*. Boulder, CO: Westview Press.

Villa, R. A., & Thousand, J. S. (Eds.). (1995). *Creating an inclusive school*. Alexandria, VA: Association for Supervision and Curriculum Development.

Viswanathan, G. (Ed.). (2001). *Power, politics, and culture: Interviews with Edward W. Said*. New York: Pantheon.

Vogt, L., Jordan, C., & Tharp, R. (1993). Explaining school failure, producing school success: Two cases. In E. Jacob & C. Jordan (Eds.), *Minority education: Anthropological perspectives* (pp. 53–65). Norwood, NJ: Ablex.

Wagner, M., Blackorby, J., Cameto, R., Hebbler, K., & Newman, L. (1993). *The transition experiences of young people with disabilities: A summary of findings from the national longitudinal transition study of special education students*. Menlo Park, CA: SRI International.

Walker, V. S. (1999). Culture and commitment: Challenges for the future training of education researchers. In E. C. Lagemann & L. S. Shulman (Eds.), *Issues in education research: Problems and possibilities* (pp. 224–244). San Francisco: Jossey-Bass.

Wang, M. C., & Walberg, H. J. (1988). Four fallacies of segregationism. *Exceptional Children, 55,* 128–137.

Will, M. (1984). Let us pause and reflect — but not too long. *Exceptional Children, 51*(1), 11–16.

Williams, R. (1983). *Culture and society*. New York: Columbia University Press.

Willis, P. (1977). *Learning to labor: How working class kids get working class jobs*. New York: Columbia University Press.

Zeichner, K. M., & Hoeft, K. (1996). Teacher socialization for cultural diversity. In J. Sikula, T. J. Buttery, & E. Guyton (Eds.), *The handbook of research on teacher education* (pp. 525–547). New York: Macmillan.

Author's Note: I presented various versions of this paper as keynote addresses at the International Special Education Conference (Manchester, England, July 2000), the ninth annual Inclusive Schools and Communities for Children and Youth Conference (Tarrytown, New York, May 2001), and the IDEA Summit (Washington, DC, June 2001). The analyses presented in this manuscript were refined while I received support from the Spencer Foundation/National Academy of Education (Postdoctoral Fellowship Program), the COMRISE Project under grant #H029J60006 awarded by the U.S. Department of Education (USDOE), Office of Special Education Programs (OSEP), and the National Center for Culturally Responsive Educational Systems (NCCRESt) under grant # H326E020003 awarded by the USDOE, OSEP. Endorsement of the ideas presented in this article by these funding agencies should not be inferred. I am indebted to many colleagues for their feedback on different versions of this paper, particularly to Fernando Diniz, Alan Dyson, Diane Ferguson, Phil Ferguson, Doug Fuchs, Kris Gutierrez, Beth Harry, Elizabeth Kozleski, Huong Tran Nguyen, Denis Poizat, Kim Reed, Mike Rose, Robert Rueda, Carlos Tejeda, and Stan Trent. My thinking and writing were sharpened by their insights, though I remain responsible for the manuscript's shortcomings.

The Silenced Dialogue

Power and Pedagogy in Educating Other People's Children

8

LISA D. DELPIT

A Black male graduate student who is also a special education teacher in a predominantly Black community is talking about his experiences in predominantly White university classes:

There comes a moment in every class where we have to discuss "The Black Issue" and what's appropriate education for Black children. I tell you, I'm tired of arguing with those White people, because they won't listen. Well, I don't know if they really don't listen or if they just don't believe you. It seems like if you can't quote Vygotsky or something, then you don't have any validity to speak about your *own* kids. Anyway, I'm not bothering with it anymore, now I'm just in it for a grade.

A Black woman teacher in a multicultural urban elementary school is talking about her experiences in discussions with her predominantly White fellow teachers about how they should organize reading instructions to best serve students of color:

When you're talking to White people they still want it to be their way. You can try to talk to them and give them examples, but they're so headstrong, they think they know what's best for *everybody*, for *everybody's* children. They won't listen: White folks are going to do what they want to do *anyway*.

It's really hard. They just don't listen well. No, they listen, but they don't *hear* — you know how your mama used to say you listen to the radio, but you *hear* your mother? Well they don't *hear* me.

So I just try to shut them out so I can hold my temper. You can only beat your head against a brick wall for so long before you draw blood. If I try to stop arguing with them I can't help myself from getting angry. Then I end up walking around praying all day "Please Lord, remove the bile I feel for these people so I can sleep tonight." It's funny, but it can become a cancer, a sore.

So, I shut them out. I go back to my own little cubby, my classroom, and I try to teach the way I know will work, no matter what those folk say. And when I get Black kids, I just try to undo the damage they did.

Harvard Educational Review   Vol. 58   No. 3   August 1988, 280–298

I'm not going to let any man, woman, or child drive me crazy — White folks will try to do that to you if you let them. You just have to stop talking to them, that's what I do. I just keep smiling, but I won't talk to them.

A soft-spoken Native Alaskan woman in her forties is a student in the Education Department of the University of Alaska. One day she storms into a Black professor's office and very uncharacteristically slams the door. She plops down in a chair and, still fuming, says, "Please tell people, just don't help us anymore! I give up. I won't talk to them again!"

And finally, a Black woman principal who is also a doctoral student at a well-known university on the West Coast is talking about her university experiences, particularly about when a professor lectures on issues concerning educating Black children:

> If you try to suggest that that's not quite the way it is, they get defensive, then you get defensive, then they'll start reciting research.
>
> I try to give them my experiences, to explain. They just look and nod. The more I try to explain, they just look and nod, just keep looking and nodding. They don't really hear me.
>
> Then, when it's time for class to be over, the professor tells me to come to his office to talk more. So I go. He asks for more examples of what I'm talking about, and he looks and nods while I give them. Then he says that that's just my experiences. It doesn't really apply to most Black people.
>
> It becomes futile because they think they know everything about everybody. What you have to say about your life, your children, doesn't mean anything. They don't really want to hear what you have to say. They wear blinders and earplugs. They only want to go on research they've read that other White people have written.
>
> It just doesn't make any sense to keep talking to them.

Thus was the first half of the title of this text born — "The Silenced Dialogue." One of the tragedies in the field of education is that scenarios such as these are enacted daily around the country. The saddest element is that the individuals that the Black and Native American educators speak of in these statements are seldom aware that the dialogue *has* been silenced. Most likely, the White educators believe that their colleagues of color did, in the end, agree with their logic. After all, they stopped disagreeing, didn't they?

I have collected these statements since completing a recently published article (Delpit, 1986). In this somewhat autobiographical account, entitled "Skills and Other Dilemmas of a Progressive Black Educator," I discussed my perspective as a product of a skills-oriented approach to writing and as a teacher of process-oriented approaches. I described the estrangement that I and many teachers of color feel from the progressive movement when writing-process advocates dismiss us as too "skills oriented." I ended the article suggesting that it was incumbent upon writing-process advocates — or indeed, advocates of any progressive movement — to enter into dialogue with teachers of color who may not share their enthusiasm about so-called new, liberal, or progressive ideas.

In response to this article, which presented no research data and did not even cite a reference, I received numerous calls and letters from teachers, professors, and even state school personnel from around the country, both Black and White. All of the White respondents, except one, have wished to talk more about the question of skills versus process approaches — to support or reject what they perceive to be my position. On the other hand, *all* of the non-White respondents have spoken passionately on being left out of the dialogue about how best to educate children of color.

How can such complete communication blocks exist when both parties truly believe they have the same aims? How can the bitterness and resentment expressed by the educators of color be drained so that the sores can heal? What can be done?

I believe the answer to these questions lies in ethnographic analysis, that is, in identifying and giving voice to alternative world views. Thus, I will attempt to address the concerns raised by White and Black respondents to my article "Skills and Other Dilemmas" (Delpit, 1986). My charge here is not to determine the best instructional methodology; I believe that the actual practice of good teachers of all colors typically incorporates a range of pedagogical orientations. Rather, I suggest that the differing perspectives on the debate over "skills" versus "process" approaches can lead to an understanding of the alienation and miscommunication, and thereby to an understanding of the "silenced dialogue."

In thinking through these issues, I have found what I believe to be a connecting and complex theme: what I have come to call "the culture of power." There are five aspects of power I would like to propose as given for this presentation:

1. Issues of power are enacted in classrooms.
2. There are codes or rules for participating in power; that is, there is a "culture of power."
3. The rules of the culture of power are a reflection of the rules of the culture of those who have power.
4. If you are not already a participant in the culture of power, being told explicitly the rules of that culture makes acquiring power easier.
5. Those with power are frequently least aware of — or least willing to acknowledge — its existence. Those with less power are often most aware of its existence.

The first three are by now basic tenets in the literature of the sociology of education, but the last two have seldom been addressed. The following discussion will explicate these aspects of power and their relevance to the schism between liberal educational movements and that of non-White, non-middle-class teachers and communities.[1]

1. Issues of power are enacted in classrooms.

These issues include: the power of the teacher over the students; the power of the publishers of textbooks and of the developers of the curriculum to determine the view of the world presented; the power of the state in enforcing compulsory schooling; and the power of an individual or group to determine another's intelligence or "normalcy." Finally, if schooling prepares people for jobs, and the kind of job a person has determines her or his economic status and, therefore, power, then schooling is intimately related to that power.

2. There are codes or rules for participating in power; that is, there is a "culture of power."

The codes or rules I'm speaking of relate to linguistic forms, communicative strategies, and presentation of self; that is, ways of talking, ways of writing, ways of dressing, and ways of interacting.

3. The rules of the culture of power are a reflection of the rules of the culture of those who have power.

This means that success in institutions — schools, workplaces, and so on — is predicated upon acquisition of the culture of those who are in power. Children from middle-class homes tend to do better in school than those from non-middle-class homes because the culture of the school is based on the culture of the upper and middle classes — of those in power. The upper and middle classes send their children to school with all the accoutrements of the culture of power; children from other kinds of families operate within perfectly wonderful and viable cultures but not cultures that carry the codes or rules of power.

4. If you are not already a participant in the culture of power, being told explicitly the rules of that culture makes acquiring power easier.

In my work within and between diverse cultures, I have come to conclude that members of any culture transmit information implicitly to co-members. However, when implicit codes are attempted across cultures, communication frequently breaks down. Each cultural group is left saying, "Why don't those people say what they mean?" as well as, "What's wrong with them, why don't they understand?"

Anyone who has had to enter new cultures, especially to accomplish a specific task, will know of what I speak. When I lived in several Papua New Guinea villages for extended periods to collect data, and when I go to Alaskan villages for work with Alaskan Native communities, I have found it unquestionably easier — psychologically and pragmatically — when some kind soul has directly informed me about such matters as appropriate dress, interactional styles, embedded meanings, and taboo words or actions. I contend that it is much the same for anyone seeking to learn the rules of the culture of power. Unless one has the leisure of a lifetime of "immersion" to learn them, explicit presentation makes learning immeasurably easier.

And now, to the fifth and last premise:

5. Those with power are frequently least aware of — or least willing to acknowledge — its existence. Those with less power are often most aware of its existence.

For many who consider themselves members of liberal or radical camps, acknowledging personal power and admitting participation in the culture of power is distinctly uncomfortable. On the other hand, those who are less powerful in any situation are most likely to recognize the power variable most acutely. My guess is that the White colleagues and instructors of those previously quoted did not perceive themselves to have power over the non-White speakers. However, either by virtue of their position, their numbers, or their access to that particular code of power of calling upon research to validate one's position, the White educators had the authority to establish what was to be considered "truth" regardless of the opinions of the people of color, and the latter were well aware of that fact.

A related phenomenon is that liberals (and here I am using the term "liberal" to refer to those whose beliefs include striving for a society based upon maximum individual freedom and autonomy) seem to act under the assumption that to make any rules or expectations explicit is to act against liberal principles, to limit the freedom and autonomy of those subjected to the explicitness.

I thank Fred Erickson for a comment that led me to look again at a tape by John Gumperz[2] on cultural dissonance in cross-cultural interactions. One of the episodes showed an East Indian interviewing for a job with an all-White committee. The interview was a complete failure, even though several of the interviewers appeared to really want to help the applicant. As the interview rolled steadily downhill, these "helpers" became more and more indirect in their questioning, which exacerbated the problems the applicant had in performing appropriately. Operating from a different cultural perspective, he got fewer and fewer clear clues as to what was expected of him, which ultimately resulted in his failure to secure the position.

I contend that as the applicant showed less and less aptitude for handling the interview, the power differential became ever more evident to the interviewers. The "helpful" interviewers, unwilling to acknowledge themselves as having power over the applicant, became more and more uncomfortable. Their indirectness was an attempt to lessen the power differential and their discomfort by lessening the power-revealing explicitness of their questions and comments.

When acknowledging and expressing power, one tends toward explicitness (as in yelling to your ten-year-old, "Turn that radio down!"). When de-emphasizing power, there is a move toward indirect communication. Therefore, in the interview setting, those who sought to help, to express their egalitarianism with the East Indian applicant, became more and more indirect — and less and less helpful — in their questions and comments.

In literacy instruction, explicitness might be equated with direct instruction. Perhaps the ultimate expression of explicitness and direct instruction in the primary classroom is Distar. This reading program is based on a behaviorist model in which reading is taught through the direct instruction of phonics generalizations and blending. The teacher's role is to maintain the full attention of the group by continuous questioning, eye contact, finger snaps, hand claps, and other gestures, and by eliciting choral responses and initiating some sort of award system.

When the program was introduced, it arrived with a flurry of research data that "proved" that all children — even those who were "culturally deprived" — could learn to read using this method. Soon there was a strong response, first from academics and later from many classroom teachers, stating that the program was terrible. What I find particularly interesting, however, is that the primary issue of the conflict over Distar has not been over its instructional efficacy — usually the students did learn to read — but the expression of explicit power in the classroom. The liberal educators opposed the methods — the direct instruction, the explicit control exhibited by the teacher. As a matter of fact, it was not unusual (even now) to hear of the program spoken of as "fascist."

I am not an advocate of Distar, but I will return to some of the issues that the program — and direct instruction in general — raises in understanding the differences between progressive White educators and educators of color.

To explore those differences, I would like to present several statements typical of those made with the best of intentions by middle-class liberal educators. To the surprise of the speakers, it is not unusual for such content to be met by vocal opposition or stony silence from people of color. My attempt here is to examine the underlying assumptions of both camps.

"I want the same thing for everyone else's children as I want for mine."

To provide schooling for everyone's children that reflects liberal, middle-class values and aspirations is to ensure the maintenance of the status quo, to ensure that power, the culture of power, remains in the hands of those who already have it. Some children come to school with more accoutrements of the culture of power already in place — "cultural capital," as some critical theorists refer to it (for example, Apple, 1979) — some with less. Many liberal educators hold that the primary goal for education is for children to become autonomous, to develop fully who they are in the classroom setting without having arbitrary, outside standards forced upon them. This is a very reasonable goal for people whose children are already participants in the culture of power and who have already internalized its codes.

But parents who don't function within that culture often want something else. It's not that they disagree with the former aim, it's just that they want something more. They want to ensure that the school provides their children with discourse patterns, interactional styles, and spoken and written language codes that will allow them success in the larger society.

It was the lack of attention to this concern that created such a negative outcry in the Black community when well-intentioned White liberal educators introduced "dialect readers." These were seen as a plot to prevent the schools from teaching the linguistic aspects of the culture of power, thus dooming Black children to a permanent outsider caste. As one parent demanded, "My kids know how to be Black — you all teach them how to be successful in the White man's world."

Several Black teachers have said to me recently that as much as they'd like to believe otherwise, they cannot help but conclude that many of the "progressive" educational strategies imposed by liberals upon Black and poor children could only be based on a desire to ensure that the liberals' children get sole access to the dwindling pool of American jobs. Some have added that the liberal educators believe themselves to be operating with good intentions, but that these good intentions are only conscious delusions about their unconscious true motives. One of Black anthropologist John Gwaltney's (1980) informants reflects this perspective with her tongue-in-cheek observation that the biggest difference between Black folks and White folks is that Black folks *know* when they're lying!

Let me try to clarify how this might work in literacy instruction. A few years ago I worked on an analysis of two popular reading programs, Distar and a progressive program that focused on higher-level critical thinking skills. In one of the first lessons of the progressive program, the children are introduced to the names of the letter *m* and *e*. In the same lesson they are then taught the sound made by each of the letters, how to write each of the letters, and that when the two are blended together they produce the word *me*.

As an experienced first-grade teacher, I am convinced that a child needs to be familiar with a significant number of these concepts to be able to assimilate so much new knowledge in one sitting. By contrast, Distar presents the same information in about forty lessons.

I would not argue for the pace of the Distar lessons; such a slow pace would only bore most kids — but what happened in the other lesson is that it merely provided an opportunity for those who already knew the content to exhibit that they knew it, or at most perhaps to build one new concept onto what was already known. This meant that the child who did not come to school already primed with what was to be presented would be labeled as needing "remedial" instruction from day one; indeed, this determination would be made before he or she was ever taught. In fact, Distar was "successful" because it actually *taught* new information to children who had not already acquired it at home. Although the more progressive system was ideal for some children, for others it was a disaster.

I do not advocate a simplistic "basic skills" approach for children outside of the culture of power. It would be (and has been) tragic to operate as if these children were incapable of critical and higher-order thinking and reasoning. Rather, I suggest that schools must provide these children the content that other families from a different cultural orientation provide at home. This does not mean separating children according to family background, but instead, ensuring that each classroom incorporates strategies appropriate for all the children in its confines.

And I do not advocate that it is the school's job to attempt to change the homes of poor and non-White children to match the homes of those in the culture of power. That may indeed be a form of cultural genocide. I have frequently heard schools call poor parents "uncaring" when parents respond to the school's urging that they change their home life in order to facilitate their children's learning by saying, "But that's the school's job." What the school personnel fail to understand is that if the parents were members of the culture of power and lived by its rules and codes, then they would transmit those codes to their children. In fact, they transmit another culture that children must learn at home in order to survive in their communities.

"Child-centered, whole language, and process approaches are needed in order to allow a democratic state of free, autonomous, empowered adults, and because research has shown that children learn best through these methods."

People of color are, in general, skeptical of research as a determiner of our fates. Academic research has, after all, found us genetically inferior, culturally deprived, and verbally deficient. But beyond that general caveat, and despite my or others' personal preferences, there is little research data supporting the major tenets of process approaches over other forms of literacy instruction, and virtually no evidence that such approaches are more efficacious for children of color (Siddle, 1986).

Although the problem is not necessarily inherent in the method, in some instances adherents of process approaches to writing create situations in which students ultimately find themselves held accountable for knowing a set of rules about which no one has ever directly informed them. Teachers do students no service to suggest, even implicitly, that "product" is not important. In this country, students will be judged on their product regardless of the process they utilized to achieve it. And that product, based as it is on the specific codes of a particular culture, is more readily produced when the directives of how to produce it are made explicit.

If such explicitness is not provided to students, what it feels like to people who are old enough to judge is that there are secrets being kept, that time is being wasted, that the teacher is abdicating his or her duty to teach. A doctoral student in my acquaintance was assigned to a writing class to hone his writing skills. The student was placed in the section led by a White professor who utilized a process approach, consisting primarily of having the students write essays and then assemble into groups to edit each others' papers. That procedure infuriated this particular student. He had many angry encounters with the teacher about what she was doing. In his words:

> I didn't feel she was teaching us anything. She wanted us to correct each others' papers and we were there to learn from her. She didn't teach anything, absolutely nothing.
>
> Maybe they're trying to learn what Black folks knew all the time. We understand how to improvise, how to express ourselves creatively. When I'm in a classroom, I'm not looking for that, I'm looking for structure, the more formal language.
>
> Now my buddy was in [a] Black teacher's class. And that lady was very good. She went through and explained and defined each part of the structure. This [White] teacher didn't get along with that Black teacher. She said that she didn't agree with her methods. But *I* don't think that White teacher *had* any methods.

When I told this gentleman that what the teacher was doing was called a process method of teaching writing, his response was, "Well, at least now I know that she *thought* she was doing *something*. I thought she was just a fool who couldn't teach and didn't want to try."

This sense of being cheated can be so strong that the student may be completely turned off to the educational system. Amanda Branscombe, an accomplished White teacher, recently wrote a letter discussing her work with working-class Black and White students at a community college in Alabama. She had given these students my "Skills and Other Dilemmas" article (Delpit, 1986) to read and discuss, and wrote that her students really understood and identified with what I was saying. To quote her letter:

> One young man said that he had dropped out of high school because he failed the exit exam. He noted that he had then passed the GED without a problem after three

weeks of prep. He said that his high school English teacher claimed to use a process approach, but what she really did was hide behind fancy words to give herself permission to do nothing in the classroom.

The students I have spoken of seem to be saying that the teacher has denied them access to herself as the source of knowledge necessary to learn the forms they need to succeed. Again, I tentatively attribute the problem to teachers' resistance to exhibiting power in the classroom. Somehow, to exhibit one's personal power as expert source is viewed as disempowering one's students.

Two qualifiers are necessary, however. The teacher cannot be the only expert in the classroom. To deny students their own expert knowledge *is* to disempower them. Amanda Branscombe, when she was working with Black high school students classified as "slow learners," had the students analyze rap songs to discover their underlying patterns. The students became the experts in explaining to the teacher the rules for creating a new rap song. The teacher then used the patterns the students identified as a base to begin an explanation of the structure of grammar, and then of Shakespeare's plays. Both student and teacher are experts at what they know best.

The second qualifier is that merely adopting direct instruction is not the answer. Actual writing for real audiences and real purposes is a vital element in helping students to understand that they have an important voice in their own learning processes. Siddle (1988) examines the results of various kinds of interventions in a primarily process-oriented writing class for Black students. Based on readers' blind assessments, she found that the intervention that produced the most positive changes in the students' writing was a "mini-lesson" consisting of direct instruction about some standard writing convention. But what produced the *second* highest number of positive changes was a subsequent student-centered conference with the teacher. (Peer conferencing in this group of Black students who were not members of the culture of power produced the least number of changes in students' writing. However, the classroom teacher maintained — and I concur — that such activities are necessary to introduce the elements of "real audience" into the task, along with more teacher-directed strategies.)

"It's really a shame but she (that Black teacher upstairs) seems to be so authoritarian, so focused on skills and so teacher directed. Those poor kids never seem to be allowed to really express their creativity. (And she even yells at them.)"

This statement directly concerns the display of power and authority in the classroom. One way to understand the difference in perspective between Black teachers and their progressive colleagues on this issue is to explore culturally influenced oral interactions.

In *Ways With Words*, Shirley Brice Heath (1983) quotes the verbal directives given by the middle-class "townspeople" teachers (p. 280):

- "Is this where the scissors belong?"
- "You want to do your best work today."

By contrast, many Black teachers are more likely to say:

- "Put those scissors on that shelf."
- "Put your name on the papers and make sure to get the right answer for each question."

Is one oral style more authoritarian than another?

Other researchers have identified differences in middle-class and working-class speech to children. Snow et al. (1976), for example, report that working-class mothers use more directives to their children than do middle- and upper-class parents. Middle-class parents are likely to give the directive to a child to take his bath as, "Isn't it time for your bath?" Even though the utterance is couched as a question, both child and adult understand it as a directive. The child may respond with "Aw Mom, can't I wait until . . . ," but whether or not negotiation is attempted, both conversants understand the intent of the utterance.

By contrast, a Black mother, in whose house I was recently a guest, said to her eight-year-old son, "Boy, get your rusty behind in that bathtub." Now I happen to know that this woman loves her son as much as any mother, but she would never have posed the directive to her son to take a bath in the form of a question. Were she to ask, "Would you like to take your bath now?" she would not have been issuing a directive but offering a true alternative. Consequently, as Heath suggests, upon entering school the child from such a family may not understand the indirect statement of the teacher as a direct command. Both White and Black working-class children in the communities Heath studied "had difficulty interpreting these indirect requests for adherence to an unstated set of rules" (p. 280).

But those veiled commands are commands nonetheless, representing true power, and with true consequences for disobedience. If veiled commands are ignored, the child will be labeled a behavior problem and possibly officially classified as behavior disordered. In other words, the attempt by the teacher to reduce an exhibition of power by expressing herself in indirect terms may remove the very explicitness that the child needs to understand the rules of the new classroom culture.

A Black elementary school principal in Fairbanks, Alaska, reported to me that she has a lot of difficulty with Black children who are placed in some White teachers' classrooms. The teachers often send the children to the office for disobeying teacher directives. Their parents are frequently called in for conferences. The parents' response to the teacher is usually the same: "They do what I say; if you just *tell* them what to do, they'll do it. I tell them at home that they have to listen to what you say." And so, does not the power still exist? Its veiled nature only makes it more difficult for some children to respond appropriately, but that in no way mitigates its existence.

I don't mean to imply, however, that the only time the Black child disobeys the teacher is when he or she misunderstands the request for certain behavior. There are other factors that may produce such behavior. Black children expect an authority figure to act with authority. When the teacher instead acts as a "chum," the message sent is that this adult has no authority, and the children react accordingly. One reason this is so is that Black people often view issues of power and authority differently than people from mainstream middle-class backgrounds.[3] Many people of color expect authority to be earned by personal efforts and exhibited by personal characteristics. In other words, "the authoritative person gets to be a teacher because she is authoritative." Some members of middle-class cultures, by contrast, expect one to achieve authority by the acquisition of an authoritative role. That is, "the teacher is the authority because she is the teacher."

In the first instance, because authority is earned, the teacher must consistently prove the characteristics that give her authority. These characteristics may vary across cultures, but in the Black community they tend to cluster around several abilities. The authoritative teacher can control the class through exhibition of personal power; establishes meaningful interpersonal relationships that garner student respect; exhibits a strong belief that all students can learn; establishes a standard of achievement and "pushes" the students to achieve that standard; and holds the attention of the students by incorporating interactional features of Black communicative style in his or her teaching.

By contrast, the teacher whose authority is vested in the role has many more options of behavior at her disposal. For instance, she does not need to express any sense of personal power because her authority does not come from anything she herself does or says. Hence, the power she actually holds may be veiled in such questions/commands as "Would you like to sit down now?" If the children in her class understand authority as she does, it is mutually agreed upon that they are to obey her no matter how indirect, soft-spoken, or unassuming she may be. Her indirectness and soft-spokenness may indeed be, as I suggested earlier, an attempt to reduce the implication of overt power in order to establish a more egalitarian and non-authoritarian classroom atmosphere.

If the children operate under another notion of authority, however, then there is trouble. The Black child may perceive the middle-class teacher as weak, ineffectual, and incapable of taking on the role of being the teacher; therefore, there is no need to follow her directives. In her dissertation, Michelle Foster (1987) quotes one young Black man describing such a teacher:

> She is boring, bo::ring.* She could do something creative. Instead she just stands there. She can't control the class, doesn't know how to control the class. She asked me what she was doing wrong. I told her she just stands there like she's meditating. I told her she could be meditating for all I know. She says that we're supposed to know what to do. I told her I don't know nothin' unless she tells me. She just can't control the class. I hope we don't have her next semester. (pp. 67–68)

But of course the teacher may not view the problem as residing in herself but in the student, and the child may once again become the behavior-disordered Black boy in special education.

What characteristics do Black students attribute to the good teacher? Again, Foster's dissertation provides a quotation that supports my experience with Black students. A young Black man is discussing a former teacher with a group of friends:

---

* *Editor's note:* The colons [::] refer to elongated vowels.

We had fu::n in her class, but she was mean. I can remember she used to say, "Tell me what's in the story, Wayne." She pushed, she used to get on me and push me to know. She made us learn. We had to get in the books. There was this tall guy and he tried to take her on, but she was in charge of that class and she didn't let anyone run her. I still have this book we used in her class. It's a bunch of stories in it. I just read one on Coca-Cola again the other day (p. 68).

To clarify, this student was *proud* of the teacher's "meanness," an attribute he seemed to describe as the ability to run the class and pushing and expecting students to learn. Now, does the liberal perspective of the negatively authoritarian Black teacher really hold up? I suggest that although all "explicit" Black teachers are not also good teachers, there are different attitudes in different cultural groups about which characteristics make for a good teacher. Thus, it is impossible to create a model for the good teacher without taking issues of culture and community context into account.

And now to the final comment I present for examination:

"Children have the right to their own language, their own culture. We must fight cultural hegemony and fight the system by insisting that children be allowed to express themselves in their own language style. It is not they, the children, who must change, but the schools. To push children to do anything else is repressive and reactionary."

A statement such as this originally inspired me to write the "Skills and Other Dilemmas" article. It was first written as a letter to a colleague in response to a situation that had developed in our department. I was teaching a senior-level teacher education course. Students were asked to prepare a written autobiographical document for the class that would also be shared with their placement school prior to their student teaching.

One student, a talented young Native American woman, submitted a paper in which the ideas were lost because of technical problems — from spelling to sentence structure to paragraph structure. Removing her name, I duplicated the paper for a discussion with some faculty members. I had hoped to initiate a discussion about what we could do to ensure that our students did not reach the senior level without getting assistance in technical writing skills when they needed them.

I was amazed at the response. Some faculty implied that the student should never have been allowed into the teacher education program. Others, some of the more progressive minded, suggested that I was attempting to function as gatekeeper by raising the issue and had internalized repressive and disempowering forces of the power elite to suggest that something was wrong with a Native American student just because she had another style of writing. With few exceptions, I found myself alone in arguing against both camps.

No, this student should not have been denied entry to the program. To deny her entry under the notion of upholding standards is to blame the victim for the crime. We cannot justifiably enlist exclusionary standards when the reason this student lacked the skills demanded was poor teaching at best and institutionalized racism at worst.

However, to bring this student into the program and pass her through without attending to obvious deficits in the codes needed for her to function effectively as a teacher is equally criminal — for though we may assuage our own consciences for not participating in victim blaming, she will surely be accused and convicted as soon as she leaves the university. As Native Alaskans were quick to tell me, and as I understood through my own experience in the Black community, not only would she not be hired as a teacher, but those who did not hire her would make the (false) assumption that the university was putting out only incompetent Natives and that they should stop looking seriously at any Native applicants. A White applicant who exhibits problems is an individual with problems. A person of color who exhibits problems immediately becomes a representative of her cultural group.

No, either stance is criminal. The answer is to *accept* students but also to take responsibility to *teach* them. I decided to talk to the student and found out she had recognized that she needed some assistance in the technical aspects of writing soon after she entered the university as a freshman. She had gone to various members of the education faculty and received the same two kinds of responses I met with four years later: faculty members told her either that she should not even attempt to be a teacher, or that it didn't matter and that she shouldn't worry about such trivial issues. In her desperation, she had found a helpful professor in the English Department, but he left the university when she was in her sophomore year.

We sat down together, worked out a plan for attending to specific areas of writing competence, and set up regular meetings. I stressed to her the need to use her own learning process as insight into how best to teach her future students those "skills" that her own schooling had failed to teach her. I gave her some explicit rules to follow in some areas; for others, we devised various kinds of journals that, along with readings about the structure of the language, allowed her to find her own insights into how the language worked. All that happened two years ago, and the young woman is now successfully teaching. What the experience led me to understand is that pretending that gatekeeping points don't exist is to ensure that many students will not pass through them.

Now you may have inferred that I believe that because there is a culture of power, everyone should learn the codes to participate in it, and that is how the world should be. Actually, nothing could be further from the truth. I believe in a diversity of style, and I believe the world will be diminished if cultural diversity is ever obliterated. Further, I believe strongly, as do my liberal colleagues, that each cultural group should have the right to maintain its own language style. When I speak, therefore, of the culture of power, I don't speak of how I wish things to be but of how they are.

I further believe that to act as if power does not exist is to ensure that the power status quo remains the same. To imply to children or adults (but of course the adults won't believe you anyway) that it doesn't matter how you talk or how you write is to ensure their ultimate failure. I prefer to be honest with my students. Tell them that their language and cultural style is unique and wonderful but that there is a political power game that is also being played, and if they want to be in on that game there are certain games that they too must play.

But don't think that I let the onus of change rest entirely with the students. I am also involved in political work both inside and outside of the educational system, and that political work demands that I place myself to influence as many gatekeeping points as possible. And it is there that I agitate for change — pushing gatekeepers to open their doors to a variety of styles and codes. What I'm saying, however, is that I do not believe that political change toward diversity can be effected from the bottom up, as do some of my colleagues. They seem to believe that if we accept and encourage diversity within classrooms of children, then diversity will automatically be accepted at gatekeeping points.

I believe that will never happen. What will happen is that the students who reach the gatekeeping points — like Amanda Branscombe's student who dropped out of high school because he failed his exit exam — will understand that they have been lied to and will react accordingly. No, I am certain that if we are truly to effect societal change, we cannot do so from the bottom up, but we must push and agitate from the top down. And in the meantime, we must take the responsibility to *teach*, to provide for students who do not already possess them, the additional codes of power.[4]

But I also do not believe that we should teach students to passively adopt an alternate code. They must be encouraged to understand the value of the code they already possess as well as to understand the power realities in this country. Otherwise they will be unable to work to change these realities. And how does one do that?

Martha Demientieff, a masterly Native Alaskan teacher of Athabaskan Indian students, tells me that her students, who live in a small, isolated, rural village of less than two hundred people, are not aware that there are different codes of English. She takes their writing and analyzes it for features of what has been referred to by Alaskan linguists as "Village English," and then covers half a bulletin board with words or phrases from the students' writing, which she labels "Our Heritage Language." On the other half of the bulletin board she puts the equivalent statements in "standard English," which she labels "Formal English."

She and the students spend a long time on the "Heritage English" section, savoring the words, discussing the nuances. She tells the students, "That's the way we say things. Doesn't it feel good? Isn't it the absolute best way of getting that idea across?" Then she turns to the other side of the board. She tells the students that there are people, not like those in their village, who judge others by the way they talk or write.

> We listen to the way people talk, not to judge them, but to tell what part of the river they come from. These other people are not like that. They think everybody needs to talk like them. Unlike us, they have a hard time hearing what people say if they don't talk exactly like them. Their way of talking and writing is called "Formal English."
>
> We have to feel a little sorry for them because they have only one way to talk. We're going to learn two ways to say things. Isn't that better? One way will be our Heritage way. The other will be Formal English. Then, when we go to get jobs, we'll be able to talk like those people who only know and can only really listen to one way. Maybe after we get the jobs we can help them to learn how it feels to have another

language, like ours, that feels so good. We'll talk like them when we have to, but we'll always know our way is best.

Martha then does all sorts of activities with the notions of Formal and Heritage or informal English. She tells the students,

> In the village, everyone speaks informally most of the time unless there's a potlatch or something. You don't think about it, you don't worry about following any rules — it's sort of like how you eat food at a picnic — nobody pays attention to whether you use your fingers or a fork, and it feels *so* good. Now, Formal English is more like a formal dinner. There are rules to follow about where the knife and fork belong, about where people sit, about how you eat. That can be really nice, too, because it's nice to dress up sometimes.

The students then prepare a formal dinner in the class, for which they dress up and set a big table with fancy tablecloths, china, and silverware. They speak only Formal English at this meal. Then they prepare a picnic where only informal English is allowed.

She also contrasts the "wordy" academic way of saying things with the metaphoric style of Athabaskan. The students discuss how book language always uses more words, but in Heritage language, the shorter way of saying something is always better. Students then write papers in the academic way, discussing with Martha and with each other whether they believe they've said enough to sound like a book. Next, they take those papers and try to reduce the meaning to a few sentences. Finally, students further reduce the message to a "saying" brief enough to go on the front of a T-shirt, and the sayings are put on little paper T-shirts that the students cut out and hang throughout the room. Sometimes the students reduce other authors' wordy texts to their essential meanings as well.

The following transcript provides another example. It is from a conversation between a Black teacher and a Southern Black high school student named Joey, who is a speaker of Black English. The teacher believes it very important to discuss openly and honestly the issues of language diversity and power. She has begun the discussion by giving the student a children's book written in Black English to read.

Teacher: What do you think about that book?

Joey: I think it's nice.

Teacher: Why?

Joey: I don't know. It just told about a Black family, that's all.

Teacher: Was it difficult to read?

Joey: No.

Teacher: Was the text different from what you have seen in other books?

Joey: Yeah. The writing was.

Teacher: How?

Joey: It use more of a southern-like accent in this book.

Teacher: Uhm-hmm. Do you think that's good or bad?

Joey: Well, uh, I don't think it's good for people down this a way, cause that's the way they grow up talking anyway. They ought to get the right way to talk.

Teacher: Oh. So you think it's wrong to talk like that?

Joey: Well . . . [*Laughs.*]

Teacher: Hard question, huh?

Joey: Uhm-hmm, that's a hard question. But I think they shouldn't make books like that.

Teacher: Why?

Joey: Because they not using the right way to talk and in school they take off for that and li'l chirren grow up talking like that and reading like that so they might think that's right and all the time they getting bad grades in school, talking like that and writing like that.

Teacher: Do you think they should be getting bad grades for talking like that?

Joey: [*Pauses, answers very slowly.*] No . . . No.

Teacher: So you don't think that it matters whether you talk one way or another?

Joey: No, not long as you understood.

Teacher: Uhm-hmm. Well, that's a hard question for me to answer, too. It's ah, that's a question that's come up in a lot of schools now as to whether they should correct children who speak the way we speak all the time. Cause when we're talking to each other we talk like that even though we might not talk like that when we get into other situations, and who's to say whether it's —

Joey: [*Interrupting.*] Right or wrong.

Teacher: Yeah.

Joey: Maybe they ought to come up with another kind of . . . maybe Black English or something. A course in Black English. Maybe Black folks would be good in that cause people talk, I mean Black people talk like that, so . . . but I guess there's a right way and wrong way to talk, you know, not regarding what race. I don't know.

Teacher: But who decided what's right or wrong?

Joey: Well that's true . . . I guess White people did.

[*Laughter. End of tape.*]

Notice how throughout the conversation Joey's consciousness has been raised by thinking about codes of language. This teacher further advocates having students interview various personnel officers in actual workplaces about their attitudes toward divergent styles in oral and written language. Students begin to understand how arbitrary language standards are, but also how politically charged they are. They compare various pieces written in different styles, discuss the impact of different styles on the message by making translations and back translations across styles, and discuss the history, apparent purpose, and contextual appropriateness of each of the technical writing rules presented by their teacher. *And* they practice writing different forms to different audiences based on rules appropriate for each audience. Such a program not only "teaches" standard linguistic forms, but also explores aspects of power as exhibited through linguistic forms.

Tony Burgess, in a study of secondary writing in England by Britton, Burgess, Martin, McLeod, and Rosen (1975/1977), suggests that we should not teach "iron conventions . . . imposed without rationale or grounding in communicative intent, . . . [but] critical and ultimately cultural awareness" (p. 54). Courtney Cazden (1987) calls for a two-pronged approach:

1. Continuous opportunities for writers to participate in some authentic bit of the unending conversation . . . thereby becoming part of a vital community of talkers and writers in a particular domain, and
2. Periodic, temporary focus on conventions of form, taught as cultural conventions expected in a particular community. (p. 20)

Just so that there is no confusion about what Cazden means by a focus on conventions of form, or about what I mean by "skills," let me stress that neither of us is speaking of page after page of "skill sheets" creating compound words or identifying nouns and adverbs, but rather about helping students gain a useful knowledge of the conventions of print while engaging in real and useful communicative activities. Kay Rowe Grubis, a junior high school teacher in a multicultural school, makes lists of certain technical rules for her eighth graders' review and then gives them papers from a third grader to "correct." The students not only have to correct other students' work, but also tell them why they have changed or questioned aspects of the writing.

A village teacher, Howard Cloud, teaches his high school students the conventions of formal letter writing and the formulation of careful questions in the context of issues surrounding the amendment of the Alaska Land Claims Settlement Act. Native Alaskan leaders hold differing views on this issue, critical to the future of local sovereignty and land rights. The students compose letters to leaders who reside in different areas of the state seeking their perspectives, set up audioconference calls for interview/debate sessions, and, finally, develop a videotape to present the differing views.

To summarize, I suggest that students must be *taught* the codes needed to participate fully in the mainstream of American life, not by being forced to attend to hollow, inane, decontextualized subskills, but rather within the context of meaningful communicative endeavors; that they must be allowed the resource of the teacher's expert knowledge, while being helped to acknowledge their own "expertness" as well; and that even while students are assisted in learning the culture of power, they must also be helped to learn about the arbitrariness of those codes and about the power relationships they represent.

I am also suggesting that appropriate education for poor children and children of color can only be devised in consultation with adults who share their culture. Black parents, teachers of color, and members of poor communities must be allowed to participate fully in the discussion of what kind of instruction is in their children's best interest. Good liberal intentions are not enough. In an insightful study entitled "Racism without Racists: Institutional Racism in Urban Schools," Massey, Scott, and

Dornbusch (1975) found that under the pressures of teaching, and with all intentions of "being nice," teachers had essentially stopped attempting to teach Black children. In their words: "We have shown that oppression can arise out of warmth, friendliness, and concern. Paternalism and a lack of challenging standards are creating a distorted system of evaluation in the schools" (p. 10). Educators must open themselves to, and allow themselves to be affected by, these alternative voices.

In conclusion, I am proposing a resolution for the skills/process debate. In short, the debate is fallacious; the dichotomy is false. The issue is really an illusion created initially not by teachers but by academics whose world view demands the creation of categorical divisions — not for the purpose of better teaching, but for the goal of easier analysis. As I have been reminded by many teachers since the publication of my article, those who are most skillful at educating Black and poor children do not allow themselves to be placed in "skills" or "process" boxes. They understand the need for both approaches, the need to help students to establish their own voices, but to coach those voices to produce notes that will be heard clearly in the larger society.

The dilemma is not really in the debate over instructional methodology, but rather in communicating across cultures and in addressing the more fundamental issue of power, of whose voice gets to be heard in determining what is best for poor children and children of color. Will Black teachers and parents continue to be silenced by the very forces that claim to "give voice" to our children? Such an outcome would be tragic, for both groups truly have something to say to one another. As a result of careful listening to alternative points of view, I have myself come to a viable synthesis of perspectives. But both sides do need to be able to listen, and I contend that it is those with the most power, those in the majority, who must take the greater responsibility for initiating the process.

To do so takes a very special kind of listening, listening that requires not only open eyes and ears, but open hearts and minds. We do not really see through our eyes or hear through our ears, but through our beliefs. To put our beliefs on hold is to cease to exist as ourselves for a moment — and that is not easy. It is painful as well, because it means turning yourself inside out, giving up your own sense of who you are, and being willing to see yourself in the unflattering light of another's angry gaze. It is not easy, but it is the only way to learn what it might feel like to be someone else and the only way to start the dialogue.

There are several guidelines. We must keep the perspective that people are experts on their own lives. There are certainly aspects of the outside world of which they may not be aware, but they can be the only authentic chroniclers of their own experience. We must not be too quick to deny their interpretations, or accuse them of "false consciousness." We must believe that people are rational beings, and therefore always act rationally. We may not understand their rationales, but that in no way militates against the existence of these rationales or reduces our responsibility to attempt to apprehend them. And finally, we must learn to be vulnerable enough to allow our world to turn upside down in order to allow the realities of others to edge themselves into our consciousness. In other words, we must become ethnographers in the true sense.

Teachers are in an ideal position to play this role, to attempt to get all of the issues on the table in order to initiate true dialogue. This can only be done, however, by seeking out those whose perspectives may differ most, by learning to give their words complete attention, by understanding one's own power, even if that power stems merely from being in the majority, by being unafraid to raise questions about discrimination and voicelessness with people of color, and to listen, no, to *hear* what they say. I suggest that the results of such interactions may be the most powerful and empowering coalescence yet seen in the educational realm — for *all* teachers and for *all* the students they teach.

NOTES

1. Such a discussion, limited as it is by space constraints, must treat the intersection of class and race somewhat simplistically. For the sake of clarity, however, let me define a few terms: "Black" is used herein to refer to those who share some or all aspects of "core black culture" (Gwaltney, 1980, p. xxiii), that is, the mainstream of Black America — neither those who have entered the ranks of the bourgeoisie nor those who are participants in the disenfranchised underworld. "Middle-class" is used broadly to refer to the predominantly White American "mainstream." There are, of course, non-White people who also fit into this category; at issue is their cultural identification, not necessarily the color of their skin. (I must add that there are other non-White people, as well as poor White people, who have indicated to me that their perspectives are similar to those attributed herein to Black people.)
2. *Multicultural Britain: "Crosstalk,"* National Centre of Industrial Language Training, Commission for Racial Equality, London, England, John Twitchin, Producer.
3. I would like to thank Michelle Foster, who is presently planning a more in-depth treatment of the subject, for her astute clarification of the idea.
4. Bernstein (1975) makes a similar point when he proposes that different educational frames cannot be successfully institutionalized in the lower levels of education until there are fundamental changes at the postsecondary levels.

REFERENCES

Apple, M. W. (1979). *Ideology and curriculum.* Boston: Routledge & Kegan Paul.

Bernstein, B. (1975). Class and pedagogies: Visible and invisible. In B. Bernstein, *Class, codes, and control* (Vol. 3). Boston: Routledge & Kegan Paul.

Britton, J., Burgess, T., Martin, N., McLeod, A., & Rosen, H. (1975/1977). *The development of writing abilities.* London: Macmillan Education for the Schools Council, and Urbana, IL: National Council of Teachers of English.

Cazden, C. (1987, January). *The myth of autonomous text.* Paper presented at the Third International Conference on Thinking, Hawaii.

Delpit, L. D. (1986). Skills and other dilemmas of a progressive Black educator. *Harvard Educational Review, 56,* (4), 379–385.

Foster, M. (1987). *It's cookin' now: An ethnographic study of the teaching style of a successful Black teacher in an urban community college.* Unpublished doctoral dissertation, Harvard University.

Gwaltney, J. (1980). *Drylongso.* New York: Vintage Books.

Heath, S. B. (1983). *Ways with words.* Cambridge: Cambridge University Press.

Massey, G. C., Scott, M. V., & Dornbusch, S. M. (1975). Racism without racists: Institutional racism in urban schools. *Black Scholar, 7*(3), 2–11.

Siddle, E. V. (1986). *A critical assessment of the natural process approach to teaching writing.* Unpublished qualifying paper, Harvard University.

Siddle, E. V. (1988). *The effect of intervention strategies on the revisions ninth graders make in a narrative essay.* Unpublished doctoral dissertation, Harvard University.

Snow, C. E., Arlman-Rup, A., Hassing, Y., Josbe, J., Joosten, J., & Vorster, J. (1976). Mother's speech in three social classes. *Journal of Psycholinguistic Research, 5,* 1–20.

I take full responsibility for all that appears herein; however, aside from those mentioned by name in this text, I would like to thank all of the educators and students around the country who have been so willing to contribute their perspectives to the formulation of these ideas, especially Susan Jones, Catherine Blunt, Dee Stickman, Sandra Gamble, Willard Taylor, Mickey Monteiro, Denise Burden, Evelyn Higbee, Joseph Delpit Jr., Valerie Montoya, Richard Cohen, and Mary Denise Thompson.

Empowering Minority Students

A Framework for Intervention

JIM CUMMINS

During the past twenty years, educators in the United States have implemented a series of costly reforms aimed at reversing the pattern of school failure among minority students. These have included compensatory programs at the preschool level, myriad forms of bilingual education programs, the hiring of additional aides and remedial personnel, and the institution of safeguards against discriminatory assessment procedures. Yet the dropout rate among Mexican American and mainland Puerto Rican students remains between 40 and 50 percent compared to 14 percent for Whites and 25 percent for Blacks (Jusenius & Duarte, 1982). Similarly, almost a decade after the passage of the nondiscriminatory assessment provision of P.L. 94-142,[1] we find Hispanic students in Texas overrepresented by a factor of 300 percent in the "learning disabilities" category (Ortiz & Yates, 1983).

I have suggested that a major reason previous attempts at educational reform have been unsuccessful is that the relationships between teachers and students and between schools and communities have remained essentially unchanged. The required changes involve *personal redefinitions* of the way classroom teachers interact with the children and communities they serve. In other words, legislative and policy reforms may be necessary conditions for effective change, but they are not sufficient. Implementation of change is dependent upon the extent to which educators, both collectively and individually, redefine their roles with respect to minority students and communities.

The purpose of this paper is to propose a theoretical framework for examining the types of personal and institutional redefinitions that are required to reverse the pattern of minority student failure. The framework is based on a series of hypotheses regarding the nature of minority students' educational difficulties. These hypotheses, in turn, lead to predictions regarding the probable effectiveness, or ineffectiveness, of various interventions directed at reversing minority students' school failure.

Harvard Educational Review   Vol. 56   No. 1   February 1986, 18–36

The framework assigns a central role to three inclusive sets of interactions or power relations: (1) the classroom interactions between teachers and students, (2) relationships between schools and minority communities, and (3) the intergroup power relations within the society as a whole. It assumes that the social organization and bureaucratic constraints within the school reflect not only broader policy and societal factors but also the extent to which *individual educators* accept or challenge the social organization of the school in relation to minority students and communities. Thus, this analysis sketches directions for change for policymakers at all levels of the educational hierarchy and, in particular, for those working directly with minority students and communities.

THE POLICY CONTEXT

Research data from the United States, Canada, and Europe vary on the extent to which minority students experience academic failure (for reviews, see Cummins, 1984; Ogbu, 1978). For example, in the United States, Hispanic (with the exception of some groups of Cuban students), Native American, and Black students do poorly in school compared to most groups of Asian American (and White) students. In Canada, Franco-Ontarian students in English language programs have tended to perform considerably less well academically than immigrant minority groups (Cummins, 1984), while the same pattern characterizes Finnish students in Sweden (Skutnabb-Kangas, 1984).

The major task of theory and policy is to explain the pattern of school success and failure among minority students. This task applies both to students whose home language and culture differ from those of the school and wider society (language minority students) and to students whose home language is a version of English but whose cultural background is significantly different from that of the school and wider society, such as many Black and Hispanic students from English language backgrounds. With respect to language-minority students, recent policy changes in the United States have been based on the assumption that a major cause of students' educational difficulty is the switch between the language of the home and the language of the school. Thus, the apparently plausible assumption that students cannot learn in a language they do not understand gave rise in the late sixties and early seventies to bilingual education programs in which students' home language was used in addition to English as an initial medium of school instruction (Schneider, 1976).

Bilingual programs, however, have met with both strong support and vehement opposition. The debate regarding policy has revolved around two intuitively appealing assumptions. Those who favor bilingual education argue that children cannot learn in a language they do not understand, and, therefore, L1 (first language) instruction is necessary to counteract the negative effects of a home/school linguistic mismatch. The opposition contends that bilingual education is illogical in its implication that less English instruction will lead to more English achievement. It makes more sense, the opponents argue, to provide language-minority students with maximum exposure to English.

Despite the apparent plausibility of each assumption, these two conventional wisdoms (the "linguistic mismatch" and "insufficient exposure" hypotheses) are each patently inadequate. The argument that language minority students fail primarily as a result of a home/school language switch is refuted by the success of many minority students whose instruction has been totally through a second language. Similarly, research in Canada has documented the effectiveness of "French immersion programs" in which English background (majority language) students are instructed largely through French in the early grades as a means of developing fluent bilingualism. In spite of the home/school language switch, students' first language (English) skills develop as well as those of students whose instruction has been totally through English. The fact that the first language has high status and is strongly reinforced in the wider society is usually seen as an important factor in the success of these immersion programs.[2]

The opposing "insufficient exposure" hypothesis, however, fares no better with respect to the research evidence. In fact, the results of virtually every bilingual program that has been evaluated during the past fifty years show either no relationship or a negative relationship between amount of school exposure to the majority language and academic achievement in that language (Baker & de Kanter, 1981; Cummins, 1983a, 1984; Skutnabb-Kangas, 1984). Evaluations of immersion programs for majority students show that students perform as well in English academic skills as comparison groups despite considerably less exposure to English in school. Exactly the same result is obtained for minority students. Promotion of the minority language entails no loss in the development of English academic skills. In other words, language minority students instructed through the minority language (for example, Spanish) for all or part of the school day perform as well in English academic skills as comparable students instructed totally through English.

These results have been interpreted in terms of "interdependence hypothesis," which proposes that to the extent that instruction through a minority language is effective in developing academic proficiency in the minority language, transfer of this proficiency to the majority language will occur, given adequate exposure and motivation to learn the majority language (Cummins, 1979, 1983a, 1984). The interdependence hypothesis is supported by a large body of research from bilingual program evaluations, studies of language use in the home, immigrant student language learning, correlational studies of L1-L2 (second language) relationships, and experimental studies of bilingual information processing (for reviews, see Cummins, 1984; McLaughlin, 1985).

It is not surprising that the two conventional wisdoms inadequately account for the research data, since each involves only a one-dimensional linguistic explanation. The variability of minority students' academic performance under different social and educational conditions indicates that many complex, interrelated factors are at work (Ogbu, 1978; Wong-Fillmore, 1983). In particular, sociological and anthropological research suggests that status and power relations between groups are an important part of any comprehensive account of minority students' school failure (Fishman, 1976; Ogbu, 1978; Paulston, 1980). In addition, a variety of factors related to educational quality and cultural mismatch also appear to be important in mediating minority students' academic progress (Wong-Fillmore, 1983). These factors have been integrated into the design of a theoretical framework that suggests the changes required to reverse minority student failure.

A THEORETICAL FRAMEWORK

The central tenet of the framework is that students from "dominated" societal groups are "empowered" or "disabled" as a direct result of their interactions with educators in the schools. These interactions are mediated by the implicit or explicit role definitions that educators assume in relation to four institutional characteristics of schools. These characteristics reflect the extent to which 1) minority students' language and culture are incorporated into the school program; 2) minority community participation is encouraged as an integral component of children's education; 3) the pedagogy promotes intrinsic motivation on the part of students to use language actively in order to generate their own knowledge; and 4) professionals involved in assessment become advocates for minority students rather than legitimizing the location of the "problem" in the students. For each of these dimensions of school organization the role definitions of educators can be described in terms of a continuum, with one end promoting the empowerment of students and the other contributing to the disabling of students.

The three sets of relationships analyzed in the present framework — majority/minority societal group relations, school/minority community relations, educator/minority student relations — are chosen on the basis of hypotheses regarding the relative ineffectiveness of previous educational reforms and the directions required to reverse minority group school failure. Each of these relationships will be discussed in detail.

INTERGROUP POWER RELATIONS

When the patterns of minority student school failure are examined from an international perspective, it becomes evident that power and status relations between minority and majority groups exert a major influence on school performance. An example frequently given is the academic failure of Finnish students in Sweden, where they are a low-status group, compared to their success in Australia, where they are regarded as a high-status group (Troike, 1978). Similarly, Ogbu (1978) reports that the outcast Burakumin perform poorly in Japan but as well as other Japanese students in the United States.

Theorists have explained these findings using several constructs. Cummins (1984), for example, discusses the "bicultural ambivalence" (or lack of cultural identification) of students in relation to both the home and school cultures. Ogbu (1978) discusses the "caste" status of minorities that fail academically and ascribes their failure to economic and social discrimination combined with the internalization of the inferior status attributed to them by the dominant group. Feuerstein (1979) attributes academic failure to the disruption of intergenerational transmission processes caused by the alienation of a group from its own culture. In all three conceptions, widespread school failure does not occur in minority groups that are positively oriented towards both their own and the dominant culture, that do not perceive themselves as inferior to the dominant group, and that are not alienated from their own cultural values.

Within the present framework, the *dominant* group controls the institutions and reward systems within society; the *dominated* group (Mullard, 1985) is regarded as inherently inferior by the dominant group and denied access to high-status positions within the institutional structure of the society. As described by Ogbu (1978), the dominated status of a minority group exposes them to conditions that predispose children to school failure even before they come to school. These conditions include limited parental access to economic and educational resources, ambivalence toward cultural transmission and primary language use in the home, and interactional styles that may not prepare students for typical teacher/student interaction patterns in school (Heath, 1983; Wong-Fillmore, 1983). Bicultural ambivalence and less effective cultural transmission among dominated groups are frequently associated with a historical pattern of colonization and subordination by the dominant group. This pattern, for example, characterizes Franco-Ontarian students in Canada, Finns in Sweden, and Hispanic, Native, and Black groups in the United States.

Different patterns among other societal groups can clearly be distinguished (Ogbu & Matute-Bianchi, in press). Detailed analysis of patterns of intergroup relations go beyond the scope of this paper. However, it is important to note that the minority groups characterized by widespread school failure tend overwhelmingly to be in a dominated relationship to the majority group.[3]

Empowerment of Students

Students who are empowered by their school experiences develop the ability, confidence, and motivation to succeed academically. They participate competently in instruction as a result of having developed a confident cultural identity as well as appropriate school-based knowledge and interactional structures (Cummins, 1983b; Tikunoff, 1983). Students who are disempowered or "disabled" by their school experiences do not develop this type of cognitive/academic and social/emotional foundation. Thus, student empowerment is regarded both as a mediating construct influencing academic performance and as an outcome variable itself.[4]

Although conceptually the cognitive/academic and social/emotional (identity-related) factors are distinct, the data suggest that they are extremely difficult to separate in the case of minority students who are "at risk" academically. For example, data from both Sweden and the United States suggest that minority students who immigrate relatively late (about ten years of age) often appear to have better academic prospects than students of similar socioeconomic status born in the host country (Cummins, 1984; Skutnabb-Kangas, 1984). Is this because their L1 cognitive/academic skills on arrival provide a better foundation for L2 cognitive/academic skills acquisition, or alternatively, because they have not experienced devaluation of their identity in the societal institutions, namely schools of the host country, as has been the case of students born in that setting?

Similarly, the most successful bilingual programs appear to be those that emphasize and use the students' L1 (for reviews, see Cummins 1983a, 1984). Is this success due to better promotion of L1 cognitive/academic skills or to the reinforcement of cultural identity provided by an intensive L1 program? By the same token, is the failure of many minority students in English-only immersion programs a function of cognitive/academic difficulties or of students' ambivalence about the value of their cultural identity (Cohen & Swain, 1976)?

These questions are clearly difficult to answer; the point to be made, however, is that for minority students who have traditionally experienced school failure, there is sufficient overlap in the impact of cognitive/academic and identity factors to justify incorporating these two dimensions within the notion of "student empowerment," while recognizing that under some conditions each dimension may be affected in different ways.

Schools and Power

Minority students are disabled or disempowered by schools in very much the same way that their communities are disempowered by interactions with societal institutions. Since equality of opportunity is believed to be a given, it is assumed that individuals are responsible for their own failure and are, therefore, made to feel that they have failed because of their own inferiority, despite the best efforts of dominant-group institutions and individuals to help them (Skutnabb-Kangas, 1984). This analysis implies that minority students will succeed educationally to the extent that the patterns of interaction in school reverse those that prevail in the society at large.

Four structural elements in the organization of schooling contribute to the extent to which minority students are empowered or disabled. As outlined in Figure 1, these elements include the incorporation of minority students' culture and language, inclusion of minority communities in the education of their children, pedagogical assumptions and practices operating in the classroom, and the assessment of minority students.

Cultural/linguistic incorporation. Considerable research data suggest that, for dominated minorities, the extent to which students' language and culture are incorporated into the school program constitutes a significant predictor of academic success (Campos & Keatinge, 1984; Cummins, 1983a; Rosier & Holm, 1980). As outlined earlier, students' school success appears to reflect both the more solid cognitive/academic foundation developed through intensive L1 instruction and the reinforcement of their cultural identity.

Included under incorporation of minority group cultural features is the adjustment of instructional patterns to take account of culturally conditioned learning styles. The Kamehameha Early Education Program in Hawaii provides strong evidence of the importance of this type of cultural incorporation. When reading instruction was changed to permit students to collaborate in discussing and interpreting texts, dramatic improvements were found in both reading and verbal intellectual abilities (Au & Jordan, 1981).

An important issue to consider at this point is why superficially plausible but patently inadequate assumptions, such as the "insufficient exposure" hypothesis, continue to dominate the policy debate when virtually all the evidence suggests that incorporation of minority students' language and culture into the school program will at least not impede academic progress. In other words, what social function do such arguments serve? Within the context of the present framework, it is suggested that a major reason for the vehement resistance to bilingual programs is that the incorporation of minority languages and cultures into the school program confers status and power (jobs, for example) on the minority group. Consequently, such programs contravene the established pattern of dominant/dominated group relations. Within democratic societies, however, contradictions between the rhetoric of equality and the re-

FIGURE I

Empowerment of Minority Students: A Theoretical Framework

SOCIETAL CONTEXT

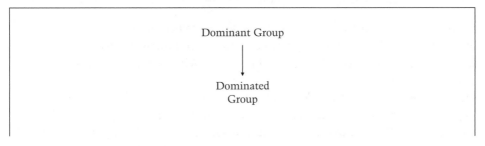

Dominant Group

Dominated
Group

SCHOOL CONTEXT

Educator Role Definitions

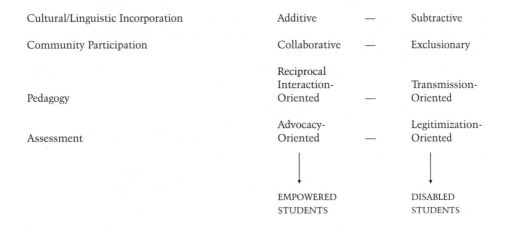

Cultural/Linguistic Incorporation	Additive	—	Subtractive
Community Participation	Collaborative	—	Exclusionary
Pedagogy	Reciprocal Interaction-Oriented	—	Transmission-Oriented
Assessment	Advocacy-Oriented	—	Legitimization-Oriented
	EMPOWERED STUDENTS		DISABLED STUDENTS

ality of domination must be obscured. Thus, conventional wisdoms such as the insufficient exposure hypothesis become immune to critical scrutiny, and incompatible evidence is either ignored or dismissed.

Educators' role definitions in relation to the incorporation of minority students' language and culture can be characterized along an "additive-subtractive" dimension.[5] Educators who see their role as adding a second language and cultural affiliation to their students' repertoire are likely to empower students more than those who see their role as replacing or subtracting students' primary language and culture. In addition to the personal and future employment advantages of proficiency in two languages, there is considerable, though not conclusive, evidence that subtle educational advantages result from continued development of both languages among bilingual students. Enhanced metalinguistic development, for example, is frequently found in association with additive bilingualism (Hakuta & Diaz, 1985; McLaughlin, 1984).

It should be noted that an additive orientation does not require the actual teaching of the minority language. In many cases a minority language class may not be possible, for reasons such as low concentration of particular groups of minority students. Educators, however, communicate to students and parents in a variety of ways the extent to which the minority language and culture are valued within the context of the school. Even within a monolingual school context, powerful messages can be communicated to students regarding the validity and advantages of language development.

Community participation. Students from dominated communities will be empowered in the school context to the extent that the communities themselves are empowered through their interactions with the school. When educators involve minority parents as partners in their children's education, parents appear to develop a sense of efficacy that communicates itself to children, with positive academic consequences.

Although lip service is paid to community involvement through Parent Advisory Committees (PAC)[6] in many education programs, these committees are frequently manipulated through misinformation and intimidation (Curtis, 1984). The result is that parents from dominated groups retain their powerless status, and their internalized inferiority is reinforced. Children's school failure can then be attributed to the combined effects of parental illiteracy and lack of interest in their children's education. In reality, most parents of minority students have high aspirations for their children and want to be involved in promoting their academic progress (Wong-Fillmore, 1983). However, they often do not know how to help their children academically, and they are excluded from participation by the school. In fact, even their interaction through L1 with their children in the home is frequently regarded by educators as contributing to academic difficulties (Cummins, 1984).

Dramatic changes in children's academic progress can be realized when educators take the initiative to change this exclusionary pattern to one of collaboration. The Haringey project in Britain illustrates just how powerful the effects of simple interventions can be (Tizard, Schofield, & Hewison, 1982). In order to assess the effects of parental involvement in the teaching of reading, the researchers established a project in the London borough of Haringey whereby all children in two primary level experimental classes in two different schools read to their parents at home on a regular basis. The reading progress of these children was compared with that of children in two classes in two different schools who were given extra reading instruction in small groups by an experienced and qualified teacher who worked four half-days at each school every week for the two years of the intervention. Both groups were also compared with a control group that received no treatment.

All the schools were in multiethnic areas, and there were many parents who did not read English or use it at home. It was found, nevertheless, to be both feasible and practicable to involve nearly all the parents in educational activities such as listening to their children read, even when the parents were nonliterate and largely non-English-speaking. It was also found that, almost without exception, parents welcomed the project, agreed to hear their children read, and completed a record card showing what had been read.

The researchers report that parental involvement had a pronounced effect on the students' success in school. Children who read to their parents made significantly greater progress in reading than those who did not engage in this type of literacy sharing. Small-group instruction in reading, given by a highly competent specialist, did not produce improvements comparable to those obtained from the collaboration with parents. In contrast to the home collaboration program, the benefits of extra reading instruction were least apparent for initially low-achieving children.

In addition, the collaboration between teachers and parents was effective for children of all initial levels of performance, including those who, at the beginning of the study, were failing in learning to read. Teachers reported that the children showed an increased interest in school learning and were better behaved. Those teachers involved in the home collaboration found the work with parents worthwhile, and they continued to involve parents with subsequent classes after the experiment was concluded. It is interesting to note that teachers of the control classes also adopted the home collaboration program after the two-year experimental period.

The Haringey project is one example of school/community relations; there are others. The essential point, however, is that the teacher's role in such relations can be characterized along a *collaborative-exclusionary* dimension. Teachers operating at the collaborative end of the continuum actively encourage minority parents to participate in promoting their children's academic progress both in the home and through involvement in classroom activities. A collaborative orientation may require a willingness on the part of the teacher to work closely with mother-tongue teachers or aides in order to communicate effectively, in a noncondescending way, with minority parents. Teachers with an exclusionary orientation, on the other hand, tend to regard teaching as *their* job and are likely to view collaboration with minority parents as either irrelevant or detrimental to children's progress.

Pedagogy. Several investigators have suggested that many "learning disabilities" are pedagogically induced in that children designated "at risk" frequently receive intensive instruction which confines them to a passive role and induces a form of "learned helplessness" (Beers & Beers, 1980; Coles, 1978; Cummins, 1984). This process is illustrated in a microethnographic study of fourteen reading lessons given to West Indian Creole-speakers of English in Toronto, Canada (Ramphal, 1983). It was found that teachers' constant correction of students' miscues prevented students from focusing on the meaning of what they were reading. Moreover, the constant corrections fostered dependent behavior because students knew that whenever they paused at a word the teacher would automatically pronounce it for them. One student was interrupted so often in one of the lessons that he was able to read only one sentence, consisting of three words, uninterrupted. In contrast to a pattern of classroom interaction which promotes instructional dependence, teaching that empowers will aim to liberate students from instruction by encouraging them to become active generators of their knowledge. As Graves (1983) has demonstrated, this type of active knowledge generation can occur when, for example, children create and publish their own books within the classroom.

Two major pedagogical orientations can be distinguished. These differ in the extent to which the teacher retains exclusive control over classroom interaction as opposed to sharing some of this control with students. The dominant instructional model in North American schools has been termed a transmission model (Barnes, 1976; Wells, 1982). This model incorporates essentially the same assumptions about teaching and learning that Freire (1970, 1973) has termed a "banking" model of education. This transmission model will be contrasted with a "reciprocal interaction" model of pedagogy.

The basic premise of the transmission model is that the teacher's task is to impart knowledge or skills that she or he possesses to students who do not yet have these skills. This implies that the teacher initiates and controls the interaction, constantly orienting it towards the achievement of instructional objectives. For example, in first- and second-language programs that stress pattern repetition, the teacher presents the materials, models the language patterns, asks questions, and provides feedback to students about the correctness of their response. The curriculum in these types of programs focuses on the internal structure of the language or subject matter. Consequently, it frequently focuses predominantly on surface features of language or literacy such as handwriting, spelling, and decoding, and emphasizes correct recall of content taught by means of highly structured drills and workbook exercises. It has been argued that a transmission model of teaching contravenes central principles of language and literacy acquisition and that a model allowing for reciprocal interaction among students and teachers represents a more appropriate alternative (Cummins, 1984; Wells, 1982).[7]

A central tenet of the reciprocal interaction model is that "talking and writing are means to learning" (Bullock Report, 1975, p. 50). The use of this model in teaching requires a genuine dialogue between student and teacher in both oral and written modalities, guidance and facilitation rather than control of student learning by the teacher, and the encouragement of student/student talk in a collaborative learning context. This model emphasizes the development of higher level cognitive skills rather than just factual recall, and meaningful language use by students rather than the correction of surface forms. Language use and development are consciously integrated with all curricular content rather than taught as isolated subjects, and tasks are presented to students in ways that generate intrinsic rather than extrinsic motivation. In short, pedagogical approaches that empower students encourage them to assume greater control over setting their own learning goals and to collaborate actively with each other in achieving these goals.

The development of a sense of efficacy and inner direction in the classroom is especially important for students from dominated groups whose experiences so often orient them in the opposite direction. Wong-Fillmore (1983) has reported that Hispanic students learned considerably more English in classrooms that provided opportunities for reciprocal interaction with teachers and peers. Ample opportunities for expressive writing appear to be particularly significant in promoting a sense of academic efficacy among minority students (Cummins, Aguilar, Bascunan, Fiorucci, Sanaoui, & Basman, in press). As expressed by Daiute (1985):

> Children who learn early that writing is not simply an exercise gain a sense of power that gives them confidence to write — and write a lot. . . . Beginning writers who are confident that they have something to say or that they can find out what they need to know can even overcome some limits of training or development. Writers who don't feel that what they say matters have an additional burden that no skills training can help them overcome. (pp. 5–6)

The implications for students from dominated groups are obvious. Too often the instruction they receive convinces them that what they have to say is irrelevant or wrong. The failure of this method of instruction is then taken as an indication that the minority student is of low ability, a verdict frequently confirmed by subsequent assessment procedures.

Assessment. Historically, assessment has played the role of legitimizing the disabling of minority students. In some cases assessment itself may play the primary role, but more often it has been used to locate the "problem" within the minority student, thereby screening from critical scrutiny the subtractive nature of the school program, the exclusionary orientation of teachers toward minority communities, and transmission models of teaching that inhibit students from active participation in learning.

This process is virtually inevitable when the conceptual base for assessment is purely psychoeducational. If the psychologist's task is to discover the causes of a minority student's academic difficulties and the only tools at his or her disposal are psychological tests (in either L1 or L2), then it is hardly surprising that the child's difficulties will be attributed to psychological dysfunctions. The myth of bilingual handicaps that still influences educational policy was generated in exactly this way during the 1920s and 1930s.

Recent studies suggest that despite the appearance of change brought about by P.L. 94-142, the underlying structure of assessment processes has remained essentially intact. Mehan, Hertweck, and Meihls (in press), for example, report that psychologists continued to test children until they "found" the disability that could be invoked to "explain" the student's apparent academic difficulties. Diagnosis and placement were influenced frequently by factors related to bureaucratic procedures and funding requirements rather than to students' academic performance in the classroom. Rueda and Mercer (1985) have also shown that designation of minority students as "learning disabled" as compared to "language impaired" was strongly influenced by whether a psychologist or a speech pathologist was on the placement committee. In other words, with respect to students' actual behavior, the label was essentially arbitrary. An analysis of more than four hundred psychological assessments of minority students revealed that although no diagnostic conclusions were logically possible in the majority of assessments, psychologists were most reluctant to admit this fact to teachers and parents (Cummins, 1984). In short, the data suggest that the structure within which psychological assessment takes place orients the psychologist to locate the cause of the academic problem within the minority student.

An alternative role definition for psychologists or special educators can be termed an "advocacy" or "delegitimization" role.[8] In this case, their task must be to delegitimize the traditional function of psychological assessment in the educational disabling of minority students by becoming advocates for the child in scrutinizing critically the societal and educational context within which the child has developed (Cazden, 1985). This involves locating the pathology within the societal power relations between dominant and dominated groups, in the reflection of these power relations between school and communities, and in the mental and cultural disabling of minority students that takes place in classrooms. These conditions are a more probable cause of the 300 percent overrepresentation of Texas Hispanic students in the learning disabled category than any intrinsic processing deficit unique to Hispanic children. The training of psychologists and special educators does not prepare them for this advocacy or delegitimization role. From the present perspective, however, it must be emphasized that discriminatory assessment is carried out by well-intentioned individuals who, rather than challenging a socioeducational system that tends to disable minority students, have accepted a role definition and an educational structure that makes discriminatory assessment virtually inevitable.[9]

EMPOWERING MINORITY STUDENTS: THE CARPINTERIA EXAMPLE

The Spanish-only preschool program of the Carpinteria School District, near Santa Barbara, California, is one of the few programs in the United States that explicitly incorporates the major elements hypothesized in previous sections to empower minority students. Spanish is the exclusive language of instruction, there is a strong community involvement component, and the program is characterized by a coherent philosophy of promoting conceptual development through meaningful linguistic interaction.

The proposal to implement an intensive Spanish-only preschool program in this region was derived from district findings showing that a large majority of the Spanish-speaking students entering kindergarten each year lacked adequate skills to succeed in the kindergarten program. On the School Readiness Inventory, a districtwide screening measure administered to all incoming kindergarten students, Spanish-speaking students tended to average about eight points lower than English-speaking students (approximately 14.5 compared to 23.0, averaged over four years from 1979 to 1982) despite the fact that the test was administered in students' dominant language. A score of 20 or better was viewed by the district as predicting a successful kindergarten year for the child. Prior to the implementation of the experimental program, the Spanish-background children attended a bilingual preschool program — operated either by Head Start or the Community Day Care Center — in which both English and Spanish were used concurrently but with strong emphasis on the development of English skills. According to the district kindergarten teachers, children who had attended these programs often mixed English and Spanish into a "Spanglish."

The major goal of the experimental Spanish-only preschool program was to bring Spanish-dominant children entering kindergarten up to a level of readiness for school similar to that attained by English-speaking children in the community. The project also sought to make parents of the program participants aware of their role as the child's first teacher and to encourage them to provide specific types of experiences for their children in the home.

The preschool program itself involved the integration of language with a large variety of concrete and literacy-related experiences. As summarized in the evaluation report: "The development of language skills in Spanish was foremost in the planning and attention given to every facet of the pre-school day. Language was used constantly for conversing, learning new ideas, concepts and vocabulary, thinking creatively, and problem-solving to give the children the opportunity to develop their language skills in Spanish to as high a degree as possible within the structure of the pre-school day" (Campos & Keatinge, 1984, p. 17).

Participation in the program was on a voluntary basis and students were screened only for age and Spanish-language dominance. Family characteristics of students in the experimental program were typical of other Spanish-speaking families in the community; more than 90 percent were of low socioeconomic status, and the majority worked in agriculture and had an average educational level of about the sixth grade.

The program proved to be highly successful in developing students' readiness skills, as evidenced by the average score of 21.6 obtained by the 1982–1983 incoming kindergarten students who had been in the program, compared to the score of 23.2 obtained by English-speaking students. A score of 14.6 was obtained by Spanish-speaking students who experienced the regular bilingual preschool program. In 1983–1984 the scores of these three groups were 23.3, 23.4, and 16.0, respectively. In other words, the gap between English-background and Spanish-background children in the Spanish-only preschool had disappeared; however, a considerable gap remained for Spanish-background students for whom English was the focus of pre-school instruction.

Of special interest is the performance of the experimental program students on the English and Spanish versions of the Bilingual Syntax Measure (BSM), a test of oral syntactic development (Hernandez-Chavez, Burt, & Dulay, 1976). Despite the fact that they experienced an exclusively Spanish preschool program, these students performed better than the other Spanish-speaking students in English (and Spanish) on entry to kindergarten in 1982 and at a similar level in 1983. On entrance to grade one in 1983, the gap had widened considerably, with almost five times as many of the experimental-program students performing at level 5 (fluent English) compared to the other Spanish-background students (47 percent v. 10 percent) (Campos & Keatinge, 1984).

The evaluation report suggests that

> although project participants were exposed to less *total* English, they, because of their enhanced first language skill and concept knowledge, were better able to comprehend the English they were exposed to. This seems to be borne out by comments made by kindergarten teachers in the District about project participants. They are making comments like, "Project participants appear more aware of what is happening around them in the classroom," "They are able to focus on the task at hand better" and "They demonstrate greater self-confidence in learning situations." All of these traits would tend to enhance the language acquisition process. (Campos & Keatinge, 1984, p. 41)

Campos and Keatinge (1984) also emphasize the consequences of the preschool program for parental participation in their children's education. They note that, according to the school officials, "the parents of project participants are much more aware of and involved with their child's school experience than non-participant parents of Spanish speakers. This is seen as having a positive impact on the future success of the project participants — the greater the involvement of parents, the greater the chances of success of the child" (p. 41).

The major relevance of these findings for educators and policymakers derives from their demonstration that educational programs *can* succeed in preventing the academic failure experienced by many minority students. The corollary is that failure to provide this type of program constitutes the disabling of minority students by the school system. For example, among the students who did not experience the experimental preschool program, the typical pattern of low levels of academic readiness and limited proficiency in both languages was observed. These are the students who are likely to be referred for psychological assessment early in their school careers. This assessment will typically legitimize the inadequate educational provision by attributing students' difficulties to some vacuous category, such as learning disability. By contrast, students who experienced a preschool program in which (a) their cultural identity was reinforced, (b) there was active collaboration with parents, and (c) meaningful use of language was integrated into every aspect of daily activities were developing high levels of conceptual and linguistic skills in *both* languages.

CONCLUSION

In this article I have proposed a theoretical framework for examining minority students' academic failure and for predicting the effects of educational interventions. Within this framework the educational failure of minority students is analyzed as a function of the extent to which schools reflect or counteract the power relations that exist within the broader society. Specifically, language-minority students' educational progress is strongly influenced by the extent to which individual educators become advocates for the promotion of students' linguistic talents, actively encourage community participation in developing students' academic and cultural resources, and implement pedagogical approaches that succeed in liberating students from instructional dependence.

The educator/student interactions characteristic of the disabling end of the proposed continua reflect the typical patterns of interaction that dominated societal groups have experienced in relation to dominant groups. The intrinsic value of the group is usually denied, and "objective" evidence is accumulated to demonstrate the group's "inferiority." This inferior status is then used as a justification for excluding the group from activities and occupations that entail societal rewards.

In a similar way, the disabling of students is frequently rationalized on the basis of students' "needs." For example, minority students need maximum exposure to English in both the school and the home; thus, parents must be told not to interact with children in their mother tongue. Similarly, minority children need a highly structured drill-oriented program in order to maximize time spent on tasks to compensate for their deficient preschool experiences. Minority students also need a comprehensive diagnostic/prescriptive assessment in order to identify the nature of their "problem" and possible remedial interventions.

This analysis suggests a major reason for the relative lack of success of the various educational bandwagons that have characterized the North American crusade against underachievement during the past twenty years. The individual role definitions of educators and the institutional role definitions of schools have remained largely unchanged despite "new and improved" programs and policies. These programs and policies, despite their cost, have simply added a new veneer to the outward facade of the structure that disables minority students. The lip service paid to initial L1 instruction, community involvement, and nondiscriminatory assessment, together with the emphasis on improved teaching techniques, has succeeded primarily in deflecting attention from the attitudes and orientation of educators who interact on a daily basis with minority students. It is in these interactions that students are disabled. In the absence of individual and collective educator role redefinitions, schools will continue to reproduce, in these interactions, the power relations that characterize the wider society and make minority students' academic failure inevitable.

To educators genuinely concerned about alleviating the educational difficulties of minority students and responding to their needs, this conclusion may appear overly bleak. I believe, however, that it is realistic and optimistic, as directions for change are clearly indicated rather than obscured by the overlay of costly reforms that leave the underlying disabling structure essentially intact. Given the societal commitment to maintaining the dominant-dominated power relationships, we can predict that educational changes threatening this structure will be fiercely resisted. This is in fact the case for each of the four structural dimensions discussed earlier.[10]

In order to reverse the pattern of widespread minority group educational failure, educators and policymakers are faced with both a personal and a political challenge. Personally, they must redefine their roles within the classroom, the community, and the broader society so that these role definitions result in interactions that empower rather than disable students. Politically, they must attempt to persuade colleagues and decisionmakers — such as school boards and the public that elects them — of the importance of redefining institutional goals so that the schools transform society by empowering minority students rather than reflect society by disabling them.

NOTES

1. The Education for All Handicapped Children Act of 1975 (Public Law 94-142) guarantees to all handicapped children in the United States the right to a free public education, to an individualized education program (IEP), to due process, to education in the least segregated environment, and to assessment procedures that are multidimensional and nonculturally discriminatory.

2. For a discussion of the implications of Canadian French immersion programs for the education of minority students, see California State Department of Education (1984).

3. Ogbu (1978), for example, has distinguished between "caste," "immigrant," and "autonomous" minority groups. Caste groups are similar to what have been termed "dominated" groups in the present framework and are the only category of minority groups that tends to fail academically. Immigrant groups have usually come voluntarily to the host society for economic reasons and, unlike caste minorities, have not internalized negative attributions of the dominant group. Ogbu gives Chinese and Japanese groups as examples of "immigrant" minorities. The cultural resources that permit some minority groups to resist discrimination and internalization of negative attributions are still a matter of debate and speculation (for a recent treatment, see Ogbu & Matute-Bianchi, in press). The final category distinguished by Ogbu is that of "autonomous" groups who hold a distinct cultural identity but who are not subordinated economically or politically to the dominant group (for example, Jews and Mormons in the United States).

   Failure to take account of these differences among minority groups both in patterns of academic performance and sociohistorical relationships to the dominant group has contributed to the confused state of policymaking with respect to language minority students. The bilingual education policy, for example, has been based on the implicit assumption that the linguistic mismatch hypothesis was valid for all language minority students, and, consequently, the same types of intervention were necessary and appropriate for all students. Clearly, this assumption is open to question.

4. There is no contradiction in postulating student empowerment as both a mediating and an outcome variable. For example, cognitive abilities clearly have the same status in that they contribute to students' school success and can also be regarded as an outcome of schooling.

5. The terms "additive" and "subtractive" bilingualism were coined by Lambert (1975) to refer to the proficient bilingualism associated with positive cognitive outcomes on the one hand, and the limited bilingualism often associated with negative outcomes on the other.

6. PACs were established in some states to provide an institutional structure for minority parent involvement in educational decisionmaking with respect to bilingual programs. In California, for example, a majority of PAC members for any state-funded program was required to be from the program target group. The school plan for use of program funds required signed PAC approval.

7. This "reciprocal interaction" model incorporates proposals about the relation between language and learning made by a variety of investigators, most notably in the Bullock Report (1975), and by Barnes (1976), Lindfors (1980), and Wells (1982). Its application with respect to the promotion of literacy conforms closely to psycholinguistic approaches to reading (Goodman & Goodman, 1977; Holdaway, 1979; Smith, 1978) and to the recent emphasis on encouraging expressive writing from the earliest grades (Chomsky, 1981; Giacobbe, 1982; Graves, 1983; Temple, Nathan, & Burris, 1982). Students' microcomputing networks such as the *Computer Chronicles Newswire* (Mehan, Miller-Souviney, & Riel, 1984) represent a particularly promising application of reciprocal interaction model of pedagogy.

8. See Mullard (1985) for a detailed discussion of delegitimization strategies in anti-racist education.

9. Clearly, the presence of processing difficulties that are rooted in neurological causes is not being denied for either monolingual or bilingual children. However, in the case of children from dominated minorities, the proportion of disabilities that are neurological in origin is likely to represent only a small fraction of those that derive from educational and social conditions.

10. Although for pedagogy the resistance to sharing control with students goes beyond majority/ minority group relations, the same elements are present. If the curriculum is not predetermined and presequenced, and the students are generating their own knowledge in a critical and creative way, then the reproduction of the societal structure cannot be guaranteed — hence the reluctance to liberate students from instructional dependence.

REFERENCES

Au, K. H., & Jordan, C. (1981). Teaching reading to Hawaiian children: Finding a culturally appropriate solution. In H. Trueba, G. P. Guthrie, & K. H. Au (Eds.), *Culture and the bilingual classroom: Studies in classroom ethnography* (pp. 139–152). Rowley, MA: Newbury House.

Baker, K. A., & de Kanter, A. A. (1981). *Effectiveness of bilingual education: A review of the literature.* Washington, DC: U.S. Department of Education, Office of Planning and Budget.

Barnes, D. (1976). *From communication to curriculum.* New York: Penguin.

Beers, C. S., & Beers, J. W. (1980). Early identification of learning disabilities: Facts and fallacies. *Elementary School Journal, 81,* 67–76.

Bethell, T. (1979, February). Against bilingual education. *Harper's,* pp. 30–33.

Bullock Report. (1975). *A language for life* (Report of the Committee of Inquiry appointed by the Secretary of State for Education and Science under the Chairmanship of Sir Alan Bullock). London: HMSO.

California State Department of Education. (1984). *Studies on immersion education: A collection for United States educators.* Sacramento: Author.

Campos, J., & Keatinge, B. (1984). *The Carpinteria preschool program: Title VII second year evaluation report.* Washington, DC: Department of Education.

Cazden, C. B. (1985, April). *The ESL teacher as advocate.* Plenary presentation to the TESOL Conference, New York.

Chomsky, C. (1981). Write now, read later. In C. Cazden (Ed.), *Language in early childhood education* (2nd ed., pp. 141–149). Washington, DC: National Association for the Education of Young Children.

Cohen, A. D., & Swain, M. (1976). Bilingual education: The immersion model in the North American context. In J. E. Alatis & K. Twaddell (Eds.), *English as a second language in bilingual education* (pp. 55–64). Washington, DC: TESOL.

Coles, G. S. (1978). The learning disabilities test battery: Empirical and social issues. *Harvard Educational Review, 48,* 313–340.

Cummins, J. (1979). Linguistic interdependence and the educational development of bilingual children. *Review of Educational Research 49,* 222–251.

Cummins, J. (1983a) *Heritage language education: A literature review.* Toronto: Ministry of Education.

Cummins, J. (1983b). Functional language proficiency in context: Classroom participation as an interactive process. In W. J. Tikunoff (Ed.), *Compatibility of the SBIS features with other research on instruction for LEP students* (pp. 109–131). San Francisco: Far West Laboratory.

Cummins, J., Aguilar, M., Bascunan, L., Fiorucci, S., Sanaoui, R., & Basman, S. (in press). Literacy development in heritage language program. Toronto: National Heritage Language Resource Unit.

Curtis, J. (1984). *Bilingual education in Calistoga: Not a happy ending.* Report submitted to the Instituto de Lengua y Cultura, Elmira, NY.

Daiute, C. (1985). *Writing and computers*. Reading, MA: Addison-Wesley.

Feuerstein, R. (1979). *The dynamic assessment of retarded performers: The learning potential assessment device, theory, instruments, and techniques*. Baltimore: University Park Press.

Fishman, J. (1976). *Bilingual education: An international sociological perspective*. Rowley, MA: Newbury House.

Freire, P. (1970). *Pedagogy of the oppressed*. New York: Seabury.

Freire, P. (1973). *Education for critical consciousness*. New York: Seabury.

Giacobbe, M. E. (1982). Who says children can't write the first week? In R. D. Walshe (Ed.), *Donald Graves in Australia: "Children want to write"* (pp. 99–103). Exeter, NH: Heinemann Educational Books.

Goodman, K. S., & Goodman, Y. M. (1977). Learning about psycholinguistic processes by analyzing oral reading. *Harvard Educational Review, 47*, 317–333.

Graves, D. H. (1983). *Writing: Teachers and children at work*. Exeter, NH: Heinemann Educational Books.

Hakuta, K., & Diaz, R. M. (1985). The relationship between degree of bilingualism and cognitive ability: A critical discussion and some new longitudinal data. In K. E. Nelson (Ed.), *Children's language* (Vol. 5, pp. 319–345). Hillsdale, NJ: Erlbaum.

Heath, S. B. (1983). *Ways with words*. Cambridge, Eng.: Cambridge University Press.

Hernandez-Chavez, E., Burt, M., & Dulay, H. (1976). *The bilingual syntax measure*. New York: The Psychological Corporation.

Holdaway, D. (1979). *The foundations of literacy*. Sydney, Australia: Ashton Scholastic.

Jusenius, C., & Duarte, V. L. (1982). *Hispanics and jobs: Barriers to progress*. Washington, DC: National Commission for Employment Policy.

Lambert, W. E. (1975). Culture and language as factors in learning and education. In A. Wolfgang (Ed.), *Education of immigrant students* (pp. 55–83). Toronto: O.I.S.E.

Lindfors, J. W. (1980). *Children's language and learning*. Englewood Cliffs, NJ: Prentice-Hall.

McLaughlin, B. (1984). Early bilingualism: Methodological and theoretical issues. In M. Paradis & Y. Lebrun (Eds.), *Early bilingualism and child development* (pp. 19–46). Lisse: Swets & Zeitlinger.

McLaughlin, B. (1985). *Second language acquisition in childhood: Vol. 2. School-age children*. Hillsdale, NJ: Erlbaum.

Mehan, H., Hertweck, A., & Meihls, J. L. (1986). *Handicapping the handicapped: Decision making in students' educational careers*. Palo Alto: Stanford University.

Mehan, H., Miller-Souviney, B., & Riel, M. M. (1984). Research currents: Knowledge of text editing and control of literacy skills. *Language Arts, 65*, 154–159.

Mullard, C. (1985, January). *The social dynamic of migrant groups: From progressive to transformative policy in education*. Paper presented at the OECD Conference on Educational Policies and the Minority Social Groups, Paris.

Ogbu, J. U. (1978). *Minority education and caste*. New York: Academic Press.

Ogbu, J. U., & Matute-Bianchi, M. E. (in press). Understanding sociocultural factors: Knowledge, identity and school adjustment. In California State Department of Education (Ed.), *Sociocultural factors and minority student achievement*. Sacramento: Author.

Ortiz, A. A., & Yates, J. R. (1983). Incidence of exceptionality among Hispanics: Implications for manpower planning. *NABE Journal, 7*, 41–54.

Paulston, C. B. (1980). *Bilingual education: Theories and issues*. Rowley, MA: Newbury House.

Ramphal, D. K. *An analysis of reading instruction of West Indian Creole-speaking students*. Unpublished doctoral dissertation, Ontario Institute for Studies in Education, 1983.

Rosier, P., & Holm, W. (1980). *The Rock Point experience: A longitudinal study of a Navajo school*. Washington, DC: Center for Applied Linguistics.

Rueda, R., & Mercer, J. R. (1985, June). *Predictive analysis of decision making with language-minority handicapped children*. Paper presented at the BUENO Center 3rd Annual Symposium on Bilingual Education, Denver.

Schneider, S. G. (1976). *Revolution, reaction or reform: The 1974 Bilingual Education Act*. New York: Las Americas.

Skutnabb-Kangas, T. (1984). *Bilingualism or not: The Education of minorities*. Clevedon, Eng.: Multilingual Matters.

Smith, F. (1978). *Understanding reading* (2nd ed.). New York: Holt, Rinehart & Winston.

Temple, C. A., Nathan, R. G., & Burris, N. A. (1982). *The beginning of writing*. Boston: Allyn & Bacon.

Tikunoff, W. J. (1983). Five significant bilingual instructional features. In W. J. Tikunoff (Ed.), *Compatibility of the SBIS features with other research on instruction for LEP students* (pp. 5–18). San Francisco: Far West Laboratory.

Tizard, J., Schofield, W. N., & Hewison, J. (1982). Collaboration between teachers and parents in assisting children's reading. *British Journal of Educational Psychology, 52*, 1–15.

Troike, R. (1978). Research evidence for the effectiveness of bilingual education. *NABE Journal, 3*, 13–24.

Wells, G. (1982). Language, learning and the curriculum. In G. Wells, (Ed.), *Language, learning and education* (pp. 205–226). Bristol, Eng.: Centre for the Study of Language and Communication, University of Bristol.

Wong-Fillmore, L. (1983). The language learner as an individual: Implications of research on individual differences for the ESL teacher. In M. A. Clarke & J. Handscombe (Eds.), *On TESOL '82: Pacific perspectives on language learning and teaching* (pp. 157–171). Washington, DC: TESOL.

Discussions at the Symposium on "Minority Languages in Academic Research and Educational Policy" held in Sandbjerg Slot, Denmark, April 1985, contributed to the ideas in the article. I would like to express my appreciation to the participants at the Symposium and to Safder Alladina, Jan Curtis, David Dolson, Norm Gold, Monica Heller, Dennis Parker, Verity Saifullah Khan, and Tove Skutnabb-Kangas for comments on earlier drafts. I would also like to acknowledge the financial support of the Social Sciences and Humanities Research Council (Grant No. 431-79-0003), which made possible participation in the Sandbjerg Slot Symposium.

Part Three:
Inclusive Practice in a
Standards-Based World

8

"It is not special education but the total educational system that must change." —Alan Gartner and Dorothy Kerzner Lipsky

To many observers, the Individuals with Disabilities Education Act (IDEA) exemplifies successful education policymaking at its best. When P.L. 94-142, IDEA's predecessor, was passed in 1975, it was estimated that one million students with disabilities in the United States were being denied access to public schooling (U.S. Department of Education, 1998). Meanwhile, students with disabilities who were in the public schools frequently found themselves on the receiving end of substandard programs and segregated classes, and without access to the general education curriculum. Regrettably, this served to perpetuate the worst stereotypes about students with disabilities and their capacity for academic achievement.

In just one generation's time, however, this picture has changed substantially. Today, because of the impact of IDEA, millions of children with disabilities who were once served in segregated settings or not served at all are being educated in public schools. In fact, the concept of educating students with disabilities in the "least restrictive environment" (LRE) — which was introduced in the original 1975 federal special education law — continues to grow and gain predominance in public schools, helping to transform the view of special education as a place into special education as a service that is connected to and integrated into all aspects of schooling. In 1997, the reauthorization of IDEA refined the notion of LRE to include access to the general education curriculum, and in so doing raised expectations for the academic achievement of students with disabilities.

These developments in special education law and policy have much in common with the emergence of the standards and accountability movement in U.S. public education. Indeed, both are based on the same basic premise: that all students can achieve at a high academic level.[1] Despite the congruence of IDEA and the No Child Left Behind Act of 2001 (NLCB) around standards-based accountability, many educators perceive a dichotomy between special education and the standards and accountability movement. For example, the basic precepts of special education policy and pedagogy prize flexibility, individualization, and collaboration of school personnel and families in addressing the educational needs of students with disabilities. Yet some of the effects of the standards movement have been to increase the use of standardized assessments, promote narrower curricula, and encourage top-down management of educational practice. As a result, educators may feel challenged when trying to implement inclusive education in an environment of rigorous standards and high-stakes tests.

The articles in this section are aimed at helping researchers, policymakers, and practitioners overcome these challenges and build on the ways special education and the standards and accountability movement do, in fact, cohere. In their seminal 1987 article, "Beyond Special Education: Toward a Quality System for All Students," Alan Gartner and Dorothy Kerzner Lipsky assess the first decade of P.L. 94-142's implementation. While lauding its manifold accomplishments, the authors contend that the implementation of the law has led to unintended negative consequences that ultimately inhibit the academic achievement of students with disabilities. Specifically, the authors criticize the establishment of separate educational programs for students with disabilities, arguing that such segregated settings — from "pull-out" resource-room classes to stand-alone schools — are inappropriate for most students and foster a culture of low expectations for their academic potential. The authors argue that school systems must fundamentally change by adopting the position that students with disabilities are capable of achieving in the regular classroom setting, provided they receive the proper support and services — in other words, in inclusionary classrooms. Their call for radical restructuring is grounded in the premise that students with disabilities can and should achieve to high standards — forecasting the core beliefs now commonly accepted in today's standards-based world.

Similarly, in "The Special Education Paradox: Equity as the Way to Excellence," Thomas Skrtic argues for inclusion from a macro-level, organizational perspective. He maintains that excellence and equity are not competing goals. Rather, he asserts that schools and school systems can achieve both by transforming themselves from bureaucracies into "adhocracies," which emphasize collaboration, active problem-solving, and innovative thinking among school personnel to address issues related to educating students with disabilities. Skrtic concludes that an "adhocratic" approach that combines the expertise of teachers, administrators, and families — rather than a professional/bureaucratic approach that tends to isolate these groups — is more likely to promote both equity and achievement for students with disabilities.

Finally, in "Complexity, Accountability, and School Improvement," Jennifer O'Day examines district- and school-level responses to standards-based reform, pointing out in particular the challenges that schools face in implementing various accountability mechanisms. While this article does not focus directly on special education, we include it here because schools are now accountable for ensuring that students with disabilities meet high academic standards. Schools face the same implementation challenges in educating students with disabilities that they do for all students. Specifically, O'Day compares a "bureaucratic" accountability structure that focuses on student outcomes as measures of successful practice to a "professional" accountability model that puts a premium on three core activities: the process of instruction in classrooms, the development of knowledge among school staff, and the enhancement of collaborative professional interchanges between teachers. She finds that the professional accountability model is much better suited to promote student and school progress, including achievement on high-stakes assessments. Her rationale for supporting this approach echoes much of what Skrtic writes about his "adhocracy" approach. As such, this article is highly relevant in addressing the needs of students with disabilities in present-day schools, and of those who educate them.

Taken together, the pieces in this section stand for one main proposition: In order to maximize the ability of students with disabilities to thrive and achieve in a standards-based environment, schools must radically reorganize around collaborative practices that engage students and families, build the capacity of teachers and administrators to think in new ways, and fully embrace the tenets of inclusive education. The optimistic news is that to the extent the authors in this section find a gap between special education and the standards and accountability movement, that gap lies in the traditional and rigid structures and practices of schools rather than in the values promoted by education reform today. The challenge — which we urge all educators to embrace — is to transform the structures of yesteryear that may yet remain in their schools into the new systems and beliefs that allow *all* students to fulfill their potential.

NOTE

1. In recognition of this premise, the 1997 reauthorization of IDEA required all schools to include students with disabilities in large-scale standardized assessments, with appropriate accommodations. Similarly, the No Child Left Behind Act of 2001 also requires that all students with disabilities be included in standardized testing, and that their scores on these assessments be a factor in determining whether a school or school district has made "adequate yearly progress."

REFERENCE

U.S. Department of Education. (1998). *To assure the free appropriate public education of all students with disabilities: Twentieth annual report to Congress on the implementation of the Individuals with Disabilities Education Act.* Washington, DC: Government Printing Office.

Beyond Special Education

Toward a Quality System for All Students

———— *8* ————

ALAN GARTNER
DOROTHY KERZNER LIPSKY

Thank you for your letter in which you ask about data concerning children who had been certified as handicapped and have returned to regular education.

While these are certainly very interesting data you request, these data are not required in State Plans nor has the Office of Special Education Programs collected them in any other survey.

> — *Letter to Alan Gartner from Patricia J. Guard,*
> *Deputy Director, Office of Special Education Programs,*
> *U.S. Department of Education, November 7, 1986.*

The decision not to collect "interesting data" can conceivably be made for various reasons. For instance, policymakers may believe that the data are not important, or they may fear the results, or believe that the collection process is not worth the potential benefit. No doubt collecting decertification data might be difficult, and most likely would show an embarrassingly low level of return to general education. We believe, however, that the major reason such data are not collected has to do with beliefs and attitudes — some implicit, some explicit — generally held about the purposes of special education and about special education students.

The faults of current special education practice, as we will detail in the following pages, are myriad. It incorporates a medical view of disability that characterizes the disability as inherent in the individual and thus formulates two separate categories of people, handicapped and nonhandicapped, as useful and rational distinctions. This arbitrary division of students provides the rationale for educating students with handicapping conditions in separate programs, and even in completely separate systems.[1] The assumptions underlying separate programs have produced a system that is both segregated and second class.

Harvard Educational Review Vol. 57 No. 4 November 1987, 367–395

The needs of students with handicapping conditions have led some parents and professionals to accept the notion of separate, if quality, education. We will argue that the current system has proven to be inadequate because it is a system that is not integrated, and that we must learn from our mistakes and attempt to create a new type of unitary system, one that incorporates quality education for all students.

It is our belief that the attitudes and assumptions about the disabled and disability require change, as do the inadequacies in general and special education practice. The need for such changes is both consequence and cause of a unitary system, thereby encouraging the production of an education model for all students — supple, variegated, and individualized — in an integrated setting.

While special education programs of the past decade have been successful in bringing unserved students into public education and have established their right to education, these programs have failed both to overcome the separation between general and special education and to make the separate system significant in terms of student benefits. This article first examines developments of the past decade, then analyzes the current failures, and, finally, formulates recommendations that will improve these programs in the future.

BACKGROUND TO THE LAW

There are many possible beginnings for a discussion of the current status of education of students with handicapping conditions. We start with *Brown v. Board of Education* (347 U.S. 483). In doing so, we wish to make three points: (1) to note the importance of education to the "life and minds" of children; (2) to set the framework concerning the inherent inequality of separate education; and (3) to recognize that advocacy efforts in the 1960s and 1970s on behalf of persons with disabilities were drawn from the context of the civil rights movement. One of the tactics which the disability rights movement learned from the Black civil rights movement was how to produce change in policies and practices through use of both the legal system and the legislature. Indeed, many see developments in special education as the logical outgrowth of civil rights efforts of an earlier period.

Between 1966 and 1974, a series of federal laws focusing on children with disabilities and the services they needed were enacted. Together, these laws can be seen as capacity building: preparing personnel, launching a set of discretionary grant programs, establishing the Bureau of Education for the Handicapped in what was then the U.S. Office of Education, providing capital funds, developing regional centers for deaf-blind children, and establishing authority for research and demonstration projects.

The concerns of adults with disabilities were addressed in the Rehabilitation Act of 1973. The Act provided a comprehensive program of vocational rehabilitation and independent living, established a federal board to coordinate and monitor access to public buildings and transportation, prohibited discrimination in employment, required affirmative action by federal agencies and federal contractors, and, almost as an afterthought, proclaimed a national mandate prohibiting discrimination against the handicapped by recipients of federal assistance (Section 504).[2]

Parents of children with disabilities were essential contributors in the legislative strategy and took the lead in litigation. Here the parent groups followed the precedent of *Brown* in its assertion of the essential importance of education. Two key decisions, *Pennsylvania Association of Retarded Citizens (PARC) v. Commonwealth* (334 F. Supp. 1257) and *Mills v. Board of Education* (348 F. Supp. 866), in 1971 and 1972, respectively, rejected reasons school districts had given for excluding students with handicapping conditions. In *PARC*, the federal district court overturned a Pennsylvania law that had relieved schools of the responsibility of enrolling "uneducable" or "untrainable" children. Basing its opinion on extensive expert testimony, the court ruled that mentally retarded children could benefit from education. In *Mills*, the federal district court ruled that a district's financial exigencies could not be the basis for excluding students with handicaps; they could not be made to take last place in the queue for funds.

The process of enacting P.L. 94–142, The Education for All Handicapped Children Act, began in the spring of 1974. Building both on the earlier legislative efforts and court cases, as well as a growing number of state laws extending the right to attend school to students with disabilities, Representative John Brademas (D-IND) introduced H.R. 7217, and six months later Senator Jennings Randolph (D-WV) introduced S. 6. The Senate bill was passed by a vote of 83 to 10 on June 18, 1975, and the House bill by a vote of 375 to 44 on July 29th. The key issues in the conference committee were: 1) funding levels, involving a cap on the number of students who could be counted as handicapped for funding purposes (as well as an internal cap on the number of learning disabled students); 2) the respective roles of state education departments and local school districts; 3) services for children aged three to five; 4) the requirement of an individualized education plan (IEP) for each student; and 5) the date for full implementation of the law. The conference report was passed in the House on November 18 and in the Senate the next day with overwhelming majorities (only seven votes against in each chamber). After some suspense about whether President Gerald Ford would veto the bill because of its cost, he signed it into law ten days later.[3]

PUBLIC LAW 94–142

As it presently exists, there is a duality inherent in P.L. 94–142. It contains a mixture both of attention to the needs of individual students and of provisions designed to solve problems that children with handicapping conditions experienced because the public school system, and other public agencies, failed to address the issue properly. One of its authors suggests that six basic principles are incorporated in the law: 1) the right of access to public education programs; 2) the individualization of services; 3) the principle of "least restrictive environment"; 4) the scope of broadened services to be provided by the schools and a set of procedures for determining them; 5) the general guidelines for identification of disability; and 6) the principles of primary state and local responsibilities.[4]

In the previous decade, federal law, state statutes, and court decisions had begun to reduce the exclusion of children with disabilities from public education programs or the charging of their parents for services otherwise provided at no cost to non-disabled children. Often, exclusions were based on categorical statements about classes of "uneducable" children or in deference to professional judgments on a child's educability. The law eliminated this exclusion of children with disabilities: it stated in the unambiguous language of its title that "all handicapped children" were to be provided with a free public education. Henceforth, no child was to be rejected as uneducable.

Once students with handicaps were included in public education, Congress wanted to assure that each student, particularly one with severe handicaps, would receive services based upon individual need, not upon categories of handicap or pre-existing service offerings. The law explicitly required a multidisciplinary individual evaluation that was nondiscriminatory, and the development of an individualized education plan (IEP).

While each student's placement was to be individually determined, the law, in keeping with its philosophic acceptance of the concepts of "normalization," expressed a strong presumption that students with disabilities be placed in regular classes whenever possible, where they could receive specialized services as necessary.[5] Only when regular classroom placements did not meet individual students' needs would they be placed in separate classes or settings. This was expressed in the law's requirement that students be educated in the "least restrictive environment" (LRE).

The law, while rejecting the traditional medical model of disability, recognized that some of these students needed more than educational services alone to be successful in school.[6] Hence the concept of "related services" was developed, incorporating those services — including counseling, physical and occupational therapy, and some medical services — necessary to enable students to take advantage of and benefit from the educational program. In addition to describing the scope of services to be provided, the law established a process for determining students' handicapping condition, educational placement, and related services, which incorporated parental involvement and required substantial due process procedures and appeal rights.

During the course of the congressional debate, there was considerable dispute about the total number of students who would be eligible for services, and, foreshadowing a continuing issue, the number of those defined as having specific learning disabilities within that overall figure. For funding purposes, caps of 12 percent and 2 percent of the total school population, respectively, were set. Procedural guidelines were set for identification, assessment, and placement of students, with particular emphasis on nondiscrimination and procedural due process.

As was to be expected, the respective roles of the state and local educational agencies and the flow of money were key issues in the congressional consideration. While the House bill required that funds go directly to local educational agencies (LEAs), the Council of Chief State School Officers argued in favor of state responsibility for monitoring local school districts and gained a victory for the state educational agencies (SEAs). Funds were to flow through SEAs, with requirements that annual increasing percentages be passed on to the local level. Also, while recognizing that other state agencies might provide services to the students, particularly the severely impaired, the SEA had responsibility for assuring that the educational services were provided, regardless of who provided or paid for them or where the student received them.

THE CURRENT SITUATION

While there was considerable concern about the feasibility of implementing P.L. 94–142, and some difficulty in doing so at the compliance level, by and large it has been accomplished:

- Over 650,000 more students are being served now than when the law was enacted. During the 1985–1986 school year, somewhat over 4.37 million students received services under the provisions of P.L. 94–142.[7] This comprised approximately 11 percent of the total public school enrollment (a slight drop from the previous year), with percentages in some states pushing against the 12 percent cap. Generally, educators believe that few, if any, students needing services have not been identified.
- There has been a substantial increase in the funds devoted to special education, from $100 million in FY 1976 to $1.64 billion in FY 1985, for P.L. 94–142. However, the promised federal contribution (40% of the average per pupil cost by 1982) has never been met. Current figures are around 8.5 percent,[8] with states (54%) and local governments (37%) providing the difference.
- While there are some exceptions, such as students in prisons, from migrant families, and in some institutional settings, for the most part location of the student does not seem to be a factor in the availability of services. The overall responsibility of SEAs has been achieved, perhaps more so in special education than in other areas of SEA–LEA joint responsibility. With New Mexico's submission of a state plan in August 1984, all fifty states are presently participating under P.L. 94–142.

In these areas, the implementation of the law has been successful. And to turn now, more extensively, to areas of lesser achievement is neither to gainsay that achievement nor deny its rightness.

While consideration of each of the issues in the conduct of special education is required, we will focus here on only those areas in special education that have emerged as the most troubling. These include referral and assessment procedures, placement options, educational programs, Least Restrictive Environment (LRE), and parental participation.

REFERRAL AND ASSESSMENT PROCEDURES

Perhaps no area in special education has received as much concern as have procedures used for the referral, assessment, and eventual placement of students. Together, these activities raise substantive issues: 1) cost, a key factor in the congressional capping of the number of students (at 12%) who could be counted for funding purposes; 2) professional judgment, particularly with regard to identification of students with learning disabilities; and 3) discrimination, as seen in the disproportionate number of minority and limited-English-proficient students referred for evaluation and placed in certain categories. These issues can be framed as a sequence of questions:

1. Who is being referred and on what basis?
2. What is the nature of the assessment?
3. What are the bases of the placement?
4. What is the likelihood, once a student is placed in a special education setting, that appropriate programs and services will be provided?
5. What is the likelihood, once these programs are provided, that the student will return to general education?

Aside from those students with obvious physical handicaps who are identified before entering a classroom, referral occurs, for the most part, "when student behavior and academic progress varies from the school norm. . . ."[9] The assumption in such cases is that there is something wrong with the student. In particular, referral is more likely to occur in cases where the student is a member of a minority group or from a family whose socioeconomic status varies from the district's norm.[10] Further,

> decisions about special education classification are not only functions of child characteristics but rather involve powerful organizational influences. The number of programs, availability of space, incentives for identification, range and kind of competing programs and services, number of professionals, and federal, state, and community pressures all affect classification decisions.[11]

Referral rates vary widely. This is apparent from examining two different sets of data from twenty-eight large cities. As a percentage of total student enrollment, referral rates range from 6 percent to 11 percent. The figures for assessment vary even more widely. For the same twenty-eight cities, the percentage of students who are referred and then placed in special education ranges from 7.8 percent to 91.8 percent.[12]

The most extensive study of the evaluation process reports that results are barely more accurate than a flip of the coin, with the evaluation process often providing a psychological justification for the referral.[13] The leading researchers conclude that current classification procedures are plagued with major conceptual and practical problems.[14]

While P.L. 94–142 includes eleven different classifications of handicapping conditions,[15] "most diagnoses of students placed in special education programs are based on social and psychological criteria. These include measured intelligence, achievement, social behavior and adjustment, and communication and language problems. Furthermore, many of the measuring criteria used in classification lack reliability or validity. . . ."[16] According to one observer, when test results do not produce the desired outcome, evaluators often change the yardstick: "If the test scores indicate the child is ineligible, but the teacher really feels the child needs help, we try to select other tests that might make the child eligible. . . ." The tests then become "a means of corroborating referral decisions. Testing, therefore, does not drive decisions but is driven by decisions."[17]

The major classification problems concern those students labeled as learning disabled. The number of students classified as learning disabled rose 119 percent between 1976–1977 and 1984–1985, at a time when the overall special education population rose 16 percent. The growth has been slowed in the past two school years. In 1985–1986, students labeled as learning disabled accounted for 42.8 percent of the students — aged three through twenty-one — receiving special education services.[18] The percentage of special education students labeled as learning disabled varied from 30 percent to 67 percent among the fifty states, and from 0 percent to 73 percent among thirty large cities.[19]

In what can be fairly called a form of classification plea bargaining, this growth in those labeled as learning disabled has been accompanied by a decline (by some 300,000 between 1976–1977 and 1983–1984) in those labeled as mentally retarded. The Department of Education gently explains, "These decreases in the number of children classified as mentally retarded are the result of an increasing sensitivity to the negative features of the label itself and to the reaction on the part of local school systems to allegations of racial and ethnic bias as a result of the use of discriminatory or culturally biased testing procedures."[20]

The problem is not only the excessive numbers of students classified as learning disabled; there are even more troubling issues as to the accuracy of the label:

- More than 80 percent of the student population could be classified as learning disabled by one or more definitions presently in use.[21]
- Based upon the records of those already certified as learning disabled and those not, experienced evaluators could not tell the difference.[22]
- Students identified as learning disabled cannot be shown to differ from other low achievers with regard to a wide variety of school-related characteristics.[23]
- A study of special education in Colorado concluded: "The single most important finding is that more than half the children do not meet statistical or valid clinical criteria for the identification of perceptual or communicative disorders."[24]

Summarizing national data on the subject, the authors of one study remarked, "At least half of the learning disabled population could be more accurately described as slow learners, as children with second-language backgrounds, as children who are naughty in class, as those who are absent more often or move from school to school, or as average learners in above-average school systems."[25]

Such results are not surprising, given reports concerning the inadequacy and inappropriateness of the measuring instruments, the disregard of results in decision-making, and, often, the evaluators' incompetence and biases.[26] A decade later, there is nothing to warrant changing Nicholas Hobbs's assessment that the classification system of students with disabilities is "a major barrier to the efficient and effective delivery of services to them and their families and thereby impedes efforts to help them."[27] The standard for assessment, in special education as elsewhere, should be validity and reliability on a series of axes.

PLACEMENT OPTIONS

While referral and assessment procedures vary widely, and students are "placed" in special education programs based upon such discrepant outcomes, P.L. 94–142 is clear concerning least restrictive environment (LRE) criteria, namely, that "removal from the regular education environment" is to occur "only when the nature and severity of the handicap is such that education in regular classes with the use of supplementary aids cannot be achieved satisfactorily" [Sec. 612 (5) (B)]. There is, however, wide variability in the implementation of the federal law at the local level. This is shown in Table 1, which presents data showing the percentage of students with the four most frequent handicapping conditions who are placed in regular classes, the placement favored by the law. These four categories together account for 95 percent of all students classified as "handicapped."

Overall, 74 percent of special education students are in pull-out or separate programs. For each handicapping condition the variation among states is substantial. For the students labeled as learning disabled (LD), 16 percent are in regular classes, with a range from 0.06 percent to 98 percent — in effect, from a bare handful in Arizona to nearly all students in Alabama. For those students labeled as speech-impaired, the national average is 64 percent of the students in regular classes, ranging from zero percent in Mississippi to nearly all in Alabama. For those students labeled as mentally retarded (MR), the national average is 5 percent in regular classes, and ranges from zero percent in five states to 50 percent in New Hampshire. Finally, for those students labeled emotionally disturbed (ED), the national average is 12 percent in regular classes, and ranges from zero percent in four states to 74 percent in Alabama.

Such results indicate that students with seemingly identical characteristics qualify for different programs, depending on where they reside and how individuals on school staffs evaluate them. Most often, these are pull-out programs, despite evidence about their lack of efficacy.[28]

Patterns of service often appear to relate more to the systems of funding than to indices of pupil benefit. For example, each of the states with the highest percentage of the students in these four categories placed in regular classes used the same type of funding formula ("cost" basis), while in all but one case the states with the lowest percentage of students in the four categories in regular classes used another type of formula ("unit" basis).[29]

The consequence in New York, for example, was to reward LEAs for assigning students to more restrictive rather than less restrictive placements, and for assigning them outside of the public school system to private schools.[30] In other words, rather than encouraging and supporting the mandate of the law to place students in the least restrictive environment, current New York State Education Department practice rewards the opposite.

Some have argued that such funding practices explain both the growth of special education and the absence of decertification or the return of students to general education once they have met their IEP objectives in special education. While funding patterns no doubt have their consequences, we will argue that a set of attitudes is more important in producing the current pattern. Here it is sufficient to note that among twenty-six large cities, fewer than 5 percent of students in special education return to general education, with a range of zero to 13.4 percent.[31] No national figures, however, have been collected on the number of students who were certified as handicapped and who have returned to general education.

TABLE 1

Percentage of Students with Handicapping Conditions in Regular Classes

	All Conditions	Learning Disabled	Speech Impaired	Mentally Retarded	Emotionally Disturbed
U.S. average	69	78	96	31	44
State with highest percentage in regular classes	90	99	100	84	88
State with lowest percentage in regular classes	36	35	75	3	8

Source: Seventh Annual Report to the Congress on the Implementation of the Education of the Handicapped Act, Table 6C3.

EDUCATIONAL PROGRAMS

The basic premise of special education is that students with deficits will benefit from a unique body of knowledge and from smaller classes staffed by specially trained teachers using special materials. We will address these assumptions of a segregated special education system in the concluding section of this paper; here we cite recent research findings that support an integrated setting.

There is no compelling body of evidence that segregated special education programs have significant benefits for students. On the contrary, there is substantial and growing evidence that goes in the opposite direction.[32] In fifty recent studies comparing the academic performance of mainstreamed and segregated students with handicapping conditions, the mean academic performance of the integrated group was in the 80th percentile, while the segregated students scored in the 50th percentile.[33]

A review of programs for academically handicapped students found no consistent benefits of full-time special education programs. Rather, it found full- or part-time regular class placements more beneficial for students' achievements, self-esteem, behavior, and emotional adjustment.[34] A study in one state found that 40 percent to 50 percent of students labeled as learning disabled did not realize the expected benefits from special education.[35]

In summarizing impediments to achieving national policy in the education of students with mild handicaps, a recent study rejects the prevalent "pull-out" strategy as ineffective, and concludes, "This split-scheduling approach . . . is neither administratively nor instructionally supportable when measured against legal requirements, effective schools research or fiscal consideration."[36]

A careful review of the literature on effective instruction strongly indicates that the general practice of special education runs counter to the basic effectiveness tenets in teaching behaviors, organization of instruction, and instructional support.[37] Furthermore,

there appear to be at least three discrepancies between the suggestions for best practice and the observation of actual teaching practice for mildly handicapped students:

(a) there is almost no instruction presented to these students that might be classified as involving high level cognitive skills, (b) there is a small amount of time spent in activities that could be considered direct instruction with active learner response and teacher feedback, and (c) students receive a low frequency of contingent teacher attention.[38]

While these shortcomings are true as well in general education classes, the needs of students appropriately classified as handicapped make the absence of the desired practices even more consequential.

At the classroom level, the time special education students spend on academic tasks is not greater than that for general education students: about forty-five minutes of engaged time per day.[39] And, most often, there is little qualitatively different in special education instruction in the areas of additional time on task, curriculum adaptation, diverse teaching strategies, adaptive equipment, or advanced technology. Classrooms, despite their small size, remain "teacher-centric."

The limited expectation for student learning in special education programs is reflected in the following results of a study of special education in large cities: 1) only seven of thirty-one cities evaluate "student achievement/outcomes"; 2) only three of thirty-one cities conduct "longitudinal student outcome studies"; and 3) only nine of the twenty-four special education directors whose districts do not conduct such evaluations believe "student achievement/outcome studies" are needed.[40] Thus, combining the numbers of special education directors whose districts conduct such evaluations and those who do not, but say they are needed, fifteen of the thirty-one directors of large-city special education programs neither collect student outcome data nor believe that such evaluations are needed. While the failure to evaluate outcomes does not in and of itself indicate limited expectations, at the least it does indicate a lack of concern with outcomes, which we believe comes from limited expectations of student capacity.

LEAST RESTRICTIVE ENVIRONMENT

We have previously addressed the topic of separation in the context of instructional placement; in this section, we will focus on separation as one aspect of the overall least restrictive environment (LRE) mandate. The two are inextricably entwined: LRE placement is not a mandate in itself; rather, students are to receive services in an appropriate placement in the least restrictive environment.

This formulation is based on the premise that while many types of placement might be appropriate for a student, the one to be chosen should be the least restrictive, that is, the one which allows maximum integration of students with their peers. Putting it the opposite way, the Sixth Circuit Court of Appeals directed: in situations "where a segregated facility is considered superior, the court should determine whether the services which make that placement superior could feasibly be provided in a non-segregated setting. If they can, the placement in the segregated school would be inappropriate under the Act."[41] Further, the Department of Education has stated that the type of placement must not be based on any of the following factors, either

alone or in combination: category of handicapping condition, configuration of the service delivery system, availability of educational or related services, availability of
space, or curriculum content or methods of curriculum delivery.[42]

Despite such statements from the Office of Special Education and Rehabilitation
Services, the reality in schools turns out to be far different. When the first figures
were collected in 1976–1977, 67 percent of the students who were served under P.L.
94-142 were served in general classes, 25 percent in special classes. A decade later,
the figures were essentially the same.[43] While overall there have been no changes in
the direction of increasing the proportion of students receiving services in general education, the change has been in the opposite direction for the mentally retarded.[44]

The New York State Association for Retarded Children (NYSARC) has charged the
State Education Department (SED) with failure to enforce the law, noting, among
other charges, that in Nassau County on Long Island, "out of 320 special education
classes, 308 are in segregated facilities." The response of the official charged with enforcing the law gives a somewhat peculiar reading to the SED's sense of its obligations
here. "It's a question of where do you draw the line. . . . [While NYSARC is strongly in
favor of placing students in integrated settings], many other people in New York State
feel differently."[45] The continuing support in New York of its Board of Cooperative
Education Services (BOCES), and similar intermediate units in other states, which
cluster special education students in separate settings, no doubt will be an arena of
future contention about the least restrictive environment.

An extensive study in Massachusetts not only mirrors the national data on the absence of integrated placements, but also reveals a significant trend toward more restrictive placements, especially in the past five years.[46] In its most recent report to
Congress on the implementation of P.L. 94–142, the Department of Education, reporting on the eighteen states reviewed in the past year, indicated that "virtually every
state had significant problems in meeting its LRE requirements. . . ."[47] Indeed, all
eighteen states were out of compliance with the law in this area. Despite such findings, only seven states reported a need to improve their LRE performances.[48]

As we have learned in the area of race relations, integration is a more complex
matter than achieving mere physical proximity. Not only are there administrative
barriers when one organization operates its programs in the buildings of another, but
there is also the day-to-day, period-to-period reality of the students' education. A
unique analysis of "mainstreaming" in the Pittsburgh schools gives dramatic evidence of its actual limitations.[49] The district classifies approximately 6 percent of its
students as mildly to moderately disabled, serving them in thirty-eight of the district's fifty-six elementary schools. Based on an examination of their academic schedules, "the percent of [special] students assigned to regular classes ranged from 3 to 7
percent. This means that over 90 percent of the mildly handicapped elementary students . . . were *never* assigned to regular education academic classes" (emphasis in the
original).[50] Participation is limited in three ways: 1) scheduling students for fewer
than the full number of periods in the week, 2) having students attend several different general education classes for the same subject, and 3) assigning students to inappropriate (by age or level) general education classes.[51] Thus, fewer than one-tenth of
mildly handicapped students participated in the mainstream, and of this small num-

ber, less than half participated in the mainstream class on a full basis. Given such program limitations, it is no surprise that only 1.4 percent of the students return to general education.[52]

In a review of mainstreaming in high schools, there was a large discrepancy between reported availability and actual utilization of general classroom education. Although special education teachers indicated that general classroom opportunities were available for their students with disabilities, according to the students' parents only one-third of the students were actually benefiting from this opportunity. Teachers cited the following impediments to mainstreaming special education students: 1) students lack entry-level skills required in general education classrooms; 2) general education classroom teachers resist mainstreaming efforts; and 3) supportive resources, such as modified curricula, are not available.[53]

PARENTAL INVOLVEMENT

Parents were central to the passage of P.L. 94–142 — to the enactment of prior and subsequent state laws as well as to the maintenance of strong regulations to implement them. While their rights are specifically cited in federal and state laws, parental involvement in student assessment, program development, and the evaluation of students' progress is limited.[54]

Research studies report that most parents are far from fulfilling their roles of providing information, participating in decisions, or serving as advocates.[55] One study reported that in 70 percent of the cases, parents provided no input to IEP development.[56] A more recent study reports that only half of the parents attended IEP meetings,[57] and that when they did, professionals believed they contributed little.[58] Other professionals suggest that perhaps parents "feel intimidated or are provided only limited opportunity" to become involved.[59] This point is emphasized in the most recent Department of Education report to Congress, which notes, "several studies have reported that in the majority of IEP conferences, the IEP was completely prepared prior to the meeting. . . ." The report concludes, "Presenting parents with what may appear to be decisions the school has already reached rather than recommendations, and the failure to directly communicate and provide appropriate opportunities for involvement, can obviously limit parent participation in the IEP decision making process."[60]

Parents of children with disabilities often feel as if they share their children's labels and are thereby perceived by others as part of the overall problem and in need of professional services for themselves.[61] Thus, should parents at an IEP conference express frustration or anger at the lack of educational or related services being provided to their children, professionals, rather than addressing the specific problem areas or providing the required services, are often quick to "diagnose" the parent as overwhelmed and over-protective and in need of psychological services to combat "their problems." If, on the other hand, parents lead an active life and have less time to devote to their children's education or therapeutic program than the professionals deem appropriate, this behavior is often diagnosed as a form of parental denial that requires psychological treatment for the family members. In addition:

The belief that parents displace their anger onto the professional is a kind of "Catch-22." That is, whenever the parent disagrees with or confronts the professional, that behavior can be dismissed as an expression of inadequate adjustment, frustration, displaced anger, or a host of psychological problems. Any interpretation is possible other than that the parent may be correct![62]

The narratives of parents of children with disabilities repeatedly describe the power struggles surrounding their involvement in the students' education and the devaluing or denigration of their knowledge about their children.[63] Their concerns are often dismissed, their requests are often patronized, and their reports of the child's home behavior are often distrusted.[64] While not all parent-professional relationships are characterized by these factors, the pattern does appear to be endemic, in keeping with the historic role of the clinical or medical model in special education. Further, this attitude often leads to an over-valuing of the knowledge of so-called experts. Thus, professionals invariably refer children with problems and their parents to specialist rather than generalist service providers or mutual support groups. Summarizing the growing parent literature: "The narratives repeatedly express anger, frustration, and resentment . . . at the unnecessary burdens they and their children face because of social attitudes and behavior toward disabilities."[65]

A WORLD OF DISABLING ATTITUDES

The National Council on the Handicapped, appointed by President Reagan, has reiterated what people with disabilities have been saying for years: their major obstacles arise from external rather than internal barriers. The Council cites with approval the statement of an expert United Nations panel:

> Despite everything we can do, or hope to do, to assist each physically or mentally disabled person achieve his or her maximum potential in life, our efforts will not succeed until we have found the way to remove the obstacles to this goal directed by human society — the physical barriers we have created in public buildings, housing, transportation, houses of worship, centers of social life and other community facilities — the social barriers we have evolved and accepted against those who vary more than a certain degree from what we have been conditioned to regard as normal. More people are forced into limited lives and made to suffer by these man-made [*sic*] obstacles than by any specific physical or mental disability.[66]

Individuals with disabilities make the point even more directly:

> In his classic article entitled "What does it mean when a retarded person says, 'I'm not retarded'?" Bogdan tells of people labelled retarded who say, "I have never really thought of myself as retarded. I never really had that ugly feeling deep down," and another who says, "The worst word I have been called is retarded." The single largest self advocacy organization of people labelled retarded calls itself "People First." Marsha Saxton, a person with Spina Bifida, reports, "As I see it, I'm not lucky or unlucky. I'm just the way I am. But I'm not disabled, I always thought. Or handicapped." Denise Karuth, who also has a physical disability, . . . writes, "Put your

handkerchiefs away. I'm a lot more like you than you probably imagine." The message in each of these instances ... is that a disability is only one dimension of a person, not all-defining and not inherently a barrier to being recognized as fully human.[67]

A quarter of a century ago, Erving Goffman addressed this issue. He wrote, "By definition, of course, we believe the person with a stigma is not quite human."[68] The point has been made more recently by Ved Mehta. "You see, we are confronted with a vast ignorance in the world about the handicapped [so that] they would not understand if we acted like normal people."[69]

In a variety of ways, persons with disabilities are neither treated like nor viewed as "normal people." More often, they are treated "specially" either for their own good or for someone else's, but always according to an externally imposed standard. From the many examples of this, two are noted here.

Airlines have asserted that for the safety of passengers who are blind (and sometimes, they argue, for the safety of nondisabled passengers), persons with disabilities *must* preboard, wait to deplane, sit in special seats and not in others, and receive special briefings. To the extent that any database is used to justify these requirements, it was created using blindfolded sighted persons in trial evacuations of planes. One need not suggest the likelihood that persons who are blind would be more rather than less able to maneuver in a smoky airplane than sighted persons (blindfolded or not!) to see that the requirements as to special treatment are both unnecessary and demeaning.[70]

The cases of "Baby Doe" in Indiana and "Baby Jane Doe" in New York have drawn considerable attention to professional attitudes toward disability and how they affect the treatment of newborns. Among the major issues raised is "quality of life." For example, in order to determine which babies with spina bifida should be provided "active vigorous treatment" as opposed to "supportive care only," doctors at the University of Oklahoma Health Sciences Center reported in 1983 on a formula they used to determine quality of life: $QL = NE \times (H + S)$. "QL" stands for quality of life; "NE" for natural endowment; "H" for contribution from home and family; and "S" for contribution from society.[71] Those infants for whom the equation predicted a high quality of life were given "active" medically indicated treatment; those for whom it predicted a low score received "no active" medical treatment: no surgery to close the spinal lesion or to drain fluid from the brain, no antibiotics to treat infection. "Of the 24 infants who did not get active, vigorous treatment, none survived. . . . All but one of the infants who received active, vigorous treatment survived. The exception was killed in an automobile accident."[72] What we have here, masquerading as an objective medical judgment, is a means test for care and a determination about one person's quality of life based on an outside person's assessment of a family's and society's "contribution."

Given public attitudes and policies such as these, persons with disabilities have increasingly developed a new perspective. This has been reflected recently in writings by disability-rights activists[73] and others in the independent-living movement. For them, "the problem of disability is not only of physical impairment but also of unnecessary dependence on relatives and professionals, of architectural barriers and of unprotected rights."[74] This formulation is echoed in the report of the first national survey of self-perceptions of Americans with disabilities:[75]

- An overwhelming majority, 74 percent, say they feel at least some sense of common identity with other people with disabilities. (Table 56)
- Nearly half, 45 percent, feel that disabled persons are a minority group in the same sense as Blacks and Hispanics. This figure rises to 56 percent of those disabled between birth and adolescence and 53 percent of those 44 years of age and younger. (Table 57)

This emerging and growing involvement of adults with disabilities can have a major impact in the field of special education. These individuals will be less likely to tolerate an educational system that fails to recognize the capabilities of handicapped students and to prepare them to deal with the realities of the outside world.

SPECIAL EDUCATION: DISABLING ATTITUDES IN PRACTICE

It is the attitudinal milieu more than the individual's physical condition that influences society's response to persons with disabilities. An all-or-nothing concept of disability requires proof of total incapacity in order to gain entitlement to various benefit programs.[76] Further, the media portrays disabled persons as either the heroic individual or the pathetic cripple, rather than as a human being with a multiplicity of qualities. Together these images of disability burden policy, including the education of students with disabilities.[77]

This point was recognized by Justice William Brennan, writing for the Supreme Court in *School Board of Nassau County v. Arline*, who said, "Congress acknowledged that society's accumulated myths and fears about disability and disease are as handicapping as are the physical limitations that flow from actual impairment."[78]

Society's attitudes toward disability are deeply ingrained in professional practice. This is particularly evident in the social-psychological literature, where disability is based on the following assumptions: 1) disability is biologically based; 2) disabled persons face endless problems, which are caused by the impairment; 3) disabled persons are "victims"; 4) disability is central to the disabled person's self-concept and self-definition; and 5) disability is synonymous with a need for help and social support.[79]

Similar assumptions hold true in special education. Here the child and family are considered impaired, instruction is disability focused, professional personnel are often trained and certified to work with specific disabilities, and attention to societal issues is often considered too political and not the business of educational institutions. The assumptions underlying such beliefs can be tersely summarized: "1) Disability is a condition that individuals have; 2) disabled/typical is a useful and objective distinction; and 3) special education is a rationally conceived and coordinated system of services that help children labeled disabled. . . ."[80] This view of students labeled as handicapped, however, adversely affects expectations regarding their academic achievement. It causes them to be separated from other students; to be exposed to a watered-down curriculum; to be excused from standards and tests routinely applied to other students; to be allowed grades that they have not earned; and, in some states, to be permitted special diplomas.[81]

The rationale given for such watered-down expectations is that they are in the best interest of the child. Professionals often suggest that a child be placed in an environment where he or she will be "safe . . . because he would never be asked to do things there 'we know he cannot do.'" Many parents recognize, however, that a "safe" place may not be the best learning environment. Writing about their experience with Chicago-area schools, which identified their young son as being in need of special education, Lori and Bill Granger conclude:

> The trap of Special Education was now open and waiting for the little boy. It is a beguiling trap. Children of Special Education are children of Small Expectations, not great ones. Little is expected and little is demanded. Gradually, these children — no matter their IQ level — learn to be cozy in the category of being "special." They learn to be less than they are.[82]

Not only do "small expectations" excuse students from academic performance; they have also led state education departments, school systems, and the courts to excuse them from the social and behavioral expectations and standards set for other students. The medical or clinical model that undergirds special education inextricably leads to the belief that persons with a handicap, especially the severely disabled, are not capable of making choices or decisions. This conceptualization diminishes "our ability to see them as individuals capable of ever making a choice, let alone the right choice. Seldom, if ever, is the person with the handicapping condition involved in the process of determining how their behavior, or the behavior of those around them, will be modified. The end result is more control for the caregivers and less control for the person being cared for."[83] Having denied individuals with disabilities autonomy and decisionmaking authority — in effect denying them the respect given to people whom society respects — we then excuse their behavior, ascribing it to the disability.[84]

GENERAL EDUCATION

It is not special education but the total educational system that must change. The origin, growth, and shape of special education have in many ways been defined by general education and the attitudes and behaviors of mainstream educators toward students with handicapping conditions. Whatever the rationale or the benign purpose claimed, children with disabilities have been denied access to public education, or, when given access, have received an education that is not equal to that given other children.

The growth of special education in the past decade has occurred not only in response to the exclusion of students with handicapping conditions. Additional factors have fueled this growth, including: 1) cutbacks in Chapter I (formerly Title I) programs and other school remedial efforts that strained local school system resources (in the same period as and coincidental with the implementation of P.L. 94–142); 2) the development of remedial and pull-out programs for students with "problems" — slow learners, "disadvantaged," limited-English proficient (miscalled bilingual), new immigrants, and gay and lesbian students;[85] and 3) given the increased emphasis on accountability, the referral of "low achievers" to special education programs, thus excluding them from test-score analyses in school districts.

Another factor promoting exclusion has been a narrowing of the definition of what is considered "normal." In special education, "this often means referral based on race, sex, physical appearance, and socioeconomic status. . . ."[86] A recent study in ten states noted that referral occurs when student behavior and academic achievement vary negatively from the school norm, and for minority students, when their socioeconomic status is lower than the norm of the community.[87] Additionally, the role of school psychologists, given their training and the present educational philosophy, gives professional rationale for special education placements and for the ever-growing identification of deviant, or to use the more recent term, "at-risk" students.[88] The obverse of this has consequences for those students who remain in regular classroom programs. "Every time a child is called mentally defective and sent off to the special education class for some trivial defect, the children who are left in the regular classroom receive a message: no one is above suspicion; everyone is being watched by the authorities; nonconformity is dangerous."[89]

The problem is not special education or general education alone. "In a sense, regular and special education teachers have colluded to relieve regular teachers of responsibilities for teaching children functioning at the bottom of their class."[90] The pressure to "succeed" with high test scores, and with the very large class sizes that make individual attention extremely difficult, makes it more likely that teachers will seek uniformity of students rather than diversity. To put it more sharply, there is, in effect, a "deal" between special and general education. The former asserts a particular body of expertise and a unique understanding of "special" students, thus laying claim both to professional obligation and student benefit. The latter, because of the lack of skills and resources or prejudice, is often happy to hand over "these" students to a welcoming special education system. This includes not only those with the traditional handicapping conditions, but increasing numbers of students labeled "learning disabled," a category that, at present, incorporates such a multitude of students that, under one or another definition, it may incorporate as many as 80 percent of the general education student body. The "deal is sanctioned, on one hand, by the clinicians who provide an intrapsychic justification for the referral, and, on the other hand, by those in the role of advocacy who see increasing numbers of students in special education as providing evidence of their effectiveness."[91]

NEXT STEPS

No discussion of a future education system for students with handicapping conditions can begin without acknowledgment of what has been achieved. As one of the P.L. 94–142 drafters writes, however:

If the law has been massively successful in assigning responsibility for students and setting up mechanisms to assure that schools carry out these responsibilities, it has been less successful in removing the barriers between general and special education. It did not anticipate that the artifice of delivery systems in schools might drive the maintenance of separate services and keep students from the mainstream.[92]

A part of this separation is revealed in special educators' decrying the absence of attention to special education in the raft of national reports about education. Indeed, nearly an entire issue of *Exceptional Children* addressed this topic. The inattention to special education is described and the alleged trade-off between excellence and equity deplored.[93] Stephen Lilly suggests, however, that the reason special education is ignored is that "current special education policies and practices for students labelled mildly handicapped are neither conceptually sound nor of sufficient quality to be included in the 'ideal' educational system described by these authors." Thus, rather than deploring the inattention, he applauds it, saying that "until we are willing to examine our flawed assumptions about children and teachers and become integral members of the general education community, we cannot expect either to be featured in reform reports or to be involved in construction of the next era of public education in the United States."[94]

We have, in the preceding pages, examined some of the flawed assumptions about disability. Before turning to ideas for reform, this section will highlight some critiques of special education that are pertinent to the development of new designs. On the one hand, the Heritage Foundation has criticized the very premises of P.L. 94–142 by saying that it "rests on the questionable assumption that the responsibility for disabled individuals is primarily society's as a civil right," and has questioned its major program direction, saying that "public schools should not be required to educate those children who cannot, without damaging the main purposes of public education, function in a normal classroom setting."[95] At the opposite extreme, the National Coalition of Advocates for Students criticized the lack of access to education for various groups, including students with handicaps. They did so, however, without questioning "the underlying separateness of regular education and special education systems."[96]

A different level of critique is represented by those who argue that the current pattern of special education, by serving some inappropriately, "robs the genuinely handicapped of funds and services they need to deal with their very real problems."[97] In particular, for those labeled learning disabled, inappropriate expenditures are claimed, both in the cost of assessments and in the expense of providing low student-teacher ratios and individualized programs.[98]

In a seeming backlash against the poor quality of services for those with low-incidence handicaps, there is a call from some for a return to separate services. These include: a proposed resolution at the annual convention of the National Federation of the Blind to (re)establish specialized schools for the blind; a proposal from a group of superintendents of residential schools and state directors of special education to (re)establish residential schools for deaf and blind students;[99] the accreditation for the first time of a special education school by a regional accrediting association;[100] and the approval by the New York State Education Department for the construction of a segregated high school for students with physical disabilities.

While the return to more restrictive settings may be understood in light of current special education services, the more predominant reaction of professionals and parents is to propose reforms designed to preclude or limit services to inappropriately labeled students and/or to lower the "barriers" between general and special education.

While no one can argue for the inappropriate labeling of students, one can also empathize with the directors of special education programs who see such students "dumped" into their programs. More disturbing, however, are efforts to impose an arbitrary "cap" on the number of students referred, to cut a "bargain" with general education, or to tighten criteria. While "tightening eligibility criteria may seem to make the problem go away . . . the main effect might be either to (a) redirect referred students into other categorical services or programs; or (b) disguise as nonhandicapped the portion of students for whom technical eligibility cannot be demonstrated."[101]

ALTERNATIVE DELIVERY SYSTEMS

An alternative way to serve students with mild and moderate handicaps is to integrate them into general education programs at the building level. Indeed, a number of states and districts are implementing experimental programs using such an approach, especially for students categorized as having "learning problems."[102] A report to the Secretary of the U.S. Department of Education noted that present practices suffer from 1) fragmented approaches ("Many students who require help and are not learning effectively fall 'through the cracks' of a program structure based on preconceived definitions of eligibility. . . ."); 2) a dual system ("The separate administrative arrangements for special programs contribute to a lack of coordination, raise questions about leadership, cloud areas of responsibility, and obscure lines of accountability within schools."); 3) stigmatization of students (producing in students "low expectations of success, failure to persist on tasks, the belief that failures are caused by personal inadequacies, and a continued failure to learn effectively"); and 4) placement decisions becoming a battleground between parents and schools. In light of such practices, the panel called for experimental programs for students with learning problems, which incorporate increased instructional time, support systems for teachers, empowerment of principals to control all programs and resources at the building level, and new instructional approaches that involve "shared responsibility" between general and special education.[103]

While clearly an improvement over the present special education practice, this broad proposal nonetheless continues a dual-system approach for a smaller (more severely impaired) population.[104] As described a decade ago, such students will continue to be faced with consequences of negative attitudes and lowered expectations, with teachers making comparisons between them "in relation to degrees of handicap rather than comparing [their] skill levels to the criteria of nonhandicapped skill performance."[105]

The data in the earlier sections of this article concerning least restrictive environment and mainstreaming focused on students with mild and moderate handicapping conditions. This reflects both the preponderance of students in special education and the major emphasis in the research literature. There is, however, an increasing body of work concerning the integration of students with severe handicaps into regular schools.[106] The Association for Persons with Severe Handicaps (TASH) has been in the forefront of these efforts,[107] and a recent book gives guidance on the conduct of programs to integrate severely impaired students into regular programs,[108] as does a recent Council for Exceptional Children report.[109]

According to this research, the education of students with severe disabilities in an integrated setting requires first and foremost an attitude change from seeing the education of students with disabilities as different or "special" and the education of "nondisabled" students as normal and expected.

Major work in the integration of students with severe multiple disabilities in classes at age-appropriate schools has been carried out by the California Research Institute on the Integration of Students with Severe Disabilities (CRI). In the past five years, they have worked with over two hundred classes serving more than two thousand students with severe handicaps in twenty San Francisco Bay Area school districts. By integration, CRI means: 1) placement of classes in general school buildings which are the chronologically age-appropriate sites for the students; 2) a balanced ratio (from 5% to 20%) of such classes in a school; 3) structured opportunities for regular and sustained interactions between severely disabled and nondisabled students; 4) participation of the severely disabled students in all non-academic activities of the school; and 5) implementation of a functional life-skills curriculum for severely disabled students. The rationale for educating students with severe disabilities in integrated settings is to ensure their normalized community participation by providing them with systematic instruction in the skills that are essential to their success in the social and environmental contexts in which they will ultimately use these skills. Thus, a key feature of the CRI model is the mixing of classroom, school, and community-based learning situations.[110]

This type of integration is a far cry from the "dumping" of students back into general education settings, rightly decried by parents and advocates after their long-fought battles. It is also vastly different from the segregated programs that have proven ineffective for many students.

A new framework for education is needed; its entire organization must be reconceptualized. Within this new framework, it would be appropriate to question programs of special education as a separate means of educating students who are deemed unable to profit from school simply because of their handicapping conditions. The growth in the numbers of those categorized as having handicapping conditions was coincidental with the post-Sputnik concern for American competitiveness in the Cold War; young people who failed to keep up with rising standards were categorized as "slow learners," "mentally retarded," "emotionally disturbed," "culturally deprived," and "learning disabled." There was a disproportionate percentage of students from minority and low-income families in the first four categories, while White and middle-class students constituted the bulk of students in the last category.

This discriminatory way of categorizing served the function of preserving class and skin color privileges as the schools performed their assigned sorting function. And, in the current wave of school reform, "members of advantaged social groups will still advocate treating their failing children in ways that maintain their advantaged status as much as possible."[111] In essence,

> we are talking about the distribution of advantage and disadvantage in society through the differential provision of opportunities to acquire knowledge or to acquire the status that goes with having been exposed to a certain kind of knowledge. There is no question of simply doing it more or less effectively. Effectiveness in such situations only has a meaning when it relates to some set of recognized values or ideals.[112]

It is not simply a matter of using the present measurement instruments more sensitively or more discretely. Nearly three-quarters of a century ago, in a series of essays concerning the use of new IQ tests to measure officer candidates for World War I, Walter Lippmann wrote of his fear that these tests would be used to label children as inferior, and consign them to a second-class life. "It is not possible, I think, to imagine a more contemptible proceeding than to confront a child with a set of puzzles, and after an hour's monkeying with them, proclaim to the child, or to his parents, that here is a C-minus individual. It would not only be a contemptible thing to do. It would be a crazy thing to do. . . ."[113]

Drawing from an older history, one can learn from the experience on Martha's Vineyard in the eighteenth and nineteenth centuries, when it was the home of the highest concentration in the United States of people who were deaf. They were full participants in community life as workers, friends, neighbors, and family members:

> The fact that a society could adjust to disabled individuals, rather than requiring them to do all the adjusting, as is the case in American society as a whole, raises important questions about the rights of the disabled and the responsibilities of those who are not. The Martha's Vineyard experience suggests strongly that the concept of a handicap is an arbitrary social category. And if it is a question of definition, rather than a universal given, perhaps it can be redefined, and many of the cultural preconceptions summarized in the term "handicapped," as it is now used, eliminated.
>
> The most important lesson to be learned from Martha's Vineyard is that disabled people can be full and useful members of a community if the community makes an effort to include them.[114]

How then does one shape an educational system to include students with disabilities, one which is both consonant with and builds toward an inclusive society? Clearly, it is not done by taking students from the general education setting and labeling them as "deficient," nor is it done, as in special education, by focusing on the setting in which instruction takes place. Rather, research indicates that we must focus on the features of instruction that can produce improved learning for students.[115] Current practices, however, mean the "dumbing down" of the curriculum: "Instead of adapting instruction to individual differences to maximize common goal attainment.

. . special education programs . . . in the extreme, become merely dead ends where common goals have been dropped altogether."[116]

An important step toward a restructured unitary system is expressed in a concept called "Rights without Labels": namely, the provision of needed services for students without the deleterious consequences of classification and labeling. A joint statement issued by the National Association of School Psychologists, the National Association of Social Workers, and the National Coalition of Advocates for Students suggests guidelines to encourage the education of (at least mild to moderately handicapped) students in general education settings.[117]

Regardless of the conceptual undergirding or the organizational arrangements of education for students with handicapping conditions, special education practice needs substantial improvement. In maintaining a separate special education system, however, no matter how refined or improved, education will continue to operate based on a set of organizational and individual assumptions that disabled and nondisabled youngsters require two distinct sets of services, which in turn require distinct funding, service delivery, and organization. While P.L. 94–142 requires educational services for students with handicapping conditions, it does not require a special education system.

There is an alternative to separate systems: a merged or unitary system. The conception of a unitary system requires a "paradigm shift," a fundamental change in the way we think about differences among people, in the ways we choose to organize schools for their education, and in how we view the purpose of that education.[118] It rejects the bimodal division of handicapped and nonhandicapped students, and recognizes that individuals vary — that single-characteristic definitions fail to capture the complexity of people. Moreover, it rejects the belief, common to all human services work that incorporates a medical or deviancy model, that the problem lies in the individual and the resolution lies in one or another treatment modality. The unitary system, in contrast, requires adaptations in society and in education, not solely in the individual:

> No longer would there be a need to approach differences in human capabilities or characteristics as disabilities on which to base categorical groupings. In a merged system, an individual difference in visual ability, for example, could be viewed as only one of numerous characteristics of a student, rather than the overriding educational focus of a student's life. . . . It would not dictate differential placement and treatment according to a categorical affiliation which is often inherent in the disabilities approach to education.[119]

In a merged or unitary system, effective practices in classrooms and schools would characterize education for all students. No longer would there be an education system that focuses on the limitations of "handicapped" students, a teacher's incapacity to teach students because of a lack of special credentials, or instruction that is determined by the label attached to students. Nor would blame be placed on students or on family characteristics. Rather, the focus would be on effective instruction for all students based on the belief that "substantial student improvements occur when teachers accept the responsibility for the performance of all their students and when they structure their classrooms so that student success is a primary product of the interaction that takes place there."[120]

At present, students are hampered in their intellectual growth by the lack of appropriate supports available to them and their families. Appropriate supports could include: assessment based on multidimensional axes; psychosocial evaluations directed toward instruction; instructional practices that utilize current research; classrooms and schools designed to incorporate effective schools research; enhanced staff and curriculum development; early intervention and transition programs; and post-secondary education, training, work, and community living options.[121] A new system means curriculum adaptations and individualized educational strategies that would allow both general and special education students to take more difficult courses. Another phenomenon that now distinguishes general from special education is that in general education, "in order to help young people make wise course choices, schools are increasingly requiring students to take courses that match their grade level and abilities. Schools are also seeing to it that the materials used in those courses are intellectually challenging." Moreover: "the more rigorous the course of study, the more a student achieves, within the limits of his capacity. Student achievement also depends on how much the school emphasizes a subject and the amount of time spent on it: the more time expended, the higher the achievement. Successful teachers encourage their students' best efforts."[122]

Fundamental to the work in school effectiveness (exemplified best by the late Ron Edmonds's efforts in New York City's public schools) is the principle that school improvement must involve both quality and equity. In other words, the results of school reform must benefit *all* students. The effective schools research identified five factors that characterize schools that achieve quality and equity: 1) high expectations for all students, and staff acceptance of responsibility for students' learning; 2) instructional leadership on the part of the principal; 3) a safe and orderly environment conducive to learning; 4) a clear and focused mission concerning instructional goals shared by the staff; and 5) frequent monitoring of student progress.[123] Work on effective instructional techniques, including teacher-directed instruction, increased academic engaged time, use of reinforcement, and individual instruction has paralleled much of the effective schools research.

While tutoring programs have involved students with handicaps for some time,[124] more recently, programs have been developed in which students with handicaps serve as tutors for other students with handicaps and for those without.[125] This serves to integrate students with handicaps, to promote respect for their capacity, and to enable them to learn by teaching.[126]

Recent reports on cross-cultural education can provide additional features worth emulating in a new unitary system. In Japan, for example, reports note the importance of clear purpose, strong motivation, and high standards; the importance of parental involvement and reinforcement between home and school; and the importance of maximum time devoted to learning and its effective use. Perhaps most central is the belief that differences in student achievement come not from innate differences in ability but from level of effort, perseverance, and self-discipline, each of which the school can encourage and teach.[127] While innate differences are limiting for some students appropriately labeled as handicapped, they are not limiting for most students in special education today.

In the United States, there is a body of "adaptive education" approaches and specific educational practice attuned to individual differences that have been shown to be effective for students with handicapping conditions.[128] Asserting the legal duty to provide effective schooling, lawyers at the Public Interest Law Center of Philadelphia put it succinctly: "Play school is out. Schooling is a profession. The law requires that practice in the schools measure up to the art of what has been demonstrated by the professional to be possible. What is done must be calculated to be effective."[129] In the Adaptive Learning Environments Model (ALEM) and similar programs, there is a design that integrates both those who are labeled as handicapped and those who are not and that benefits both.[130]

The ultimate rationale for quality education of students in an integrated setting is based not only on law or pedagogy, but also on values. What kinds of people are we? What kind of society do we wish to develop? What values do we honor? The current failure to provide a quality education to all students and the perpetuation of segregated settings expresses one set of answers to these questions. To change the outcome, we need to develop another set of values. As Walter Lippmann said in 1922, "If a child fails in school and then fails in life, the schools cannot sit back and say: 'You see how accurately I predicted this.' Unless we are to admit that education is essentially impotent, we have to throw back the child's failure at the school, and describe it as a failure not by the child but by the school."[131]

While there is neither agreement among educators nor commitment by policymakers to a unitary system of quality education for all students, especially commitment in terms of money, we believe "we can, whenever and wherever we choose, successfully teach all children whose schooling is of interest to us. We already know more than we need in order to do this. Whether we do it must finally depend on how we feel about the fact that we haven't done it so far."[132]

NOTES

1. Nomenclature in the field of disability is often confusing and changing. Generally, disability refers to the individual's condition, while handicap refers to the consequence in society. Thus, for example, the individual with quadriplegia is disabled by the paralysis of his or her legs, but handicapped by the absence of a ramp to the local library. In special education, however, given the title of the major federal law P.L. 94–142, "The Education for All Handicapped Children Act," the term, 'handicapped' is used synonymously with disabled. We will, therefore, use the terms "students with handicapping conditions" and "persons with a disability" interchangeably. We do not use the words handicapped or disabled, nor refer to a particular condition, such as deaf or blind, as an adjective. Rather than saying "The deaf boy," we say, "The boy who is deaf." This makes the point that deafness is but one of the boy's characteristics, and not the most important.

2. For a study of the passage of Section 504, and the tortuous process of the issuance of regulations implementing it, see Richard K. Scotch, *From Good Will to Civil Rights: Transforming Federal Disability Policy* (Philadelphia: Temple University Press, 1984).

3. There is not one in-depth study of the law's development and passage. For a brief survey, see Roberta Weiner, *P.L. 94–142: Impact on the Schools* (Washington, DC: Capitol Publications, 1985).

4. Lisa J. Walker, "Procedural Rights in the Wrong System: Special Education Is Not Enough," in *Images of the Disabled/Disabling Images,* ed. Alan Gartner and Tom Joe (New York: Praeger, 1987), pp. 98–102.

5. Coined in 1959, normalization as a concept was introduced in the United States a decade later. Generally, it means giving people with disabilities opportunities to live in as normal a fashion as possible. See, in particular, R. B. Kugel and W. Wolfensberger, *Changing Patterns in Residential Services for the Mentally Retarded* (Washington, DC: President's Committee on Mental Retardation, 1969) and W. Wolfensberger, *The Principle of Normalization in Human Services* (Toronto: National Institute on Mental Retardation, 1971).

6. The medical model views disability as located within the individual, and, thus, primary emphasis is devoted to the etiology or causes of conditions and the placement of persons in separate diagnostic categories. From this perspective, efforts to improve the functional capabilities of individuals are regarded as the exclusive solution to disability.

7. *Ninth Annual Report to the Congress on the Implementation of the Education of the Handicapped Act* (Washington, DC: U. S. Department of Education, 1987), Table EA1.

8. *Ninth Annual Report,* Table EJ1.

9. Walker, "Procedural Rights in the Wrong System," p. 105.

10. Among myriad studies, see especially Patricia Craig, *Status of Handicapped Students* (Menlo Park, CA: SRI, 1978) and *Barriers to Excellence: Our Children at Risk,* report of the National Coalition of Advocates for Students (New York, 1985).

11. B. K. Keogh, "Learning Disabilities: Diversity in Search of Order," in *The Handbook of Special Education: Research and Practice,* vol 2., *Mildly Handicapped Conditions,* ed. Margaret C. Wang, Maynard C. Reynolds, and Herbert J. Walberg (Oxford: Pergamon, in press).

12. *Special Education: Views from America's Cities* (Washington, DC: The Council of Great City Schools, 1986), Tables 8 and 9.

13. James E. Ysseldyke et al., "Generalizations from Five Years of Research on Assessment and Decision-Making," *Exceptional Education Quarterly, 4* (1983), 75–93.

14. James E. Ysseldyke et al., "A Logical and Empirical Analysis of Current Practice in Classifying Students as Handicapped," *Exceptional Children, 50* (1983), 160–166.

15. Deaf, deaf-blind, hard of hearing, mentally retarded, multihandicapped, orthopedically impaired, other health impaired, seriously emotionally disturbed, specific learning disabled, speech impaired, and visually handicapped.

16. Margaret C. Wang, Maynard C. Reynolds, and Herbert J. Walberg, "Rethinking Special Education," *Educational Leadership, 44* (1986), 27.

17. Richard White and Mary Lynne Calhoun, "From Referral to Placement: Teachers' Perceptions of Their Responsibilities," *Exceptional Children, 53* (1987), 467.

18. Keogh, "Learning Disabilities."

19. Betty Binkard, "State Classifications of Handicapped Students: A National Comparative Data Report," *Counter-Point* 12 (1986), and *A Study of Special Education,* Table 2. Both the state and city data are for the 1984–85 school year but are not strictly comparable.

20. *Seventh Annual Report to Congress on the Implementation of the Education of the Handicapped Act* (Washington, DC: U. S. Department of Education, 1985), p. 4.

21. James E. Ysseldyke, "Classification of Handicapped Students," in *Handbook of Special Education: Research and Practice,* vol. 1, *Learner Characteristics and Adaptive Education,* ed. Margaret C. Wang, Maynard C. Reynolds, and Herbert J. Walberg (Oxford: Pergamon, in press).

22. W. A. Davis and L. A. Shepard, "Specialists' Use of Test and Clinical Judgment in the Diagnosis of Learning Disabilities," *Learning Disabilities Quarterly, 19* (1983), 128–138.

23. James E. Ysseldyke et al., *Similarities and Differences between Underachievers and Students Labelled Learning Disabled: Identical Twins with Different Mothers* (Minneapolis: University

of Minnesota, Institute for Research and Learning Disabilities, 1979) and James E. Ysseldyke et al., "Similarities and Differences between Low Achievers and Students Classified as Learning Disabled," *Journal of Special Education*, 16 (1982), 73–85.

24. Lorrie A. Shepard and L. A. Smith, *Evaluation of the Identification of Perceptual Communicative Disorders in Colorado* (Boulder: University of Colorado, 1981), p. 28.

25. Lorrie A. Shepard, L. A. Smith, and C. P. Vojir, "Characteristics of Pupils Identified as Learning Disabled," *Journal of Special Education*, 16 (1983), 73–85.

26. Davis and Shepard, "Specialists' Use of Tests and Clinical Judgment in the Diagnosis of Learning Disabilities"; James E. Ysseldyke et al., "Technical Adequacy of Tests Used by Professionals in Simulated Decision-Making," *Psychology in the Schools*, 17 (1980), 202–209; James E. Ysseldyke et al., "Declaring Students Eligible for Learning Disability Services: Why Bother with the Data?" *Learning Disability Quarterly*, 5 (1982), 37–44; James E. Ysseldyke and B. Algozzine, "LD or not LD: That's Not the Question!" *Journal of Learning Disabilities*, 16 (1983), 29–31; James E. Ysseldyke and B. Algozzine, *Introduction to Special Education* (Boston: Houghton Mifflin, 1984).

27. Nicholas Hobbs, "An Ecologically Oriented Service-Based System for Classification of Handicapped Children," in *The Ecosystem of the "Risk" Child*, ed. E. Salzmeyer, J. Antrobus, and J. Gliak (New York: Academic Press, 1980), p. 274.

28. C. Carlberg and Kenneth Kavale, "The Efficacy of Special versus Regular Class Placement for Exceptional Children: A Meta Analysis," *Journal of Special Education*, 14 (1980), 295–309. See also P. Johnston, R. L. Allington, and P. Afflerbach, "The Congruence of Classroom and Remedial Reading Evaluation," *Elementary School Journal*, 85 (1985), 465–478.

29. "Funding formulas that create incentives for more restrictive and separate class placement or that support particular configurations of services based on special education teacher allocations maintain an inflexible program structure and fail to allow models that encourage students to remain in general classrooms with resource room or individualized help. . . . States that provide financial incentives for separate placements, or which traditionally have had dual systems of services, place students disproportionately in more restrictive placements." Walker, "Procedural Rights in the Wrong System," p. 110.

30. Based upon a study of the effects of the state's funding formulae on the New York City public schools conducted by Lynn Weikart, Chief Administrator, Office of Finance and Management, Division of Special Education, 1981–83. The study found that the net cost to the school system — that is, program cost less state reimbursement — was greater when the student was placed in a more rather than less restrictive environment. In other words, while (generally) more restrictive placements cost more, the reimbursement was sufficiently greater so that the net cost to the school system favored more restrictive placements.

31. *Special Education*, Table 13. Again, these numbers must be viewed with some skepticism. Internal evidence suggests that the figures on students exiting from special education may, at least in some instances, be too high by at least half.

32. Dorothy Kerzner Lipsky and Alan Gartner, "Capable of Achievement and Worthy of Respect: Education for the Handicapped as if They Were Full-Fledged Human Beings," *Exceptional Children*, 54 (1987), 61.

33. Weiner, *P.L. 94-142*, p. 42.

34. Nancy A. Madden and Robert L. Slavin, *Count Me In: Academic Achievement and Social Outcomes of Mainstreaming Students with Mild Academic Handicaps* (Baltimore: The Johns Hopkins University Press, 1982), p. 1.

35. R. Bloomer et al., *Mainstreaming in Vermont: A Study of the Identification Process* (Livonia, NY: Brador Publications, 1982).

36. George J. Hagerty and Marty Abramson, "Impediments to Implementing National Policy Change for Mildly Handicapped Students," *Exceptional Children*, 53 (1987), 316.

37. William E. Bickel and Donna Diprima Bickel, "Effective Schools, Classrooms, and Instruction: Implications for Special Education," *Exceptional Children*, 52 (1986), 489–500.

38. Catherine V. Morsink et al., "Research on Teaching: Opening the Door to Special Education Classrooms," *Exceptional Children, 53* (1986), 38.

39. James E. Ysseldyke, "Current Practices in Making Psychoeducational Decisions about Learning Disabled Students," *Journal of Learning Disabilities, 16* (1983), 226–233.

40. *Special Education,* Table 21.

41. Roncker v. Walter 700 F. 2d 1058 (1983), *cert. denied,* 104 S. Ct. 196 (1983).

42. *Standards and Guidelines for Compliance with Federal Requirements for the Education of the Handicapped* (Washington, DC: Office of Special Education Programs, U. S. Department of Education, 1986), p. 24.

43. Walker, "Procedural Rights in the Wrong System," p. 104.

44. National Center for Education Statistics, *The School-Age Handicapped* (Washington, DC: Government Printing Office, 1985), p. 20.

45. "Special Ed Students Kept in Restrictive Environments, Disability Groups Say," *Education of the Handicapped* (29 October 1986), pp. 5–6.

46. *Out of the Mainstream: Education of Disabled Youth in Massachusetts* (Boston: Massachusetts Advocacy Center, 1987).

47. "Improved Special Education Monitoring Unearthing More Flaws, ED Says," *Education Daily* (21 April 1987), p. 3.

48. *Ninth Annual Report,* p. 166.

49. Janet Sansone and Naomi Zigmond, "Evaluating Mainstreaming through an Analysis of Students' Schedules," *Exceptional Children, 52* (1986), 452–458.

50. Sansone and Zigmond, "Evaluating Mainstreaming," p. 455.

51. The opportunity "to provide preparation periods for special education teachers . . . seems to be the decisive factor in these assignments." Sansone and Zigmond, "Evaluating Mainstreaming," p. 455.

52. *Special Education,* Table 13.

53. Andrew S. Halpern, "Transition: A Look at the Foundations," *Exceptional Children, 51* (1985), 483.

54. Despite myriad studies concerning P.L. 94–142, there has not been a systematic study nor an in-depth evaluation of parental involvement in the education of their children. Rick Rodgers, *Caught in the Act: What LEA's Tell Parents under the 1981 Education Act* (London: Centre for Studies on Integration in Education, 1986) is a model for this.

55. B. L. Baker and R. P. Brightman, "Access of Handicapped Children to Educational Services," in *Children, Mental Health, and the Law,* ed. N. D. Repucci, L. A. Withorn, E. P. Mulvey, and J. Monahan (Beverly Hills, CA: Sage, 1984), p. 297.

56. *A National Survey of Individualized Education Programs (IEPs) for Handicapped Children* (Triangle Park, NC: Research Triangle Institute, 1980).

57. C. A. Scanlon, J. Arick, and N. Phelps, "Participation in the Development of the IEP: Parents' Perspective," *Exceptional Children, 47* (1981), 373.

58. S. Goldstein, B. Strickland, A. P. Turnbull, and L. Curry, "An Observational Analysis of the IEP Conference," *Exceptional Children, 46* (1980), 278–286.

59. C. E. Meyers and Jan Blacher, "Parents' Perception of Schooling for Severely Handicapped Children: Home and Family Variables," *Exceptional Children, 53* (1987), 441.

60. *Ninth Annual Report,* p. 71.

61. See, for example, Philip M. Ferguson and Dianne L. Ferguson, "Parents and Professionals," in *Introduction to Special Education,* ed. Peter Knoblock (Boston: Little, Brown, in press); Seymour B. Sarason and John Doris, *Educational Handicap, Public Policy, and Social History* (New York: Free Press, 1979); H. Rutherford Turnbull, III, and Ann P. Turnbull, eds., *Parents Speak Out: Then and Now,* 2nd ed. (Columbus, OH: Charles C. Merrill, 1985); Philip M. Ferguson and Adrienne Asch, "What We Want for Our Children: Perspectives of Parents and Adults with Disabilities," in *Schooling and Disability,* ed. Douglas Biklen, Philip M. Ferguson, and Allison Ford (Chicago: National Society for the Study of Education, in press).

62. Dorothy Kerzner Lipsky, "A Parental Perspective on Stress and Coping," *American Journal of Orthopsychiatry, 55* (1985), 616.

63. Ferguson and Asch, "What We Want for Our Children."

64. A recent version of this is reported in Lori Granger and Bill Granger, *The Magic Feather* (New York: E. P. Dutton, 1986). Diagnosticians, having decided that the Grangers' child could not read, refused to heed the parents' report that he read at home; therefore, they failed to ask him to read, but rather only subjected him to batteries of tests to explain why he could not read.

65. Ferguson and Asch, "What We Want for Our Children."

66. "Report of the United Nations Expert Group Meeting on Barrier-Free Design," *International Rehabilitation Review 26* (1975), 3.

67. Douglas Biklen, "The Culture of Poverty: Disability Images in Literature and Their Analogies in Public Policy," *Policy Studies Journal,* forthcoming.

68. Erving Goffman, *Stigma: Notes on the Management of Spoiled Identities* (Englewood Cliffs, NJ: Prentice-Hall, 1963).

69. Ved Mehta, "Personal History," *The New Yorker, 60,* 53 (1985), 61.

70. A new law, P.L. 99–435, states: "No air carrier may discriminate against any otherwise qualified handicapped individual, by reason of such handicap, in the provision of air travel." Of course, the question here is the interpretation, should differential service be provided, as to whether it is "by reason of such handicap." *The Braille Monitor,* the National Foundation of the Blind's publication, provides extensive treatment of this topic from the perspective of an organization of the blind.

71. Richard Gross, Alan Cox, and Michael Pollay, "Early Management and Decision Making for the Treatment of Myelomeningocele," *Pediatrics* (1983).

72. Nat Hentoff, "The Awful Privacy of Baby Doe," *Atlantic Monthly* (1985), 59.

73. See particularly, Michelle Fine and Adrienne Asch, "Disability beyond Stigma: Social Interaction, Discrimination, and Activism," *Journal of Social Issues,* forthcoming; William Gliedeman and William Roth, *The Unexpected Minority: Handicapped Children in America* (New York: Harcourt Brace Jovanovich, 1980); Harlan Hahn, "Paternalism and Public Policy," *Society* (1983), 36–42; Robert Funk, "Disability Rights: From Caste to Class in the Context of Civil Rights"; and Harlan Hahn, "Civil Rights for Disabled Americana: The Formulation of a Political Agenda," in *Images of the Disabled/Disabling Images,* ed. Alan Gartner and Tom Joe (New York: Praeger, 1987).

74. Gerben DeJong and Raymond Lifchez, "Physical Disability and Public Policy," *Scientific American, 248* (1983), 40–49.

75. Louis Harris and Associates, *Disabled Americans' Self-Perceptions: Bringing Disabled Americans into the Mainstream* (New York: Louis Harris and Associates, 1986).

76. National Council on the Handicapped, *Toward Independence: A Report to the President and to the Congress of the United States* (Washington, DC: The Council, 1986), pp. 22–29.

77. For a description of these images as expressed in literature, the press, television, and the movies and a discussion of the ways in which the images play themselves out in policies in employment, education, health care, everyday living, and the treatment of newborns, see *Images of the Disabled/Disabling Images,* ed. Alan Gartner and Tom Joe (New York: Praeger, 1987).

78. "On Cases of Contagion," *New York Times,* 4 March 1987, p. A21.

79. Fine and Asch, "Disability beyond Stigma."

80. Robert Bogdan and J. Kugelmass, "Case Studies of Mainstreaming: A Symbolic Interactionist Approach to Special Schooling," in *Special Education and Societal Interests,* ed. L. Barton and S. Tomlinson (London: Croom-Helm, 1984), p. 173.

81. These are annotated "regular" diplomas which denote that the student has achieved the goals and objective of her/his IEP. Such diplomas may reduce the pressure upon school districts to provide educational services that enable all students, including those labeled as handicapped, to earn a diploma.

     And where so-called minimum competency tests are used as diploma requirements, there are questions as to adequate notice, common courses of study, and the appropriateness of the competencies used, as well as test validity. Martha M. McCarthy, "The Application of Competency Testing Mandates to Handicapped Students," *Harvard Educational Review, 53* (1983), 146–164.

82. Granger and Granger, *The Magic Feather,* pp. 26, 27.

83. Doug Guess, Holly Anne Benson, and Ellin Siegel-Causey, "Concepts and Issues Related to Choice-Making and Autonomy among Persons with Severe Disabilities;" *Journal of the Association for Persons with Severe Handicaps, 10* (1985), 83. The authors' suggestion that the opportunity for choice-making may have a positive effect upon an individual's learning appears to be correct. Analysis of programs involving persons with severe handicaps indicates that those which involve opportunities for choice are more effective; that is, increase the subject's learning. Alan Gartner, "TASH Reflects Changes," *TASH Newsletter* (October, 1986), p. 12.

84. The approved process in carrying out disciplinary action for students with handicapping procedures involves the same clinical procedure which labeled the child; it must be used to determine whether the misconduct in question was a manifestation of the handicapping condition.

85. We favor the inclusion of all children in the public schools and believe that all can and should be educated in integrated settings. We oppose segregated schemes, such as that developed recently by the New York City Board of Education, which responded to the abuse of gay and lesbian students by setting up a separate and segregated school for them, rather than by meeting its obligation to provide safe settings for all students.

86. Walker, "Procedural Rights in the Wrong System," p. 105.

87. *A Policy-Oriented Study of Special Education's Service Delivery Systems Research* (Triangle Park, NC: Research Triangle Institute, 1984).

88. *School Psychology: A Blueprint for Training and Practice* (Minneapolis: National School Psychology Inservice Training Network, 1984), pp. 7–9.

89. Granger and Granger, *The Magic Feather,* p. xii.

90. Shepard, "The New Push for Excellence," p. 328.

91. Lipsky and Gartner, "Capable of Achievement," p. 59.

92. Walker, "Procedural Rights in the Wrong System," p. 109.

93. Marleen Pugach and Mara Sapon-Shevin, "New Agendas for Special Education Policy: What the National Reports Haven't Said," *Exceptional Children, 53* (1987), 295–299, and Mara Sapon-Shevin, "The National Education Reports and Special Education: Implications for Students," *Exceptional Children, 53* (1987), 300–307.

94. M. Stephen Lilly, "Lack of Focus on Special Education in Literature on Educational Reform," *Exceptional Children, 53* (1987), 326, 327.

95. Heritage Foundation, "The Crisis: Washington Shares the Blame," *The Heritage Foundation Backgrounder* (Washington, DC: The Heritage Foundation, 1984), pp. 1, 12.

96. Sapon-Shevin, "The National Education Reports," p. 304.

97. Granger and Granger, *The Magic Feather,* p. xi.

98. *Special Education,* p. 52.

99. "Deaf, Blind Need Both Segregated and Mainstreamed Services, Experts Say," *Education Daily,* 9 December 1986, p. 4.

100. "Kennedy Institute First Special Ed School to Receive Accreditation," *Education Daily,* 26 November 1986, p. 2.

101. Michael M. Gerber, "The Department of Education's Sixth Annual Report to Congress on P.L. 94–142: Is Congress Getting the Full Story?" *Exceptional Children, 51* (1984), 213.

102. Margaret C. Wang, Maynard C. Reynolds, and Herbert J. Walberg, "Rethinking Special Education," *Education Leadership* (1986), 26–31.

103. *Educating Students with Learning Problems — A Shared Responsibility,* A Report to the Secretary (Washington, DC: Office of Special Education and Rehabilitative Services, 1986), pp. 7–9.

104. See Susan Stainback and William Stainback, "Integration versus Cooperation: A Commentary on 'Educating Children with Learning Problems: A Shared Responsibility,'" *Exceptional Children, 54* (1987), 66–68.

105. L. Brown et al., "Toward the Realization of the Least Restrictive Educational Environments for Severely Handicapped Students," *AAESPH Review, 2* (1977), 198.

106. "Integration is *not* mainstreaming. . . . Children [with severe handicaps] who are integrated spend the majority of each school day in a special education classroom, although they join non-handicapped peers for certain nonacademic activities. The education needs of the two groups are too disparate to warrant putting them together for academic activities. But integration provides a supportive environment in which nonhandicapped children and severely handicapped youngsters can play and grow as well as learn from one another." Mary Frances Hanline and Carola Murray, "Integrating Severely Handicapped Children into Regular Public Schools," *Phi Delta Kappan* (December 1984), 274.

107. Bud Fredericks, "Back to the Future: Integration Revisited," *TASH Newsletter, 13,* No. 6 (1987), 1.

108. Douglas Biklen, *Achieving the Complete School: Strategies for Effective Mainstreaming* (New York: Teachers College Press, 1985).

109. Susan Stainback and William Stainback, *Educating Students with Severe Handicaps in Regular Schools* (Reston, VA: The Council for Exceptional Children, 1985).

110. Wayne Sailor, Lori Goetz, Jacki Anderson, Pam Hunt, and Kathy Gee, "Integrated Community Intensive Instruction" in *Generalization and Maintenance in Applied Settings,* ed. R. Horner, G. Dunlap, and R. Koegel (Baltimore: Paul H. Brookes, in press); Wayne Sailor, Ann Halvorsen, Jacki Anderson, Lori Goetz, Kathy Gee, Kathy Doering, and Pam Hunt, "Community Intensive Instruction" in *Education of Learners with Severe Handicaps,* ed. R. Horner, L. Meyer, and H. Fredericks (Baltimore: Paul H. Brookes, 1986).

111. Christine E. Sleeter, "Learning Disabilities: The Social Construction of a Special Education Category," *Exceptional Children, 53* (1986), 52.

112. F. Inglis, "Ideology and the Curriculum: The Value Assumptions of Systems Builders," *Policy Sciences, 18* (1985), 5.

113. Cited in Granger and Granger, *The Magic Feather,* p. v.

114. Nora Ellen Groce, *Everyone Here Spoke Sign Language: Hereditary Deafness on Martha's Vineyard* (Cambridge: Harvard University Press, 1985), p. 108.

115. Sapon-Shevin, "The National Education Reports," p. 303.

116. R. E. Snow, "Placing Children in Special Education: Some Comments," *Educational Researcher, 13* (1984), 13.

117. The statement is available from the Advocacy Center for the Elderly and Disabled, 1001 Howard Avenue, New Orleans, LA 70113.

118. Thomas S. Kuhn, ed., *The Structure of Scientific Revolutions* (Chicago: University of Chicago Press, 1962).

119. William Stainback and Nancy Stainback, "A Rationale for the Merger of Special and Regular Education," *Exceptional Children, 51* (1984), 109.

120. B. Algozzine and L. Maheady, "When All Else Fails, Teach!" *Exceptional Children, 52* (1985), 498.

121. Our focus in this article has been on school services. However, we cannot fail to note that whatever the many inadequacies of the education for students with handicapping conditions, services for those who have "aged out" of the P.L. 94–142 entitlement are far fewer. For example, a recent article notes that while approximately 50,000 mentally impaired students, those with IQs of 70 and below, leave school each year, there are only "roughly 5,000 places in training and support programs nationwide. . . ." William Celis, III, "Generation of Retarded Youth Emerges from Public Schools — But Little Awaits," *Wall Street Journal,* 16 January 1987, p. 25.

122. *What Works: Research about Teaching and Learning* (Washington, DC: U. S. Department of Education, 1986), p. 59.

123. Ronald Edmonds, "Effective Schools for the Urban Poor," *Educational Leadership, 37* (1979), 15–27, and "Some Schools Work and More Can," *Social Policy, 9,* No. 5 (1979), 26–31.

124. Joseph R. Jenkins and Linda M. Jenkins, *Cross Age and Peer Tutoring: Help for Children with Learning Problems* (Reston, VA: The Council for Exceptional Children, 1981).

125. R. T. Osguthorpe and T. E. Scruggs, "Special Education Students as Tutors: A Review and Analysis," *Remedial and Special Education,* 7, No. 4 (1986), 15–26.

126. Alan Gartner, Mary Conway Kohler, and Frank Riessman, *Children Teach Children: Learning by Teaching* (New York: Harper & Row, 1971).

127. *Japanese Education Today* (Washington, DC: U.S. Department of Education, 1987).

128. Margaret C. Wang and Herbert J. Walberg, eds., *Adapting Instruction to Individual Differences* (Berkeley, CA: McCutchan, 1985).

129. Frank J. Laski, Thomas K. Gilhool, and Stephen F. Gold, "A Legal Duty to Provide Effective Schooling," Adaptive Instruction Conference, 3 June 1983, p. 8.

130. Margaret C. Wang, Stephen Peverly, and Robert Randolph, "An Investigation of the Implementation and Effects of a Full-Time Mainstreaming Program," *Remedial and Special Education,* 5 (1984), 21–32. The authors of this article were responsible for the introduction of the Adaptive Learning Environments Model (ALEM) program into the New York City public schools when, respectively, they were Executive Director and Chief Administrator for Program Development, Division of Special Education. We did this at the behest of the Chancellor, Frank J. Macchiarola, whose support of the program expressed his belief that all students can learn and that it was the obligation of the school system to enable that to happen. Basically, the ALEM program involved the full-time mainstreaming of students certified as handicapped in a program that adapted curricula to each student's needs, paced learning at an individual rate, and taught students to take responsibility for their own learning.

131. Walter Lippmann, "The Reliability of Intelligence Tests," *The New Republic* (1922), reprinted in *The I. Q. Controversy,* ed. N. J. Block and Gerald Dworkin (New York: Random House, 1976), p. 17.

132. Edmonds, "Some Schools Work and More Can," p. 29.

The Special Education Paradox

Equity as the Way to Excellence

—————— *8* ——————

THOMAS M. SKRTIC

> The final result of political action often, no, even regularly, stands in
> completely inadequate and often even paradoxical relation to its original
> meaning.   — Max Weber, *Politics as a Vocation*[1]

Although the Education for All Handicapped Children Act of 1975 (EHA) marked the end of a successful policy revolution in which the spirit of mainstreaming was formalized in law, the special education community knew that if the law was to amount to anything more than "a comprehensive set of empty promises" (Abeson & Zettel, 1977, p. 115), an implementation revolution would also have to be mounted and won (Abeson & Zettel, 1977; National Advisory Committee on the Education of the Handicapped, 1976; Weintraub, 1977). The strategy for winning the implementation revolution was to follow the letter of the law because special education professionals and advocates were convinced that the EHA "would only work if [they] and others made it work by using the procedures set forth in the law" (Weintraub, 1977, p. 114). At the time, of course, this appeared to be a prudent course of action. But the tragic irony is that the letter of the law has become the principal barrier to achieving the spirit of the law (see, for example, Gartner & Lipsky, 1987; Reynolds, Wang, & Walberg, 1987, Skrtic, Guba, & Knowlton, 1985; Stainback & Stainback, 1984; Walker, 1987).

Although no one in the special education community is questioning the spirit of the EHA, or the fact that some important implementation battles have been won, there is widespread concern that the implementation revolution has been lost (see, for example, Gartner & Lipsky, 1987; Reynolds, Wang, & Walberg, 1987; Stainback & Stainback, 1984; Will, 1986a). In fact, the sense of defeat is so pervasive that many of those who had been staunch supporters of the EHA are calling for a new revolution. This new revolution, which has come to be known as the Regular Education Initiative (REI), represents a number of proposals for achieving the spirit of the EHA for stu-

Harvard Educational Review   Vol. 61   No. 2   May 1991, 148–206

dents with disabilities by extending its rights and resources to all students. Although there is opposition to the REI within the special education community, even its detractors agree that there are serious problems with the EHA and that, in principle, the REI has some appealing features (for example, Kauffman, Gerber, & Semmel, 1988; Keogh, 1988). However, those who oppose the REI are rightfully concerned that a new revolution could mean a loss of hard-won rights and, in the worst case, a full-circle return to the unacceptable conditions that existed before the EHA (Kauffman, 1988, 1989b; Kauffman, Gerber, & Semmel, 1988).

The REI debate parallels the earlier mainstreaming debate in at least three ways. First, in both cases, the ethics and efficacy of special education practices are criticized and a new approach is proposed. In the 1960s, the practices associated with the segregated special classroom were criticized for being racially biased, instructionally ineffective, and socially and psychologically damaging, and mainstreaming (and eventually the EHA) emerged as the solution (Abeson & Zettel, 1977; Christophos & Renz, 1969; Deno, 1970; Dunn, 1968; Johnson, 1962). In the current debate, the practices associated with mainstreaming and the EHA are under attack for virtually the same reasons (Heller, Holtzman, & Messick, 1982; Hobbs, 1980; Wang, Reynolds, & Walberg, 1987a), and the REI is being advocated as the new solution.

The second parallel is that both debates take place during a period of apparent reform in public education, the character of which is seen as consistent with the proposed special education reform. In the 1960s, advocates of mainstreaming argued that nascent structural reforms and instructional innovations in public education (for example, team teaching, open classrooms, individualized instruction) were consistent with the mainstreaming concept (Dunn, 1968). Today, the REI proponents are arguing that calls for school restructuring and the availability of new instructional technologies (for example, cooperative learning, teacher collaboration) are consistent with their reform proposals (Lipsky & Gartner, 1989a; Pugach & Lilly, 1984; Stainback, Stainback, & Forest, 1989; Wang 1989a,b; Wang, Reynolds, & Walberg, 1985, 1986).[2]

The third parallel explains the first two: both debates are forms of *naïve pragmatism*, a mode of analysis and problem resolution that is premised on an unreflective acceptance of the assumptions that lie behind social practices. As such, naive pragmatism is "socially reproductive, instrumentally and functionally reproducing accepted meanings and conventional organizations, institutions, and ways of doing things for good or ill" (Cherryholmes, 1988, p. 151). Thus, the problem with the mainstreaming and REI debates is that their criticism stops at the level of special education practices; neither one questions the assumptions in which these practices are grounded. In the case of the mainstreaming debate, the result was that the new practices associated with the EHA and mainstreaming simply reproduced the special education problems of the 1960s in the 1980s (Skrtic, 1987a, 1988b). Moreover, although the REI debate implicates these assumptions and thus is less naive than the mainstreaming debate, it does not explicitly recognize the connection between special education practices and assumptions, and thus promises to reproduce the problems of the 1980s in the 1990s and beyond (Skrtic, 1988b, 1991).

It is a given, of course, that resolving social problems always requires one to be pragmatic. But being pragmatic in a just and productive way, in a way that does not merely reproduce and extend the original problems, requires a critical form of pragmatism, a mode of inquiry that accepts the fact that our assumptions themselves require evaluation and reappraisal (Cherryholmes, 1988). The advantage today is that revolutionary developments in the social disciplines are providing the conceptual and methodological insights for analyzing social practices from the perspective of their grounding assumptions.[3] Although the REI and mainstreaming debates are forms of naive pragmatism, by appropriating these insights and applying them to special education practices, it is possible to address the field's past and present problems in terms of *critical pragmatism*, a mode of analysis in which the grounding assumptions of social practices are themselves treated as problematic (Cherryholmes, 1988; Skrtic, 1991). Moreover, by conducting such an analysis of special education, and by extending it and its implication to public education per se, it is possible to address the broader question of educational reform in a way that reconciles the historical contradiction between the social goals of educational excellence and educational equity.

In subsequent sections I apply a form of critical pragmatism to three interrelated practices and their grounding assumptions.[4] The practices are: a) special education as a professional practice, b) special education as an institutional practice of public education, and c) public education as a social practice of our society. Because ultimately I am concerned with the legitimacy of public education, my approach is to subject it to an immanent critique, a form of criticism that asks whether public education's institutional *practices* are consistent with its democratic *ideals*. As such, I am interested in restoring the legitimacy of public education — that is, in transforming the real (actual practices) into the ideal — by forcing the reader to consider whether it is living up to its own standards.[5]

To carry out the immanent critique of public education, I conduct critical readings of three discourses, each of which surrounds, shapes, and legitimizes one of the three practices noted above. The discourses are: a) the REI debate in the field of special education, b) the discourse on school organization and adaptability in the field of educational administration,[6] and c) the discourse on school failure in the institution of public education. The purpose of reading the discourses critically is to deconstruct them — and thus the practices they legitimize — by exposing their silences, inconsistencies, contradictions, and incompleteness relative to their grounding assumptions.[7] The purpose of deconstructing the discourses and practices is to show that their grounding assumptions are inadequate and in need of reappraisal, that alternative assumptions are possible and desirable, and, most important, that choosing grounding assumptions is a political and moral act with implications for ethical practice and a just society.

The significance of the REI debate is that, when read critically, it provides the grounds to deconstruct special education as a professional practice, which, in conjunction with a critical reading of the discourse on school organization and adaptability, provides the grounds to deconstruct special education as an institutional practice of public education. The broader significance of deconstructing the institutional practice of special education is that, together with a critical reading of the discourse on educational excellence in general education,[8] it deconstructs the discourse on school failure in the institution of public education. Ultimately, without the legitimizing effect of the discourse on school failure, the immanent contradiction between its institutional practices and democratic ideals deconstructs twentieth-century public education and prepares the way for reconstructing it according to its traditional democratic ideals and the changing historical conditions of the twenty-first century.

The remainder of this article is divided into seven major sections. The first section is a genealogy of the twentieth-century discourse on school failure, which provides an overview of my basic argument and identifies the assumptions that ground the professional and institutional practices and discourses of public education — the assumptions that I believe need to be reappraised.[9] In the second section I deconstruct special education as a professional practice by showing that a critical reading of the REI debate delegitimizes its grounding assumptions. The third section is a critical reading of the discourse on school organization and adaptability. On the basis of this reading, I introduce an alternative way to conceptualize school organization and the problem of change, which I use in the fourth section to deconstruct special education as an institutional practice of public education. In the fifth section I combine my analysis of special education with a critical reading of the discourse on educational excellence in general education. My aim in this section is to show how these critical readings converge to delegitimize the discourse on school failure and, ultimately, to deconstruct the institution of public education. After section five, my focus shifts to reconstructing public education. In the sixth section I propose an alternative organizational configuration for schooling that is both excellent and equitable, and in the final section I consider the implications of this particular configuration for the emerging political and economic relevancies of the twenty-first century.

FUNCTIONALISM AND THE PROBLEM OF SCHOOL FAILURE

Functionalism, the dominant mode of theorizing in the social disciplines (Bernstein, 1976; Rorty, 1979) and the professions (Glazer, 1974; Schön, 1983), including general education (Bowles & Gintis, 1976; Feinberg & Soltis, 1985; Giroux, 1981), educational administration (Griffiths, 1983, 1988), and special education (Heshusius, 1982; Iano, 1986; Skrtic, 1986), presupposes that social reality is objective, inherently orderly, and rational, and thus that social and human problems are pathological (Foucault, 1954/1976, 1961/1973; Ritzer, 1980). As such, the functionalist worldview institutionalized the mutually reinforcing theories of *organizational rationality* and *human pathology* in society and in public education. As a result, when industrialization and compulsory school attendance converged to produce large numbers of students who were difficult to teach in traditional classrooms, the problem of school failure was reframed as two interrelated problems — inefficient organizations and defective students. This distorted the problem by largely removing it from the general education discourse and compartmentalizing it into two separate but mutually reinforcing discourses. The first one was in the developing field of educational administration, which, in the interest of maximizing organizational efficiency, was compelled to rationalize its orientation according to the precepts of scientific management (Callahan, 1962). The second was in the new field of special education, which emerged as a means to remove and contain the most recalcitrant students in the interest of maintaining order in the rationalized school plant (Lazerson, 1983; Sarason & Doris, 1979).

The discourses of all three fields are shaped by explicit presuppositions grounded in their respective foundations of professional knowledge, as well as by implicit presuppositions grounded in the social norms of human pathology and organizational rationality. Because its professional knowledge is grounded in scientific management, educational administration presupposes explicitly that school organizations are rational (Clark, 1985; Griffiths, 1983) and implicitly that school failure is pathological (Skrtic, 1991).[10] Conversely, special education's professional grounding in psychology and biology (medicine) means that it presupposes explicitly that school failure is pathological (Mercer, 1973; Skrtic, 1986) and implicitly that school organizations are rational (Skrtic, 1987a, 1988b). Given that its professional grounding is in psychology *and* scientific management (Cherryholmes, 1988; Oakes, 1985, 1986a,b; Spring, 1980), the general education discourse is grounded explicitly and implicitly in both presuppositions.

Taken together, these presuppositions yield four mutually reinforcing assumptions that shape the discourses and practices of all three fields and thus of public education itself. In the language of the special education discourse, these assumptions are that: a) disabilities are pathological conditions that students have, b) differential diagnosis is objective and useful, c) special education is a rationally conceived and coordinated system of services that benefits diagnosed students, and d) progress results from rational technological improvements in diagnostic and instructional practices (Bogdan & Knoll, 1988; Bogdan & Kuglemass, 1984; Mercer, 1973; Skrtic, 1986).[11] Inquiry in all three fields is dominated by functionalist methodologies (Griffiths, 1983, 1988; Lincoln & Guba, 1985; Poplin, 1987; Skrtic, 1986), which favor data over theory and assume, more or less, that empirical data are objective and self-evident (Churchman, 1971; Mitroff & Pondy, 1974). Thus, each discourse is a form of naive pragmatism that produces and interprets empirical data on student outcomes and school effects intuitively, according to the four taken-for-granted assumptions about disability, diagnosis, special education, and progress. This reproduces the status quo in all three fields, which reaffirms the four assumptions and, ultimately, reinforces the functionalist presuppositions of organizational rationality and human pathology in public education and society.

Thus, the institutional practice of special education (and the very notion of student disability) is an artifact of the functionalist quest for rationality, order, and certainty in the field of education, a quest that is both intensified and legitimized by the institutional practice of educational administration.[12] As such, special education distorts the problem of school failure and, ultimately, prevents the field of education from entering into a productive confrontation with uncertainty. And because uncertainty is a necessary precondition for growth of knowledge and progress in communal activities such as the physical sciences (Kuhn, 1970), the social sciences (Barnes,

1982; Bernstein, 1983), and the professions (Schön, 1983; Skrtic, 1991), the object-ification and legitimization of school failure as student disability prevents public edu-cation from moving beyond its functionalist practices. The problem in special educa-tion and educational administration has been that, although both fields have experienced enough uncertainty to call their traditional practices into question,[13] they have lacked a critical discourse for addressing their problems in a reflective man-ner (Bates, 1980, 1987; Foster, 1986; Skrtic, 1986, 1991; Tomlinson, 1982). The problem in general education, however, is more fundamental. Not only has it lacked a critical discourse (Cherryholmes, 1988; Giroux, 1981, 1983; Sirotnik & Oakes, 1986), it has been largely prevented from having to confront uncertainty altogether, precisely because of the objectification of school failure as student disability. Ultimately, the problem is that this distortion of school failure prevents public education from seeing that it is not living up to its democratic ideals.

Public education in a democracy must be both excellent and equitable. If America was to avoid tyranny and remain free, Jefferson argued, public education must pro-duce excellent (intelligent, imaginative, reflective) citizens and assure that "[persons] of talent might rise whatever their social and economic origins" (Greer, 1972, p. 16). The problem with the Jeffersonian ideal, however, is that its democratic ends are con-tradicted by the bureaucratic means that were used to actualize universal public edu-cation in this century. As such, the failure of public education to be either excellent or equitable can be understood in terms of the inherent contradiction between democ-racy and bureaucracy in the modern state (Weber, 1922/1978). Special education, then, can be understood as the institutional practice that emerged to contain this contradiction in public education. And because social institutions are best under-stood from their dark side — from the perspective of the institutional practices that emerge to contain their failures (Foucault, 1983) — special education is a particularly insightful vantage point for deconstructing twentieth-century public education. The paradox in all of this is that, when read critically, special education provides the struc-tural and cultural insights that are necessary to begin reconstructing public education for the historical conditions of the twenty-first century and, ultimately, for recon-ciling it with its democratic ideals.

SPECIAL EDUCATION AS A PROFESSIONAL PRACTICE

Although the REI is generally thought of as a 1980s phenomenon, the first criticism of the EHA and mainstreaming, in the language of what was to become the REI, ap-peared in 1976 (Reynolds, 1976; Reynolds & Birch, 1977), barely a year after the EHA had been signed into law and nearly two full years before it was to become fully effec-tive.[14] The next papers promoting the REI appeared in the early 1980s, and since then a body of supporting literature has been produced by four teams of writers whose names have become synonymous with the pro-REI position.[15] This literature contains two lines of argument: one against the current special education system, and one for certain general and special education reforms intended to correct the situation.

The arguments against the current system address an array of technical and ethical problems associated with the elaborate classification system required by the EHA, as well as instructional problems associated with the pull-out approach implied by mainstreaming. Although the reforms for addressing these problems are unique to particular teams of REI proponents, all four teams agree that the EHA and mainstreaming are fundamentally flawed, particularly for students who are classified as mildly to moderately handicapped (hereafter, mildly handicapped); that is, students classified as learning disabled, emotionally disturbed, and mentally retarded, who make up over two-thirds of the 4.5 million students served under the law.[16] Although the field's initial reaction to the REI was mixed, a full-blown controversy developed in 1988 when several leading figures in the three mild disability subfields published a *tour de force* response criticizing the REI.[17] Since then, the controversy has become a heated debate over the ethics and efficacy of the current system of special education on the one hand, and the wisdom and feasibility of the REI reform proposals on the other.[18]

Criticism of the Current System

The debate over current practices is important because it is implicitly a debate over the adequacy of special education's grounding assumptions, which are recast below in the form of questions.

Are Mild Disabilities Pathological?

Although the debate has been quite heated, there is virtually no disagreement on this point.[19] Both the REI proponents (Gartner & Lipsky, 1987; Pugach & Lilly, 1984; Stainback & Stainback, 1984; Wang, Reynolds, & Walberg, 1986, 1987b) and opponents (for example, Braaten, Kauffman, Braaten, Polsgrove, & Nelson, 1988; Bryan, Bay, & Donahue, 1988; Council for Children with Behavioral Disorders, 1989; Kauffman, Gerber, & Semmel, 1988; Keogh, 1988) agree that there are students for whom the mildly handicapped designation is an objective distinction based on a pathology, but that because of a number of definitional and measurement problems, as well as problems related to the will or capacity of teachers and schools to accommodate student diversity, many students identified as mildly handicapped are not truly disabled in the pathological sense, a situation that is particularly true for students identified as learning disabled. Moreover, both sides in the debate agree that there are additional students in school who remain unidentified and thus unserved; while some of these students have mild pathological disabilities, there are others who do not but nonetheless require assistance. Although the REI proponents recognize that many of these students, including those who have or are thought to have mild disabilities, present difficult problems for classroom teachers, their point is simply that neither the general education system nor the special education system is sufficiently adaptable to accommodate their individual needs (for example, Gartner & Lipsky, 1987; Pugach & Lilly, 1984; Wang, Reynolds, & Walberg, 1986), a point with which most REI opponents agree (Bryan, Bay, & Donahue, 1988; Kauffman, 1988; Kauffman, Gerber, & Semmel, 1988; Keogh, 1988).[20]

Is Diagnosis Objective and Useful?

The REI proponents argue that differential diagnosis does not result in objective distinctions, either between the disabled and nondisabled designations or among the three mild disability classifications (Gartner & Lipsky, 1987; Stainback & Stainback, 1984; Wang, Reynolds, & Walberg, 1986, 1987a). As noted above, the REI opponents generally agree that the disabled-nondisabled distinction is not objective. Moreover, they also agree that distinctions among the three mild disability classifications are not objective because, in addition to measurement and definitional problems, the process for making these decisions in schools is "embedded in a powerful economic, political, and philosophical network" (Keogh, 1988, p. 20; see also Council for Children with Behavioral Disorders, 1989; Gerber & Semmel, 1984; Hallahan & Kauffman, 1977; Kauffman, 1988, 1989a,b).

On the matter of the utility of differential diagnosis, the REI proponents argue that there are no instructionally relevant reasons for making the disabled-nondisabled distinction, or for distinguishing among the three mild disability classifications. Their point is that all students have unique learning needs and, moreover, that students in the three mild disability classifications, as well as those in the other special needs classifications, can be taught using similar instructional methods (for example, Lipsky & Gartner, 1989a; Reynolds, Wang, & Walberg, 1987; Stainback & Stainback, 1984, 1989; Wang, 1989a,b; Wang, Reynolds, & Walberg, 1986, 1987a). Here, too, most of the REI opponents agree, admitting that "effective instructional and management procedures will be substantially the same for nonhandicapped and most mildly handicapped students" (Kauffman, Gerber, & Semmel, 1988, p. 8; see also Gerber, 1987; Hallahan & Kauffman, 1977).[21]

Is Special Education a Rational System?

The REI proponents argue that the only rational justification for the existence of the special education system is that it confers instructional benefit on students who are designated as handicapped (Lilly, 1986; Lipsky & Gartner, 1987; Reynolds, 1988; Reynolds, Wang, & Walberg, 1987; Stainback & Stainback, 1984; Wang, Reynolds, & Walberg, 1987a), a position with which the REI opponents agree (Kauffman, Gerber, & Semmel, 1988; Keogh, 1988). On this basis, the REI proponents believe that, given the weak effects of special education instructional practices and the social and psychological costs of labeling, the current system of special education is, at best, no more justifiable than simply permitting most students to remain unidentified in regular classrooms and, at worst, far less justifiable than regular classroom placement in conjunction with appropriate in-class support services (Lipsky & Gartner, 1987, 1989a; Pugach & Lilly, 1984; Stainback & Stainback, 1984; Wang, Reynolds, & Walberg, 1987a). Thus, the REI proponents reject the idea that special education is a rational system.

Although none of the REI opponents argue that special education has been shown to lead to direct *instructional* benefit (see, for example, Keogh, 1988; Hallahan, Keller, McKinney, Lloyd, & Bryan, 1988),[22] some of them argue that the handicapped designation is beneficial in a *political* sense. That is, they justify the current system of special education on the political grounds that it targets otherwise unavailable resources and personnel to designated students. Such targeting, they argue, is essential if these students are to receive instructional assistance in the context of the resource allocation process in schools (Council for Children with Behavioral Disorders, 1989; Kauffman, 1988, 1989b; Kauffman, Gerber, & Semmel, 1988). As noted, the REI opponents recognize that to be justifiable, special education must confer instructional benefit on designated students, and that, at present, special education interventions do not confer such benefits. In effect, then, the REI opponents who justify special education on political grounds are saying that, although special education is not an instructionally rational system in its current form, it is a politically rational system. This is so, they maintain, because the nonadaptability and political inequality of the general education system makes the pull-out logic of mainstreaming and the targeting function of the EHA absolute necessities if designated students are to receive instructional assistance in school, even though the assistance they receive does not appear to be effective.

As we will see below, in response to the question of the nature of progress, the REI opponents (including those who justify special education on political grounds) argue that the special education system can be improved incrementally through additional research and development. Thus, their position on the nature of special education cannot be separated from their position on the nature of progress in the field. In effect, when their positions on the third and fourth assumptions are considered together, the REI opponents are saying that, although special education is not an instructionally rational system *at present*, it is a politically rational system that can be rendered instructionally rational *in the future*, given the assumption of the possibility of rational-technical progress. Thus, let us say for present purposes that the REI opponents are arguing that special education *is* an instructionally rational system, given the caveat that, to be rational in an instructional sense, rational-technical progress *must* be possible.[23]

Is Progress Rational and Technical?

This question asks whether progress can be made under the current system through incremental technological improvements in its associated diagnostic and instructional practices. The REI proponents argue that the diagnostic and instructional practices of the current system are fundamentally flawed and thus cannot and should not be salvaged. They believe that these practices and the entire system must be replaced through a fundamental restructuring of the special and general education systems (Lilly, 1986; Lipsky & Gartner, 1987, 1989a; Pugach & Lilly, 1984; Reynolds, Wang, & Walberg, 1987; Stainback & Stainback, 1984; Stainback, Stainback, & Forest, 1989), which is an argument against the possibility of rational-technical change. Although the REI opponents recognize that there are serious problems with the current special education system, they believe that incremental progress is possible through additional research and development aimed at improving special education diagnostic and instructional practices while maintaining the current system (Braaten, Kauffman, Braaten, Polsgrove, & Nelson, 1988; Bryan, Bay, & Donahue, 1988; Council for Children with Behavioral Disorders, 1989; Hallahan, Keller, McKinney, Lloyd, & Bryan, 1988; Kauffman, 1988, 1989b; Kauffman, Gerber, & Semmel, 1988; Keogh, 1988; Lloyd, Crowley, Kohler, & Strain, 1988). This, of course, is an argument for the possibility of rational-technical change.

At this point in the critical reading, the REI proponents and opponents reject the two grounding assumptions associated with the presupposition of human pathology, the explicit disciplinary grounding of special education's professional knowledge and practice since the field's inception. Moreover, the REI proponents also reject the two assumptions associated with the normative presupposition of organizational rationality. Thus, by rejecting the field's entire framework of grounding assumptions and presuppositions, the arguments of the REI proponents deconstruct special education as a professional practice. However, by arguing that special education is a politically (if not an instructionally) rational system that can be improved in a rational-technical manner, the REI opponents retain the third and fourth assumptions and thus hold out some hope for the legitimacy of the field.

Although the REI proponents and opponents agree that the field's grounding assumptions about the nature of disability and diagnosis are inadequate, their disagreement over the nature of special education and progress has resulted in total disagreement over an appropriate course of ameliorative action. On one hand, the REI proponents believe that, given the negative evidence on the ethics and efficacy of special education practices and the nonadaptability of the general education system, a completely new system should be formed by restructuring the two systems into a single adaptable one. On the other hand, the REI opponents believe that, negative evidence on the adequacy of special education notwithstanding, the current system and its associated practices should be retained for political purposes, given the nonadaptability of the general education system and the fact that special education practices can be improved. Thus, the REI debate turns on the question of whether school organizations can and will be restructured into the adaptable system envisioned by the REI advocates.

The REI Proposals

There are four REI proposals, each of which, to one degree or another, calls for eliminating the EHA classification system and the pull-out approach of mainstreaming. Each also proposes restructuring the separate general and special education systems into a new system in which, depending on the proposal, most or all students who need help in school are provided with in-class assistance.[24] Although the REI proponents generally agree that this restructured system should be "flexible, supple and responsive" (Lipsky & Gartner, 1987, p. 72), a "totally adaptive system" (Reynolds & Wang, 1983, p. 199) in which professionals personalize instruction through "group problem solving . . . shared responsibility, and . . . negotiation" (Pugach & Lilly, 1984,

p. 52), they disagree on which students should be integrated into the new system on a full-time basis.[25]

Whom to Integrate?

Each of the four teams of REI proponents believes that all students currently served in compensatory and remedial education programs, as well as every other student who needs help in school but is not currently targeted for it, should remain in the regular classrooms of the restructured system on a full-time basis and receive whatever assistance they need in those classrooms. Where they differ, however, is with respect to which students currently classified as handicapped under the EHA should be served in this manner.

The Lilly and Pugach proposal is the least inclusive. In addition to those students noted above, it includes only "the vast majority of students served as 'mildly handicapped'" (Lilly, 1986, p. 10) under the EHA, whereas students with moderate, severe, and profound disabilities would be taught by special educators in separate settings within regular school buildings.[26] The Reynolds and Wang proposal is somewhat more inclusive in that it maintains that "most students with special learning needs" (Wang, Reynolds, & Walberg, 1985, p. 13; Reynolds & Wang, 1983) should be in these regular classrooms on a full-time basis, while reserving the option of separate settings for some students, presumably those with severe and profound disabilities.[27]

The Gartner and Lipsky proposal includes all students currently served under each EHA classification, except those with the most severely and profoundly handicapping conditions. These students would receive their primary instruction in separate classrooms located in regular, age-appropriate school buildings (Gartner & Lipsky, 1987). Finally, in what is the most inclusive proposal, Stainback and Stainback (1984) argue for the integration of all students, including those with the most severely and profoundly disabling conditions, while recognizing the need to group students, "in some instances, into specific courses and classes according to their instructional needs" (p. 108).

What to Merge?

Although the strategy for creating the adaptable system necessary to implement the REI proposals is most often characterized as a merger of the general and special education systems, only the Stainback and Stainback and Gartner and Lipsky proposals actually call for a merger of the two systems at the classroom level.[28] The other two teams propose a merger of instructional support personnel above the classroom level. Toward this end, Reynolds and Wang (1983) propose eliminating the categorical special needs pull-out programs through a two-step merger. The first merger is within special education, among the programs serving the three traditional mild disability classifications. The second is between this merged or noncategorical special education program and the other "compensatory services that are provided for disadvantaged, bilingual, migrant, low-English-proficiency, or other children with special needs" (1983, p. 206). Supported by paraprofessionals, these generic specialists form a school-based support team that works "mostly in the regular classrooms . . . to supply technical and administrative support to regular classroom teachers" (1983, p. 206).[29]

The Lilly and Pugach proposal merges the special education resource and support programs that currently provide services "for the mildly handicapped, and primarily for the learning disabled" (Pugach & Lilly, 1984, p. 54) with the traditional general education support service of remedial education.[30] They recognize the need for support services, but propose a single, coordinated system of services based in general education and provided largely in regular classrooms, rather than the current array of special pull-out programs (Lilly, 1986; Pugach & Lilly, 1984). Although the Reynolds and Wang and Lilly and Pugach proposals modify the current notion of instructional support services by replacing the categorical pull-out approach with a noncategorical or remedial model of in-class support services, both of them retain the traditional notion of a classroom, in the sense of one teacher with primary responsibility for a group of students.[31]

Although the Stainback and Stainback proposal calls for merger at the classroom level, it actually merges general and special education subject areas, not special education and general instructional programs or personnel. It calls for disbanding special education programs and integrating the residual personnel into the general education system according to an instructional specialization. Each teacher in this system would have "a strong base in the teaching/learning process" (Stainback & Stainback, 1984, p. 107) and a particular specialization in a traditional general education subject (for example, science or reading) or a special education subject (for example, supported employment), and each would work individually in a separate classroom (Stainback & Stainback, 1987a; Stainback, Stainback, & Forest, 1989). As with the first two proposals, this one provides support services above the classroom level. Here, however, the support personnel are organized as subject-area specialists rather than generic specialists, which modifies the current categorical pull-out approach by replacing it with in-class subject area support services. As in the case of the other two support services models, this one retains the traditional notion of a classroom in which one teacher has primary responsibility for a group of students (see Stainback & Stainback, 1984, 1987a).

The Gartner and Lipsky proposal calls for a merged or unitary system in which education is "both one and special for all students" (Lipsky & Gartner, 1987, p. 73). Such a system would mean the complete abandonment of a separate special education system for students with mild to moderate disabilities. Although in their original proposal Gartner and Lipsky also emphasized the support services level (Gartner & Lipsky, 1987), in a recent clarification and extension (Lipsky & Gartner, 1989a) they emphasize the classroom level by linking their proposal for a restructured system to the excellence movement in general education, which is, for them, the effective schools movement (Edmonds, 1979; Lezotte, 1989). As such, their basic assertion is that, through broad adoption of the principles and practices identified in the effective schools research, "the education of students labeled as handicapped can be made effective" (Lipsky & Gartner, 1989a, p. 281). They build their case for the effective schools approach by combining Edmonds's (1979) assertion that, if some schools are effective, all schools can be effective, with Gilhool's (1976) parallel assertion about effective integration of students with disabilities. They conclude that effective schools, and thus effective education for students labeled handicapped, is a matter of will and commitment on the part of teachers and schools to adopt the principles and practices contained in the effective schools literature.[32]

Reactions to the REI Proposals

The REI opponents argue against the possibility of an adaptable system on historical and political grounds and conclude that special needs have not, are not, and simply cannot be met in regular classrooms. Kauffman (1988) and others (Council for Children with Behavioral Disorders, 1989) argue that, historically, the separate special education system emerged precisely because of the nonadaptability of regular classrooms and that, since nothing has happened to make contemporary classrooms any more adaptable (see Keogh, 1988), the REI most likely will lead to rediscovering the need for a separate system in the future. In their political or microeconomic criticism of the REI reform proposals, Kauffman, Gerber, & Semmel (1988; see also Gerber, 1988b; Gerber & Semmel, 1985) argue that "teachers, whether in regular or special class environments, cannot escape the necessary choice between higher means [that is, maximizing mean performance by concentrating resources on the most able learners] and narrower variances [that is, minimizing group variance by concentrating resources on the least able learners] as long as resources are scarce and students differ" (Gerber & Semmel, 1985, p. 19, cited in Kauffman, Gerber, & Semmel, 1988, p. 10). This is true, they argue, "whenever a teacher instructs a group of students . . . [except] when new resources are made available or more powerful instructional technologies are employed" (Kauffman, Gerber, & Semmel, 1988, p. 10).

Although these are compelling arguments, they ignore the fact that the REI proposals call for creating a system of adaptable classrooms by making new resources available and introducing more powerful instructional technologies, the exact conditions that can narrow group variances without negatively affecting class means, according to the microeconomic argument itself. Thus, these are not arguments against the REI proposals; implicitly, they are compelling arguments against the traditional notion of a classroom. In fact, by arguing that both regular and special education classrooms are nonadaptable in a microeconomic sense, the REI opponents make a stronger case against the current system of special education than the REI proponents. Moreover, by arguing that the regular classroom has not changed and that neither it nor the special classroom can change, the REI opponents contradict their position on the possibility of rational-technical change, and thus their implicit support of the third and fourth assumptions.[33]

As we have seen, on the question of the adequacy of the current system of special education, the REI proponents reject all four of the field's grounding assumptions, while the opponents reject the two about disability and diagnosis but retain the two about special education and progress. In their criticism of the REI proposals, however, the REI opponents reverse their position on the two assumptions about special education and progress, and thus implicitly agree with the REI proponents that all four of the field's grounding assumptions are inadequate. At this point, then, the arguments for and against the field's current practices and those against the REI proposals reject all four grounding assumptions and thus deconstruct special education as a professional practice. Nevertheless, although the deconstruction of special education appears to be complete, we will see in a subsequent section that the REI proponents reverse their position on the third and fourth assumptions as well.

As we know, in their criticism of the current system the REI proponents argue against the rationality of special education (and thus of the traditional organization of schools). However, when their reform proposals are considered from an organizational perspective (see below), they actually reproduce and extend the traditional organization of schools and call for a rational-technical approach to change. Thus, both sides in the REI debate reject the first two assumptions and thus the presupposition of human pathology that serves as the field's explicit disciplinary grounding, but they are contradictory and inconsistent about the third and fourth assumptions and thus about the presupposition of organizational rationality that serves as the field's implicit normative grounding. Therefore, let us reserve judgment on whether the arguments in the REI debate deconstruct special education as a professional practice until we have considered the notion of organizational rationality in greater depth.

In the following section I address the legitimacy of the presupposition of organizational rationality by way of a critical reading of the discourse on school organization and adaptability in the field of educational administration. On the basis of this reading, I introduce two alternative ways to conceptualize school organization and the problem of change, which I combine in subsequent sections to carry out my deconstructions of the institutional practice of special education and the discourse on school failure, as well as my deconstruction and reconstruction of the institution of public education.

THE DISCOURSE ON SCHOOL ORGANIZATION AND ADAPTABILITY

Generally speaking, there are two sources of insight into school organization and adaptability: the prescriptive discourse of educational administration, and the theoretical discourse of the multidisciplinary field of organization analysis. The field of educational administration is grounded in the notion of scientific management, an extremely narrow view that presupposes that organizations are rational and that organizational change is a rational-technical process (Burrell & Morgan, 1979; Scott, 1981). Although scientific management is a purely functionalist approach for organizing and managing industrial firms, it was applied to schools and other social organizations during the social efficiency movement at the turn of the century (Callahan, 1962; Haber, 1964), and has remained the grounding formulation of educational administration ever since.[34]

The theoretical discourse of organization analysis is grounded in the social disciplines and thus, in principle, provides a much broader range of perspectives on organization and change. Ultimately, however, the theories produced in the field of organization analysis are shaped by the various modes of theorizing or paradigms that have been available to and, more important, historically favored by social scientists (Burrell & Morgan, 1979).[35] Because functionalism has been the favored mode of theorizing in the social sciences, the theoretical discourse on organization, like the prescriptive discourse of educational administration, has been dominated by the functionalist paradigm, and thus by the presupposition of organizational rationality (Burrell & Morgan, 1979). However, over the past thirty years the same revolutionary developments in the social disciplines that were noted previously have produced a number of new theories of organization that are grounded in other modes of social theorizing that had been underutilized in organizational research.[36]

One important substantive outcome of these developments has been a shift in emphasis on the question of the nature of organization and change itself. Whereas the functionalist notion of rational organizations (that is, prospective and goal-directed) and rational-technical change had been the exclusive outlook in organization analysis, many of the newer theories are premised on the idea that organizations are nonrational entities (that is, quasi-random, emergent systems of meaning or cultures) in which change is a nonrational-cultural process (Pfeffer, 1982; Scott, 1981). Methodologically, the trend in organization analysis, as in the social sciences generally, has been away from the traditional foundational notion of one best theory or paradigm for understanding organization. Thus, the contemporary discourse in organization analysis is characterized by theoretical diversity (Burrell & Morgan, 1979; Pfeffer, 1982; Scott, 1981) and, at the margins at least, by an antifoundational methodological orientation (Morgan, 1983).[37]

Drawing on these substantive and methodological developments, the following analysis considers school organization and adaptability from two general frames of reference that, together, include several theories of organization and change drawn from each of the modes of theorizing found in the social disciplines. The *structural* frame of reference includes configuration theory (Miller & Mintzberg, 1983; Mintzberg, 1979) and what will be referred to as "institutionalization theory" (Meyer & Rowan, 1977, 1978; Meyer & Scott, 1983). By combining these two theories, we can understand school organization as an inherently nonadaptable, two-structure arrangement. The *cultural* frame of reference includes what will be referred to as paradigmatic (Brown, 1978; Golding, 1980; Jonsson & Lundin, 1977; Rounds, 1979, 1981) and cognitive theories of organization (Weick, 1979, 1985), which, when combined, provide a way to understand school organizations as cultures or corrigible systems of meaning. The two frames of reference are presented separately below and then integrated in the next major section where the relationship between organization structure and culture is used to reconsider the four grounding assumptions of special education as an institutional practice of public education.[38] Although the reader no doubt will begin to see in the following analysis some of the organizational implications that I will emphasize in subsequent sections, at this point I will refrain from commenting on those implications. My aim here is merely to set the stage for the sections to follow.

The Structural Frame of Reference[39]

The central idea in configuration theory is that organizations structure themselves into somewhat naturally occurring configurations according to the type of work that they do, the means they have available to coordinate their work, and a variety of situational factors. Given these considerations, school organizations configure themselves as professional bureaucracies (Mintzberg, 1979), even though in this century they have been managed and governed as machine bureaucracies (Callahan, 1962; Meyer & Rowan, 1978; Weick, 1982). According to institutionalization theory, organizations like schools deal with this contradiction by maintaining two structures: a material structure that conforms to the technical demands of their work and a normative structure that conforms to the cultural demands of their institutionalized environments. By combining the insights of configuration theory and institutionalization theory, school organizations can be understood in terms of two organizations, one inside the other. On the outside, their normative structure conforms to the machine bureaucracy configuration, the structure that people expect because of the social norm of organizational rationality. On the inside, however, the material structure of schools conforms to the professional bureaucracy configuration, the structure that configures itself around the technical requirements of their work.

Differences between the Machine and Professional Bureaucracies

The differences between the two organizations stem from the type of work that they do and thus the way they can distribute it among workers (division of labor) and subsequently coordinate its completion. Organizations configure themselves as machine bureaucracies when their work is simple; that is, when it is certain enough to be *rationalized* (or task-analyzed) into a series of separate subtasks, each of which can be prespecified and done by a different worker. Because it can be completely prespecified, simple work can be coordinated by standardizing the work processes through *formalization*, or the specification of precise rules for doing each subtask. Organizations configure themselves as professional bureaucracies when their work is complex; that is, when it is ambiguous and thus too uncertain to be rationalized and formalized. Because their work is too uncertain to be broken apart and distributed among a number of workers, division of labor in the professional bureaucracies is achieved through *specialization*. That is, in the professional bureaucracy (which typically does client-centered work) clients are distributed among the workers, each of whom specializes in the skills that are needed to do the total job with his or her assigned client cohort. Given this form of division of labor, complex work is coordinated by standardizing the skills of the workers, which is accomplished through *professionalization*, or intensive education and socialization carried out in professional schools.

The logic behind rationalization and formalization in the machine bureaucracy is premised on minimizing discretion and separating theory from practice. The theory behind the work rests with the technocrats who rationalize and formalize it; they do the thinking and the workers simply follow the rules. Conversely, specialization and professionalization are meant to increase discretion and to unite theory and practice in the professional. This is necessary because containing the uncertainty of complex work within the role of a particular professional specialization requires the professional to adapt the theory behind the work to the particular needs of his or her clients (Schein, 1972). In principle, professionals know the theory behind their work and have the discretion to adapt it to the actual needs of their clients. In practice, however, the standardization of skills is circumscribed; it provides professionals with a finite repertoire of standard programs that are applicable only to a finite number of contingencies or presumed client needs. Given adequate discretionary space (see below), there is room for some adjustment. However, when clients have needs that fall on the margins or outside of the professional's repertoire of standard programs, they either must be forced artificially into the available programs or sent to a different professional specialist, one who presumably has the right standard programs (Perrow, 1970; Weick, 1976). A fully open-ended process — one that seeks a truly creative solution to each unique need — requires a problem-solving orientation. But professionals are performers, not problem solvers. They perfect the programs they have; they do not invent new ones for unfamiliar contingencies. Instead of accommodating heterogeneity, professionals screen it out by squeezing their clients' needs into their standard programs or by squeezing them out of the professional-client relationship altogether (Segal, 1974; Simon, 1977).

An organization's division of labor and means of coordination shape the nature of interdependency or coupling among its workers (March & Olsen, 1976; Thompson, 1967; Weick, 1976). Because machine bureaucracies distribute and coordinate their work by rationalizing and formalizing it, their workers are highly dependent on one another and thus, like links in a chain, they are tightly coupled. However, specialization and professionalization create a loosely coupled form of interdependency in the professional bureaucracy, a situation in which workers are not highly dependent on one another. Because specialization requires close contact with the client and professionalization requires little overt coordination or communication among workers (everyone knows roughly what everyone else is doing by way of their common professionalization), each professional works closely with his or her clients and only loosely with other professionals (Weick, 1976, 1982).

Managing Professional Bureaucracies Like Machine Bureaucracies

Given the prescriptive discourse of educational administration and the social norm of organizational rationality, traditional school management (Weick, 1982) and governance (Meyer & Rowan, 1978; Mintzberg, 1979) practices force school organizations to adopt the rationalization and formalization principles of the machine bureaucracy, even though they are ill-suited to the technical demands of doing complex work. In principle, this drives the professional bureaucracy toward the machine bureaucracy configuration because, by misconceptualizing teaching as simple work that can be rationalized and formalized, it violates the theory/practice requirement and discretionary logic of professionalization. Thus, by separating theory and practice and reducing professional discretion, the degree to which teachers can personalize instruction is reduced. Complex work cannot be rationalized and formalized, except in misguided ways that force the professionals "to play the machine bureaucratic game — satisfying the standards instead of serving the clients" (Mintzberg, 1979, p. 377).

Fortunately, however, the imposition of rationalization and formalization does not work completely in school organizations because, from the institutionalization perspective, these structural contingencies are built into the outer machine bureaucracy structure of schools, which is decoupled from their inner professional bureaucracy structure where the work is done. That is, the outer machine bureaucracy structure of schools acts largely as a myth that, through an assortment of symbols and ceremonies, embodies the rationalization and formalization but has little to do with the way the work is actually done. This decoupled arrangement permits schools to do their work according to the localized judgments of professionals — the logic behind specialization and professionalization — while protecting their legitimacy by giving managers and the public the appearance of the rationalized and formalized machine bureaucracy that they expect.

But decoupling does not work completely either because, from the configuration perspective, no matter how contradictory they may be, misplaced rationalization and formalization require at least overt conformity to their percepts and thus circumscribe professional thought and action (Dalton, 1959; Mintzberg, 1979). Decoupling notwithstanding, managing and governing schools as if they were machine bureaucracies increases rationalization and formalization and thus decreases professional thought and discretion, which reduces even further the degree to which teachers can personalize instruction.

Similarities between the Machine and Professional Bureaucracies

Even though they are different in the respects noted above, the machine and professional bureaucracies are similar in one important way: both are inherently non-adaptable structures because they are premised on standardization. All bureaucracies are performance organizations; that is, structures that are configured to perfect the programs they have been standardized to perform. Of course, the standardization of skills is intended to allow for enough professional thought and discretion to accommodate client variability. However, even with adequate discretionary space, there is a limit on the degree to which professionals can adjust their standard programs and, moreover, they can only adjust the standard programs that are in their repertoires. In a professional bureaucracy, coordination through standardization of skills itself circumscribes the degree to which the organization can accommodate variability. A fully open-ended process of accommodation requires a problem-solving organization, a configuration premised on inventing new programs for unique client needs. But the professional bureaucracy is a performance organization; it screens out heterogeneity by forcing its clients' needs into one of its existing specializations, or by forcing them out of the system altogether (Segal, 1974).

Because bureaucracies are performance organizations, they require a stable environment. They are potentially devastated under dynamic conditions, when their environments force them to do something other than what they were standardized to do. Nevertheless, machine bureaucracies can change by restandardizing their work processes, a more or less rational-technical process of rerationalizing their work and reformalizing worker behavior. However, when its environment becomes dynamic, the professional bureaucracy cannot respond by making rational-technical adjustments in its work because its coordination rests within each professional, not in its work processes. At a minimum, change in a professional bureaucracy requires a change in what each professional does, because each professional does all aspects of the work individually and personally with his or her clients. Nevertheless, because schools are managed and governed as if they were machine bureaucracies, attempts to change them typically follow the rational-technical approach (Elmore & McLaughlin, 1988; House, 1979), which assumes that changes in, or additions to, the existing rationalization and formalization will result in changes in the way the work gets done. Of course, this fails to bring about the desired changes because the existing rationalization and formalization are located in the decoupled machine bureaucracy structure. However, because such changes or additions require at least overt conformity, they act to extend the existing rationalization and formalization. This, of course, drives the organization further toward the machine bureaucracy configuration, which reduces teacher thought and discretion even further, leaving students with even less personalized and thus even less effective services.

Even though schools are nonadaptable structures, their status as public organizations means that they must respond to public demands for change. From the institutionalization perspective, schools deal with this problem by using their outer machine bureaucracy structure to deflect change demands. That is, they relieve pressure for change by signaling the environment that a change has occurred, thereby creating the illusion that they have changed when, in fact, they remain largely the same (Meyer, 1979; Rowan, 1980; Zucker, 1981). One way that school organizations signal change is by building symbols and ceremonies of change into their outer machine bureaucracy structure, which, of course, is decoupled from the actual work. Another important signal of change is the ritual or decoupled subunit. Not only are the two structures of schools decoupled, but the various units(classrooms and programs) are decoupled from one another as well. As we know from the configuration perspective, this is possible because specialization and professionalization create precisely this sort of loosely coupled interdependency within the organization. As such, schools can respond to pressure for change by simply adding on separate classrooms or programs — that is, by creating new specializations — to deal with the change demand. This response acts to buffer the organization from the change demand because these subunits are decoupled from the rest of the organization, thus making any substantive reorganization of activity unnecessary (Meyer & Rowan, 1977; Zucker, 1981).

The Cultural Frame of Reference

Organization theorists working from the cultural frame of reference think of organizations as bodies of thought, as schemas, cultures, or paradigms. Their theories are premised on the idea that humans construct their social realities through intersubjective communication (see Berger & Luckmann, 1967). As such, the cognitive and paradigmatic perspectives on organization and change are concerned with the way people construct, deconstruct, and reconstruct meaning and how this relates to the way action and interaction unfold over time in organizations. Cognitive theories emphasize the way people create and recreate their organizational realities; paradigmatic theories emphasize the way organizational realities create and recreate people. Together, these theories reflect the interactive duality of the cultural frame of reference — people creating culture and culture creating people (Pettigrew, 1979).

Organizations as Paradigms

Paradigmatic theorists conceptualize organizations as paradigms or shared systems of meaning. They are concerned with understanding the way existing socially constructed systems of meaning affect and constrain thought and action in organizations. From this perspective, an organizational paradigm is a system of beliefs about cause-effect relations and standards of practice and behavior. Regardless of whether these paradigms are true, they guide and justify action by consolidating disorder into an image of orderliness (Brown, 1978; Clark, 1972). From this perspective, organizational change requires a paradigm shift, which is difficult because the paradigm self-justifies itself by distorting new information so it is seen as consistent with the prevailing view. Nevertheless, when sufficient anomalies build up to undermine the prevailing paradigm, a new one emerges and action proceeds again under the guidance of the new organizing framework (Golding, 1980; Jonsson & Lundin, 1977).[40]

One way that anomalies are introduced into organizational paradigms is when values and preferences in society change. However, to the degree that the new social values are inconsistent with the prevailing paradigm, resistance emerges in the form of political clashes and an increase in ritualized activity, which act to reaffirm the paradigm that has been called into question (Rounds, 1979; see also Lipsky, 1975; Perrow, 1978; Zucker, 1977). Another way that anomalies are introduced is through the availability of technical information that indicates that the current paradigm is not working, which can bring about a paradigm shift in one of two ways (Rounds, 1981). The first way is through a confrontation between an individual (or a small constituency group), who rejects the most fundamental assumptions of the current paradigm on the basis of information that the system is not working, and the rest of the organization's members, who are acting in defiance of the negative information to preserve the prevailing paradigm. The second way is when an initially conservative action is taken to correct a generally recognized flaw in what is otherwise assumed to be a viable system. Here, the corrective measure exposes other flaws that, when addressed, expose more flaws, and so on, until enough of the system is called into question to prepare the way for a radical reconceptualization of the entire organization.

Organizations as Schemas

From the cognitive perspective, an organization is a cognitive entity, a paradigm or human schema, "an abridged, generalized, corrigible organization of experience that serves as an initial frame of reference for action and perception" (Weick, 1979, p. 50). That is, although an organizational paradigm orients the thought and action of its members, the members are active in creating and recreating the paradigm. Through activity, selective attention, consensual validation, and luck, people in organizations unrandomize streams of random experience enough to form a paradigm that — correct or not — structures the field of action sufficiently so that meaningful activity can proceed (Weick, 1979, 1985). Members' sampling of the environment, and thus the paradigms they construct, are shaped by prior beliefs and values, which act as filters through which they examine their experiences. Moreover, activity in organizations, which from the cognitive perspective is the pretext for sense-making, is shaped by material structures like formalization, professionalization, and bureaucracy itself. These structural contingencies shape members' organizational realities because they influence the contacts, communication, and commands that they experience and thus affect the streams of experience, beliefs, values, and actions that constitute their organizational paradigms. Furthermore, the paradigm and its values and beliefs also "constrain contacts, communication, and commands. These constraints constitute and shape organizational processes that result in structures" (Weick, 1979, p. 48). Thus, from this perspective, organization is a mutually shaping circularity of structure and culture. Depending on where one enters the circle, organization is a continuous process in which structural contingencies shape the work activities of organizational members, which, in turn, shapes the members' value orientation and thus the nature of the organizational paradigms they construct to interpret the organization's structural contingencies.

From this perspective, school organizations are "underorganized systems" (Weick, 1985, p. 106), ambiguous settings that are shaped and reshaped by values and beliefs (see also Cohen, March, & Olsen, 1972). Change occurs in such contexts when organizational members believe, correctly or not, that a change in the environment was caused by their own actions. Although this may be an error, when environments are sufficiently malleable, acting on a mistaken belief can set in motion a sequence of activities that allows people to construct the reality that the belief is true. From the cognitive perspective, confident action based on a presumption of efficacy reinforces beliefs about efficacy contained in the paradigm. For good or ill, things are done in certain ways in ambiguous, underorganized systems because people believe their assumptions and presuppositions. And, because believing is seeing in these settings, things change when these beliefs change (Weick, 1985).

Thus, the very underorganized nature of schools that prevents change from a structural perspective is the precise condition that makes change possible from a cultural perspective. Under conditions of increased ambiguity and uncertainty, the presuppositions that underwrite the prevailing paradigm are called into question. Change occurs when someone or something introduces new presuppositions that explain the ambiguity and thus reduce the uncertainty (Brown, 1978; Golding, 1980; Rounds, 1981; Weick, 1979). The recognition of an important, enduring ambiguity — an unresolvable anomaly in the prevailing paradigm — is an occasion when an organization may redefine itself. From the cultural perspective, organizations like schools are human constructions grounded in values. Schools change when apparently irresolvable ambiguities are resolved by confident, forceful, persistent people who manage to convince themselves and others to adopt a new set of presuppositions, which introduces innovation because the values embedded in these presuppositions create a new set of contingencies, expectations, and commitments (Weick, 1985).

SPECIAL EDUCATION AS AN INSTITUTIONAL PRACTICE

The structural and cultural frames of reference on school organization and adaptability are combined in this section and used to reconsider the four grounding assumptions relative to special education as an institutional practice of public education. The first three assumptions are addressed below. Following that, the fourth assumption is considered by way of an organizational analysis of the EHA and the REI proposals.

School Organization, Student Disability, and Special Education[41]

The participants in the REI debate reject the assumptions that mild disabilities are pathological and that diagnosis is objective and useful, recognizing instead that many students are identified as handicapped simply because they have needs that cannot be accommodated in the regular classrooms of the general education system. This contradiction can be understood from an organizational perspective by redescribing student disability as an organizational pathology resulting from the inherent structural and cultural characteristics of traditional school organizations.

Structurally, schools are nonadaptable at the classroom level because professionalization ultimately results in "convergent thinking, in the deductive reasoning of the professional who sees the specific situation in terms of the general concept" (Mintzberg, 1979, p. 375). Given a finite repertoire of standard programs, students whose needs fall outside the standard programs must be forced into them or out of the classroom, a situation that is compounded by the rational-technical approach to school management, which, by introducing unwarranted rationalization and formalization, reduces professional thought and discretion and, thus, the degree to which teachers can personalize their standard programs. The same phenomenon can be understood culturally by thinking of the standard programs as a paradigm of practice that persists because anomalies are distorted to preserve its validity. The principal distortion, of course, is the institutional practice of special education, which reaffirms the paradigm by removing students for whom it does not work. In effect, this prevents teachers from recognizing anomalies in their paradigms and thus, ultimately, removes a valuable source of innovation from the system.[42] Moreover, rationalization and formalization compound and further mystify the situation because they conflict with the values that ground the paradigm and thus increase ritualized activity, which further reduces thought and personalization.

Thus, whether we think of schools from the structural or the cultural frame of reference, the implication is that the first two grounding assumptions are inadequate and incomplete. In organizational terms, student disability is neither a human pathology nor an objective distinction; it is an organizational pathology, a matter of not fitting the standard programs of the prevailing paradigm of a professional culture, the legitimacy of which is artificially reaffirmed by the objectification of school failure as a human pathology through the institutional practice of special education.

The participants in the REI debate reject the assumption that special education is an instructionally rational system and recognize that, at best, it is a politically rational system for targeting otherwise unavailable educational services to designated students, even though the targeting process stigmatizes the students and the services do not necessarily benefit them instructionally. This contradiction can be understood from an organizational perspective by reconceptualizing the institutional practice of special education as an organizational artifact that emerged to protect the legitimacy of a nonadaptable bureaucratic structure faced with the changing value demands of a dynamic democratic environment.

Even though specialization, professionalization, rationalization, and formalization make schools nonadaptable structures, these organizations maintain their legitimacy under dynamic social conditions by signaling to the public that changes have occurred through symbols, ceremonies, and decoupled subunits. As such, the segregated special classroom emerged in conjunction with compulsory school attendance to preserve the legitimacy of the prevailing organizational paradigm by symbolizing compliance with the public demand for universal public education.[43] Structurally, special education is not a rational system; it is a nonrational system, an institutional practice that functions as a legitimizing device. Culturally, it distorts the anomaly of school failure and thus preserves the prevailing paradigm of school organization, which ultimately reaffirms the functionalist presuppositions of organizational rationality and human pathology in the profession of education and in society.[44]

School Organization and Progress

Both sides in the REI debate agree that most mild disabilities are not pathological and that diagnosis is neither objective nor useful. As such, the arguments put forth in the debate reject the presupposition of human pathology as a grounding for the institutional practice of special education. However, the two sides disagree over an appropriate course of action because of a conceptual confusion about the nature of special education and progress resulting from the presupposition of organizational rationality. As we have seen, this confusion among the REI opponents is evident in their defense of the current system of special education and their criticism of the REI proposals. The same sort of confusion among the REI proponents can be illustrated at this point by considering their reform proposals from an organizational perspective, which I will turn to after analyzing the EHA. Before considering either reform measure, however, it will be helpful to introduce a third organizational configuration.

The Adhocracy

As we know, the professional bureaucracy is nonadaptable because it is premised on the principle of standardization (of skills), which configures it as a performance organization for perfecting standard programs. Conversely, the adhocracy configuration is premised on the principle of innovation rather than standardization and, as such, configures itself as a problem-solving organization for inventing new programs. It is the organizational form that configures itself around work that is so ambiguous and uncertain that neither the standard programs nor the skills for doing it are known (Mintzberg, 1979).[45]

Perhaps the best example of this configuration is the National Aeronautics and Space Administration (NASA) during its Apollo phase in the 1960s. Given its mission to put an American on the moon, it configured itself as an adhocracy because at that time there were no standard programs for this sort of manned space flight. At that point in its history, NASA had to rely on its workers to invent and reinvent these programs on an ad hoc basis — on the way to the moon, as it were. Although NASA employed professional workers, it could not use specialization and professionalization to distribute and coordinate its work because there were no specialties that had perfected the standard programs for doing the type of work that was required, and thus no professional fields whose existing repertoires of standard programs could contain its uncertainty. As such, during its Apollo phase, NASA's division of labor and means of coordination were premised on *collaboration* and *mutual adjustment*, respectively.

Under such an arrangement, division of labor is achieved by deploying professionals from various specializations on multidisciplinary project teams, a situation in which team members work collaboratively on the team's project and assume joint responsibility for its completion. Under mutual adjustment, coordination is achieved through informal communication among team members as they invent and reinvent novel solutions to problems on an ad hoc basis, a process that requires them to adapt, adjust, and revise their conventional theories and practices relative to those of their colleagues and the teams' progress on the tasks at hand (Chandler & Sayles, 1971; Mintzberg, 1979). Together, the structural contingencies of collaboration and mutual adjustment give rise to a *discursive coupling* arrangement that is premised on reflective thought, and thus on the unification of theory and practice in the team of workers (Burns & Stalker, 1966). By contrast, during its current Space Shuttle phase, NASA configures itself as a professional bureaucracy (Romzek & Dubnick, 1987), a performance organization that perfects a repertoire of standard launch and recovery programs that were invented during its Apollo phase. This transformation from the adhocracy to the professional bureaucracy configuration begins when the organization assumes that it has solved all or most of its problems and thus that the programs it has invented can be standardized and used as solutions in the future. The difference between the two configurations is that, faced with a problem, the adhocracy "engages in creative effort to find a novel solution; the professional bureaucracy pigeonholes it into a known contingency to which it can apply a standard program. One engages in divergent thinking aimed at innovation; the other in convergent thinking aimed at perfection" (Mintzberg, 1979, p. 436).

Finally, under the organizational contingencies of collaboration, mutual adjustment, and discursive coupling, accountability in the adhocracy is achieved through a presumed community of interests — a sense among the workers of a shared interest in a common goal, in the well-being of the organization with respect to progress toward its mission — rather than through an ideological identification with a professional culture (professional bureaucracy) or a formalized relationship with an organization (machine bureaucracy) (Burns & Stalker, 1966; Chandler & Sayles, 1971; Romzek & Dubnick, 1987). Thus, rather than the *professional-bureaucratic* mode of accountability that emerges in two-structure configurations like schools, the organizational contingencies of the adhocracy give rise to a *professional-political* mode of accountability, a situation in which work is controlled by experts who, although they act with discretion, are subject to sanctions that emerge within a political discourse among professionals and client constituencies (Burns & Stalker, 1966; Chandler & Sayles, 1971).[46]

The Education for All Handicapped Children Act

From an organizational perspective, the basic problem with the EHA is that it attempts to force an adhocratic value orientation on a professional bureaucracy by treating it as if it were a machine bureaucracy.[47] The EHA's ends are adhocratic because it seeks a problem-solving organization in which interdisciplinary teams of professionals and parents collaborate to invent personalized programs, or, in the language of the EHA, individualized educational plans (IEPs). But this orientation contradicts the value orientation of the professional bureaucracy in every way, given that it is a performance organization in which individual professionals work alone to perfect standard programs. Culturally, this value conflict produces resistance in the form of political clashes, which undermine the ideal of collaboration, as well as an increase in ritualized activity, which, by further mystifying the prevailing paradigm of practice, intensifies the problem of professionalization and thus deflects the ideas of problem solving and personalization.[48] Moreover, because the EHA's means are completely consistent with the value orientation of the machine bureaucracy structure — rationalization of instructional programs, (see below) and formalization of procedures — the EHA extends and elaborates the existing rationalization and formalization in schools. Structurally, this both decouples the adhocratic ends of the EHA from the actual work and further reduces professional thought and discretion, a process that intensifies professionalization and thus reduces personalization. This results in even more students who fall outside the standard programs, many of whom must be identified as handicapped to protect the legitimacy of the prevailing paradigm. Moreover, because there is a legal limit on the number of students who can be identified as handicapped under the EHA, as well as a political limit on the amount of school failure society will tolerate, the EHA, in conjunction with other rational-technical reforms associated with the excellence movement, helped to create the new "at-risk" category of student causalities, which, at this point, is decoupled from both general education and special education.[49]

Because the EHA requires at least overt conformity, a number of symbols of compliance have emerged, two of which are important for present purposes. The symbol of compliance for programs that serve students with severe and profound disabilities is the traditional decoupled subunit, the segregated special classroom. These programs are simply added to the existing school organization and, to one degree or another, decoupled from the basic operation. Because the nature of the needs of the students in these programs is beyond the standard programs of any single profession and thus requires an interdisciplinary approach, their efficacy depends on school organizations providing the team of professionals that is required. Beyond this, these programs have very little to do with the basic school operation.[50]

The symbol of compliance for most students identified as mildly handicapped is the resource room, a new type of decoupled subunit. From an organizational perspective, the resource room is even more problematic than the special classroom because it violates the logic of the professional bureaucracy's means of coordination and division of labor.[51] Under the mainstreaming model, the responsibility for the student's instructional program is divided among one or more regular classroom teachers and a special education resource teacher. This contradicts the division of labor because it requires that the student's instructional program be rationalized and assigned to more than one professional. Of course, this is justified implicitly on the assumption that the professionals will work collaboratively to integrate the program. But the collaboration required to integrate the student's instructional program contradicts the logic of professionalization and thus the loosely coupled from of interdependency among workers. Because professionalization locates virtually all of the necessary coordination within the teacher, there is no need for collaboration in schools, and thus it rarely occurs.[52]

Given the adhocratic spirit of the EHA, it was intended to decrease the effects of student disability by increasing personalized instruction and regular classroom integration. However, given the bureaucratic value orientation of schools and of the procedural requirements of the law itself, the result has been an increase in the number of students classified as disabled, a disintegration of instruction, and a decrease in personalization in regular and special classrooms.[53]

The Regular Education Initiative Proposals[54]

The problem with the REI proposals is that each of them reproduces and extends the value contradictions of the EHA. This is so because, even though they reject the two assumptions associated with the notion of human pathology, ultimately they retain the assumptions that school organizations are rational and that changing them is a rational-technical process. In organizational terms, the result is that, although the REI proposals call for an adhocratic value orientation, they retain the professional bureaucracy inner configuration of schools and extend their machine bureaucracy outer configuration. They retain the professional bureaucracy configuration because, by retaining the classroom teacher, each proposal retains a specialized division of labor and a professionalized means of coordination — a combination that yields loose coupling and thus deflects the ideal of collaboration.

In principle, as long as the work in schools is distributed through specialization and coordinated through professionalization, there is no need for teachers to collaborate. Collaboration emerges when work is distributed on the basis of a collaborative division of labor and coordinated through mutual adjustment, an arrangement that is premised on a team approach to problem solving and yields a form of interdependency premised on reflective discourse. Although the Reynolds and Wang, Lilly and

Pugach, and Stainback and Stainback proposals call for collaborative problem solving between a classroom teacher and a support services staff, by retaining the notion of a classroom and placing the support services staff above it, they actually extend the rationalization and formalization of the machine bureaucracy configuration and thus undermine the ideals of problem solving and personalized instruction. That is, placing the support staff above the classroom teacher implies that the theory of teaching is at the support level while the mere practice of teaching takes place in the classroom, an administrative arrangement that maintains the misplaced convention of separating theory from practice. Moreover, this politicizes and thus undermines the ideal of collaboration, because placing support personnel above the practice context makes them technocrats rather than support staff (Mintzberg, 1979). In an actual machine bureaucracy, technocrats are the people with the theory; they control and define the activities of the other workers. This is not collaboration in an organizational sense; it is bureaucratic control and supervision. In professional bureaucracies, where the notion of a technocracy within the organization violates the logic of professionalization (Mintzberg, 1979), technocrats are resisted, particularly change agents and other school improvement personnel (Wolcott, 1977).

The same problems are inherent in the Gartner and Lipsky proposal, which retains the regular classroom and proposes to make it effective for all students by implementing the principles of effective schools research through school improvement projects. Here the assumption is that the theory of effective teaching, which is known by the school improvement and effective schools specialists apart from and prior to the classroom context, is contained in the principles identified in effective schools research and that implementing these principles in the practice context is simply a matter of the teacher making a commitment to follow them. In principle, imposing such standards from above, their apparent efficacy in some other context notwithstanding, can only lead to an extension of existing rationalization and formalization, and thus to an increase in ritualized activity. Ultimately, this leads to an increase in professionalization and a corresponding decrease in personalization.[55] Finally, the Stainback and Stainback proposal compounds both of these problems. Not only does it retain the notions of a classroom and the separation of theory and practice, thus politicizing and undermining the ideals of collaboration and problem solving, but by creating a system of individual subject area specializations, it disintegrates the student's instructional program across even more teachers than the mainstreaming approach. Ironically, the REI proposal that promotes total integration of students implies a virtually complete disintegration of instruction.

Although the arguments put forth in the REI debate reject the assumption of human pathology and thus represent progress relative to the mainstreaming debate, the outcome is the same. The adhocratic values of the REI proponents are distorted by the bureaucratic value orientation of school organization. Moreover, because they retain the presupposition of organizational rationality, their adhocratic ends are deflected by the bureaucratic value orientation of their own proposals.

Earlier in the analysis we saw that a critical reading of the REI debate rejected the presupposition of human pathology and thus left the legitimacy of special education as a professional practice hanging on the adequacy of the presupposition of organizational rationality. At this point, however, we have seen that a critical reading of the discourse on school organization and adaptability, in conjunction with an organizational analysis of the EHA and the REI proposals, rejects the presuppositions of human pathology and organizational rationality. Such a reading deconstructs special education, both as a professional practice and as an institutional practice of public education. In terms of the adequacy of its grounding assumptions, special education cannot be considered a rational and just response to the problem of school failure.

PUBLIC EDUCATION AND THE DISCOURSE ON SCHOOL FAILURE

To this point in the analysis we have been concerned with special education, first as a professional practice from the vantage point of the REI debate, then as an institutional practice from the perspective of school organization and adaptability. The focus of this section is the implications of the deconstruction of special education for the discourse on school failure and, ultimately, for the legitimacy of the institutional practice of public education. Considering these implications, however, will require broadening the analysis to include the voice of the general education community and what it has to say about school failure from the perspective of educational excellence. If we think of the mainstreaming and REI debates in special education as two debates within a broader discourse on educational equity, and the effective schools and school restructuring debates in general education as two debates within a broader discourse on educational excellence, we can begin to see how the equity and excellence discourses parallel, mirror, and, ultimately, converge upon one another.[56]

The first parallel is that the initial debate within each discourse is an extreme form of naive pragmatism that merely reproduces the problems it sets out to solve. As in the case of mainstreaming and the EHA, the new practices that emerged out of the effective schools debate reproduced the original problems (Clark & Astuto, 1988; Cuban, 1983, 1989; Slavin, 1989; Stedman, 1987; Timar & Kirp, 1988; Wise, 1988). The second parallel is that the failure of the first debate within each discourse gives rise to the second debate, which, although it is less naive, is also a form of naive pragmatism that promises to reproduce current problems in the future. As we will see below, although the restructuring debate is less naive than the effective schools debate, it does not explicitly recognize the connection between general education practices and the four assumptions. As such, like the REI debate in special education, it promises to reproduce the general education problems of the 1980s in the 1990s and beyond (see Cuban, 1983, 1989; Skrtic, 1991; Wise, 1988). Although the restructuring debate parallels the REI debate in this second respect, the effects of this pattern in the two debates are mirror images of one another.

As we know, the REI debate implicates school organization in the problem of student disability. Thus, the first way that the two debates mirror each other is that, by pointing to the emergence and persistence of homogeneous grouping — curriculum tracking, in-class ability grouping, and compensatory pull-out programs — as an indication of deep structural flaws in traditional school organization (Cuban, 1989; Oakes, 1985, 1986a, 1986b; Stedman, 1987; Wise, 1988), the restructuring debate implicates student disability in the problem of school organization. The second way that the REI and restructuring debates mirror each other is that, although both of them reject two of the four assumptions and question the other two, in the final analysis they retain the assumptions that they question. We saw this pattern for both the REI proponents and opponents relative to the assumptions about the rationality of school organization and change. The mirror image of this contradiction in the restructuring debate is that, although it rejects the two assumptions about the rationality of school organization and change, it questions but retains the two assumptions about the nature of school failure and diagnosis. That is, although it criticizes the institutional practice of tracking, and even the overrepresentation of minority students in certain special education programs, it does not criticize special education as an institutional practice (see Goodlad, 1984; Oakes, 1986a,b; Sizer, 1984), and thus retains the assumptions that school failure is pathological and that diagnosis is objective and useful.[57]

The restructuring debate does not recognize special education as a form of tracking because its criticism of homogeneous grouping stops at the point of presumed pathology, which is the third and, for present purposes, most important way that the two debates mirror one another. Whereas the REI debate rejects the presupposition of human pathology but retains that of organizational rationality, the restructuring debate rejects organizational rationality but retains human pathology. The significance here, of course, is that the two debates — and thus the discourses on excellence and equity in public education — converge to reject both of the functionalist presuppositions that ground the twentieth-century discourse on school failure, and thus they deconstruct it.

The broader significance of the deconstruction of the discourse on school failure is that it provides the grounds for an immanent critique of the institution of public education. That is, confronted with the fact that its practices are neither excellent nor equitable, public education must account for itself without recourse to the distorting and legitimizing effects of the functionalist discourse on school failure. Ultimately, to be able to continue making the claim that it embodies the Jeffersonian ideal of democratic education, public education must reconstruct itself to be both excellent and equitable.

EXCELLENCE, EQUITY, AND ADHOCRACY

We can turn from deconstruction to reconstruction by considering the moments of truth contained in the convergence between excellence and equity in the REI and restructuring debates. As we know, the REI proponents call for virtually eliminating the regulatory requirements of the EHA. The corresponding argument among the proponents of restructuring is for eliminating scientific management as the approach to administration and change (for example, Boyer, 1983; Cuban, 1983, 1989; Goodlad, 1984; Oakes, 1985, 1986a, 1986b; Sirotnik & Oakes, 1986; Sizer, 1984; Wise, 1988). In organizational terms, the first convergence is that both sets of proponents are arguing for the elimination of rationalization, formalization, and tight coupling — the misplaced structural contingencies of the machine bureaucracy. The second convergence is between the REI proponents' arguments for merging the general and special education systems and the arguments of the restructuring proponents for merging the various general education tracks. Here, both sets of proposals are calling for the elimination of specialization, professionalization, and loose coupling — the structural contingencies of the professional bureaucracy configuration. In practical terms, both sets of proponents seek an adaptable system in which increased teacher discretion leads to more personalized instruction through collaborative problem solving among professionals and client constituencies (Boyer, 1983; Cuban, 1983, 1989; Goodlad, 1984; McNeil, 1986; Oakes, 1985; Sizer, 1984). Of course, because the restructuring proponents retain the assumption of pathology, there are differences between the two sets of proposals. But these are differences in degree, not in kind. In organizational terms, the participants in both debates are arguing for the introduction of collaboration, mutual adjustment, and discursive coupling — the structural contingencies of the adhocratic form. In principle, both sets of reform proposals require an adhocratic school organization and professional culture.

The REI opponents' position on equity is that, given the nonadaptability of regular classrooms and school organizations, the targeting function of the EHA and the pullout logic of mainstreaming must be maintained for political purposes, diagnostic and instructional inadequacies notwithstanding. The moment of truth in this position is the argument that, as long as resources are constant and students differ, no teacher, whether in a general or special education classroom, can escape the necessary choice between excellence (higher class means) and equity (narrower class variances), unless more powerful instructional technologies are available. In organizational terms, this is true because the structural contingencies of rationalization and formalization circumscribe a finite set of resources relative to a prespecified set of activities and outcomes, while those of specialization and professionalization circumscribe a finite repertoire of standard programs relative to a finite set of presumed client needs. Thus, students whose needs fall on the margins or outside of these standard programs must be either squeezed into them or squeezed out of the classroom. Given the inevitability of human diversity, a professional bureaucracy can do nothing but create students who do not fit the system. In a professional bureaucracy, all forms of tracking — curriculum tracking and in-class ability grouping in general education, as well as self-contained and resource classrooms in special, compensatory, remedial, and gifted education — are organizational pathologies created by specialization and professionalization and compounded by rationalization and formalization. Students are subjected to — and subjugated by — these practices because, given their structural and cultural contingencies, traditional school organizations cannot accommodate diversity and so must screen it out.

The problem with the REI opponents' argument, however, is that it assumes that nonadaptability is inherent in schooling, rather than in its traditional bureaucratic organization. Student diversity is not an inherent problem for school organizations; it is only a problem when they are premised on standardization and thus configure themselves as performance organizations that perfect standard programs for known contingencies. As we have seen, the adhocratic form is premised on innovation. It configures itself as a problem-solving organization for inventing novel programs for unfamiliar contingencies. Regardless of its causes and its extent, student diversity is not a liability in a problem-solving organization; it is an asset, an enduring uncertainty, and thus the driving force behind innovation, growth of knowledge, and progress.

The problem with the REI and restructuring proposals in this regard is that, although their ends require the adhocratic configuration, their means reproduce the professional bureaucracy configuration. This is so because, by retaining the notion of a classroom, they retain a specialized division of labor, a professionalized means of coordination, and thus a loosely coupled form of interdependency. Both reform approaches eliminate rationalization and formalization — and thus the misplaced machine bureaucracy outer structure of schools — while retaining specialization and professionalization — and thus the professional bureaucracy inner structure.

From an organizational perspective, the argument for eliminating rationalization and formalization is an argument for uniting theory and practice in the professional. The problem with this move in the REI and restructuring proposals, however, is that by retaining the professional bureaucracy configuration, they unite theory and practice in the *individual professional* rather than in a *team of professionals*.[58] From a structural perspective, innovation is "the building of new knowledge and skills, [which] requires the combination of different bodies of existing ones" (Mintzberg, 1979, p. 434). This requires a division of labor and a means of coordination that "break through the boundaries of conventional specialization," creating a situation in which "professionals must amalgamate their efforts [by joining] forces in multidisciplinary teams, each formed around a specific project of innovation" (Mintzberg, 1979, pp. 434–435). From a cultural perspective, repertoires or paradigms of practice are social constructions; innovation occurs when new paradigms emerge through confrontations over uncertainty within social groups (Brown, 1978; Rounds, 1981; Weick, 1979). From an organizational perspective, professional innovation is not a solitary act; when it does occur, it is a social phenomenon that takes place within a reflective discourse.

The problem of uniting theory and practice in the individual professional can be illustrated by considering the genealogy of special education as a professional and institutional practice.[59] The first special classroom teachers were general education teachers who thus had to invent new programs for students who, by definition, had needs that fell outside their repertoires of standard programs. Moreover, because special classrooms were decoupled from the machine bureaucracy structure and thus were relatively free from its rationalization and formalization, theory and practice were united in the special classroom teacher. However, because these teachers were decoupled from other regular and special classroom teachers and thus lacked the structural contingencies of collaboration, mutual adjustment, and discursive coupling, they were denied the structural conditions necessary for the emergence of an adhocratic mode of professional practice. The inadequacy of special education practices throughout this century illustrates the problem with freeing teachers from the outer machine bureaucracy structure of school organizations while retaining the inner professional bureaucracy structure. Although such a move may permit teachers to invent new repertoires, it will not assure that the repertoires they invent will be any more effective, ethical, or, in the long run, much different from what they had been doing before being set free.[60]

From a structural perspective, the REI and restructuring proponents are right about eliminating the rationalization and formalization associated with scientific management and the EHA. At a minimum, achieving their adhocratic ends will require merging theory and practice. However, if merging theory and practice is to have the adhocratic effects they desire, they will have to do more than merge general education tracks and the general and special education systems in the ways that they have proposed. Achieving their adhocratic ends will require merging theory and practice *in conjunction with* eliminating specialization and professionalization. This will require eliminating the classroom, which, in structural terms, is an organizational artifact of the structural contingencies of the professional bureaucracy configuration and, in practical terms, the principal barrier to the introduction of collaboration, mutual adjustment, and discursive coupling, the structural contingencies of the adhocracy configuration. Furthermore, from a cultural perspective, achieving their adhocratic ends will require that an adhocratic professional culture emerge and be sustained within public education. To emerge, such a culture will require the structural contingencies of the adhocratic form. To be sustained, it will require an enduring source of uncertainty because, as we saw in the case of NASA, without problems to solve, adhocracies revert to bureaucracies.[61]

In political terms, the institution of public education cannot be democratic unless its practices are excellent and equitable. In organizational terms, its practices cannot be excellent and equitable unless school organizations are adhocratic. In structural and cultural terms, school organizations cannot be adhocratic — and thus cannot be excellent, equitable, *or* democratic — without the uncertainty of student diversity. In the adhocratic school organization, educational equity is the precondition for educational excellence.

HISTORY, EDUCATION, AND DEMOCRACY

Although the evidence on educational excellence, equity, and adaptability is overwhelmingly negative, there are schools that are relatively effective, equitable, and adaptable, including some that have met or surpassed the intent of the EHA and the spirit of mainstreaming.[62] One way to explain this contradictory evidence theoretically is to think of schools as ambiguous, underorganized systems that are shaped by values. Of course, given the organizational history of public education, the value orientation of school organizations and their members tends to be bureaucratic. On occasion, however, someone, some group, or some event increases ambiguity enough to cast doubt on the prevailing paradigm and, under conditions of increased ambiguity, someone or some group, acting on a different set of values, manages to decrease the ambiguity by redefining the organization for themselves and others. In fact, it is just this sort of organizational phenomenon that one finds in successful schools. Their success turns on human agency, on the values, expectations, and actions of the people who work in them.[63] Schools can be effective, equitable, and adaptable, but when they are, they are operating more like adhocracies than bureaucracies. And they are operating this way because the people in them are thinking and acting more like problem solvers than performers. They are acting and thinking this way because someone or some group reduced uncertainty by reframing an ambiguous situation in terms of adhocratic values, a subtle process of deconstruction and reconstruction in which organizational members construct a new set of structural and cultural contingencies for themselves and their clients.

Although such an interpretation of today's successful schools provides further support for the adhocratic form, it does not account for the fact that the traditional industrial-era definitions of excellence and equity that have shaped the research on successful schools are losing their relevance with the emergence of post-industrialism. To assess the implications of post-industrialism for public education and the adhocratic form, it will be helpful to consider the arguments put forth in the social reconstruction debate, one of several debates within the progressive education movement earlier in this century (see Kliebard, 1988; Kloppenberg, 1986).

The proponents of social reconstruction were concerned that bureaucracy was distorting democracy. As Weber (1922/1978) explained, democracy and bureaucracy grow coincidentally because actualizing democratic government requires the bureaucratic administrative form. The problem is that, although democracy is supposed to be dynamic, the bureaucracy on which it depends resists change, a problem that, for Weber, was the central and irresolvable fact of the modern state. In *The Public and Its Problems*, Dewey (1927/1988b) argued that, although industrialization had intensified the problem of bureaucracy, it also provided an opportunity to recover democracy. According to Dewey (1899, 1927/1988b), the problem of bureaucracy is intensified by industrialization because it places more of life — particularly work and education — under the bureaucratic form. This reduces the need for problem solving and discourse, which stunts the growth of reflective thought and, ultimately, undercuts the ability of the public to govern itself. The opportunity posed by industrialization was that it created an expanding network of social interdependencies that Dewey (1929–30/1988a) believed made possible and begged for a way of developing a new sense of *social* individualism to replace the *possessive* form of individualism of the eighteenth and nineteenth centuries.

For Dewey (1897, 1916, 1927/1988b) and other progressive reformers (see Kloppenberg, 1986), the only meaningful response to the problem and opportunity of the industrial era was to restore the public for democracy through a cultural transformation, which was to be actualized by instituting progressive education in the public schools. Dewey's (1897, 1899, 1916) notion of progressive education was particularly well-suited to this end because, as a pedagogy grounded in the antifoundational epistemology of American pragmatism, it was premised on the belief that education in a democracy should both cultivate a sense of social responsibility by developing an awareness of interdependency, and engender a critical attitude toward received knowledge by promoting an appreciation of uncertainty. The problem, of course, was that the value orientation of progressive education is pluralistic and adhocratic, which contradicts the individualistic and bureaucratic value orientation of public education. Thus, the circularity in the progressive argument for transforming society through education was and still is that:

> If the problems facing society can be traced to its individualism . . . and reform must proceed by means of education, how can reformers get around the awkward fact that the educational system is imbued with precisely the values that they have isolated as the source of the problem? (Kloppenberg, 1986, p. 377)

No one grasped the circularity problem better than Weber (1922/1978). Whereas the problem of an unreflective public lay in the contradiction between democracy and bureaucracy in the modern state, he argued that the circularity of trying to solve it through education meant confronting an even greater problem in the logic of modernity itself: the contradiction among democracy, bureaucracy, education, and professionalization. Weber explained that the ever-increasing push to further bureaucratize government and the economy creates the need for more and more experts and thus continually increases the importance of specialized knowledge. But the logic of expertise contradicts democracy because it creates "the struggle of the 'specialist' type of man against the older type of 'cultivated' man" (1922/1978, p. 1090). And since the progressive project is premised on restoring democracy by educating the cultivated citizen, it is stymied because public education itself becomes increasingly bureaucratized in the interest of training specialized experts. Thus, democracy continues to decline, not only because the bureaucratic form resists change, but because the cultivated citizen continues to disappear. As more of life comes under the control of the professional bureaucracy's standard problem solutions, the need to solve problems and to engage in discourse diminishes even further. This tendency stunts the growth of reflective thought in society and in the professions, which not only undercuts the ability of the public to govern itself democratically, but also the ability of the professions to see themselves critically.

The advantage today is that post-industrialism is premised on an even greater and more pervasive form of interdependency and social responsibility. Whereas the network of social interdependencies of industrialization stopped at the boundaries of industrial organizations themselves, post-industrialization extends the network into the very core of the post-industrial organizational form (Drucker, 1989; Naisbitt & Aburdene, 1985; Reich, 1983). The key difference is that industrial organization depended on the machine bureaucracy configuration and thus on the separation of theory and practice and an unreflective, mechanical form of interdependency among workers. However, post-industrial organization depends on the adhocratic form; on collaboration, mutual adjustment, and discursive coupling, and on a political form of accountability premised on a community of interests among workers, managers, and, ultimately, among the organization's members, consumers, and host community (Drucker, 1989; Mintzberg, 1979; Reich, 1983, 1990).

Reich (1990, p. 201) characterized the adhocracies of the post-industrial economy as "environments in which people can identify and solve problems for themselves," as contexts in which individual skills are integrated into a group. . . . Over time, as group members work through various problems . . . they learn about each other's abilities. They learn how they can help one another perform better, what each can contribute to a particular project, and how they can best take advantage of one another's experience. (Reich, 1990, p. 201)

The system of education needed for the post-industrial economy is one that prepares young people "to take responsibility for their continuing education, and to collaborate with one another so that their combined skills and insights add up to something more than the sum of their individual contributions" (Reich, 1990, p. 202). As such, educational excellence in the post-industrial era is more than basic numeracy and literacy; it is a capacity for working collaboratively with others and for taking responsibility for learning (Drucker, 1989; Naisbitt & Aburdene, 1985; Reich, 1983). Moreover, educational equity is a precondition for excellence in the post-industrial era, for collaboration means learning collaboratively with and from persons with varying interests, abilities, skills, and cultural perspectives, and taking responsibility for learning means taking responsibility for one's own learning and that of others. Ability grouping and tracking have no place in such a system because they "reduce young people's capacities to learn from and collaborate with one another" and work against developing a community of interests, a situation that is precluded unless "unity and cooperation are the norm" in schools (Reich, 1990, p. 208).

Given the relevancies of the post-industrial era, the successful school is one that prepares young people to work responsibly and interdependently under conditions of uncertainty. It does this by promoting in its students a sense of social responsibility, an awareness of interdependency, and an appreciation of uncertainty. It achieves these things by developing its students' capacity for experiential learning through collaborative problem solving and reflective discourse within a community of interests. The successful school in the post-industrial era is one that produces cultivated citizens by providing all of its students with the experience of a progressive education in an adhocratic setting. Given the emerging historical conditions of the twenty-first century, and the fact that democracy *is* collaborative problem solving through reflective discourse within a community of interests, the adhocratic school organization provides more than a way to reconcile the social goals of educational excellence and educational equity. It provides us with an opportunity to resume the critical project of American pragmatism in public education and, thus, with another chance to save democracy from bureaucracy.

NOTES

1. Max Weber (1919/1946, p. 117).
2. Although the special education community has responded favorably to what is being referred to as the school restructuring phase (see Elmore, 1987; notes 8 and 56) of the excellence movement, the push for higher standardized test scores during the early phase of the excellence movement (see Wise, 1988) was viewed negatively (see Pugach & Sapon-Shevin, 1987; Shepard, 1987).

3. The developments in the social disciplines include the general trend away from objectivism and toward subjectivism (see, e.g., Bernstein, 1976; Schwartz & Ogilvy, 1979) and, more important, the reemergence of antifoundationalism (see, e.g., Bernstein, 1983; Lyotard, 1979/1984; Skinner, 1985). Whereas social inquiry historically has been dominated by the objectivist conceptualization of science and the foundational view of knowledge and thus by a monological quest for the truth about the social world, contemporary scholars are calling for dialogical social analysis — an antifoundational discourse open to multiple interpretations of social life (see, e.g., Bernstein, 1983; Rorty, 1979; Riceour, 1981). The reemergence of antifoundationalism has led to a revival of interest in philosophical pragmatism, particularly in the work of John Dewey (see Antonio, 1989; Kloppenberg, 1986) and his contemporary appropriators (e.g., Rorty, 1979, 1982), as well as increased attention to the work of contemporary Continental philosophers like Derrida (1972/1982a) and Foucault (1980). An important methodological outcome of these developments has been the emergence of new antifoundational methodologies and the reappropriation of older ones (see notes 4, 5, 7, and 9). A second important outcome has been the emergence of the text as a metaphor for social life (Geertz, 1983), which implies a mode of social analysis that views human and institutional practices as discursive formations that can be read or interpreted in many ways, none of which is correct in a foundational sense, but each of which carries with it a particular set of moral and political implications. Among other things, social analysis under the text metaphor studies that which conditions, limits, and institutionalizes discursive formations; it asks how power comes to be concentrated in the hands of those who have the right to interpret reality and define normality (Dreyfus & Rabinow, 1983; see notes 4, 5, 7, and 9).

4. My version of critical pragmatism uses four antifoundational methodologies (see note 3): two reappropriated ones, immanent critique and ideal type (note 5), and two newer ones, deconstruction (note 7) and genealogy (note 9). Given its grounding in philosophical pragmatism, critical pragmatism does not seek "truth" in the foundational sense; it is, rather, a form of edification (see Cherryholmes, 1988; Rorty, 1979). As used here, it is a mode of inquiry that, by forcing us to acknowledge that what we think, do, say, write, and read as professionals is shaped by convention, helps us avoid the delusion that we can know ourselves, our profession, our clients, "or anything else, except under optional descriptions" (Rorty, 1979, p. 379). Critical pragmatism is "the same as the 'method' of utopian politics or revolutionary science (as opposed to parliamentary politics or normal science). The method is to redescribe lots and lots of things in new ways, until you . . . tempt the rising generation to . . . look for . . . new scientific equipment or new social institutions" (Rorty, 1989, p. 9). For an extended discussion of my version of critical pragmatism, see Skrtic (1991). For a somewhat different version, see Cherryholmes (1988).

5. Immanent critique is more than a method of analysis. Historically, from Hegel and Marx to more contemporary emancipation theorists in the social disciplines (e.g., Horkheimer, 1974) and education (e.g., Giroux, 1981), it has been understood as the driving force behind social progress and change, a process driven by the affinity of humans for attempting to reconcile their claims about themselves (appearances) with their actual social conditions (reality) (Hegel, 1807/1977; Kojeve, 1969). It is an emancipatory form of analysis in that it is intended to free us from our unquestioned assumptions about ourselves and our social practices, assumptions that prevent us from doing what we believe is right (Antonio, 1981; Schroyer, 1973). As a method, however, immanent critique does not on its own provide a way of identifying the ideals or actual conditions of social phenomena. For this I will use Max Weber's (1904/1949) method of ideal types.

   The ideal-typical analytic is premised on the idea that the meaning of social phenomena derives from the cultural significance (value orientation) behind human and institutional action. As such, ideal types are exaggerated mental constructs (developed from empirical and theoretical knowledge) for analyzing social phenomena in terms of their value orientation. They are not "true" in a foundational sense; they are mental constructions used as expository devices (Dallmayr & McCarthy, 1977; Mommsen, 1974; Ritzer, 1983). I use ideal types extensively in the article to draw out and emphasize the explicit and implicit value orientations in the discourses and practices considered, particularly in the characterizations of school organization that are used in the second half of the paper (see notes 38 and 39).

6. I use the term educational administration in both a narrow sense (to refer to the field and practice of educational administration) and a broad sense (to refer to the fields and practices of educational policy and educational change, or school improvement or educational reform), inclusive of the role played by persons in the fields of educational administration (narrow sense), including special education administration. By the discourse on school organization and adaptability I mean the discourse on these topics in the field of educational administration (both senses), as well as in the broader discourse on organization and change in the multidisciplinary field of organization analysis (see Scott, 1981; notes 34 and 37). I use "school organization and adaptability" rather than "school organization and change" to refer to this discourse because I am interested in the capacity for change at both the microscopic level of the individual professional and the macroscopic level of the entire organization (see notes 35 and 36).

7. Deconstruction is Derrida's (1972/1982a,b) method of reading texts by focusing on their margins (silences, contradictions, inconsistencies, and incompleteness) rather than on their central ideas or arguments. Although Derrida deconstructs philosophical texts, the method of deconstruction has been applied broadly to the texts of the social sciences and professions, including professional, institutional, and social practices and discourses (see Cherryholmes, 1988; Hoy, 1985; Ryan, 1982; Rorty, 1989). Whereas traditional analyses purport to enable us to read or interpret a text, discourse, or practice (as an accurate or true representation of the world), deconstruction tries to show that interpretation is a distinctively human process in which no single interpretation ever has enough cognitive authority to privilege it over another (see Derrida, 1972/1982a).

8. I use terms like general education, regular education, and regular classroom in reference to the typical kindergarten through twelfth grade program within public education. Although I recognize that these terms often carry "decidedly neutral or even negative connotations" (Lilly, 1989, p. 143) for professional educators outside the field of special education, I use them for ease of presentation only, particularly where clarity demands that I distinguish between general education and special education professionals, practices, and discourses, as well as between education in a broad sense (the entire field or institution of education) and education in a narrow sense (the kindergarten through twelfth grade program).

   Although I use the term special education in the narrow sense of the professional field (or institutional practice) of special education, the implications of much of what I have to say in the first half of the paper apply equally well to students in the other special needs programs (e.g., compensatory, remedial, and migrant education), as well as students who are tracked in one way or another within the general education program (see note 12). In the second half of the article references to the other special needs programs and tracking practices in general education are made explicit. By "the discourse on educational excellence" in the field of general education I mean what general educators think, do, say, read, and write about educational excellence, a discourse that (over the past decade) can be understood in terms of two related debates — what I will refer to as the "effective schools" and "school restructuring" debates (see note 56). Although it plays a key role in special education classification practices under the EHA, I have not included the field of school psychology in the present analysis. For a separate treatment, see Skrtic (1990a).

9. Genealogy is Foucault's (1980, 1983) approach for analyzing what conditions, limits, and institutionalizes social practices and discourses. He used genealogy to study "the way modern societies control and discipline their populations by sanctioning the knowledge claims and practices of the human sciences: medicine, psychiatry, psychology, criminology, sociology and so on" (Philip, 1985, p. 67; Foucault, 1961/1973, 1963/1975, 1975/1979). The key difference between genealogy and traditional historical analysis is that the genealogist is far less interested in the events of history than in the "norms, constraints, conditions, conventions, and so on" (Dreyfus & Rabinow, 1983, p. 108) that produced them.

10. My use of the qualifiers "explicit" and "implicit" here is a bit misleading. It is more accurate to think of all three discourses as being grounded in unquestioned presuppositions. Explicit here refers to the idea that certain presuppositions are an explicit part of the profession's knowledge tradition relative to other ones that are merely implicit norms in society. This problem will come up again (see note 19) because the degree of implicitness and explicitness of guiding assumptions is a key part of the subject matter of this type of inquiry (see notes 4, 5, 7, and 9).

    Although one could argue that the field of educational administration implicitly assumes that school failure is pathological on the grounds that historically it has avoided topics on school effects and student outcomes (Bridges, 1982; Erickson, 1979), human pathology is explicit in the conceptualization of administration that grounds the field. The Getzels-Guba model of administration (Getzels & Guba, 1957), "the most successful theory in educational administration" (Griffiths, 1979, p. 50), is, in part, an extension of Barnard's (1938) conceptualization of administration (Campbell, Fleming, Newell, & Bennion, 1987) that assumes a cooperative (rational) organization in which uncooperativeness is pathological (Burrell & Morgan, 1979).

11. The same assumptions in the language of the general education and educational administration discourses are that: a) school failure is a (psychologically or sociologically) pathological condition that students have, b) differential diagnosis (identification by ability, need, and/or interest) is objective and useful, c) special programming (homogeneous grouping in general education tracks and segregated and pull-out classrooms in special, compensatory, gifted, and remedial education) is a rationally conceived and coordinated system of practices and programs that benefits diagnosed students, and d) progress in education (increases in academic achievement and efficiency) results from incremental technological improvements in differential diagnosis and intervention practices and programs (see Bridges, 1982; Cherryholmes, 1988; Erickson, 1979; McNeil, 1986; Oakes, 1985, 1986a,b; Sirotnik & Oakes, 1986; Spring, 1980).

12. Although I am emphasizing the institutional practice of special education here, we will see in subsequent sections that, from an organizational perspective, all practices that group or track students in general education (e.g., in-class ability grouping, curriculum tracking), as well as the other institutional practices that remove students from the general program (e.g., compensatory, gifted, remedial education), are artifacts of functionalist assumptions about organizational rationality and human and social pathology.

13. Although the introductory discussion dichotomized the mainstreaming debate and the REI debate as if there were a period between them when the field was completely certain about the adequacy of mainstreaming and the EHA, it is more accurate to think of the field of special education as being in a more or less constant state of self-criticism since the early 1960s. Criticism subsided somewhat during the period shortly before and after the enactment of the EHA, but it did not disappear (see, e.g., Keogh & Levitt, 1976; MacMillan & Semmel, 1977; Reynolds, 1976; Reynolds & Birch, 1977). The field of educational administration (narrow sense) has been in a constant state of self-criticism since at least the early 1950s (Clark, 1985; Cunningham, Hack, & Nystrand, 1977; Griffiths, 1959, 1983, 1988; Halpin, 1970; Halpin & Hayes, 1977; Hayes & Pharis, 1967; Spring, 1980). Driven by the persistent anomaly of little or no substantive change or improvement in public education, the field of educational change or school improvement has been characterized by the same sort of self-criticism since the early 1960s (Elmore & McLaughlin, 1988; House, 1979; Lehming & Kane, 1981; note 36).

14. Hallahan, Kauffman, Lloyd, and McKinney (1988), key opponents of the REI, argue that the concept first appeared in Reynolds and Wang (1981), which, in revised form (Wang, Reynolds, & Walberg, 1985, 1986), subsequently received formal recognition from Madeleine C. Will (1985, 1986a,b), the Assistant Secretary for the Office of Special Education and Rehabilitative Services in the Reagan administration. This is an important connection because, in subsequent criticism of the REI, a major argument has been that it is "entirely consistent with Reagan-Bush policies aimed at decreasing federal support for education, including the education of vulnerable children and youth" (Kauffman, 1989a, p. 7). Although Wang (Wang & Walberg, 1988), a key proponent of the REI, agrees that Will (1986a) provided the original policy state-

ment for the REI, she contends that the REI itself is grounded in empirical evidence on the inadequacies of the current system contained in Heller, Holtzman and Messick (1982); Hobbs (1975, 1980); and Wang, Reynolds, and Walberg (1987a). Thus, the REI opponents tend to characterize the REI as a political outcome of conservative ideology, while the proponents characterize it as a logical outcome of empirical research. Nevertheless, it is perhaps more accurate to think of it as a logical outcome of Maynard Reynolds's liberal strategy of "progressive inclusion" (Reynolds & Rosen, 1976), the idea that the entire history of special education is or should be one of incremental progress toward more normalized instructional placements. In 1976, Reynolds, one of the architects of the "continuum of placements" model that underwrites mainstreaming (Reynolds, 1962; see also Deno, 1970) and a key REI proponent, rejected the pull-out logic of mainstreaming in favor of making "regular classrooms . . . more diverse educational environments, [thus reducing] the need to . . . use separate . . . educational environments" (Reynolds, 1976, p. 8). He proposed to do this "through the redistribution of resources and energies, through training, and, finally, through the redistribution of students" (1976, p. 18). Thus, although there probably is a moment of truth in both the REI proponents' and opponents' characterizations of the motivation behind the REI, Reynolds formulated the concept and started the debate before either the empirical data were available or the conservative ideology held much sway in Washington.

15. Besides Will's (1984, 1985, 1986a,b) statements on or related to the REI, and several attempts to place the REI in perspective (e.g., Davis, 1989; Davis & McCaul, 1988; Lieberman, 1984, 1988; Sapon-Shevin, 1988; Skrtic, 1987a,b, 1988b), the vast majority of the literature promoting the REI has been produced by eight individuals working either alone or in teams of two (or, at times, with other colleagues). I will refer to them as REI proponents according to the following two-person teams: a) Maynard Reynolds and Margaret Wang (Reynolds, 1988; Reynolds & Wang, 1981, 1983; Reynolds, Wang, & Walberg, 1987; Walberg & Wang, 1987; Wang, 1981, 1988, 1989a,b; Wang & Reynolds, 1985, 1986; Wang, Reynolds, & Walberg, 1985, 1986, 1987a,b, 1988, 1989; Wang & Walberg, 1988); b) M. Stephen Lilly and Marleen Pugach (Lilly, 1986, 1987, 1989; Pugach & Lilly, 1984); c) Susan Stainback and William Stainback (Stainback & Stainback, 1984, 1985a,b, 1987a,b, 1989; Stainback, Stainback, Courtnage, & Jaben, 1985; Stainback, Stainback, & Forest, 1989); and d) Alan Gartner and Dorothy Kerzner Lipsky (Gartner, 1986; Gartner & Lipsky, 1987, 1989; Lipsky & Gartner, 1987, 1989a,b). The analysis of the REI proponents' arguments against the EHA and for their REI proposals is based on virtually all of the literature cited in a) through d) above, as well as some additional related work done by these authors and others, as noted.

16. In their criticism of the current system of special education, all four teams of REI proponents refer, more or less, to a common body of EHA implementation research, virtually all of which is reviewed or cited in Wang, Reynolds, and Walberg (1987a) and Gartner and Lipsky (1987). The 4.5 million figure represents an increase of about 20 percent in the number of students identified as handicapped since 1976–1977, much of which has resulted from increases in the number of students identified as learning disabled, a classification that currently represents over 43 percent of all students identified as handicapped and that, despite attempts to tighten eligibility criteria, has increased over 140 percent since 1977 (U.S. Department of Education, 1988; Gerber & Levine-Donnerstein, 1989). In addition to these three classifications, the mildly handicapped designation includes students with mild forms of speech and language problems and students with physical and sensory impairments that are not accompanied by other severely disabling conditions, such as severe mental retardation (Reynolds & Lakin, 1987). When these additional students are included in the count, estimates of the proportion of students considered mildly handicapped range from 75–90 percent of those students classified as handicapped in school (Algozzine & Korinek, 1985; Shepard, 1987; Wang, Reynolds, & Walberg, 1989).

17. The first published reactions to the REI (Lieberman, 1985; Mesinger, 1985) were decidedly negative, but focused exclusively on Stainback and Stainback (1984). These were followed by reactions from three subgroups within the field that, although sensitive to current problems

and generally supportive of reform, merely called for more information (Teacher Education Division of the Council for Exceptional Children, 1986, 1987), proposed a mechanism for interpreting information and building a consensus (Skrtic, 1987b), or specified several preconditions of reform (Heller & Schilit, 1987). Neither these reactions nor those of others who have criticized the REI in part (e.g., Davis, 1989); Davis & McCaul, 1988; Lieberman, 1984, 1988; Sapon-Shevin, 1988; Skrtic, 1987a, 1988b) or in whole (e.g., Vergason & Anderegg, 1989) have had much impact on the course of events. The controversy over the REI began with the publication of a special issue of the *Journal of Learning Disabilities* (*JLD*) in 1988 and has been sustained by several other articles since then that have been written by some of the same authors. Together, the *JLD* articles and these other pieces include: a) Braaten, Kauffman, Braaten, Polsgrove, & Nelson (1988); b) Bryan, Bay, & Donahue (1988); c) Council for Children with Behavioral Disorders (1989); d) Gerber (1988a, 1988b); e) Hallahan, Kauffman, Lloyd, and McKinney (1988); f) Hallahan, Keller, McKinney, Lloyd, and Bryan (1988); g) Kauffman (1988, 1989a,b); h) Kauffman, Gerber, and Semmel (1988); i) Keogh (1988); j) Lloyd, Crowley, Kohler, and Strain (1988); k) McKinney and Hocutt (1988); and l) Schumaker and Deshler (1988). My analysis of the REI opponents' assessment of the adequacy of the current system of special education and their criticism of the REI proponents' proposals for reform is drawn from the literature cited in a) through l) above, as well as from some additional work done by these authors and others, as noted.

18. The controversial nature of the current debate and the degree to which it has divided the field is clear in some of the more recent encounters in the literature. In these pieces the REI advocates characterize the opponents as segregationists (Wang & Walberg, 1988) and compare the current system of special education to slavery (Stainback & Stainback, 1987b) and apartheid (Lipsky & Gartner, 1987), whereas the REI opponents characterize the proponents as politically naive liberals and the REI as the Reagan-Bush "trickle-down theory of education of the hard-to-teach" (Kauffman, 1989b, p. 256).

19. There is no argument over the fact that most disabilities in the severe to profound range are associated with observable patterns of biological symptoms or syndromes, and are thus comprehensible under the pathological model (Mercer, 1973). In any event, the issue relative to these students, as in the case of the students identified as mildly handicapped, is whether they are being served adequately and ethically under the current system (see note 25). In most cases, students classified as mildly handicapped, and particularly those classified as learning disabled, emotionally disturbed, and mildly mentally retarded, do not show biological signs of pathology (Algozzine, 1976, 1977; Apter, 1982; Hobbs, 1975; Mercer, 1973; Rhodes, 1970; Rist & Harrell, 1982; Ross, 1980; Schrag & Divorky, 1975; Skrtic, 1988b; Swap, 1978).

It should be clear that the participants in the REI debate are not speaking explicitly to the four assumptions (see note 10). Indeed, that is the problem with the debate, as noted. Thus, from this point on in the article (including endnotes), I will at times omit the qualifiers "implicit" and "explicit" when discussing the implications of REI proponents' and opponents' arguments for the four grounding assumptions, particularly when including them is cumbersome, as it is in this section because the discussion includes two other levels of implicitness. First, there is the nature of agreement (implicit or explicit) between the REI proponents' and opponents' assessments of current practices, a level I will retain in text. Second, there is the nature of the unquestioned presuppositions that ground the field (explicit in the professional knowledge tradition or an implicit social norm) (see note 10), which I will not retain in text. So, when I say that the REI proponents or opponents "reject" or "retain" an assumption or presupposition, it should be understood that they do so implicitly. The same will hold true (relative to the four assumptions) for the arguments of the participants in the effective schools and school restructuring debates in general education, which will be addressed in subsequent sections (see notes 8 and 56). In all cases where it seems necessary for clarity, however, I will use the qualifiers in the text or in a note.

20. A further argument of the REI proponents relative to the nonadaptability of the general education system is that the existence of the special education system is a barrier to the development

of a responsive capacity within general education, both in public schools and in teacher education (Lilly, 1986, 1989; Pugach, 1988; Pugach & Lilly, 1984; Reynolds, 1988). This assertion relative to public schools is addressed extensively in subsequent sections from an organizational perspective (see also Skrtic & Ware, in press). For my position on this assertion relative to teacher education, see Thousand (1990).

On the related matter of the attribution of student failure, both the REI opponents and proponents agree that an exclusively student-deficit orientation is inappropriate. Although some of the REI opponents argue that the proponents lean too far toward an exclusively teacher-deficit orientation (Kauffman, Gerber, & Semmel, 1988; Keogh, 1988), the REI proponents clearly recognize the responsibility of the student in the learning process (Gartner, 1986; Walberg & Wang, 1987; Wang, 1989b).

21. The only REI opponent who makes a case for the potential instructional relevance of differential diagnosis considers it to be an empirical question that, if answered in the negative, should signal the discontinuance of the practice of differential diagnosis and the categorical approach to special education (Keogh, 1988). Although Bryan, Bay, and Donahue (1988, p. 25) do not make an explicit argument for the instructional relevance of differential diagnosis, by arguing that "one cannot assume that any two learning disabled children would be any more similar than a learning disabled child and a normally achieving child, or a normally achieving child and an underachieving child" they actually make an implicit argument against the instructional utility of differential diagnosis and thus implicitly agree with the REI proponents' position that all students have unique learning needs and interests, even those within the traditional mild disability categories.

22. Although there is general agreement among the REI opponents that the instructional effectiveness of special education interventions has not been demonstrated, two arguments are put forth in favor of instruction delivered in special education settings. The first one is that teachers in general education are unable to meet the diverse needs of students with learning disabilities in their classrooms (Bryan, Bay, & Donahue 1988). The second argument rests on the speculation that more powerful instructional techniques might be more easily implemented in special education settings than in regular classrooms (Hallahan, Keller, McKinney, Lloyd, & Bryan, 1988; see also Hallahan & Keller, 1986).

23. The argument that the current system is politically rational cannot be divorced from the argument that progress is rational-technical because, although targeting students for services that are instructionally ineffective at present but will be rendered effective in the future may be politically justifiable, targeting them for ineffective services that will not be rendered effective in the future is not justifiable, politically or ethically (see note 33).

As for the question of whether special education is a rationally coordinated system of services, the REI proponents argue that it is coordinated with neither the general education system nor with the other special needs programs. They characterize the entire special needs enterprise, including the special education system, in terms of disjointed incrementalism — a collection of disjointed programs, each with its own clients, personnel, administrators, budget, and regulations, which have been added to schools incrementally over time (Reynolds & Birch, 1977; Reynolds & Wang, 1983; Reynolds, Wang, & Walberg, 1987; Wang, Reynolds, & Walberg, 1985, 1986). Although the REI opponents are generally silent on the issue of coordination, Kauffman, Gerber, and Semmel (1988) respond by linking it to their argument for the political rationality of the current system. Although they recognize the lack of coordination, they consider it to be an unavoidable consequence of the politically rational targeting function of the EHA, a function that is fundamental to the very notion of categorical programs.

24. Although she has been a major figure in the REI debate, Will (1985, 1986a, 1986b) has not offered a specific proposal as such (see notes 14, 15, 27, and 28).

25. This issue actually separates the four teams of REI advocates into two camps. The Gartner and Lipsky and Stainback and Stainback teams have distanced themselves from the other two teams and from the REI itself, nothing that, while it has resulted in some positive momentum for reform, ultimately it is merely "blending at the margin" (Lipsky & Gartner, 1989a, p. 271)

because it maintains two separate systems. For Stainback and Stainback (1989, p. 43), the REI concept is too restrictive because it "does not address the need to include in regular classrooms and regular education those students labeled severely and profoundly handicapped" (see also notes 19 and 27).

26. The Lilly and Pugach proposal excludes students classified as mildly handicapped who have "developmental learning disabilities" (Pugach & Lilly, 1984, p. 53), that is, learning disabilities that are presumed to be pathological (Kirk & Chalfant, 1983).

27. Reynolds and Wang reserve the option of separate settings because they believe that "surely there will be occasions to remove some students for instruction in special settings" (Wang, Reynolds, & Walberg, 1985, p. 13). Will's (1986a) position in this regard is similar to those of Lilly and Pugach and Reynolds and Wang, in that her version of a restructured system continues to rely on separate instructional settings for some students, a position that has been criticized by Stainback and Stainback (1987b) and Gartner and Lipsky (1987, p. 385) as perpetuating "a dual system approach for a smaller (more severely impaired) population."

28. Each team of REI proponents, as well as Will (1986a,b), takes a unique stance on this point, both in terms of the degree to which general and special education should be merged and the level or levels of the institution of public education at which merger should take place. Although neither Will nor any of the four teams of proponents speaks to each of the following levels, taken together they address changes at or have implications for: a) the U.S. Department of Education, b) research and development centers, c) teacher education programs, d) local education agencies, e) school buildings, and f) classrooms. Although she is somewhat contradictory on the matter (see Gartner & Lipsky, 1987; Stainback & Stainback, 1987b; note 27), Will (1986a, p. 415) calls for "enhanced component parts," better cooperation, and shared responsibility between the two systems at all levels, particularly at levels a) and e); she does not, however, call for outright merger of the two systems at any level. In the analysis of these proposals in text, the notion of merger is addressed at the building and classroom levels only (see notes 29 and 30).

29. Above the regular classroom teachers and generic specialists, Reynolds and Wang (1983) propose a merger of district-level consultants who would provide the classroom teachers and generic specialists with consultation and training on generic topics (Wang, Reynolds, & Walberg, 1985).

30. In addition to merging special and remedial education at the building level, the Lily and Pugach plan (Pugach & Lilly, 1984, p. 54) proposes a merger at the level of teacher education. Their plan would merge "what is now special education for the mildly handicapped [in departments of special education] with what are currently departments of elementary and secondary education or curriculum and instruction" (p. 53) for the purpose of "providing instruction of the highest quality . . . for advanced preparation of support services specialists at the graduate level" (p. 54), as well as undergraduate instruction for persons in preparation for the role of regular classroom teacher.

31. Other than the recommended use of more powerful instructional technologies — such as cooperative learning, curriculum-based assessment, and peer tutoring (Lloyd, Crowley, Kohler, & Strain, 1988; Thousand & Villa, 1988, 1989) — and professional problem-solving mechanisms — such as teacher assistance teams (Chalfant, Pysh, & Moultrie, 1979) and collaborative consultation (e.g., Pugach, 1988) — the primary difference at the classroom level is that students who would have been removed under the current system remain in the classroom on a full-time basis where they, their teachers, and any other students who need assistance are provided with in-class support services.

32. Drawing on the work of Edmonds (1979), Gilhool (1976, 1989), Allington and McGill-Franzen (1989), and Lezotte (1989), Gartner and Lipsky argue that a) all students, including those with special needs, can learn effectively from the same pedagogy; b) this generic pedagogy is known and available in the principles and practices contained in the effective schools research; and c) these principles and practices are replicable through school improvement programs. Ironically,

although they argue that effective education for students labeled as handicapped is a matter of will and commitment on the part of teachers and schools, Gartner and Lipsky call for reformulating the EHA into a new mandate "that requires a unitary system [that] is 'special' for all students." That is, they call for transforming the EHA into "an effective schools act for all students" (1989a, p. 282).

33. The explicit historical and political arguments against the possibility of change presented in Council for Children with Behavioral Disorders (1989), Kauffman (1988), and Kauffman, Gergel, and Semmel (1988) contradict the implicit arguments for the possibility of incremental change through research and development presented in Braaten, Kauffman, Braaten, Polsgrove, and Nelson (1988); Bryan, Bay, and Donahue (1988); Council for Children with Behavioral Disorders (1989); Hallahan, Keller, McKinney, Lloyd, and Bryan (1988); Kauffman (1988); Kauffman, Gerber, and Semmel (1988); Keogh (1988); and Lloyd, Crowley, Kohler, and Strain (1988). It is obvious, of course, that by contradicting their position on the possibility of rational-technical change, the REI opponents reverse their position on the fourth assumption. However, this also reverses their position on the third assumption because, on political and ethical grounds, their position on the third and fourth assumptions cannot be separated (see note 23).

34. There was an attempt in the mid-1950s to ground education administration (narrow sense) in the theoretical discourse of the social sciences (Griffiths, 1959; Hayes & Pharis, 1967), but it failed (Cunningham, Hack, & Nystrand, 1977; Halpin, 1970; Halpin & Hayes, 1977). As a result, the field continues to be grounded in the prescriptive discourse of scientific management (Clark, 1985; Griffiths, 1983; Spring, 1980). Although this orientation has been criticized by persons in the field (e.g., Clark, 1985) and others (e.g., Spring, 1980), and arguments from within the field for a critical orientation have emerged (e.g., Bates, 1980, 1987; Foster, 1986), the field continues to be dominated by the prescriptive discourse of scientific management and by functionalist conceptualizations of organization, administration, and inquiry (Clark, 1985; Griffiths, 1988; Lincoln, 1985).

35. These modes of theorizing can be understood in terms of two dimensions of metatheoretical assumptions: a) an objectivism-subjectivism dimension that corresponds to various presuppositions about the nature of science and b) a microscopic-macroscopic dimension that reflects various presuppositions about the nature of society. Counterposing the two dimensions forms four modes of theorizing or paradigms of social scientific thought: a) functionalism (micro-objectivist), the dominant mode in the West; b) interpretivism (micro-subjectivist); c) structuralism (macro-objectivist); and d) humanism (macro-subjectivist) (Burrell & Morgan, 1979; Ritzer, 1980, 1983). Each paradigm represents a unique way to understand the social world, including organization and change (Burrell & Morgan, 1979; Morgan, 1983). In terms of the theoretical discourse in the field of organization analysis, the objectivism-subjectivism dimension corresponds to assumptions about the nature of action in organizations, ranging from the objectivist notion of rational action to the subjectivist notion of nonrational action. The microscopic-macroscopic dimension corresponds to assumptions about the level at which organizational activity is most appropriately analyzed, ranging from theories that emphasize organizing processes at the micro-level of individuals and small groups to those that emphasize organization structure at the macro-level of total organization (Pfeffer, 1982; Scott, 1981).

36. One major development has been a series of paradigm shifts. Referring to the four paradigm matrix in note 35, the three shifts include: a) one in the 1960s from the micro-objectivist to the macro-objectivist paradigm, b) one in the 1970s at the microscopic level of analysis from the micro-objectivist to the micro-subjectivist paradigm, and c) one in the 1980s at the macroscopic level of analysis from the macro-objectivist to the macro-subjectivist paradigm (Burrell & Morgan, 1979; Pfeffer, 1982; Scott, 1981). A related development has been the emergence of several theories that implicitly or explicitly bridge paradigms (see Skrtic, 1988b, 1991), each of which facilitates the integration of theoretical insights from two or more paradigms (see note 38). Although educational administration (narrow sense) continues to be dominated by the ra-

tional-technical perspective on organization and change, there has been a shift in the field of educational change from the rational-technical to the nonrational-cultural perspective on change (House, 1979). This shift has been driven by three decades of uncertainty surrounding the apparent inability to actually bring about meaningful change in school organizations (Boyd & Crowson, 1981; Cuban, 1989; Elmore & Mc Laughlin, 1988; Lehming & Kane, 1981; Wise, 1988). As a result, the nonrational-cultural perspective increasingly has become the favored outlook on change (e.g., Goodlad, 1975; House, 1979; Sarason, 1971/1982; Sirotnik & Oakes, 1986; notes 37 and 38).

37. In the interest of space, I conduct my deconstruction of the discourse on school organization and adaptability in the field of educational administration indirectly. That is, I spend most of the available space in this section on the antifoundational interpretation of school organization and adaptability that I will use in subsequent sections to deconstruct the institutional practice of special education, the discourse on school failure, and the institution of public education. Nevertheless, virtually everything that is presented in this section and the ones to follow can be read as a deconstruction of the discourse on school organization and adaptability in the field of educational administration because it delegitimizes the presupposition of organizational rationality, the explicit grounding of the field of educational administration. For a more direct deconstruction of the discourse of school organization and adaptability in the field of educational administration, see Skrtic (1988b, 1991). For additional critical analyses that can be read as deconstructions, see Bates (1980, 1987), Foster (1986), House (1979), and Sirotnik and Oakes (1986).

38. The structural and cultural frames of reference do not correspond to the rational-technical and nonrational-cultural perspectives (see notes 35 and 36). Indeed, the particular combination of theories in each frame of reference was selected to avoid this dichotomy, as well as those between objectivism-subjectivism and microscopic-macroscopic. This is the sense in which the present analysis is antifoundational and dialogical. Such an analysis gives a voice to a variety of perspectives, while recognizing that none of the perspectives, including its own, are "true" in a foundational sense (see Skrtic, 1988b, 1991, in press).

39. Throughout this section all of the material relative to configuration theory (e.g., nature of work, division of labor, coordination of work, interdependency or coupling among workers) is drawn from Mintzberg (1979) and Miller and Mintzberg (1983), except where noted otherwise. All of the material relative to institutionalization theory (e.g., material and normative structures, decoupled structures and subunits, and myth, symbol, and ceremony) is drawn from Meyer and Rowan (1977, 1978) and Meyer and Scott (1983), except where noted otherwise.

    Within both the structural and the cultural frames of reference I treat each theory and the images of organization and change that emerge from them (and from combining them) as ideal types (see note 5), as exaggerated mental constructs for analyzing traditional school organization in terms of its value orientation. My aim in this section of the paper is to combine these ideal types to form two larger ideal types — one structural and one cultural. In subsequent sections, I combine the structural and cultural ideal types into a larger ideal type and use it to carry out my deconstruction and reconstruction of public education.

40. The process of organizational change from this perspective is similar to a Kuhnian (1970) paradigm shift: long periods of stability that are maintained by the self-reinforcing nature of the organization's current paradigm (what Kuhn would call the long period of normal science) and occasional periods of change in which unreconcilable anomalies eventually destroy the prevailing paradigm (what Kuhn would call revolutionary science and the shift to a new paradigm).

41. Other than a few citations that clarify and extend my theoretical arguments on organization and change, virtually all of the citations in this section refer to empirical and interpretive evidence that supports the theoretical claims made in text.

42. For empirical evidence that teachers rarely view their instructional practices as a potential source of the problem in special education referrals, and that the special education referral and classification process is oriented to place the blame for failure on the student rather than on the

standard programs in use, see Bennett and Rogosta (1984), Sarason and Doris (1979), White and Calhoun (1987), and Ysseldyke, Thurlow, Graden, Wesson, Algozzine, and Deno (1983).

43. For historical evidence on the conditions under which the special classroom emerged, see Lazerson (1983) and Sarason and Doris (1979). For empirical evidence on the disjunction between the special classroom and the rest of the school enterprise, see Deno (1970), Dunn (1968), Johnson (1962), and Reynolds (1962). See Chandler and Plakos (1969), MacMillan (1971), Wright (1967), and Mercer (1973) for empirical evidence on the overrepresentation of students from minority groups in segregated special classrooms after *Brown v. Board of Education* (1954), which, of course, is another example of the use of the special classroom to protect legitimacy. Indeed, the organizational isolation of the special classroom and the overrepresentation of students from minority groups in these classrooms were two of the major arguments for the EHA (Christophos & Renz, 1969; Deno, 1970; Dunn, 1968; Johnson, 1962). From an organizational perspective, the problem of over-representation of students from minority groups in special education classrooms and programs, both before (e.g., Christophos & Renz, 1969; Dunn, 1968) and after the EHA (e.g., Heller, Holtzman, & Messick, 1982), can be understood as school organizations using an existing decoupled subunit to maintain legitimacy in the face of failing to meet the needs of disproportionate numbers of these students in regular classrooms.

44. In organizational terms, although special education is a nonrational system, it is a politically rational system in two opposite senses: it protects students from the nonadaptability of school organizations, in the REI opponents' sense; and it protects school organizations from the uncertainty of student diversity, in the sense developed here. I will return to these ideas, and particularly to the moment of truth in the REI opponents' political justification for special education, in subsequent sections.

45. Recognition of the adhocratic configuration, or what were called "organic" organizations, occurred in the 1960s (Pugh, Hickson, Hinnings, MacDonald, Turner, & Lupton, 1963). Because these organizations operated in dynamic, uncertain environments, where innovation and adaptation were necessary for survival, they configured themselves as the inverse of the bureaucratic form (Burns & Stalker, 1966; Woodward, 1965). Mintzberg (1979) called them adhocracies following Toffler (1970), who popularized the term in *Future Shock*.

46. Although I will not pursue the issue of accountability in any great depth here, the mode of accountability that emerges in the adhocracy represents an alterative to the two extreme positions on accountability that have shaped the current debate on school restructuring, what Timar and Kirp (1988, p. 130) called the "romantic decentralist" (i.e., professional) and the "hyperrationalist" (i.e., bureaucratic) modes of accountability (see also Murphy, 1989; Timar & Kirp, 1989), as well as Conley's (1990, p. 317) middle ground "constrained decisionmaker" position. Modes of accountability are shaped by the logic of the division of labor, means of coordination, and form of interdependency in organizations. There is no way out of the professional-bureaucratic dilemma as long as schools are configured as professional bureaucracies. The constrained decision-maker position merely tries to strike a balance between the two extremes while leaving the current configuration of schools intact. The key to accountability in the adhocracy is that it avoids all three positions by assigning responsibility to groups of professionals, thus politicizing discretion within a discourse among professionals and client constituencies. For a somewhat more extended treatment of this topic, see Kiel and Skrtic (1988) and Skrtic (1991); see also note 58.

47. The EHA is completely consistent with the third and fourth assumptions; it is a rational-technical mechanism for change that assumes that schools are machine bureaucracies — that is, organizations in which worker behavior is controlled by procedural rules and thus subject to modification through revision and extension of formalization and supervision (see Elmore & McLaughlin, 1982). Its requirements for classification, parent participation, individualized educational plans, and least restrictive environment placements are perceived to be new technologies for diagnosis and intervention. Moreover, its requirement for a comprehensive system of

personnel development, what Gilhool (1989, p. 247) called "probably the most important provision of the act," assumes that "there [are] known procedures for effectively educating disabled children," and that the problem is simply that "the knowledge of how to do so [is] not widely distributed." This, of course, assumes the possibility of rational-technical change through dissemination of practices and training (see notes 35 and 36).

48. For empirical and interpretive evidence on the degree to which the EHA has resulted in an increase in political clashes, a decrease in collaboration, and an increase in the number of students identified as handicapped, see note 15 and Bogdan (1983); Lortie (1978); Martin (1978); Patrick and Reschly (1982); Singer and Butler (1987); Skrtic, Guba, and Knowlton (1985); and Weatherley (1979). For empirical and interpretive evidence that the EHA's adhocratic goal of personalized instruction contradicts its bureaucratic means of uniform procedures, see Singer and Butler (1987); Skrtic, Guba, and Knowlton (1985); and Wright, Cooperstein, Renneker, and Padilla (1982). For empirical and interpretive evidence that special education has itself conformed to the two-structure, machine-professional bureaucracy configuration to deal with this contradiction, see Singer and Butler (1987); Skrtic, Guba, and Knowlton (1985); and Weatherley (1979). As Singer and Butler noted, the EHA "has created a *dual* locus of organizational control," an arrangement in which information necessary for "legal or monitoring purposes, quick-turnaround defense of special education priorities . . . or public relations in the wider community" are managed centrally in the office of the special education director; whereas instructional decisions "have become or have remained more decentralized" in the hands of professionals (p. 139).

49. On the rational-technical nature of the excellence movement (note 56), see Bacharach (1990), Cuban (1983), Meier (1984), Resnick and Resnick (1985), and Wise (1988). For example, Wise (1988, p. 329) characterized it generally as "state control, with its emphasis on producing standardized results through regulated teaching." See Cuban (1989) on the relationship among school reform, the at-risk category, and the graded school, "the core processes" of which are "labeling, segregating, and eliminating those who do not fit" (p. 784). The graded school, of course, is the traditional school organization, that is, the actual case of the idealized professional bureaucracy configuration presented here.

50. The degree of decoupling, as well as the availability of the requisite personnel, depends in large measure on the local history of special education services, which reflects the value orientation embedded in political cultures at the state, local, and school organization levels. For empirical and interpretive evidence on this point see McDonnell and McLaughlin (1982); Skrtic, Guba, and Knowlton (1985); Noel and Fuller (1985); and Biklen (1985). Although there are exceptions (Biklen, 1985; Thousand, Fox, Reid, Godek, & Williams, 1986), students classified as having severe and profound disabilities and the professionals who serve them continue to be located in segregated classrooms, a matter of great concern in the work of Stainbeck and Stainback (see note 15) and others (e.g., Biklen, 1985; Thousand, Fox, Reid, Godek, & Williams, 1986). When these classrooms are located in regular school buildings, they follow the organizational from of the traditional decoupled subunit, which historically has existed as an adhocratic space outside the bureaucratic configuration of general education. The needs of the students in these programs typically are so variable that the notion of a standard program is virtually precluded. Moreover, the complexity of the diagnostic and instructional problems is so great that interdisciplinary collaboration is essential. Given the extreme ambiguity and complexity of the work in these programs, the fact that they are decoupled from the machine bureaucracy structure, and the degree to which collaboration, mutual adjustment, and discursive coupling characterize the work (see Sailor & Guess, 1983), these programs are prototypical of the adhocratic form in public education. See Skrtic (1991) for an extended discussion of this point.

51. Although regular classroom placement to the maximum extent possible is required for these students under the EHA, they are identified as handicapped because they cannot be accommodated within existing standard programs in particular regular classrooms (Skrtic, Guba, &

Knowlton, 1985; Walker, 1987). As such, depending on the degree to which the particular school is more adhocratically or bureaucratically oriented, mainstreaming for these students more or less represents symbolic integration, primarily in nonacademic classrooms and activities. For empirical and interpretive evidence on this point, see Biklen (1985); Carlberg and Kavale (1980); Skrtic, Guba, and Knowlton (1985); and Wright, Cooperstein, Renneker, and Padilla (1982).

52. In principle, teachers working collaboratively in the interest of a single student for whom they share responsibility violates the logic of loose coupling and the sensibility of the professional culture (Bidwell, 1965; Mintzberg, 1979; Weick, 1976) and thus, in principle, collaboration should not be expected to any meaningful degree in professional bureaucracies. At a minimum, mainstreaming and the resource room model require reciprocal coupling (Thompson, 1967), which is not the type of interdependency that specialization and professionalization yield. For empirical evidence that collaboration among regular teachers and between regular and special education teachers is rare, fleeting, and idiosyncratic in the professional bureaucracy, see Bishop (1977); Lortie (1975, 1978); Skrtic, Guba, and Knowlton (1985); Tye and Tye (1984); and notes 48 and 53.

53. Although the adhocratic ends of the EHA are distorted because of the bureaucratic nature of the law and its implementation context, schools appear to be complying with its procedural requirements because of the adoption of practices that, although they may be well-intended and in some respects may actually result in positive outcomes, serve largely to symbolize (e.g., IEPs and resource rooms) and ceremonialize (e.g., IEP staffings and mainstreaming) compliance with the letter of the law rather than conformance with its spirit. For empirical evidence on the symbolic and ceremonial nature of the IEP document and staffing process, resource room programs, and mainstreaming, see Carlberg and Kavale (1980); Gerardi, Grohe, Benedict, and Coolidge (1984); Schenck (1980); Schenck and Levy (1979); Ysseldyke, Thurlow, Graden, Wesson, Algozzine, and Deno (1983); and notes 51 and 48. Moreover, from a policy perspective, symbolic compliance with procedural requirements can lead monitors and implementation researchers to faulty conclusions. For example, Singer and Butler (1987, p. 151) observed that "federal demands have equilibrated rapidly with local capacity to respond," and thus concluded that the EHA demonstrates that "a federal initiative *can* result in significant social reform at the local level." Although they are correct in asserting that such equilibration has resulted in "a basically workable system" (p. 151), they fail to recognize that equilibration is largely a process of institutionalizing the necessary symbols and ceremonies of compliance (Rowan, 1980; Zucker, 1977, 1981), which, given the contradiction between their bureaucratic orientation and the EHA's adhocratic ends, renders the system workable for school organizations but not necessarily for the intended beneficiaries of the federal initiative.

54. Citations for the proposals of the four teams of REI proponents have been omitted in this section. The proposals analyzed here are those described in the section, "Special Education as a Professional Practice," and its corresponding notes. The same format is followed in the remainder of the article for references to the REI proponents' and opponents' arguments for and against the REI and the current system of special education, as well as for the REI proponents' reform proposals.

55. For empirical evidence that the excellence movement has resulted largely in extensions of rationalization and formalization, see Clark and Astuto (1988), Timar and Kirp (1988), and note 49. For empirical evidence that the excellence movement, in general, and the effective schools movement (see note 56), in particular, have increased ritualization and professionalization and decreased personalization, see Cuban (1983, 1989), Slavin (1989), Stedman (1987), and Wise (1988). For example, Cuban noted that, under the effective schools formula, curriculum and instruction in many schools have become more standardized and thus less personalized. The problem is that advocates of effective schools, although well meaning, "seldom [question] the core structures of the graded schools within which they [work]. Their passion was (and is) for making those structures more efficient" (Cuban, 1989, p. 784).

56. By the "effective schools" debate I mean the earlier phase of the excellence movement, which was shaped by the thinking in *A Nation at Risk* (National Commission on Excellence in Education, 1983) and generally seeks excellence through means that are quantitative and top-down: quantitative in that they simply call for more of the existing school practices; top-down in that their bureaucratic value orientation turns the goal of higher standards into more standardization for producing standardized results (e.g., Wise, 1988; notes 49 and 55). The proponents of this approach do not question traditional school organization, they simply want to make it more efficient (e.g., Cuban, 1989; notes 49 and 55). By the "school restructuring" debate I mean the more recent phase of the excellence movement, which was shaped by the thinking in books like *High School* (Boyer, 1983), *A Place Called School* (Goodlad, 1984), and *Horace's Compromise* (Sizer, 1984). The participants in this debate (see, e.g., Bacharach, 1990; Clark, Lotto, & Astuto, 1984; Cuban, 1983, 1989; Elmore, 1987; Elmore & McLaughlin, 1988; Lieberman & Miller, 1984; McNeil, 1986; Oakes, 1985; Sergiovanni & Moore, 1989; Sirotnik & Oakes, 1986; Wise, 1988) generally seek excellence through means that are qualitative and bottom-up: qualitative in that they call for fundamental changes in the structure of school organizations; bottom-up in that they call for an increase in professional discretion, adult-adult collaboration, and personalization of instruction.

57. Although tracking as such is criticized, neither students labeled handicapped nor special education as an institutional practice receive much attention in the restructuring debate or the effective schools debate (Lilly, 1987; Pugach & Sapon-Shevin, 1987; Shepard, 1987).

58. The best articulation of this position within the restructuring debate is Schön's (1983, 1987, 1988, 1989) argument for developing reflective practitioners by eliminating the "normal bureaucratic emphasis on technical rationality" (Schön, 1983, p. 338) in schools and thus permitting teachers to become "builders of repertoire rather than accumulators of procedures and methods" (1988, p. 26). Although Schön clearly recognized that the reflective practitioner requires a reflective organization (Schön, 1983, 1988), he conceptualized the reflective practitioner as an individual professional engaged in a monological discourse with a problem situation, rather than a team of professionals engaged reflectively in a dialogical discourse with one another. As such, Schön retains the structural contingencies of specialization and professionalization and thus the professional bureaucracy configuration. For a deconstruction of Schön's notion of the reflective practitioner, see Skrtic (1991). Beyond the problem of innovation, eliminating rationalization and formalization while retaining specialization and professionalization creates a professional mode of accountability, which places virtually all decisions about the adequacy of practice in the hands of individual professionals. From an organizational perspective, this is a problem in a structural sense because the convergent thinking and deductive reasoning of professionals and professions means that they tend to see the needs of their clients in terms of the skills they have to offer them (Mintzberg, 1979; Perrow, 1970; Segal, 1974). In a cultural sense, professionals and professions tend to distort negative information about their paradigms to make it consistent with their prevailing paradigms of practice (see, e.g., Brown, 1978; Rounds, 1979, 1981; Weatherley & Lipsky, 1977; Weick, 1985; see also note 46).

59. For genealogies (note 9) of special education's professional knowledge, practice, and value orientation, see Skrtic (1986, 1988a, 1991). For histories of special education see, for example, Lazerson (1983), and Sarason and Doris (1979).

60. For evidence on the ethics and efficacy of special education practices before the EHA, see note 43. For evidence on these practices after the EHA, see notes 15, 17, 48, 51, and 53.

61. See Cherryholmes (1988) for a discussion of critical pragmatism (note 4) as a mode of professional practice and discourse in public education. See Skrtic (1991) for a discussion of it as a means of developing and sustaining an adhocratic professional culture. Critical practice is "continual movement between construction of a practice . . . and deconstruction of that practice, which shows its incompleteness and contradictions. . . . Critical discourse is continual movement between the constitution of a methodology designed to [construct, deconstruct, and reconstruct practices] and subsequent criticism of that approach" (Cherryholmes, 1988, pp.

96–97). The goal of critical pragmatism is education or self-formation (Gadamer, 1975), a pedagogical process of remaking ourselves as we think, write, read, and talk more about our practices and discourses.

62. For the negative evidence on educational excellence, equity, and adaptability see, for example, Cuban (1979), Edgar (1987), Elmore and McLaughlin (1988), Goodlad (1984), Lehming and Kane (1981), McNeil (1986), Oakes (1985), Sizer (1984), and note 15. For empirical and interpretive evidence that some schools are more effective, equitable, and adaptable than others, as well as discussions of contributing factors, see Berman and McLaughlin (1974–1978); Brophy (1983); Clark, Lotto, and Astuto (1984); Goodlad (1975); Lieberman and Miller (1984); McNeil (1986); and note 63. For the same type of evidence and discussions relative to the EHA and mainstreaming, see Biklen (1985); Skrtic, Guba, and Knowlton (1985); Thousand, Fox, Reid, Godek, and Williams (1986); Wright, Cooperstein, Renneker, and Padilla (1982); and note 63.

63. For empirical and interpretive evidence on the place of human agency in successful schools, see Biklen (1985); Brophy (1983); Clark, Lotto, and Astuto (1984); Lieberman and Miller (1984); McNeil (1986); Singer and Butler (1987); Skrtic, Guba, and Knowlton (1985); and Thousand, Fox, Reid, Godek, and Williams (1986).

REFERENCES

Abeson, A., & Zettel, J. (1977). The end of the quiet revolution: The Education for All Handicapped Children Act of 1975. *Exceptional Children, 44*(2), 115–128.

Algozzine, B. (1976). The disturbing child: What you see is what you get? *Alberta Journal of Education Research, 22*, 330–333.

Algozzine, B. (1977). The emotionally disturbed child: Disturbed or disturbing? *Journal of Abnormal Child Psychology, 5*(2), 205–211.

Algozzine, B., & Korinek, L. (1985). Where is special education for students with high prevalence handicaps going? *Exceptional Children, 51*(5), 388–394.

Allington, R. L., & McGill-Franzen, A. (1989). Different programs: Indifferent instruction. In D. K. Lipsky & A. Gartner (Eds.). *Beyond separate education: Quality education for all* (pp. 75–97). Baltimore, MD: Paul H. Brookes.

Antonio, R. J. (1981). Immanent critique as the core of critical theory: Its origins and developments in Hegel, Marx, and contemporary thought. *British Journal of Sociology, 32*(3), 330–345.

Antonio, R. J. (1989). The normative foundations of emancipatory theory: Evolutionary versus pragmatic perspectives. *American Journal of Sociology, 94*(4), 721–748.

Apter, S. J. (1982). *Troubled children, troubled systems*. New York: Pergamon Press.

Bacharach, S. B. (Ed.). (1990). *Education reform: Making sense of it all*. Boston: Allyn & Bacon.

Barnard, C. I. (1938). *Functions of the executive*. Cambridge: Harvard University Press.

Barnes, B. (1982). *T. S. Kuhn and social science*. New York: Columbia University Press.

Bates, R. J. (1980). Educational administration, the sociology of science, and the management of knowledge. *Educational Administration Quarterly, 16*(2), 1–20.

Bates, R. J. (1987). Corporate culture, schooling, and educational administration. *Educational Administration Quarterly, 23*(4), 79–115.

Bennett, R. E., & Ragosta, M. (1984). *A research context for studying admissions tests and handicapped populations*. Princeton, NJ: Educational Testing Service.

Berger, P. L., & Luckmann, T. (1967). *The social construction of reality*. New York: Doubleday.

Berman, P., & McLaughlin, M. W. (1974–1978). *Federal programs supporting educational change* (Vols. 1–8). Santa Monica, CA: Rand.

Bernstein, R. J. (1976). *The restructuring of social and political theory*. Philadelphia: University of Pennsylvania Press.

Bernstein, R. J. (1983). *Beyond objectivism and relativism: Science, hermeneutics, and praxis*. Philadelphia: University of Pennsylvania Press.

Bidwell, C.E. (1965). The school as formal organization. In J. G. March (Ed.), *Handbook of organizations* (pp. 972–1022). Chicago: Rand McNally College Publishing.

Biklen, D. (1985). *Achieving the complete school: Strategies for effective mainstreaming*. New York: Columbia University Press.

Bishop, J. M. (1977). Organizational influences on the work orientations of elementary teachers. *Sociology of Work and Occupation, 4,* 171–208.

Bogdan, R. (1983). Does mainstreaming work? is a silly question. *Phi Delta Kappan, 64,* 425–434.

Bogdan, R., & Knoll, J. (1988). The sociology of disability. In E. L. Meyen & T. M. Skrtic (Eds.), *Exceptional children and youth: An introduction* (pp. 449–477). Denver: Love Publishing.

Bogdan, R., & Kugelmass, J. (1984). Case studies of mainstreaming: A symbolic interactionist approach to special schooling. In L. Barton & S. Tomlinson (Eds.), *Special education and social interests* (pp. 173–191). New York: Nichols.

Bowles, S., & Gintis, H. (1976). *Schooling in capitalist America*. New York: Basic Books.

Boyd, W. L., & Crowson, R. L. (1981). The changing conception and practice of public school administration. In D. C. Berliner (Ed.), *Review of research in education* (pp. 311–373). Itasca, IL: F. E. Peacock.

Boyer, E. L. (1983). *High school*. New York: Harper & Row.

Braaten, S. R., Kauffman, J. M., Braaten, B., Polsgrove, L., & Nelson, C. M. (1988). The regular education initiative: Patent medicine for behavioral disorders. *Exceptional Children, 55*(1), 21–27.

Bridges, E. M. (1982). Research on the school administrator: The state of the art, 1967–1980. *Educational Administration Quarterly, 18*(3), 12–33.

Brophy, J. E. (1983). Research in the self-fulfilling prophesy and teacher expectations. *Journal of Educational Psychology, 75*(5), 631–661.

Brown v. Board of Education (1954). 347 U.S. 483, 74 S. Ct. 686, 98 L. Ed. 873.

Brown, R. H. (1978). Bureaucracy as praxis: Toward a political phenomenology of formal organizations. *Administrative Science Quarterly, 23*(2), 365–382.

Bryan, T., Bay, M., & Donahue, M. (1988). Implications of the learning disabilities definition for the regular education initiative. *Journal of Learning Disabilities, 21*(1), 23–28.

Burns, T., & Stalker, G. M. (1966). *The management of innovation* (2nd ed.). London: Tavistock.

Burrell, G., & Morgan, G. (1979). *Sociological paradigms and organizational analysis*. London: Heinemann.

Callahan, R. (1962). *Education and the cult of efficiency*. Chicago: University of Chicago Press.

Campbell, R. F., Fleming, T., Newell, L. J., & Bennion, J. W. (1987). *A history of thought and practice in educational administration*. New York: Teachers College Press.

Carlberg, C., & Kavale, K. (1980). The efficacy of special versus regular class placement for exceptional children: A meta-analysis. *Journal of Special Education, 14,* 295–309.

Chalfant, J., Pysh, M., & Moultrie, R. (1979). Teacher assistance teams: A model of within-building problem solving. *Learning Disabilities Quarterly, 2,* 85–86.

Chandler, J. T., & Plakos, J. (1969). *Spanish-speaking pupils classified as educable mentally retarded*. Sacramento: California State Department of Education.

Chandler, M. D., & Sayles, L. R. (1971). *Managing large systems*. New York: Harper & Row.

Cherryholmes, C. H. (1988). *Power and criticism: Poststructuralist investigations in education*. New York: Teachers College Press.

Christophos, F., & Renz, P. (1969). A critical examination of special education programs. *Journal of Special Education, 3*(4), 371–380.

Churchman, C. W. (1971). *The design of inquiry systems*. New York: Basic Books.

Clark, B. R. (1972). The organizational saga in higher education. *Administrative Science Quarterly, 17,* 178–184

Clark, D. L. (1985). Emerging paradigms in organizational theory and research. In Y.S. Lincoln (Ed.), *Organizational theory and inquiry: The paradigm revolution* (pp. 43–78). Beverly Hills, CA: Sage.

Clark, D. L., & Astuto, T. A. (1988). *Education policy after Reagan — What next?* (Occasional Paper No. 6). Charlottesville: University of Virginia, Policy Studies Center of the University Council for Educational Administration.

Clark, D. L., Lotto, L. S., & Astuto, T. A. (1984). Effective schools and school improvement: A comparative analysis of two lines of inquiry. *Educational Administration Quarterly, 20*(3),41–68.

Cohen, M. D., March, J. G., & Olsen, J. P. (1972). A garbage can model of organizational choice. *Administrative Science Quarterly, 17*(2), 1–25.

Conley, S. C. (1990). Reforming paper pushers and avoiding free agents: The teacher as a constrained decision maker. In S. B. Bacharach (Ed.), *Education reform: Making sense of it all*. Boston: Allyn & Bacon.

Council for Children with Behavioral Disorders. (1989). Position statement on the regular education initiative. *Behavioral Disorders, 14*, 201–208.

Cuban, L. (1979). Determinants of curriculum change and stability, 1870–1970. In J. Schaffarzick & G. Sykes (Eds.), *Value conflicts and curriculum issues*. Berkeley, CA: McCutchan.

Cuban, L. (1983). Effective schools: A friendly but cautionary note. *Phi Delta Kappan, 64*(10), 695–696.

Cuban, L. (1989). The "at-risk" label and the problem of urban school reform. *Phi Delta Kappan, 70*(10), 780–784 and 799–801.

Cunningham, L. L., Hack, W. G., & Nystrand, R. O. (Eds.). (1977). *Educational administration: The developing decades*. Berkeley, CA: McCutchan.

Dallmayr, F. R., & McCarthy, T. A. (1977). *Understanding and social inquiry*. Notre Dame, IN: University of Notre Dame Press.

Dalton, M. (1959). *Men who manage*. New York: Wiley.

Davis, W. E. (1989). The regular initiative debate: Its promises and problems. *Exceptional Children, 55*(5), 440–446.

Davis, W. E., & McCaul, E. J. (1988). *New perspectives on education: A review of the issues and implications of the regular education initiative*. Orono, ME: Institute for Research and Policy Analysis on the Education of Students with Learning and Adjustment Problems.

Deno, E. (1970). Special education as developmental capital. *Exceptional Children, 37*(3), 229–237.

Derrida, J. (1982a). *Dissemination* (B. Johnson, Trans.). London: Athlone Press. (Original work published 1972)

Derrida, J. (1982b). *Margins of philosophy* (A. Bass, Trans.). Chicago: University of Chicago Press. (Original work published 1972)

Dewey, J. (1897). My pedagogic creed. *School Journal, 54*(3), 77–80.

Dewey, J. (1899). *The school and society*. Chicago: University of Chicago Press.

Dewey, J. (1916). *Democracy and education*. New York: Macmillan.

Dewey, J. (1988a). Individualism, old and new. In J. A. Boydston (Ed.), *John Dewey: The later works, 1925–1953. Vol. 5: 1929–1930* (pp. 41–123). Carbondale: Southern Illinois University Press. (Original work published 1929–1930)

Dewey, J. (1988b). The public and its problems. In J. A. Boydston (Ed.), *John Dewey: The later works, 1925–1953. Vol. 2: 1925–1927* (pp. 235–372). Carbondale: Southern Illinois University Press. (Original work published 1927)

Dreyfus, H. L., & Rabinow, P. (Eds.). (1983). *Michel Foucault: Beyond structuralism and hermeneutics*. Chicago: University of Chicago Press.

Drucker, P. F. (1989). *The new realities*. New York: Harper & Row.

Dunn, L. M. (1968). Special education for the mildly retarded — Is much of it justifiable? *Exceptional Children, 35*(1), 5–22.

Edgar, E. (1987). Secondary programs in special education: Are many of them justified? *Exceptional Children, 53*, 555–561.

Edmonds, R. (1979). Some schools work and more can. *Social Policy, 9*(5), 26–31.

Elmore, R. F. (1987). *Early experiences in restructuring schools: Voices from the field*. Results in Education series. Washington, DC: National Governors Association.

Elmore, R. F., & McLaughlin, M. W. (1982). Strategic choice in federal education policy: The compliance-assistance trade-off. In A. Lieberman and M. W. McLaughlin (Eds.). *Policy making in education: Eighty-first yearbook of the National Society for the Study of Education* (pp. 159–194). Chicago: University of Chicago Press.

Elmore, R.F., & McLaughlin, M. W. (1988). *Steady work: Policy, practice, and the reform of American education.* Santa Monica, CA: Rand.

Erickson, D. A. (1979). Research on educational administration: The state-of-the-art. *Educational Researcher, 8*(3), 9–14.

Feinberg, W., & Soltis, J. F. (1985). *School and society.* New York: Teachers College Press.

Foster, W. (1986). *Paradigms and promises: New approaches to educational administration.* Buffalo, NY: Prometheus Books.

Foucault, M. (1973). *Madness and civilization: A history of insanity in the age of reason* (R. Howard, Trans.). New York: Vintage/Random House. (Original work published 1961)

Foucault, M. (1975). *The birth of the clinic: An archeology of medical perception* (A. M. Sheridan Smith, Trans.). New York: Vintage/Random House. (Original work published 1963)

Foucault, M. (1976). *Mental illness and psychology.* Berkeley: University of California Press. (Original work published 1954)

Foucault, M. (1979). *Discipline and punish: The birth of the prison* (A.M. Sheridan Smith, Trans.). New York: Vintage/Random House. (Original work published 1975)

Foucault, M. (1980). *Power/knowledge: Selected interviews and other writings, 1972–1977* (C. Gordon, Ed.; C. Gordon, L. Marshall, J. Mepham, & K. Soper, Trans.). New York: Pantheon Books.

Foucault, M. (1983). The subject and power. In H. L. Dreyfus & P. Rabinow (Eds.), *Michel Foucault: Beyond structuralism and hermeneutics* (pp. 208–226). Chicago: University of Chicago Press.

Gartner, A. (1986). Disabling help: Special education at the crossroads. *Exceptional Children, 53*(1), 72–79.

Gartner, A., & Lipsky, D. K. (1987). Beyond special education: Toward a quality system for all students. *Harvard Educational Review, 57*(4), 367–390.

Gartner, A., & Lipsky, D. K. (1989). *The yoke of special education: How to break it.* Rochester, NY: National Center on Education and the Economy.

Geertz, C. (1983). *Local knowledge: Further essays in interpretive anthropology.* New York: Basic Books.

Gerardi, R. J., Grohe, B., Benedict, G. C., & Coolidge, P. G. (1984). I.E.P. — More paperwork and wasted time. *Contemporary Education, 56*(1), 39–42.

Gerber, M. M. (1987). Application of cognitive-behavioral training methods to teach basic skills to mildly handicapped elementary school students. In M. C. Wang, M. C. Reynolds, & H. J. Walberg (Eds.), *Handbook of special education: Research and practice. Vol. 1: Learner characteristics and adaptive education* (pp. 167–186). Oxford, Eng.: Pergamon Press.

Gerber, M. M. (1988a). Tolerance and technology of instruction: Implications for special education reform. *Exceptional Children, 54*(4), 309–314.

Gerber, M. M. (1988b, May 4). Weighing the regular education initiative: Recent calls for change lead to slippery slope. *Education Week,* pp. 36, 28.

Gerber, M. M., & Levine-Donnerstein, D. (1989). Educating all children: Ten years later. *Exceptional Children, 56*(1), 17–27.

Gerber, M. M., & Semmel, M.I. (1984). Teacher as imperfect test: Reconceptualizing the referral process. *Educational Psychologist, 19*, 137–148.

Gerber, M. M., & Semmel, M.I. (1985). The microeconomics of referral and reintegration: A paradigm for evaluation of special education. *Studies in Educational Evaluation, 11*, 13–29.

Getzels, J. W., & Guba, E. G. (1957). Social behavior and the administrative process. *School Review, 65*, 423–441.

Gilhool, T. K. (1976). Changing public policies: roots and forces. In M. C. Reynolds (Ed.), *Mainstreaming: Origins and implications* (pp. 8–13). Reston, VA: Council for Exceptional Children.

Gilhool, T. K. (1989). The right to an effective education: From *Brown* to P. L. 94–142 and beyond. In D. K. Lipsky & A. Gartner (Eds.), *Beyond separate education: Quality education for all* (pp. 243–253). Baltimore, MD: Paul H. Brookes.

Giroux, H. A. (1981). *Ideology, culture, and the process of schooling.* Philadelphia: Temple University Press.

Giroux, H. A. (1983). Theories of reproduction and resistance in the new sociology of education: A critical analysis. *Harvard Educational Review, 58*(3), 257–293.

Glazer, N. (1974). The schools of the minor professions. *Minerva, 12*(3), 346–364.

Golding, D. (1980). Establishing blissful clarity in organizational life: Managers. *Sociological Review, 28*, 763–782.

Goldman, J., & Gardner, H. (1989). Multiple paths to educational effectiveness. In D. K. Lipsky & A. Gartner (Eds.), *Beyond separate education: Quality education for all* (pp. 121–139). Baltimore, MD: Paul H. Brookes.

Goodlad, J. I. (1975). *The dynamics of educational change*. New York: McGraw-Hill.

Goodlad, J. I. (1984). *A place called school: Prospects for the future*. New York: McGraw-Hill.

Greer, C. (1972). *The great school legend: A revisionist interpretation of American public education* New York: Basic Books.

Griffiths, D. E. (1959). *Administrative theory*. New York: Appleton-Century-Crofts.

Griffiths, D. E. (1979). Intellectual turmoil in educational administration. *Educational Administration Quarterly, 15*(3), 43–65.

Griffiths, D. E. (1983). Evolution in research and theory: A study of prominent researchers. *Educational Administration Quarterly, 19*(3), 201–221.

Griffiths, D. E. (1988). Administrative theory. In N. J. Boyan (Ed.), *Handbook of research on educational administration* (pp. 27–51). New York: Longman.

Haber, S. (1964). *Efficiency and uplight: Scientific management in the progressive era, 1890–1920* Chicago: University of Chicago Press.

Hallahan, D. P., Kauffman, J. M. (1977). Categories, labels, behavioral characteristics: ED, LD, and EMR reconsidered. *Journal of Special Education, 11*, 139–149.

Hallahan, D. P., Kauffman, J. M., Lloyd, J. W., & McKinney, J. D. (1988). Introduction to the series: Questions about the regular education initiative. *Journal of Learning Disabilities, 21*(1), 3–5.

Hallahan, D. P., & Keller, C. E. (1986). *Study of studies for learning disabilities: A research review and synthesis*. Charleston: West Virginia Department of Education.

Hallahan, D. P., & Keller, C. E., McKinney, J. D., Lloyd, J. W., & Bryan, T. (1988). Examining the research base of the regular education initiative: Efficacy studies and the adaptive learning environments model. *Journal of Learning Disabilities, 21*(1), 29–35; 55.

Halpin, A. W. (1970). Administrative theory: The fumbled torch. In A. M. Kroll (Ed.), *Issues in American education*. New York: Oxford University Press.

Halpin, A. W., & Hayes, A. E. (1977). The broken ikon, or What ever happened to theory? In L. L. Cummingham, W. G. Hack, & R. O. Nystrand (Eds.), *Educational administration: The developing decades* (pp. 261–297). Berkeley, CA: McCutchan.

Hayes, D., & Pharis, W. (1967). *National conference of professors of educational administration*. Lincoln: University of Nebraska Press.

Hegel, G. W. F. (1977). *Phenomenology of spirit*. Oxford, Eng.: Clarendon Press. (Original work published 1807)

Heller, K., Holtzman, W., & Messick, S. (1982). *Placing children in special education: A strategy for equity*. Washington, DC: National Academy of Sciences Press.

Heller, W. H., & Schilit, J. (1987). The regular education initiative: A concerned response. *Focus on Exceptional Children, 20*(3), 1–6.

Heshusius, L. (1982). At the heart of the advocacy dilemma: A mechanistic world view. *Exceptional Children, 49*(1), 6–13.

Hobbs, N. (1975). *The futures of children: Categories, labels, and their consequences*. San Francisco: Jossey-Bass.

Hobbs, N. (1980). An ecologically oriented service-based system for the classification of handicapped children. In E. Salzinger, J. Antrobus, & J. Glick (Eds.), *The ecosystem of the "risk" child* (pp. 271–290). New York: Academic Press.

Horkheimer, M. (1974). *Eclipse of reason*. New York: Seabury. (Original work published 1947)

House, E. R. (1979). Technology versus craft: A ten-year perspective on innovation. *Journal of Curriculum Studies, 11*(1), 1–15.

Hoy, D. (1985). Jacques Derrida. In Q. Skinner (Ed.), *The return of grand theory in the human sciences* (pp. 83–100). Cambridge, Eng.: Cambridge University Press.

Iano, R. P. (1986). The study and development of teaching: With implications for the advancement of special education. *Remedial and Special Education, 7*(5), 50–61.

Johnson, G. O. (1962). Special education for the mentally handicapped — A paradox. *Exceptional Children, 29*(2), 62–69.

Jonsson, S. A., & Lundin, R. A. (1977). Myths and wishful thinking as management tools. In P. C. Nystrom & W. H. Starbuck (Eds.), *Prescriptive models of organizations* (pp. 157–170). New York: Elsevier North-Holland.

Kauffman, J. M. (1988). Revolution can also mean returning to the starting point: Will school psychology help special education complete the circuit? *School Psychology Review, 17,* 490–494.

Kauffman, J. M. (1989a). *The regular education initiative as Reagan-Bush education policy: A trickle-down theory of education of the hard-to-teach.* Austin, TX: Pro-Ed Publishers.

Kauffman, J. M. (1989b). The regular education initiative as Reagan-Bush education policy: A trickle-down theory of education of the hard-to-teach. *Journal of Special Education, 23*(3), 256–278.

Kauffman, J. M., Gerber, M. M., & Semmel, M. I. (1988). Arguable assumptions underlying the regular education initiative. *Journal of Learning Disabilities, 21*(1), 6–11.

Keogh, B. K. (1988). Improving services for problem learners: Rethinking and restructuring. *Journal of Learning Disabilities, 21*(1), 19–22.

Keogh, B. K., & Levitt, M. L. (1976). Special education in the mainstream: A confrontation of limitations? *Focus on Exceptional Children, 8,* 1–11.

Kiel, D. C., & Skrtic, T. M. (1988). Modes of organizational accountability: An ideal type analysis. Unpublished manuscript, University of Kansas, Lawrence.

Kirk, S. A., & Chalfant, J. D. (1983). *Academic and developmental learning disabilities.* Denver, CO: Love Publishing.

Kliebard, H. M. (1988). The effort to reconstruct the modern American curriculum. In L. E. Beyer & M. W. Apple (Eds.), *The curriculum: Problems, politics, and possibilities* (pp. 19–31). Albany: State University of New York Press.

Kloppenberg, J. T. (1986). *Uncertain victory: Social democracy and progressivism in European and American thought, 1870–1920.* New York: Oxford University Press.

Kojeve, A. (1969). *Introduction to the reading of Hegel.* New York: Basic Books.

Kuhn, T. (1970). *The structure of scientific revolutions* (2nd ed.) Chicago: University of Chicago Press.

Lazerson, M. (1983). The origins of special education. In J. G. Chambers & W. T. Hartman (Eds.), *Special education policies: Their history, implementation, and finance.* Philadelphia: Temple University Press.

Lehming, R., & Kane, M. (1981). *Improving schools: Using what we know.* Beverly Hills, CA: Sage.

Lezotte, L. W. (1989). School improvement based on the effective schools research. In D. K. Lipsky & A. Gartner (Eds.), *Beyond separate education: Quality education for all* (pp. 25–37). Baltimore, MD: Paul H. Brookes.

Lieberman, A., & Miller, L. (1984). *Teachers, their world and their work: Implications for school improvement.* Alexandria, VA: Association for Supervision and Curriculum Development.

Lieberman, L. M. (1984). *Preventing special education . . . for those who don't need it.* Newton, MA: GloWorm Publications.

Lieberman, L. M. (1985). Special education and regular education: A merger made in heaven? *Exceptional Children, 51*(6), 513–516.

Lieberman, L. M. (1988). *Preserving special education . . . for those who need it.* Newton, MA: GloWorm Publications.

Lilly, M. S. (1986, March). The relationship between general and special education: A new face on an old issue. *Counterpoint, 6*(1), p. 10.

Lilly, M. S. (1987). Lack of focus on special education in literature on education reform. *Exceptional Children, 53*(4), 325–326.

Lilly, M. S. (1989). Teacher preparation. In D. K. Lipsky & A. Gartner (Eds.), *Beyond separate education: Quality education for all* (pp. 143–157). Baltimore: Paul H. Brookes.

Lincoln, Y. S. (Ed.) (1985). *Organizational theory and inquiry: The paradigm revolution.* Beverly Hills, CA: Sage.

Lincoln, Y. S. & Guba, E. G. (1985). *Naturalistic inquiry.* Beverly Hills, CA: Sage.

Lipsky, D. K., & Gartner, A. (1987). Capable of achievement and worthy of respect: Education for handicapped students as if they were full-fledged human beings. *Exceptional Children, 54*(1), 69–74.

Lipsky, D. K., & Gartner, A. (Eds.), (1989a). *Beyond separate education: Quality education for all.* Baltimore, MD: Paul H. Brookes.

Lipsky, D. K., & Gartner, A. (1989b). School administration and financial arrangements. In S. Stainback, W. Stainback, & M. Forest (Eds.), *Educating all students in the mainstream of regular education* (pp. 105–120). Baltimore, MD: Paul H. Brookes.

Lipsky, M. (1975). Toward a theory of street-level bureaucracy. In W. D. Hawley, M. Lipsky, S. B. Greenberg, J. D. Greenstone, I. Katznelson, K. Orren, P. E. Peterson, M. Shefter, & D. Yates (Eds.), *Theoretical perspectives on urban politics* (pp. 196–213). Englewood Cliffs, NJ: Prentice-Hall.

Lloyd, J. W., Crowley, E. P., Kohler, F. W., & Strain, P. S. (1988). Redefining the applied research agenda: Cooperative learning, prereferral, teacher consultation, and peer-mediated interventions. *Journal of Learning Disabilities, 21*(1) 43–52.

Lortie, D. C. (1975). *Schoolteacher: A sociological study.* Chicago: University of Chicago Press.

Lortie, D. C. (1978). Some reflections on renegotiation. In M. C. Reynolds (Ed.), *Futures of education for exceptional students: Emerging structures* (pp. 235–243). Reston, VA: Council for Exceptional Children.

Lyotard, J. F. (1984). *The postmodern condition: A report on knowledge.* Minneapolis: University of Minnesota Press. (Original work published 1979)

MacMillan, D. L. (1971). Special education for the mildly retarded: Servant or savant? *Focus on Exceptional Children, 2*(9), 1–11.

MacMillan, D. L. & Semmel, M. I. (1977). Evaluation of mainstreaming programs. *Focus on Exceptional Children, 9*(4), 1–14.

March, J. G., & Olsen, J. P. (1976). *Ambiguity and choice in organizations.* Bergen, Norway: Universitetsforlaget.

Martin, E. (1978). Preface. In M. C. Reynolds (Ed.), *Futures of education for exceptional students* (pp. iii–vi). Reston, VA: Council for Exceptional Children.

McDonnell, L. M., & McLaughlin, M. W. (1982). *Education policy and the role of the states.* Santa Monica, CA: Rand.

McKinney, J. D., & Hocutt, A. M. (1988). The need for policy analysis in evaluating the regular education initiative. *Journal of Learning Disabilities, 21*(1), 12–18.

McNeil, L. M. (1986). *Contradictions of control: School structure and school knowledge.* New York: Methuen/Routledge & Kegan Paul.

Meier, D. (1984). "Getting tough" in the schools. *Dissent, 31,* 61–70.

Mercer, J. (1973). *Labeling the mentally retarded: Clinical and social system perspectives on mental retardation.* Berkeley, CA: University of California Press.

Mesinger, J. F. (1985). Commentary on "A rationale for the merger of special and regular education." *Exceptional Children, 51*(6), 510–512.

Meyer, J. W., & Rowan, B. (1977). Institutionalized organizations: Formal structure as myth and ceremony. *American Journal of Sociology, 83,* 340–363.

Meyer, J. W., & Rowan, B. (1978). The structure of educational organizations. In M. W. Meyer (Ed.), *Environments and organizations* (pp. 78–109). San Francisco: Jossey-Bass.

Meyer, J. W. & Scott, W. R. (1983). *Organizational environments: Ritual and rationality.* Beverly Hills, CA: Sage.

Meyer, M. W. (1979). Organizational structure as signaling. *Pacific Sociological Review, 22*(4), 481–500.

Miller, D., & Mintzberg, H. (1983). There case for configuration. In G. Morgan (Ed.), *Beyond method: Strategies for social research* (pp. 57–73). Beverly Hills, CA: Sage.

Mintzberg, H. (1979). *The structuring of organizations*. Englewood Cliffs, NJ: Prentice-Hall.

Mitroff, I. I., & Pondy, L. R. (1974, September/October). On the organization of inquiry: A comparison of some radically different approaches to policy analysis. *Public Administration Review*, pp. 471–479.

Mommsen, W. J. (1974). *The age of bureaucracy: Perspectives on the political sociology of Max Weber*. New York. Harper & Row.

Morgan, G. (Ed.). (1983). *Beyond method: Strategies for social research*. Beverly Hills, CA: Sage.

Murphy, J. T. (1989). The paradox of decentralizing schools: Lessons from business, government, and the Catholic Church. *Phi Delta Kappan, 70*(10), 808–812.

Naisbitt, J., & Aburdene, P. (1985). *Re-inventing the corporation*. New York: Warner Books.

National Commission on Excellence in Education. (1983). *A nation at risk: The imperative for educational reform*. Washington, DC: U.S. Government Printing Office.

Noel, M. M., & Fuller, B. C. (1985). The social policy construction of special education: The impact of state characteristics on identification and integration of handicapped children. *Remedial and Special Education, 6*(3), 27–35.

Oakes, J. (1985). *Keeping track: How schools structure inequality*. New Haven: Yale University Press.

Oakes, J. (1986a). Keeping track, Part 1: The policy and practice of curriculum inequality. *Phi Delta Kappan, 68*(1), 12–17.

Oakes, J. (1986b). Keeping track, Part 2: Curriculum inequality and school reform. *Phi Delta Kappan, 68*(2), 148–154.

Patrick, J., & Reschly, D. (1982). Relationship of state education criteria and demographic variables to school-system prevalence of mental retardation. *American Journal of Mental Retardation, 86*, 351–360.

Perrow, C. (1970). *Organizational analysis: A sociological review*. Belmont, CA: Wadsworth.

Perrow, C. (1978). Demystifying organizations. In R. C. Sarri & Y. Hasenfeld (Eds.), *The management of human services* (pp. 105–120). New York: Columbia University Press.

Pettigrew, A. (1979). On studying organizational cultures. *Administrative Science Quarterly, 24*(4), 570–581.

Pfeffer, J. (1982). *Organizations and organization theory*. Marshfield, MA: Pitman Publishing.

Philip, M. (1985). Michel Foucault. In Q. Skinner (Ed.), *The return of grand theory in the human sciences* (pp. 65–81). Cambridge, Eng.: Cambridge University Press.

Poplin, M. S. (1987). Self-imposed blindness: The scientific method in education. *Remedial and Special Education, 8*(6), 31–37.

Pugach, M. (1988). The consulting teacher in the context of educational reform. *Exceptional Children, 55*(3), 266–277.

Pugach, M., & Lilly, M. S. (1984). Reconceptualizing support services for classroom teachers: Implications for teacher education. *Journal of Teacher Education, 35*(5), 48–55.

Pugach, M., & Sapon-Shevin, M. (1987). New agendas for special education policy: What the regular education reports haven't said. *Exceptional Children, 53*(4), 295–299.

Pugh, D.S., Hickson, D. J., Hinnings, C. R., MacDonald, K. M., Turner, C., & Lupton, T. (1963). A conceptual scheme for organizational analysis. *Administrative Science Quarterly, 8*(4), 289–315.

Reich, R. B. (1983). *The next American frontier*. New York: Penguin.

Reich, R. B. (1990). Education and the next economy. In S. B. Bacharach (Ed.), *Education reform: Making sense of it all* (pp. 194–212). Boston: Allyn & Bacon.

Resnick, D., & Resnick, L. (1985). Standards, curriculum, and performance: Historical and comparative perspectives. *Educational Researcher, 14*(4), 5–20.

Reynolds, M. C. (1962). A framework for considering some issues in special education. *Exceptional Children, 28*(5), 367–370.

Reynolds, M. C. (1976, November 22–23). *New perspectives on the instructional cascade*. Paper presented at the conference "The Least Restrictive Alternatives: A Partnership of General and

Special Education," sponsored by Minneapolis Public Schools, Special Education Division, Minneapolis, MN.

Reynolds, M. C. (1988). A reaction to the JLD special series on the regular education initiative. *Journal of Learning Disabilities, 21*(6), 352–356.

Reynolds, M.C., & Birch, J. W. (1977). *Teaching exceptional children in all America's schools.* Reston, VA: The Council for Exceptional Children.

Reynolds, M. C., & Lakin, K. C. (1987). Noncategorical special education: Models for research and practice. In M. C. Wang, M. C. Reynolds, & H. J. Walberg (Eds.), *Handbook of special education: Research and practice. Vol. 1: Learner characteristics and adaptive education* (pp. 331–356). Oxford, Eng.: Pergamon Press.

Reynolds, M. C., & Rosen, S. W. (1976, May). Special education: Past, present, and future. *Education Forum*, pp. 3–9.

Reynolds, M. C., & Wang, M. C. (1981, October). *Restructuring "special" school programs: A position paper.* Paper presented at the National Invitational Conference on Public Policy and the Special Education Task of the 1980s, Racine, WI.

Reynolds, M. C., & Wang, M. C. (1983). Restructuring "special" school programs: A position paper. *Policy Studies Review, 2*(1), 189–212.

Reynolds, M. C., & Wang, M. C., & Walberg, H. J. (1987). The necessary restructuring of special and general education. *Exceptional Children, 53*(5), 391–398.

Rhodes, W. C. (1970). A community participation analysis of emotional disturbance. *Exceptional Children, 36*, 306–314.

Ricoeur, P. (1981). *Paul Ricoeur: Hermeneutics and the human sciences* (J. B. Thompson, Ed. & Trans.). Cambridge, Eng.: Cambridge University Press.

Rist, R., & Harrell, J. (1982). Labeling and the learning disabled child: The social ecology of educational practice. *The American Journal of Orthopsychiatry, 52*(1), 146–160.

Ritzer, G. (1980). *Sociology; A multiple paradigm science.* Boston: Allyn & Bacon.

Ritzer, G. (1983). *Sociological theory.* New York: Alfred A. Knopf.

Romzek, B. S., & Dubnick, M. J. (1987). Accountability in the public sector: Lessons from the Challenger tragedy. *Public Administration Review, 47*(3), 227–238.

Rorty, R. (1979). *Philosophy and the mirror of nature.* Princeton, NJ: Princeton University Press.

Rorty, R. (1982). *Consequences of pragmatism.* Minneapolis: University of Minnesota Press.

Rorty, R. (1989). *Contingency, irony, and solidarity.* Cambridge, Eng.: Cambridge University Press.

Ross, A. O. (1980). *Psychological disorders of children.* New York: McGraw-Hill.

Rounds, J. (1979). *Social theory, public policy and social order.* Unpublished doctoral dissertation, University of California, Los Angeles.

Rounds, J. (1981). *Information and ambiguity in organizational change.* Paper presented at the Carnegie-Mellon Symposium on Information Processing in Organizations, Carnegie-Mellon University, Pittsburgh, PA.

Rowan, B. (1980). *Organizational structure and the institutional environment: The case of public schools.* Unpublished manuscript, Texas Christian University, Fort Worth.

Ryan, M. (1982). *Marxism and deconstruction.* Baltimore, MD: The Johns Hopkins Press.

Sailor, W., & Guess, D. (1983). *Severely handicapped students: An instructional design.* Boston: Houghton Mifflin.

Sailor, W., Halvorsen, A., Anderson, J., Goetz, L., Gee, K., Doering, K., & Hunt, P. (1986). Community intensive instruction. In R. Horner, L. Meyer, & H. Fredericks (Eds.), *Education of learners with severe handicaps* (pp. 251–288). Baltimore, MD: Paul H. Brookes.

Sapon-Shevin, M. (1987). The national education reports and special education: Implications for students. *Exceptional Children, 53*(4), 300–307.

Sapon-Shevin, M. (1988). Working towards merger together: Seeing beyond distrust and fear. *Teacher Education and Special Education, 11*(3), 103–110.

Sarason, S. B. (1971/1982). *The culture of the school and the problem of change* (orig. ed. 1971; rev. ed. 1982). Boston: Allyn & Bacon.

Sarason, S. B., & Doris, J. (1979). *Educational handicap, public policy, and social history*. New York: The Free Press.

Schein, E. H. (1972). *Professional education*. New York: McGraw-Hill.

Schenck, S. J. (1980). The diagnostic/instructional link in individualized education programs. *Journal of Special Education, 14*(3), 337–345.

Schenck, S. J., & Levy, W. K. (1979, April). *IEP's: The state of the art — 1978*. Paper presented at the annual meeting of the American Educational Research Association, San Francisco, CA.

Schön, D. A. (1983). *The reflective practitioner: How professionals think in action*. New York: Basic Books.

Schön, D. A. (1987). *Education the reflective practitioner: Toward a design for teaching and learning in the professions*. San Francisco: Jossey-Bass.

Schön, D. A. (1988). Coaching reflective practice. In P. Grimmett & G. Erickson (Eds.), *Reflection in teacher education*. New York: Teachers College Press.

Schön, D. A. (1989). Professional knowledge and reflective practice. In T. Sergiovanni & J. Moore (Eds.), *Schooling for tomorrow: Directing reforms to issues that count*. Boston: Allyn & Bacon.

Schrag, P., & Divorky, D. (1975). *The myth of the hyperactive child*. New York: Pantheon.

Schroyer, T. (1973). *The critique of domination*. Boston: Beacon Press.

Schumaker, J. B., & Deshler, D. D. (1988). Implementing the regular education initiative in secondary schools: A different ball game. *Journal of Learning Disabilities, 21*(1), 36–42.

Schwartz, P., Ogilvy, J. (1979). *The emergent paradigm: Changing patterns of thought and belief*. Menlo Park, CA: SRI International.

Scott, R. W. (1981). *Organizations: Rational, natural, and open systems*. Englewood Cliffs, NJ: Prentice-Hall.

Segal, M. (1974). Organization and environment: A typology of adaptability and structure. *Public Administration Review, 34*(3), 212–220.

Sergiovanni, T. J., & Moore, J. H. (Eds.). (1989). *Schooling for tomorrow*. Boston: Allyn & Bacon.

Shepard, L. A. (1987). The new push for excellence: Widening the schism between regular and special education. *Exceptional Children, 53*(4), 327–329.

Simon, H. A. (1977). *The new science of management decision*. Englewood Cliffs, NJ: Prentice-Hall.

Singer, J. D., & Butler, J. A. (1987). The Education for All Handicapped Children Act: Schools as agents of social reform. *Harvard Educational Review, 57*(2), 125–152.

Sirotnik, K. A., & Oakes, J. (1986). *Critical perspectives on the organization and improvement of schooling*. Boston: Kluwer-Nijhoff Publishing.

Sizer, T. R. (1984). *Horace's compromise: The dilemma of the American high school*. Boston: Houghton Mifflin.

Skinner, Q. (Ed.). (1985). *The return of grand theory in the human sciences*. Cambridge, Eng.: Cambridge University Press.

Skrtic, T. M. (1986). The crisis in special education knowledge: A perspective on perspective. *Focus on Exceptional Children, 18*(7), 1–16.

Skrtic, T. M. (1987a). An organizational analysis of special education reform. *Counterpoint, 8*(2), 15–19.

Skrtic, T. M. (1987b). The national inquiry into the future of education for students with special needs. *Counterpoint, 7*(4), 6.

Skrtic, T. M. (1988a). The crisis in special education knowledge. In E. L. Meyen & T. M. Skrtic (Eds.), *Exceptional Children and youth: An introduction* (pp. 415–447). Denver, CO: Love Publishing.

Skrtic, T. M. (1988b). The organizational context of special education. In E. L. Meyen & T. M. Skrtic (Eds.), *Exceptional children and youth: An introduction* (pp. 479–517). Denver, CO: Love Publishing.

Skrtic, T. M. (1990a, August 10–14). *School psychology and the revolution in modern knowledge*. Paper presented at the American Psychology Association Convention, Boston, MA.

Skrtic, T. M. (1990b). Social accommodation: Toward a dialogical discourse in educational inquiry. In E. G. Guba (Ed.), *The paradigm dialog: Options for inquiry in the social sciences* (pp. 125–135). Beverly Hills, CA: Sage.

Skrtic, T. M. (1991). *Behind special education: A critical analysis of professional knowledge and school organization*. Denver, CO: Love Publishing.

Skrtic, T. M. (in press). Toward a dialogical theory of school organization and adaptability: Special education and disability as organizational pathologies. In T. M. Skrtic (Ed.), *Exploring the theory/practice link in special education: A critical perspective*. Reston, VA: Council for Exceptional Children.

Skrtic, T. M., Guba, E. G., & Knowlton, H. E. (1985). *Interorganizational special education programming in rural areas: Technical report on the multisite naturalistic field study*. Washington, DC: National Institute of Education.

Skrtic, T. M., & Ware, L. P. (in press). Reflective teaching and the problem of school organization. In E. W. Ross, G. McCutcheon, & J. Cornett (Eds.), *Teacher personal theorizing: Issues, problems, and implications*. New York: Teachers College Press.

Slavin, R. E. (1989). PET and the pendulum: Faddism in education and how to stop it. *Phi Delta Kappan, 70*(10), 752–758.

Spring, J. (1980). *Education the worker-citizen: The social, economic, and political foundations of education*. New York: Longman.

Stainback, S., & Stainback, W. (1984). A rationale for the merger of special and regular education. *Exceptional Children, 51*(2), 102–111.

Stainback, S., & Stainback, W. (1985a). *Integration of students with severe handicaps into regular schools*. Reston, VA: Council for Exceptional Children.

Stainback, S., & Stainback, W. (1985b). The merger of special and regular education: Can it be done? A response to Lieberman and Mesinger. *Exceptional Children, 51*(6), 517–521.

Stainback, S., & Stainback, W. (1987a). Facilitating merger through personnel preparation. *Teacher Education and Special Education, 10*(4), 185–190.

Stainback, S., & Stainback, W. (1987b). Integration versus cooperation: A commentary on educating children with learning problems: A shared responsibility. *Exceptional Children, 54*(1), 66–68.

Stainback, S., & Stainback, W. (1989). Integration of students with mild and moderate handicaps. In D. K. Lipsky & A. Gartner (Eds.), *Beyond separate education: Qualify education for all* (pp. 41–52). Baltimore, MD: Paul H. Brookes.

Stainback, S., Stainback, W., & Forest, M. (Eds.). (1989). *Educating all students in the mainstreaming of regular education*. Baltimore, MD: Paul H. Brookes.

Stainback, W., Stainback, S., Courtnage, L., & Jaben, T. (1985). Facilitating mainstreaming by modifying the mainstream. *Exceptional Children, 52*(2), 144–152.

Stedman, L. C. (1987). It's time we changed the effective schools formula. *Phi Delta Kappan, 69*(3), 215–224.

Swap, S. (1978). The ecological model of emotional disturbance in children: A status report and proposed synthesis. *Behavioral Disorders, 3*(3), 156–186.

Teacher Education Division of the Council for Exceptional Children. (1986, October). *Message to all TED members concerning The National Inquiry into the Future of Education for Students with Special Needs*. Reston, VA: Author.

Teacher Education Division of the Council for Exceptional Children. (1987). The regular education initiative: A statement by the Teacher Education Division, Council for Exceptional Children. *Journal of Learning Disabilities, 20*(5), 289–293.

Thompson, J. D. (1967). *Organizations in action*. New York: McGraw-Hill.

Thousand, J. S. (1990). Organizational perspectives on teacher education and school renewal: A conversation with Tom Skrtic, *Teacher Education and Special Education, 13*(1), 30–35.

Thousand, J. S., Fox, T., Reid, R., Godek, J., & Williams, W. (1986). *The homecoming model: Educating students who present intensive educational challenges within regular education environments* (Monograph No. 7-1). Burlington: University of Vermont, Center for Developmental Disabilities.

Thousand, J. S., & Villa, R. A. (1988). *Enhancing success in heterogeneous classrooms and schools* (Monograph 8-1). Burlington: University of Vermont, Center for Developmental Disabilities.

Thousand, J. S., & Villa, R. A. (1989). Enhancing success in heterogeneous schools. In S. Stainback, W. Stainback, & M. Forest (Eds.), *Educating all students in the mainstream of regular education*. Baltimore, MD: Paul H. Brookes.

Timar, T. B., & Kirp, D. L. (1988). *Managing educational excellence*. New York: Falmer Press.

Timar, T. B., & Kirp, D. L. (1989). Education reforms in the 1980's: Lessons from the states. *Phi Delta Kappan, 70*(7), 504–511.

Toffler, A. (1970). *Future shock*. New York: Bantam Books.

Tomlinson, S. (1982). *A sociology of special education*. Boston: Routledge and Kegan Paul.

Tye, K. A., & Tye, B. B. (1984). Teacher isolation and school reform. *Phi Delta Kappan, 65*(5), 319–322.

U.S. Department of Education (USDE), Office of Special Education and Rehabilitative Services. (1988). *Annual report to Congress on the implementation of the Education for all Handicapped Children Act*. Washington, DC: Author.

Vergason, G. A., & Anderegg, M. L. (1989). Save the baby! A response to Integrating the Children of the Second System. *Phi Delta Kappan, 71*(1), 61–63.

Walberg, H. J., & Wang, M. C. (1987). Effective educational practices and provisions for individual differences. In M. C. Wang, M. C. Reynolds, & H. J. Walberg (Eds.). *Handbook of special education: Research and practice. Vol. 1: Learner characteristics and adaptive education* (pp. 113–128). Oxford, Eng.: Pergamon Press.

Walker, L. J. (1987). Procedural rights in the wrong system: Special education is not enough. In A. Gartner & T. Joe (Eds.), *Images of the disabled/disabling images*. New York: Praeger.

Wang, M. C. (1981). Mainstreaming exceptional children: Some instructional design and implementation considerations. *Elementary School Journal, 81*, 195–221.

Wang, M. C. (1988, May 4). A promising approach for reforming special education. *Education Week*, pp. 36, 28.

Wang, M. C. (1989a). Accommodating student diversity through adaptive instruction. In S. Stainback, W. Stainback, & M. Forest (Eds.), *Educating all students in the mainstream of regular education* (pp. 183–197). Baltimore, MD: Paul H. Brookes.

Wang, M. C. (1989b). Adaptive instruction: An alternative for accommodating student diversity through the curriculum. In D. K. Lipsky & A. Gartner (Eds.), *Beyond separate education: Quality education for all* (pp. 99–119). Baltimore, MD: Paul H. Brookes.

Wang, M. C., & Reynolds, M. C. (1985). Avoiding the "catch-22" in special education reform. *Exceptional Children, 51*(6), 497–502.

Wang, M. C., & Reynolds, M. C. (1986). "Catch 22 and disabling help": A reply to Alan Gartner. *Exceptional Children, 53*(1), 77–79.

Wang, M. C., Reynolds, M. C., & Walberg, H. J. (1985, December 5–7). *Rethinking special education*. Paper presented at the Wingspread Conference on the Education of Students with Special Needs: Research Findings and Implications for Policy and Practice, Racine, WI.

Wang, M. C., Reynolds, M. C., & Walberg, H. J. (1986). Rethinking special education. *Educational Leadership, 44*(1), 26–31.

Wang, M. C., Reynolds, M. C., & Walberg, H. J. (Eds.). (1987a). *Handbook of special education: Research and practice. Vol. 1: learner characteristics and adaptive education*. Oxford, Eng.: Pergamon Press.

Wang, M. C., & Reynolds, M. C., & Walberg, H. J. (1987b, October 1–3). *Repairing the second system for students with special needs*. Paper presented at the Wingspread Conference on the Education of Children with Special Needs: Gearing Up to Meet the Challenges of the 1990s, Racine, WI.

Wang, M. C., Reynolds, M. C., & Walberg, H. J. (1988). Integrating the children of the second system. *Phi Delta Kappan, 70*(3), 248–251.

Wang, M. C., Reynolds, M. C., & Walberg, H. J. (1989). Who benefits from segregation and murky water? *Phi Delta Kappan, 71*(1), 64–67.

Wang, M. C., & Walberg, H. J. (1988). Four fallacies of segregationism. *Exceptional Children, 55*(2), 128–137.

Weatherley, R. (1979). *Reforming special education: Policy implementation from state level to street level*. Cambridge, MA: MIT Press.

Weatherley, R., & Lipsky, M. (1977). Street-level bureaucrats and institutional innovation: Implementing special education reform. *Harvard Educational Review, 47*(2), 171–203.

Weber, M. (1946). Politics as a vocation. In H. H. Gerth & C. W. Mills (Eds. & Trans.), *From Max Weber: Essays in sociology* (pp. 77–128). Oxford, Eng.: Oxford University Press. (Original work published 1919)

Weber, M. (1949). "Objectivity" in social science and social policy. In E. A. Shils & H. A. Finch (Eds. & Trans.), *The methodology of the social sciences*. New York: Free Press. (Original work published 1904)

Weber, M. (1978). *Economy and society* (G. Roth & C. Wittich, Eds.; E. Fischoll et al., Trans.) (2 Vols.). Berkeley: University of California Press. (Original work published 1922)

Weick, K. E. (1976). Educational organizations as loosely coupled systems. *Administrative Science Quarterly, 21*(1), 1–19.

Weick, K. E. (1979). Cognitive processes in organization. In B. M. Staw (Ed.), *Research in organizational behavior* (Vol. 1, pp. 41–74). Greenwich, CT: JAI Press.

Weick, K. E. (1982). Administering education in loosely coupled schools. *Phi Delta Kappan, 63*(10), 673–676.

Weick, K. E. (1985). Sources of order in underorganized systems. In Y. S. Lincoln (Ed.), *Organizational theory and inquiry: The paradigm revolution* (pp. 106–136). Beverly Hills, CA: Sage.

Weintraub, F. J. (1977). Editorial comment. *Exceptional Children, 44*(2), 114.

White, R., & Calhoun, M. L. (1987). From referral to placement: Teachers' perceptions of their responsibilities. *Exceptional Children, 53*(5), 460–468.

Will, M. C. (1984). Let us pause and reflect — But not too long. *Exceptional Children, 51*(1), 11–16.

Will, M. C. (1985, December). *Educating children with learning problems: A shared responsibility*. Paper presented at the Wingspread Conference on the Education of Special Needs Students: Research Findings and Implications for Policy and Practice, Racine, WI.

Will, M. C. (1986a). Educating children with learning problems: A shared responsibility. *Exceptional Children, 52*(5), 411–416.

Will, M. C. (1986b). *Educating children with learning problems: A shared responsibility. A report to the secretary*. Washington, DC: U.S. Department of Education.

Wise, A. E. (1988). The two conflicting trends in school reform: Legislated learning revisited. *Phi Delta Kappan, 69*(5), 328–333.

Wolcott, H. F. (1977). *Teachers versus technocrats: An educational innovation in anthropological perspective*. Eugene, OR: Center for Educational Policy and Management.

Woodward, J. (1965). *Industrial organizations: Theory and practice*. Oxford, Eng.: Oxford University Press.

Wright, A. R., Cooperstein, R. A., Renneker, E. G., & Padilla, C. (1982). *Local implementation of P.L. 94–142: Final report of a longitudinal study*. Menlo Park, CA: SRI International.

Wright, J. S. (1967). *Hobson vs. Hansen: Opinion by Honorable J. Skelly Wright, Judge, United States Court of Appeals for the District of Columbia*. Washington, DC: West Publishing.

Ysseldyke, J., Thurlow, M., Graden, S., Wesson, C., Algozzine, B., & Deno, S. (1983). Generalization from five years of research on assessment and decision-making: The University of Minnesota Institute. *Exceptional Education Quarterly, 4*, 75–93.

Zucker, L. G. (1977). The role of institutionalization in cultural persistence. *American Sociological Review, 42*, 726–743.

Zucker, L. G. (1981). Institutional structure and organizational processes: The role of evaluation units in schools. In A. Bank & R. C. Williams (Eds.), *Evaluation and decision making* (CSE Monograph Series No. 10). Los Angeles: UCLA Center for the Study of Evaluation.

Complexity, Accountability, and School Improvement[1]

8

JENNIFER A. O'DAY

T his article, like much of the conversation among reformers and policymakers today, is about accountability. Everywhere you turn — from Congress to the statehouse to local communities and parent groups — some people are trying to make other people more accountable for some thing in education. However deafening at times, these cries for accountability should not surprise us. Public education consumes over $400 billion in public revenues. It is reasonable that the public and its representatives want to know where the money is going and what it is producing. Are educators doing what they are being paid to do? Are administrators responsible in how they are spending money? Are children engaged and learning what they need to know?

Such questions are hardly new. In the early days of the common school, for example, teachers were closely scrutinized and called to task even for such personal habits as demeanor and dress, as well as for their duties in the classroom. Meanwhile, student accountability — in the form of grades and report cards — has been around for even longer, while fiscal accountability for districts came to the fore with the rise of federal programs such as Title I in the 1960s. Yet, as many observers have noted, the current emphasis on and efforts toward educational accountability represent a departure, or evolution, from previous practice. Researchers at the Consortium for Policy Research in Education (CPRE) have labeled this evolution the "new accountability" and have analyzed its various components or manifestations.[2] Central among these are the emphasis on student outcomes as the measure of adult and system performance, a focus on the school as a basic unit of accountability, public reporting of student achievement, and the attachment of consequences to performance levels (Elmore, Abelmann, & Fuhrman, 1996; Fuhrman, 1999). Other analysts have delineated typologies of educational accountability (Adams & Kirst, 1999; Darling-Hammond & Ascher, 1991; O'Day & Smith, 1993; O'Reilly, 1996), noting differences among administrative/bureaucratic accountability and legal, professional, or market accountability systems with respect to who is holding whom accountable for

Harvard Educational Review   Vol. 72   No. 3   Fall 2002, 293–329

what. In each case, reformers and observers assume that the goal of current account-ability-based interventions is (or should be) the improvement of instruction and student learning.

This article focuses on one class of the current accountability mechanisms — those that take the school as the unit of accountability and seek to improve student learning by improving the functioning of the school organization. My goal is to place the current trends and typologies of school accountability into a theoretical framework drawn from the literature on organizational learning and adaptation. I begin with a discussion of schools as complex systems, focusing on the role of information and interaction in system change and on critical mechanisms of, and barriers to, the use of information to improve schools. In particular, I argue that accountability systems will foster improvement to the extent that they generate and focus attention on information relevant to teaching and learning, motivate individuals and schools to use that information and expend effort to improve practice, build the knowledge base necessary for interpreting and applying the new information to improve practice, and allocate resources for all of the above. The most widespread and well-developed policy approach for addressing these four tasks is the outcomes-based bureaucratic model of school accountability evident in most states and districts and codified in extreme form in the recent federal legislation, the No Child Left Behind Act (NCLB) of 2001.[3] Using the Chicago experience as an example, I discuss the promise and limitations of this most pervasive approach to school accountability in light of the theoretical framework.[4] I then consider professional accountability as a potential alternative, arguing that the combination of administrative and professional accountability is the most promising approach for fostering organizational learning and improvement in schools. In the final section I draw out several implications of the discussion for the refinement of accountability policies.[5]

SCHOOL-BASED ACCOUNTABILITY: TENSIONS AND PROBLEMS

This discussion starts from the premise that school accountability mechanisms by their very nature seek to increase student performance by improving the functioning of the school organization. Mechanisms of school accountability vary from jurisdiction to jurisdiction, but generally include the establishment of some target level of performance (aggregated across the school, though targets may include disaggregated benchmarks as well), with consequences (and sometimes assistance) meted out to the school unit for achieving or not achieving the target performance. Whatever their differences in terms of the targets or the consequences, policies that take the school as the basic unit of accountability must contend with a number of inherent problems if they are to effect organizational change. I raise three such problems here and return to them at the conclusion of this article.

Problem 1: The school is the unit of intervention, yet the individual is the unit of action. The first of these problems concerns the relationship between collective accountability and individual action. School accountability by definition targets the school unit for monitoring, intervention, and change. But schools are collections of individuals, and to the extent that the needed change involves the behavior of the members of the organization, it must occur ultimately at the individual level. That is, individual teachers, administrators, and parents must in some way change what they are doing in the hope that this will change what students do (individually and in interaction with teachers) in such a way as to increase or deepen student learning. School-level accountability approaches bank on school members' identification and interaction with their organizational environment to motivate and direct individual action. In other words, such policies assume that targeting the school unit will generate the necessary and desired changes in the behavior of individuals within that unit. This assumption leads to two questions: How will school accountability mechanisms reach beyond the collective level to mobilize such changes among individuals? What conditions need to be in place for this connection to occur?

Problem 2: External control seeks to influence internal operations. Just as individuals operate within schools, schools are nested within larger systems and environments. New accountability approaches, by their very nature, seek to influence from the outside what goes on inside schools. Moreover, such policies assume that external forces can play a determining role in changing the internal workings of schools. The limitations of such assumptions, however, have provided grist for the vast literature on policy implementation in education.[6]

The heart of the issue is the problematic relationship between external and internal sources of control and the implications of this relationship for organizational learning and improvement. Organizational systems have several mechanisms at their disposal to control the behavior of individuals and subunits. Two such mechanisms are formal rules and normative structures. Large systems — like public education — tend toward bureaucracy and reliance on rules. Teachers work a certain number of hours a day, teach their classes in a prescribed order, and follow a variety of district, state, and federal mandates. But rules decreed from on high often have little impact, especially when it comes to the core technology of teaching and learning (Elmore, 1996; Marion, 1999). One reason is that externally generated rules may come up against the power of an organization's internal norms of behavior. Normative structures inside schools, such as the privacy of classroom practice, are often the determining factor not only in the implementation of policy, but, more importantly, in the school's overall effectiveness in fostering student learning.[7] The resulting questions for school accountability policies are profound. What is the appropriate and most effective balance between external and internal control? What are the mechanisms for achieving this balance? Can external accountability measures influence the development of internal norms that are more conducive to improving student learning?

Problem 3: Information is both problematic in schools and essential to school improvement. The third problem in school accountability concerns the nature and role of information in school improvement. Indeed, information is the lifeblood of all accountability mechanisms: one accounts to someone for something, and this accounting gets done by conveying information. Current school accountability policies, such as public reporting of student test scores, assume that, armed with accurate information about the achievement of students in the school, stakeholders and participants in the instructional process will take whatever action is necessary to improve learning outcomes. But again, this simple assumption raises a host of questions, the answers to which are anything but straightforward. What are the most effective forms and uses of information in the school improvement process? What is the potential for the external accountability system to generate and disseminate the information needed to accomplish the accountability goals? What are the motivational and learning links between information on the one hand and individual and collective action?

These three problems — collective accountability versus individual action, internal versus external sources of control, and the nature and uses of information for school improvement — undergird this paper on school accountability. To illuminate their interrelationships, I turn to theories of organizational complexity and adaptation, focusing on the central role of information in both accountability and school improvement processes.

COMPLEX ADAPTIVE SYSTEMS AND CHANGE: A FRAMEWORK FOR UNDERSTANDING SCHOOL ACCOUNTABILITY

Complexity Theory and Organizations

Complex systems theory draws on parallel developments in the physical, biological, and social sciences that challenge traditional notions of linear causality and externally imposed or predetermined order.[8] Complexity theorists use the term *complex adaptive systems* (CAS) to describe "a world in which many players are all adapting to each other and where the emerging future is very hard to predict" (Axelrod & Cohen, 1999, p. xi). A few central concepts from complexity theory as applied to organizations are particularly instructive in understanding both the potential and the limitations of current approaches to school accountability.

Interaction and Interdependence in Complex Adaptive Systems   A central characteristic of complex adaptive systems is the interdependence of individual and collective behavior. CAS are defined as populations of interacting "agents" (be they cells, animals, people, organizations, or other systems), each of which pursues a limited set of strategies in response to its surroundings and in pursuit of its goals. The systemic nature of a complex adaptive system derives from the patterns of interaction and to some extent from a commonality of strategies among like agents (Axelrod & Cohen, 1999; Marion, 1999).

In a school, for example, teachers interact with students, with other teachers, with administrators, with parents, and so forth. In each of these interactions, the individual actor follows his or her own goals and strategies, which differ from those of other actors to varying degrees. One teacher may seek to develop her students' mathematical reasoning while another is more focused on keeping students safe and off the streets. These teachers' differing goals may be manifested in somewhat different strategies in the classroom. Similarly, while one student may show up because he wants to hang out with friends and avoid the truancy officer, another has his eyes on an elite university. Again, students' particular activities will vary according to their goals. This variation among individual actors and their strategies is central to the notion of complexity and adaptation.

Equally central, however, are the constraints placed on that variation by the interaction of actors within the organization and between them and the larger environment. Thus, what a teacher does in her classroom depends greatly on what her students do, and vice versa; and what individuals in one classroom do is shaped in part by their interaction with individuals in other classrooms, in the hallways, and on the grounds of the school. The more frequent and powerful those interactions are, the more influence they are likely to have on the behavior of individual actors. Conversely, the more weakly connected — or loosely coupled (Weick, 1976) — the organization, the more independent and self-determined the actions of individuals and subunits within it. The nature and strength of the patterns of interaction are thus key to understanding the relationship between individual and organizational behavior and change.

Stability and Change   In complex systems, the strategies that individual agents and organizations pursue reflect both stability and change over time — with both these characteristics being manifestations of learning. As new members come in to the organization, they become socialized into (i.e., learn) its "code" — the languages, beliefs, and routines that make up the dominant behaviors of the organization and define it as an interactive system (March, 1991); hence, the stability of the system. But organizational codes and practices also change. Such change occurs through the selection, recombination, and adaptation of strategies, based on information derived from the interactions of system members with one another and with their environment. Thus, second-grade teacher Mrs. Cardenas moves Anton to a different seat because she notices that he is distracted by activity outside the window near his current seat. Meanwhile, Mr. Arthur and his third-grade colleagues introduce cross-class reading groups, based on feedback and modeling from a literacy coordinator working with the school. And Washington Elementary selects a new mathematics curriculum after receiving notice from the school board about a new testing policy. As Huber (1991) explains: "An entity learns if, through its processing of information, the range of its potential behaviors is changed. This definition holds whether the entity is a human or other animal, a group, an organization, an industry, or a society" (p. 89).

Information and Learning   At the heart of the learning process in any complex system is the role of information and the movement of information among agents and subunits through patterns of interaction. Several characteristics of this information are important to note.

First, information and adaptation derive from variation. Without variation among the agents of a system or in the surrounding environment, there is little information on which to act. For example, students — individually and as a group — vary from teachers in knowledge and maturity, vary from each other, and vary from their prior behavior over time as they grow and learn. Much of teachers' activity is bound up with responding to these variations in and among students. At the system level, monitoring and responding to variation is also at the heart of current accountability efforts, as differences in reported test scores become the basis on which progress, success, and failure are judged.

Second, information in this model is not a static entity that is disseminated unchanged. Rather, information is dynamic, constantly changing as it is interpreted based on prior experience, recombined with other information and knowledge, and passed on through interaction with others. Interpretation is "the process though which information is given meaning" (Daft & Weick, 1984, p. 294). As such, it depends on "a person's prior cognitive map (or belief structure or mental representation or frame of reference)" (Huber, 1991, pp. 102–103), which is socially constructed and varies across organizational units having different responsibilities. One implication is that the process of spreading information will itself become a source of variation — as in the classic children's game "telephone" (Marion, 1999). In essence, the message changes each time it is passed on. Spillane (2000, 2002) has found, for example, that variation in the implementation of state standards derives in part from variation in the way that district leaders interpret and then convey those standards to school personnel, who then reinterpret them based on their own context and frames of reference.[9] A second implication is that the meaningfulness of the information generated by the system will vary in relation to the knowledge and skills of the users. To the extent that such knowledge and skills are weak or are unequally distributed, so too will be the meaning and usefulness of the accountability information.

Finally, not all information leads to learning and change. As implied above, for information to be useful, members of the system must first have access to it, through interaction with other members or the environment.[10] Moreover, if they are to incorporate the information into their cognitive maps or repertoire of strategies, they must attend to it and must have sufficient knowledge and stability to interpret it. Action does not necessarily follow, even once learning occurs, as this step often requires motivation and resources beyond those necessary for the learning itself. As I will discuss later, these elements — access, attention, knowledge, motivation, and resources — are all essential. A breakdown in any one of them may disrupt the connection between information and change.

Learning and Improvement   Even when learning and change occur, they do not necessarily lead to improvement. This may seem counterintuitive, given popular notions about learning and "learning organizations" (Senge, 1993), but this conclusion flows from the conception of learning and of complex systems just described. Complexity theorists Robert Axelrod and Michael Cohen (1999) use the term *adaptation* to indicate when learning and change lead to "improvement along some measure of success" (p. 7). This concept of adaptation is highly consistent with the goals of school accountability systems, which seek improvement in terms of specific assessments of student performance. In complex systems, however, the relationship between learning (an "increase in the range of potential behaviors)" (Huber, 1991, p. 89) and adaptation is obscured. For one thing, individual agents vary in their goals and thus in measures of success; adaptation for one might not be adaptation for others (Axelrod & Cohen, 1999).

In addition, interaction and interpretation of information make learning unreliable. Agents and organizations may misinterpret feedback from their environment, causing "superstitious learning" (Levitt & March, 1988).[11] If individuals and organizations act on that superstitious learning — for example, using it to select a strategy — the results may be maladaptive rather than adaptive; that is, they may lead to a decline rather than an improvement in relevant measures of success. Finally, learning at one point in an individual's or system's experience may inhibit learning and change at another point. As individuals and organizations gain competence in certain activities through learning, they may actually decrease their range of potential strategies (Levinthal, 1991). By repeatedly selecting strategies that have led to success in the past and interacting with other entities based on those strategies, an organization reduces variation, thus potentially reducing future learning and adaptation. The end result is that individuals and mature organizations over time may get caught in "competency traps," becoming prisoners of their own past success (Levitt & March, 1988).[12] One might argue that the general inertia of the educational system is a reflection of such competency traps.

Barriers to Improvement in Schools

This discussion of complex adaptive systems has implications for how we think about the potential relationship between accountability policies and school improvement and, more specifically, about the organizational barriers that accountability policies must overcome in order to foster successful adaptation. These barriers center on the generation, interpretation, and use of information for school and system improvement.

Too Much or Too Little Information   Teachers and schools are constantly bombarded by information and by demands to do something about that information — requests from parents, notices from the central office or federal and state departments, publishing companies, external advocates and programs, community groups, counselors, etc. In many schools, teachers' and students' work is subject to continual interruption as others try to thrust new information upon them. What's worse, much of the information is irrelevant to the improvement of instruction and learning. It merely distracts attention and resources from what is supposed to be the main work of school personnel and students. Sifting through the morass to find that which is likely to lead to improvement requires time, resources, and knowledge that school personnel may not possess. Unable to make productive choices, some teachers and schools move chaotically from one demand or source of information to another, with insufficient focus and time to learn. The classic "Christmas tree school" is an example of this pattern.[13]

Alternatively, teachers and schools may metaphorically and literally close the door on new information, shutting out the noise. This is a coping strategy that potentially allows them to focus, but it also leads to isolation. Such isolation prevents their having sufficient opportunity to encounter variation and the information it engenders, and thus little opportunity for learning. Norms of private practice in education and loose coupling (Weick, 1976) throughout the system reinforce this isolation.[14] On the one hand, loose coupling prevents failure in one unit (school or classroom) from cascading throughout the system (Marion, 1999; Weick, 1976), but at the same time it may inhibit learning that can lead to improvement.

Consider a veteran teacher typical of those in many U.S. urban schools. Extended survival in the system implies that he or she has learned and selected strategies that have been successful by at least some measure of success — perhaps student learning, perhaps social competence, perhaps simply control. As described earlier, one such strategy has been to shut out the cacophony of information and distracting interactions by literally closing the classroom door on them. Other teachers in the school, many of them also veterans in the system, have adopted a similar approach, so that the school has become a collection of virtually private domains demarcated by the walls surrounding each classroom. Moreover, protecting the sanctity of those domains has become an integral part of the school code. New teachers quickly learn this code if they intend to continue in the organization; they develop their own strategies for what they do in the classroom, leaving their colleagues to do the same. The structure of the school day and the school building reinforce this pattern. The teachers survive, and over time survival increasingly becomes the measure of success, not only for individuals but for the school as a whole. That this means of survival has been enhanced through isolation has implications for future change. In a sense, one could say the "egg-crate" structure of U.S. schooling, with its separate and isolated classroom structures designed to buffer each component from change, is a kind of competency trap. That is, separating teachers and students in independent and isolated classrooms is a strategy that has worked in the past for survival, control, and sorting, but that may not work well if the measure of success changes (e.g., to high levels of student learning for all students). The "trap" of the egg crate is that such isolation prevents teachers from taking advantage of the variation in their individual classroom strategies in order to learn from one another and select more successful ways of doing things.

On the one hand, external sources thrust an overload of information on schools and school personnel, while on the other hand, isolation creates a lack of information sharing among teachers. What seems to be needed is some middle ground — as in the story of Goldilocks and the just-right porridge. For Goldilocks, only the porridge of just the right temperature could ensure taste, consumption, and eventual satisfaction. Likewise, teachers, given the right amount of information, will be able to attend to it, interpret it, and use it for learning and adaptation. The question is, how will the accountability system ensure that school personnel receive an adequate amount of information, can interpret the information, and have the ability to focus on what is most appropriate for improving teaching and learning?

Complexity and the Problem of Attribution in Schools   The amount of information encountered is only one part of the problem. Also of concern are the kinds of information available, how that information is interpreted, and whether the interpretations will lead to learning and to selecting strategies that lead to adaptation.

Theorists (e.g., Levitt & March, 1988) tell us that organizations are oriented toward targets and adapt based on feedback (information) about those targets. Discrepancies between observed outcomes and aspirations for those outcomes can provide motivation for change (Simon, 1986). Such is certainly the assumption of outcomes-based accountability. First of all, agents within schools vary in their definition of a target (sometimes it is just getting through the day!), and schools also have multiple and changing targets. Moving a school community from an emphasis on discipline and order to a focus on student learning, for example, is difficult and represents this sort of change. Second, even taking a single generally agreed-upon goal, such as independent reading by the third grade, does not remove the ambiguity. Other targets remain, agents have differing views about what independent reading entails, and measurement is difficult.

But perhaps most important, even in an ideal situation where the goals and measures are clear, the complexity of interaction patterns inside and outside the organization and of the learning process itself makes attribution of cause and effect difficult and unreliable. Consider the following hypothetical example: Only 15 percent of third graders in Bryant Elementary are reading independently by time of the spring assessment. Do we conclude that the third-grade teachers are not teaching appropriately? And if so, in what particular ways is the instruction inadequate? Are the textbooks too difficult? Too easy? Too boring? Perhaps the low performance is due to constant interruptions during reading time or lack of order in the school. Maybe the problem is that the students do not see any reason for reading, or perhaps they speak a language other than English and do not have the requisite English vocabulary. Perhaps the real problem lies in first- or second-grade instruction, in the fear induced by violence in the neighborhood, or in the low expectations of the adults. Perhaps it is all or some combination of the above. Alternatively, if the majority of students at Bryant are doing well, we are not necessarily any closer to understanding the cause of their performance. Is it class background? School selection processes? Motivated teachers? Effective instruction? All of the above? Indeed, it is often more difficult to pinpoint the cause of success than it is of failure.

The difficulty of attribution, and thus of selection and prediction, is endemic to complex systems. Complexity theorists use terms like *circular causality* and *multiple interactions* to discuss the problem of attribution where individual actors are responding to (and providing) feedback from (and to) multiple sources (Marion, 1999; Weick, 1976). Mutual adaptation inevitably leads to mistakes in attribution.[15]

The tendency toward faulty attribution in education is commonplace. It is exacerbated by the lack of accurate, valid, and appropriately detailed information on outcomes. For example, a test given in the spring with the results reported to teachers (about their now former students) in the fall does not solve the attribution problem for teachers. That problem is also exacerbated when those involved in interpreting the results know little about the type and distribution of strategies and resources used to produce those results, or when they lack the opportunity and knowledge to reflect on and explore alternative interpretations of the information they have. As we will see, school accountability systems generally seek to address the first of these conditions — the lack of information on outcomes — but often ignore the other information needed for appropriate attribution.

Faulty Incentive and Resource Allocation Structures   Adaptation in schools is also inhibited by incentive and resource structures that undermine motivation and the opportunity for organizational learning or that preclude the adoption of more productive strategies. These inhibitors include such things as incentives that pull attention and effort to goals other than student learning,[16] insufficient time or other resources for collaboration and sharing information about instruction, and human resource systems that reward mediocrity and concentrate the most knowledgeable teachers where they are least needed. One might think about such allocation as a "strategy" of the larger system in which the unit or individual is embedded. Thus, we would ask whether the school has an effective strategy for allocating resources to foster student learning. Does the district? As with other aspects of the system, resource allocation is dependent on accurate and reliable information. Again, the goal of the accountability system should be to supply that information.

School Accountability Framework

This discussion suggests a framework for analyzing the potential impact of accountability-based interventions on school improvement. School accountability mechanisms will be successful in improving the functioning of school organizations to the extent that those interventions are able to:

- *Generate and focus attention on information relevant to teaching and learning and to changes in that information as it is continually fed back into and through the system.* Note that in order to alter what happens in classrooms, this focus must occur not only at the school level, but at the level of individual teachers as well. Interaction patterns are likely to be very important in the generation and spread of such information.
- *Motivate educators and others to attend to relevant information and to expend the effort necessary to augment or change strategies in response to this information.* Central here is the problematic relationship of collective accountability and individual action. Motivation must ultimately occur at the individual level, but it is likely to be dependent in part on the normative structures of the school as well as on individual characteristics of educators and students.
- *Develop the knowledge and skills to promote valid interpretation of information and appropriate attribution of causality at both the individual and system levels.* As discussed above, learning takes place through the interpretation of information, whether that information is data from a student assessment, research on reading instruction, or observation of a colleague's lesson. Interpretation is dependent on prior learning and is constrained and informed by such. Data often remain unused because educators lack the knowledge base for interpretation and incorporation of

the new information. If accountability systems are to be successful, they will need not only to build knowledge and skills for interpretation in the short run, but also to establish mechanisms for continued learning through use of information generated by the system.

- *Allocate resources where they are most needed.*   Information at all levels can promote the allocation of resources — human and material — to where they are most needed. A classroom teacher might reallocate resources by spending more of her time and attention on a student she sees is having trouble understanding a new concept. Similarly, district administrators might move additional resources to a low-performing school or one taking on a new challenge. To what extent does the accountability system encourage allocation (or reallocation) of resources to foster student learning based on information generated?

BUREAUCRATIC ACCOUNTABILITY AND SCHOOL IMPROVEMENT

How do current school accountability policies fare with respect to the framework outlined above? That is, to what extent do accountability policies generate and focus attention on relevant information, motivate the use of that information for individual and collective change, contribute to the knowledge base needed for appropriate interpretation of that information, and use information to provide adequate resources where needed? To answer this question requires that we first define what is meant by "current school accountability policies." Here I turn to analyses of the new accountability in education (Elmore et al., 1996), as well as the more expansive typologies of educational accountability (Adams & Kirst, 1999; Darling-Hammond & Ascher, 1991; O'Reilly, 1996).

Accountability systems, according to these and other observers, differ in large part by the way they respond to four central questions: *Who* is accountable? *To whom* are they accountable? *For what* are they accountable? And *with what consequences*? Fuhrman notes that one of the distinguishing characteristics of the new accountability in standards-based reform is that the "who" in this formulation is generally the school unit, and as previously indicated, this article focuses exclusively on school-level accountability.[17] In addition, while school accountability policies differ in their particulars from jurisdiction to jurisdiction, the "to whom" designation almost universally refers to the district and/or state agencies.[18] That is, schools as collective entities are accountable to the higher levels of the educational system. In this respect, such policies represent a form of administrative (O'Day & Smith, 1993) or bureaucratic accountability (Adams & Kirst, 1999; Darling-Hammond & Ascher, 1991). However, they differ from traditional forms of bureaucratic accountability in one very important respect: they hold schools and school personnel accountable not for delivering designated educational inputs and processes but for producing specific levels or improvements in student learning outcomes. Thus, they are examples of what might best be termed "outcome-based bureaucratic accountability."[19] In this section, I will use Chicago as an exemplar of this form of school accountability.[20]

Addressing the Framework: Outcomes-Based Accountability, Chicago Style

The Chicago Public Schools (CPS) provide a particularly useful model to illustrate this framework, since the Illinois legislature amended the Chicago School Reform Act in 1995 to include specific provisions for school accountability. Following those provisions, the Chicago School Board designated school-level targets for student performance and instituted sanctions (probation and reconstitution) for schools falling below those targets. The district has now accumulated six years of experience with school accountability. Several colleagues and I have had the opportunity to follow the design, practice, and results of this system over the past several years. Our investigation has included in-depth interviews with business, political, education, and community stakeholders; analyses of school improvement plans and the planning process; interviews and shadowing of support providers; school case studies; and multilevel analyses of survey and achievement data on all CPS elementary schools since 1994 (two years prior to the implementation of sanctions). Our data are thus both rich and varied. They provide an inroad into understanding the links between outcomes-based school accountability and school improvement.

At first glance, CPS and similar school accountability systems seem to address well the criteria laid out in the framework above. Below I discuss how the four components of the school accountability framework are reflected in the CPS accountability system.

Attention: On the most basic level, these accountability systems call attention to information on student outcomes by designating a particular indicator (or indicators) of those outcomes and by defining specific performance targets. In Chicago's case, the focus is sharpened by the district's use of a single indicator — the Iowa Test of Basic Skills (ITBS)[21] — in only two subject areas, reading and mathematics. Moreover, the targeted performance benchmark is simple, measurable, and clear: schools must have at least 20 percent of their students in grades 3–8 or 9–11 reading at or above national grade-level norms in the spring administration of the ITBS, or be declared "on probation." Attention to the outcomes is further enhanced through school planning and reporting mechanisms that single out reading and math scores and require all schools to provide information on how they will increase student performance in these areas. Such mechanisms establish priorities in the organization and thus should help school personnel sift through the usual information overload to focus on that most directly related to student achievement and improvement strategies.

Motivation: Chicago's policy, like outcomes-based policies in other jurisdictions, provides motivation for this sifting process and related improvement efforts by attaching consequences to the outcome targets. For all schools, these consequences come in the form of public and administrative scrutiny of reported school outcome data. For schools falling below the target, sanctions include the stigma of the "probation" label, decreased autonomy as local school councils lose authority to select their principals, additional requirements for planning, monitoring, and assistance, and potentially even reconstitution or reengineering, both of which entail involuntary changes in personnel.[22] Policy designers believe that even the threat of such sanctions will increase educator motivation and efforts to improve student learning.

Knowledge Development: Attending to outcome information is of little value if school personnel do not know how to interpret it, and motivation to act will produce nothing if educators do not know what actions they should take. Recognizing the need for site-based knowledge and skill development, CPS administrators instituted an elaborate program of assistance for schools, including mentoring for principals, help with business and school improvement plans, and professional and organizational development provided by external partners. A particularly interesting feature of the CPS design of external assistance is the district's response to the tension between internal and external sources of control discussed earlier. In an effort to balance these sources of control and enhance normative buy-in among school personnel, CPS allows probation schools to select their own partners from an approved list. The policy designers hoped that this selection process would both enhance motivation and ensure that support providers pay attention to the particular conditions in each school.

Resource Allocation: Finally, funding for this assistance demonstrates a major way in which the district has used information generated by the accountability system to allocate resources. Low test scores trigger the targeting of discretionary monies — initially from the district surplus and then from federal programs, including the Comprehensive School Reform Demonstration (CSRD) program and class-size reduction — to probation schools.[23] The district covers 100 percent of the cost of the first year of assistance, 50 percent of the second year, and the school bears the full cost in subsequent years. In the first two years of the probation policy, CPS spent $29 million for external support alone.[24]

Other jurisdictions, both states and other districts, have set in place similar systems — in part in response to the accountability requirements incorporated into Title I of the Elementary and Secondary Education Act (ESEA) in 1994.[25] Of course, jurisdictions vary considerably in the specifics of their policies. One important dimension of this variation is in the definition of targets. Some jurisdictions have set improvement targets for all schools and rewards for those meeting or exceeding targets. The intent is to focus and motivate improvement in both higher performing schools and lower performing ones.[26] Jurisdictions also vary in the forms of assistance provided and in the consequences attached to either high or low performance relative to the targets. Yet, despite these variations, the general school accountability model is the same in that it defines certain expected levels of performance, designates schools as high or low performing based on student assessments, requires planning to focus attention and coordinate action in the school, provides assistance in some form, and administers sanctions for continued failure to improve.

Impact of Outcomes-Based Accountability   Although experience with and research on school accountability are still in the early stages, some evidence of its impact is beginning to accumulate. Our data from Chicago (Finnigan & Gross, 2001) and CPRE research in Kentucky and Charlotte-Mecklenburg, North Carolina (Kelley, Odden, Milanowski, & Heneman, 2000), indicate that teachers are working harder in response to the accountability measures and are more focused on externally set student-learning goals. In addition, many systems (e.g., Boston, San Diego, Tennessee, and California) are using school-level data on student outcomes to allocate additional discretionary resources where they appear to be most needed. Some jurisdictions, such as New York City and Baltimore, have even put in place special monetary incentives to attract and retain highly skilled teachers and principals for the lowest performing schools (Westat, 2001).

There is also evidence of an impact on achievement, as measured by standardized tests. In each of the first four years after instituting its school accountability policy, the Chicago schools posted increased scores in both reading and mathematics, though reading scores have begun to level off since 2000 (Chicago Public Schools, 2002). Similarly, Kentucky, California, Texas, Tennessee, and other jurisdictions have claimed that their accountability policies have resulted in higher student achievement. However, some observers question whether increases in test scores really indicate higher levels of student learning or whether later scores have been artificially inflated by concentrated "teaching to the test" and increased familiarity with test questions and format.[27] In Texas and Tennessee, rising scores on the National Assessment of Educational Progress (NAEP) seem to validate similar increases on the state assessments, but in these and in all other cases it is difficult to attribute such increases to school accountability mechanisms.

Schools respond unevenly to outcomes-based accountability policies and this unevenness may be directly tied to internal conditions in schools that make them more or less able to use the information generated by the accountability systems. The CPRE research team led by Richard Elmore and Leslie Siskin, for example, has found that schools that are better positioned in terms of their socioeconomic composition (i.e., higher SES students) and their prior academic performance respond more readily and coherently to the demands of external performance-based accountability systems than those schools less well situated (DeBray, Parson, & Woodworth, 2001; Elmore, 2001). This research suggests that lower performing schools actually lose ground relative to the well-positioned schools once an external accountability system is instituted.

Our research on the lowest performing schools in Chicago extends the CPRE analysis, identifying variations in responses among schools that might all be considered less well positioned — that is, among those at similarly low socioeconomic and achievement levels.[28] The first indication of this variation is a rapid bifurcation in the achievement trends for all elementary schools placed on probation in 1996, despite comparable initial achievement. More specifically, one group of schools — those that came off the probation list by spring of 1998 — posts a significantly sharper increase in scores than those schools that remained on probation after 1998. Multilevel analysis of survey data for this rapidly improving group suggests that they differed significantly from other probation schools along several dimensions of initial school capacity: peer collaboration, teacher-teacher trust, and collective responsibility for student learning (Gwynne & Easton, 2001). Referring to the earlier discussion of organizational complexity, we might surmise that the first two of these dimensions — peer collaboration and teacher-to-teacher trust — reflect stronger patterns of interaction among the organizational agents (teachers in this case). The third dimension — collective responsibility for student learning — suggests that attention and effort in these schools were already directed to a higher degree to student learning and were bolstered by the normative structure of the school — what Elmore and his colleagues call "internal accountability" (DeBray et al., 2001; Elmore, 2001).

That schools with such patterns of interaction and attention would be more successful at adaptation makes sense in light of the earlier discussion of complexity, information, and learning, as these patterns would facilitate the dissemination, selection, and interpretation or information relevant to student learning. Meanwhile, the failure of other schools to show similar improvement and their propensity to stay on probation for as long as five years or more suggests something about the limitations of bureaucratic accountability for catalyzing school improvement in low-capacity schools — that is, in schools lacking the internal accountability structures or knowledge base to generate or use information well. Indeed, our qualitative data on the policy, assistance, and individual school response point to significant limitations of bureaucratic outcomes-based accountability for fostering school improvement.

Limitations of Bureaucratic, Outcomes-Based School Accountability

The earlier discussion of complex adaptive systems suggests that adaptation (improvement) is based on the feedback (information) agents receive from one another and from the environment, on the interpretations and dispersal of this information through patterns of interaction in the organization, and then on the invention, selection, and recombination of strategies to produce improvement along some measure of performance. Our data from Chicago indicate several ways in which bureaucratic outcomes-based accountability may inhibit — or at least fail to promote — widespread organizational adaptation.

Inadequate Information   A central limitation of school accountability in Chicago and elsewhere is that the nature and quality of the information produced and dispensed by the system are simply inadequate for effective organizational adaptation and learning. Three aspects of this inadequacy stand out.

The first limitation of the information dispensed in an outcomes-based school accountability system concerns the validity of the outcome measure on which improvement is to be based. Much of the criticism of Chicago's model of school accountability has centered on the use of a norm-referenced basic skills test that is not fully aligned with either the district or the state standards, that emphasizes fragmented and discrete skill acquisition, and that lacks validation for the types of decisions (e.g., probation and grade retention) made on the basis of its results. Validity with respect to measurement of the goals (e.g., standards) is a critical aspect of an assessment's quality: if the assessment does not measure what it purports to measure, it could actually draw attention away from the goals of the system rather than toward them. This potential problem is compounded in a situation like that in Chicago, where the use of a single measure and the attachment of consequences to that measure (see below) intensifies attention to the measure rather than to the larger goal of increased student learning. In this regard, it is important to note that the Iowa Test of Basic Skills has not been validated for the purpose of either school or student accountability.

A second limitation of Chicago's and most other school accountability systems concerns the periodicity and specificity (grain size) of the information provided by the outcome measure.[29] On the one hand, a test given once a year that reports a general indication of the content and skills that students have and have not mastered can be extremely valuable for identifying schools and subject areas that may need additional attention, resources, or, possibly, changes in strategies. An important contribution of school accountability systems in places like Chicago and Maryland, for example, is that they have directed the spotlight at failing parts of the system that can then be given additional assistance.[30] However, while such information is useful at these higher levels of aggregation, its potential for directly improving strategies in the classroom is limited. Such assessments are usually administered in the spring to measure student learning during the academic year, but the results are not available in time for the relevant teacher to alter instruction in response to the test. Even if the scores were available earlier in the year, the infrequency and lack of specificity of results is still a problem.

In short, the measure of outcomes through such a test is simply too distant from the complexities of instructional inputs for the teacher to make reasonable attributions of causality. Superstitious learning is common under such circumstances (Levitt & March, 1988). For this reason, some schools supplement the annual testing with more regular and focused assessments aligned with the ITBS. These periodic tests can give teachers more information on outcomes, though they may also underscore concerns about teaching to the test.

A third limitation of the quality of the information is an extension of the second, and concerns the appropriate balance of information about outcomes and information about processes. The implication is that the actor — whether that actor is an individual or an organization — must have valid and reliable information on both outcomes and processes. Yet, school accountability systems focus almost exclusively on outcomes, producing little in the way of reliable information on instruction or organizational practices. Some authors have argued that the production of such process-based information at aggregated levels would introduce further measurement problems and unduly constrain practice.[31] That the external accountability system does not generate information on practice might not be a problem if such information were available at the school level. Substantial research suggests that when teachers share information about instruction as well as student learning, they are better able to adapt their practice to the needs and progress of their students.[32] However, the egg-crate structure of U.S. schools impedes such adaptation; information on instructional strategies and processes is held privately by teachers and only rarely shared across the school as the basis for future learning (Lortie, 1975; McLaughlin & Talbert, 2001). Our research in Chicago suggests that bureaucratic school accountability policies are insufficient to establish the patterns of interaction that might foster more effective information sharing in low-capacity schools.

Patterns of Interaction   Indeed, if CPS is any indication, bureaucratic school accountability mechanisms serve to maintain interaction patterns that foster compliance and hierarchy over system learning. Our data reveal a fairly unidirectional (top-down) flow of information throughout the system. For example, rather than being op-portunities for collective sharing of information and knowledge, meetings between assistance providers and central office staff and between principals and district liaison personnel were reportedly occasions in which schools and those working with them were simply the recipients of information and mandates rather than sources of valu-able information in their own right. When information did flow the other way (from schools and those working with them up into the system), it focused on whether peo-ple were carrying out prescribed tasks — that is, whether external partners were pro-viding agreed-upon services, whether schools were implementing specifics of school plans, and whether teachers were understanding and using the tools and techniques disseminated by the external partners (Finnigan, O'Day, & Wakelyn, 2001).

Even those instances in which one might expect more collective problem-solving — such as in the school improvement planning process — more often than not be-came symbolic exercises in responding to formulaic requirements of the district office rather than thoughtful and inclusive learning experiences for the staff.[33] The plan-ning template was handed down from the Office of Accountability and schools com-plied, with emphasis on compliance over self-reflection being noticeably stronger in the least improving, lowest capacity schools.[34] What was perhaps most distressing was that this transmission model of information flow also characterized the profes-sional development provided by the external partners, the bulk of which consisted of traditional short workshops rather than intensive inquiry-based explorations of either content or instructional practice (Finnigan et al., 2001).

The end result is that much of the response we saw in schools involved their react-ing to directions imposed from above and outside the school rather than reflecting on internal practices. This response is perhaps unsurprising. Hierarchical control and information dissemination are characteristic of large bureaucracies like CPS, and well-established, internalized organizational codes are difficult to change (March, 1991). Moreover, the "get tough" theory of action and the urban politics underlying the school probation policy could be expected to exacerbate these tendencies. By de-fining the problem as low expectations and a lack of effort on the part of school staff, the forces that come from higher in the system and outside the schools seek to push those inside to work harder. The accompanying incentives only reinforce control and enforcement over system learning.

Maladaptive Incentive Structures   While much of the benefit of current school ac-countability schemes is supposed to be that they provide incentives to motivate im-provement, we found that the incentive structures in Chicago actually exacerbated the problem of motivation in some low-performing, low-capacity schools.

The emphasis on negative incentives (stigma of probation, threat of reconstitu-tion) tied to a single measure (ITBS) appears to have resulted in two tendencies that work against long-term improvement. First, attention in these schools became fo-cused not so much on student learning per se, but on getting off or staying off proba-tion. This goal essentially places adult desires (to remove the professional stigma and avoid administrative scrutiny) over the needs of students (Wei & Evans, 2001). Second, to achieve this goal, probation schools exhibited an emphasis on strategies to produce immediate increases in test scores, often to the neglect of longer-term success. The combination of these tendencies produced a number of dysfunctional practices.

Most common was the emphasis on test preparation in the form of intensive drill and practice to raise student scores. Some schools even redesigned their curriculum not only to reflect the general skills on the ITBS but to align the proportion of time allotted in the curriculum to a given discrete skill with the proportion of test items measuring that skill. In such cases, the test specifications became the curriculum specifications as well. Another common practice was to triage assistance (mostly test preparation) to students scoring near grade-level cutoffs in the hope that, by raising these students' scores slightly, the school could escape probation. These and similar practices suggest the allocation of resources to achieve adult ends (e.g., getting off probation), rather than to meet the greatest student needs.

Such patterns, which have been noted in prior research on high-stakes testing in education, are not uncommon in organizations in crisis.[35] A focused search for short-term strategies to satisfy a specific target is typical when an organization's performance falls below its aspirations or goals (March, 1994; Simon, 1986). When low performance is combined with negative incentives, including a threat to the organization's position or survival (as is the case of school probation), the potential for maladaptive response increases.

A comprehensive review of research on organizational response to threat (Staw, Sanderlands, & Dutton, 1981) uncovered two dominant and often maladaptive patterns, both of which are relevant to the earlier discussion of organizational learning. First, rather than expanding their use of information to find solutions to the problem, threatened organizations and individuals actually restrict their information processing, relying instead on previously held internal hypotheses and expectations. Exacerbated by stress, this reliance produces a rigidity of action rather than an expansion of strategies and adaptation. A second pattern associated with the presence of a threat is centralization of authority, which in the case of schools serves to further enhance the bureaucratic, control-oriented patterns of interaction mentioned earlier (Staw et al., 1981). Both patterns were observed in low-performing schools in Chicago. We can expect individual and system learning to be constrained under these conditions, as well as innovation and examination of existing practice and assumptions.[36]

A second limitation of the incentive structures is the unbalanced reliance on collective incentives. This a problem raised at the beginning of this article regarding the relationship between individual action and collective accountability. With a focus on schoolwide consequences, the policy offers few incentives for individuals to improve their practice. Individual teacher evaluation is not well aligned with either outcome measures or standards of practice likely to produce those outcomes. In many schools there is little accountability for individual teachers at all, and in others, teachers receive little recognition for improving their practice. One revealing example occurred at one of our case study schools in which a teacher who was working hard to improve practice was repeatedly told by her principal that she could not get an "excellent" rating because "if we had excellent teachers, this school would not be on probation." In other words, until the school as a whole was removed from probation, this teacher could not expect any reward for her individual efforts, no matter what the actual quality of her work. The effect of this proclamation was a sharp decrease in this teacher's motivation and commitment to the school. While we could attribute this result to the actions of a single principal, what becomes clear is that the policy relies on the ability of the principal (or others in the school community) to motivate the individuals on the school's staff. Where the principal is unable to provide such motivation (often the case in low-performing schools), the effect of the policy on individual teachers is likely to be weak, or even negative. Alternatively, where the principal is an effective motivator or where the connections among individuals are mutually reinforcing, the lack of individual incentives may be mitigated by the strong identification of individuals with the group. This may help to explain why probation schools with higher levels of teacher-to-teacher trust, peer collaboration, and collective responsibility improved more rapidly than others in our Chicago study (Gwynne & Easton, 2001). Perhaps other incentives are at work in these schools to motivate individual behavior.[37]

Weak Resource Allocation and Knowledge Development Strategies   As stated earlier, one of the most promising aspects of outcomes-based school accountability is the use of information to direct attention and resources where they are most needed. In Chicago, this reallocation mainly took the form of external assistance to low-performing schools. Our data indicate, however, how the potential effect of this substantial reallocation of resources was mitigated by the low intensity and lack of focus of most of the support actually provided to schools. For example, external partners[38] on average spent only one or two person-days per week in the schools, and with few exceptions their work provided neither a consistent and coherent focus on literacy instruction (the target of the policy) nor a clear strategy for organizational change (Finnigan et al., 2001). The limitations of the assistance may be attributed in part to problems of implementation, such as the weak quality control in the selection of the external partner candidates. In addition, however, the weak specification of the policy with regard to the content or goals of the assistance gave little guidance to either the schools or the support providers themselves about where to concentrate their energies. Such weak specification is common in school accountability policies in other jurisdictions as well. It derives on the one hand from a desire to respond to internal school context and on the other from the policy's emphasis on student outcomes to the neglect of information — or a theory of action — about instruction. The resulting diffuseness of the assistance, however, does little to highlight or solve problems of attribution discussed earlier. Moreover, the policy neglect of other inputs — such as reallocation of human or other resources — also weakens the potential impact.

Summary

What does this discussion of the CPS experience add up to in light of the framework and central problems of school accountability outlined earlier? On the one hand, school accountability policies like those in Chicago have clearly helped focus attention throughout the system on student outcomes and have provided data that can be used for targeting resources and assistance where they are most needed — particularly in low-performing schools. On the other hand, this outcomes-based school accountability approach suffers from a number of inherent weaknesses that make it, as it is currently construed, unlikely to effect the deep changes necessary for long-term improvement, particularly in low-performing, low-capacity schools. Four weaknesses stand out:

1. The problems of validity, periodicity, and specificity in the outcome measures, coupled with inattention to information on instructional practice, make attribution and thus learning at the school or individual teacher level difficult.
2. Most school accountability systems still operate from a bureaucratic control model and thus fail to create the interaction patterns and normative structures within schools that encourage sustained learning and adaptation. Most low-performing schools lack such patterns and structures.
3. Reliance on negative incentives undermines innovation and risk-taking in threatened schools and diverts attention to organizational survival rather than student learning. Moreover, most current incentive structures fail to foster individual motivation or to reward learning and changes in practice that might lead to sustained improvement.
4. Finally, the reallocation of assistance and resources for increasing the capacity of low-performing schools is generally inadequate and weakly specified. Unfocused assistance based on transmission models of learning does little to build the knowledge base needed for valid interpretation of information produced by the system.

While some of these shortcomings are exacerbated by poor implementation, they derive from fundamental assumptions inherent in the design of current school accountability systems. Current approaches have not solved any of the three problems outlined at the beginning of this article: the relationship between collective accountability and individual action; the tension between external and internal sources of control; and the production, spread, and use of information that can help solve problems of attribution caused by the complexity of school organizations. Thus, reliance on bureaucratic forms of accountability, even with better implementation, is unlikely to lead to the kind of improvement desired.

Is there an alternative?

PROFESSIONAL ACCOUNTABILITY: ALTERNATIVE OR ADDITION?

Perhaps the most commonly posed alternative to bureaucratic or administrative accountability in education is that of professional accountability (Adams & Kirst, 1999; Darling-Hammond & Ascher, 1991; O'Reilly, 1996). Professional accountability is rooted in the assumption that teaching is too complex an activity to be governed by bureaucratically defined rules and routines. Rather, like other professions, effective teaching rests on professionals acquiring specialized knowledge and skills and being able to apply such knowledge and skills to the specific contexts in which they work. In mature professions, the requisite knowledge is articulated in professionally determined standards of practice, and professional accountability involves members of those professions assuming responsibility for the definition and enforcement of those standards.

In education, the focus of professional accountability might be described as three-fold. First, it is centered on the process of instruction — that is, on the work of teachers as they interact with students around instructional content (Cohen & Ball, 1999; McLaughlin & Talbert, 2001). Professional accountability thus concerns the performance of adults in the system at least as much as the performance of students.[39] Second, much of the focus of professional accountability concerns ensuring that educators acquire and apply the knowledge and skills needed for effective practice. Knowledge development is front and center. Third, professional accountability involves the norms of professional interchange. These norms include placing the needs of the client (students) at the center of professional work, collaborating with other professionals to address those needs and ensure the maintenance of standards of practice, and committing to the improvement of practice as part and parcel of professional responsibility.

At the system level, mechanisms of professional accountability center on teacher preparation, teacher licensure, and peer review. At the school level, professional accountability rests both on individual educators assuming responsibility for following standards of practice and on their professional interaction with colleagues and clients. Mentoring, collaboration, and collective problem-solving in response to student needs and some form of peer review to ensure quality of practice are all aspects of school-site professional accountability. Advocates for professionally based forms of accountability argue that this approach holds the most promise for the improvement of teaching and, by extension, for the improvement of student learning.

The Promise and Limitations of Professional Accountability

The earlier discussion of complexity and organizational adaptation lends some theoretical support for the claims of advocates of professionalism. In particular, professional accountability at the school site would seem to address problems of attribution and motivation more productively than what we have seen from bureaucratically based models.

With respect to the use of information for effective attribution, three aspects of professional accountability seem most pertinent. First, professionalism draws attention both to instructional practice (agents' strategies) and to teachers' collective responsibility for student learning (outcomes). Second, norms of collaboration around instruction enhance patterns of interaction at the school site that allow for the generation and spread of information about both practice and outcomes and the dissemination of effective strategies based on analysis of that information (i.e., data-driven change). This information is naturally more fine-grained and immediate than that accumulated at higher levels of aggregation, and thus the links between specific strategies and their effects are more easily discerned. This is in part because the articulation of both outcome targets and of standards of practice allows for the testing of hypotheses about those links, particularly where experience or results run contrary to expectations (Axelrod & Cohen, 2000; Sitkin, 1992). Finally, more successful attribution is also likely because of the emphasis on professional knowledge and skills, which lay the groundwork for meaningful interpretations of the information available and more meaningful sharing of information with others. Standards of practice, constructed generally across the profession and more particularly within the professional community of the school, provide the cognitive maps for this process of meaning creation (Huber, 1991).

In addition to addressing problems of attribution, professional accountability expands the incentives for improvement, with particular emphasis on the intrinsic motivators that bring teachers into teaching in the first place, a commitment to students (clients) and an identity as an educator (O'Day, 1996). Scott (1998) has delineated three types of incentives in organizations: material incentives such as monetary rewards and job promotion or loss; community/solidarity incentives based on an identity as a member of a community or profession and a desire to maintain or gain position in that community; and purposive incentives, for example, satisfaction from achieving a valued goal such as a learning objective for students. Our work in schools on probation in Chicago suggests that school accountability policies often fail to tap into solidarity and intrinsic purposive incentives, focusing instead on the threat of material sanctions such as reassignment or job loss or on rewards (Finnigan & Gross, 2001). In contrast, research on professional communities of practice note the motivational aspects of membership in those communities and of normative structures that focus on student learning (goal attainment) and professional identity (Darling-Hammond, 1996; McLaughlin & Talbert, 2001).

Beyond the theoretical appeal of professional accountability, a growing body of empirical evidence points to aspects of professionalism as important components of school improvement. Lee and Smith (1996), for example, find a significant positive relationship between student achievement gains and teachers' collective responsibility for students' academic success in high school.[40] Meanwhile, various researchers have pointed to the positive impact on instruction and student achievement of teacher interaction and collaboration in school-based professional communities (Little, 1990; McLaughlin & Talbert, 1993, 2001; Newmann & Wehlage, 1995). Community School District 2 in New York City provides proof of the deep impact professional culture and professional development can have as a strategy for improvement and system management (Elmore, 1997). Finally, as mentioned previously, there is some recent evidence that professionally based aspects of internal school accountability and capacity are essential for a school's ability to respond effectively to outcomes-based accountability (DeBray et al., 2001; Elmore, 2001) and can help explain the differential gains among schools that are targets of accountability policies (Gwynne & Easton, 2001).

Limitations of Professional Accountability

Despite its promise, however, reliance on professional accountability alone cannot ensure that all students' needs are addressed. The most obvious limitation of such a strategy is the overall weakness of professionalism and professional accountability throughout U.S. education. Most U.S. schools are atomized structures in which responsibility rests with the individual educator rather than with the collective body or the profession as a whole (Abelmann & Elmore, 1999; Lortie, 1975). Mentoring and collaboration are simply too rare to ensure the information sharing necessary for ongoing organizational learning. In addition, teachers' knowledge and skills are not what they need to be, especially in light of more challenging goals for *all* students, and professional standards of practice are only beginning to be defined and enforced.[41] Given this situation, U.S. public school systems may well need external incentives and administrative assistance to stimulate the development of professional accountability and attention to learning objectives for all students.

A second limitation of professionalism concerns the problem of equity. Failure of professionalism is most notable in schools serving disenfranchised groups, especially schools in inner cities with large proportions of low-income students and students of color. Many of these schools have been allowed to languish for years, during which time the profession has not stepped forth to fight for the needs of these students. External administrative accountability is needed to address this failure of professionalism and help ensure equal opportunity.

Tied to the equity limitations of professionalism is the fact that outcomes-based school accountability is able to address some systemic purposes and needs more readily than professional accountability alone. For example, at more aggregated levels of the system, performance reporting and other outcomes-based accountability tools provide a useful mechanism for managing the resources necessary for instruction and school improvement. Low performance can be a marker indicating areas of greatest need. In addition, monitoring and reporting of outcomes are important avenues for informing the public about the status of the system and the degree to which it is addressing the needs of and providing opportunities to all students. This is particularly true in the United States, where neither the public nor its representatives are ready to fully trust professional educators (Cohen & Spillane, 1993).

A BETTER WAY: COMBINING THE BUREAUCRATIC AND THE PROFESSIONAL

A combination of professional and administrative/bureaucratic school accountability may be most useful to create an environment that would foster long-term school improvement. Such combinations are common in other professions. In medicine, for example, physicians establish and enforce standards of medical practice but hospitals, insurance companies, and sometimes governments pay attention to outcome (as well as process[42]) data to identify and respond to breakdowns and problems in the distribution and management of medical resources.

Similarly, some educational jurisdictions are experimenting with combinations of outcomes-based administrative accountability to identify areas of low performance and professionally based interventions and accountability to foster school adaptation to address these problems. One such example is the recently formed CEO District in Baltimore, Maryland. Maryland established outcome targets based on the Maryland

Student Performance Assessment Program, and identifies schools that are the farthest from and declining in relation to those targets. Such schools are deemed "reconstitution eligible." The preponderance of reconstitution eligible schools in Baltimore City was one factor contributing to a change in governance for the district, to a district-state partnership, and to additional funding being directed to the district (reallocation of resources based on outcomes).[43] Once in place, the new leadership of the district collected a group of the lowest performing schools into a special configuration, the CEO District, and turned to the local education fund (LEF) to assist these schools in becoming effective learning organizations.[44]

The resulting intervention incorporates many of the aspects of teacher professionalism discussed above, as well as the characteristics of adaptive organizations. These include a focus on literacy for teacher and student work and for generating and sharing information about that work; ongoing assessments through Running Records and regular evaluation of student work to provide frequent, fine-grained information about learning outcomes; team structures like regular grade-level meetings to foster teacher interaction, sharing of strategies, and collective responsibility; and ongoing professional development designed to build a "culture of shared learning" (Fund for Educational Excellence, 2001). Professional development, which is central to the intervention in the CEO District, is site based, focuses on literacy standards, and incorporates teachers' professional interchange through collective study, interclass visitations, and common planning. A client-centered focus, which is also central to notions of professionalism, is manifested throughout these endeavors, but especially in the identification of, targeted assistance to, and monitoring of all students reading below grade level. Finally, the CEO District intervention fosters a full range of incentives, from material rewards for principals and teachers for taking on the challenge of and showing progress in these schools to solidarity incentives derived from membership in a profession, and, finally, to the intrinsic purposive rewards of success with students.[45]

An interesting characteristic of this and several similar approaches is the apparent division of labor between the generation and use of information at the state level, which is following a more administrative/bureaucratic model, and that at the local level, which has a strong infusion of professionalism.[46] This division of labor suggests a necessary distinction in the balance of accountability approaches depending on the level of aggregation, and thus on the distance from or closeness to the point of instruction and school change. What seems critical here is that the bureaucratic accountability mechanisms from the more aggregated levels of the system not get in the way of the development of professional norms, structures, and standards at the school site.

The Baltimore CEO District and similar models represent only one approach to combining professional and bureaucratic accountability. What is important to note is the synergistic interplay of professional and bureaucratic accountability. On the one hand, outcomes-based targets for schools and performance reporting are critical for identifying problem areas, for allocating of resources to address those problems, and for monitoring progress. But the real action at the school site and across school sites is on developing professional knowledge through focused assistance on instruction, professional norms, and the professional patterns of interaction necessary for establishing the basis for ongoing organizational adaptation. This combination allows for a more thorough and balanced incorporation of all aspects of the accountability framework discussed earlier. It generates and draws attention to information relevant to teaching and learning (i.e., to both adult and student performance); it motivates individuals and units through intrinsic as well as extrinsic incentives to attend and to use that information; it builds the knowledge base for valid interpretations of information; and it allocates resources where they are most needed.

The combination also addresses the three underlying problems and tension in school accountability described at the beginning of this article. Recall that the first of these problems concerned the interplay between collective accountability for the school unit and the requisite change in behavior of the individuals within that unit. The addition of professional accountability at the school site strengthens the links between individual teachers and their schools by fostering interaction around common work, a sense of shared purpose, and identity as members of the school community. These ties increase individual motivation to act in accordance with the community's collectively defined endeavor. Moreover, the deprivatization of practice through sharing of student work and teacher strategies, as well as interclass visitations, provides a mechanism for developing and enforcing common standards of practice.

This latter point also has implications for the second problem identified earlier, the relationship between external and internal mechanisms of control. Attempts to control individual and group behavior by means of external rules and policies are notorious for their inevitable failure, especially in situations where tasks and environments are complex and ambiguous.[47] Resistance and superficial compliance are the common responses. In the case of education, compliance with externally produced rules can even be counterproductive, as it does not allow for the flexible application of professional knowledge to specific contexts and students. In contrast, the strong professional norms generated by the infusion of professional accountability, especially collective responsibility for student learning, become potential resources and mechanisms for orienting the entire school community toward the higher levels of student performance sought by reformers and the general public.

Finally, with respect to the third problem — the generation, flow, and use of information for organizational learning and adaptation — the combination of professional and outcomes-based school accountability holds considerable promise. Drawing on the discussion of complexity theory and the examples described above, we might posit several principles of information generation and use for accountability purposes. The first of these, which is the subject of considerable scholarship and debate, is that information on performance must be valid and accurate and must reflect the goals of teaching and learning.[48] This principle applies to all forms of accountability, regardless of target or mechanism.

With respect to school accountability and improvement, four additional principles derive from our discussion here. First, for individuals and systems to evaluate performance, make appropriate attributions, and adapt their strategies, information must be available both on student performance (achievement) and on adult performance (instructional and other relevant strategies). Second, the grain size and periodicity of the information feedback should match the level and purposes of its use. For the improvement of instructional practice at the school and classroom level, fine-grained and frequent information, including instructionally integrated diagnostic assessments of student learning and feedback on instructional practice tied to that learning, provides the basis for professional reflection. Meanwhile, at higher levels of the system, more aggregate and less frequent information feedback provides a sufficient basis for allocating resources and evaluating and refining policies. Third, because information in complex systems derives from interaction, accountability systems should foster connections within and across units to allow access to and reflection on information relevant to teaching and learning. And, finally, accountability systems must pay particular attention to developing the knowledge base necessary for valid interpretation of the information so generated.

A thoughtful combination of outcomes-based school accountability and professional accountability provides the means of addressing all these information needs and thus for fostering the data driven improvement sought by many system reformers and policymakers. Whether such a thoughtful combination is likely to come about, however, particularly in light of the highly prescriptive and stringent testing and accountability provisions of the No Child Left Behind Act, is another matter.

NOTES

1. Work for this paper was supported in part by Office of Educational Research and Improvement (Grant No. R308A60003) to the Consortium for Policy Research in Education and by two grants from the Spencer Foundation (one to the Wisconsin Center for Educational Research for the study of school probation in Chicago elementary schools and the other to Marshall S. Smith to explore implementation issues in standards-based reform). All findings, opinions, and conclusions expressed in this paper are those of the author and do not necessarily reflect the views of any of the funders.

2. The Consortium for Policy Research in Education unites five leading research institutions — the University of Pennsylvania, Harvard University, Stanford University, the University of Michigan, and the University of Wisconsin–Madison — in collaborative efforts to improve educational systems and student learning through research on educational reform, policy, and finance.

3. The No Child Left Behind Act (NCLB), the most recent reauthorization of the Elementary and Secondary Education Act (ESEA), requires annual testing of all students in grades three through eight, a twelve-year timeline to achieve universal proficiency in reading and mathematics, identification of low-performing schools based on aggregated and disaggregated test scores, and administration of severe consequences (including public school choice) for low-performing schools that fail to improve.

4. Chicago's school accountability policy is explained in greater detail in the section on bureaucratic accountability and in Note 22. In brief, the Chicago system identifies low-performing schools for "probation" based on student test results and metes out both assistance and sanctions to spur improvement in those schools. This article draws on data from a three-year study of school probation policies and practices in Chicago elementary schools.

5. While this article focuses on the explicit organizational improvement goals of school accountability, these policies have symbolic and political purposes as well. For a fuller discussion of some of the politics underlying Chicago's school probation policies, see Bennett (2001).

6. For a range of implementation discussions over the past three decades, see, for example, Berman and McLaughlin (1974), Goertz, Floden, and O'Day (1995), McLaughlin (1987), Spillane (2000), and Weatherly and Lipsky (1977).

7. See, for example, DeBray, Parson, and Woodworth (2001), Elmore (2001), McLaughlin and Talbert (1993), or Newmann and Wehlage (1995) for a discussion of the power of internal norms.

8. For popular accounts of complexity theory in the natural and social sciences, see Kauffman (1995), Lewin (1992), and Waldrop (1992).

9. See also McLaughlin and Talbert (1993) and Cohen (1990).

10. Interaction patterns among agents within the system are thus critical in understanding how information from the outside becomes available (or not) and used (or not) by its members for learning.

11. "Superstitious learning occurs when the subjective experience of learning is compelling but the connections between actions and outcomes are misspecified" (Levitt & March, 1988, p. 325).

12. It is important to note that organizational inertia is enhanced as the web of supporting relationships grows, creating codependencies among units of the organization and between it and external systems. For a discussion of how initial advantage and increasing returns serves to lock in certain solutions and strategies, see Arthur (1989) or Marion (1999).

13. The term *Christmas tree school* is often used to indicate a school that adds on multiple uncoordinated and inconsistent programs, much as a Christmas tree displays a mélange of multicolored and decorative ornaments.

14. Coupling, in organizations literature, refers to the connections and interdependence of elements of a system. According to Weick (1976), loosely "coupled events are responsive [to one another], *but* each event also preserves its own identity and some evidence of its physical or logical separateness . . . and their attachment may be circumscribed, infrequent, weak in its mutual effects, unimportant, and/or slow to respond. . . . Loose coupling also carries connotations of impermanence, dissolvability, and tacitness, all of which are potentially crucial properties of the 'glue' that holds organizations together" (p. 3).

15. Axelrod and Cohen (1999) identify three types of attribution mistakes: crediting or blaming a part when a larger ensemble of forces is responsible for a given outcome; crediting or blaming a particular ensemble of factors when a different ensemble is actually responsible; and failing to appreciate the role of context — that is, believing that what was successful in one context may be equally successful in another. Each type of mistake is common in education at every level of the system.

16. An example of such incentives would be salary increases given to teachers for taking additional course credits whether or not such coursework has any bearing on school improvement plans and strategies, any effect on teachers' actual instructional knowledge, or any impact on student performance.

17. In addition to school accountability, student accountability — in which consequences for individual students such as graduation or grade promotion are based on standardized measures of academic performance — has become an increasingly prevalent aspect of standards-based reform in the past several years. School accountability remains the lynchpin in most jurisdictions, however, as well as in the No Child Left Behind Act.

18. In the case of federal policies (e.g., Title I), *to whom* may also refer indirectly to the federal government, but still by way of the state and local education agencies (SEAs and LEAs). Similarly, where authority for a given policy derives from state law (legal accountability) and the courts are the ultimate arbiter, administration remains the responsibility of the superordinate levels of the educational bureaucracy to whom the schools are most directly accountable. From the perspective of the schools, then, these cases are almost indistinguishable from other examples of bureaucratic accountability.

19. *Note:* In this article, the terms *bureaucratic accountability, outcomes-based accountability,* and *outcomes-based bureaucratic accountability* will be used interchangeably with school accountability. This discussion excludes choice systems in which schools are held accountable directly to parents through the market.

20. It may be important here to note that the designation "outcomes-based bureaucratic accountability" differs somewhat from the terms used in prior typologies — in large part because it incorporates two somewhat different approaches to categorizing accountability systems. Adams and Kirst (1999) focus their typology on the differences in *who* is accountable *to whom.* According to these authors, "Bureaucratic accountability ensures that the preferences and decisions of organizational leaders govern the work of employees throughout the organization. It is based on the relationship between superiors and subordinates and operates through a system of supervisory control characterized by hierarchical structure, standard operating procedures, and rewards and punishments" (p. 467). Darling-Hammond (1990) agrees, underscoring the importance of standardized rules and procedures for practice, established at the top of the system and followed by teachers and others in schools. "New accountability" models do not entirely fit this description, however, as they loosen the standardization of *practice,* replacing it with standardization of *outcomes* (or progress toward the outcomes). O'Reilly (1996) tries to incorporate this distinction by developing a typology based on the operational assumptions that various approaches to accountability make in order to effect systemic change. She thus identifies four operational "theories" of accountability: performance reporting, changes in governance, market-based approaches, and professional accountability. Performance reporting comes closest to the Chicago Public Schools and similar models in that "performance reporting assumes that the collection and reporting of information on student academic performance can be used to stimulate strategies for improving teaching and learning" (p. 5). However, O'Reilly's category falls short in two respects. First, it overlaps with and is integral to other categories in the typology, confounding its interpretation. Second, it does not distinguish between performance and outcomes. While test scores may be a direct indicator of *student* performance, they are only an indirect indicator of *adult* performance. Campbell and his colleagues underscore the importance of distinguishing between performance (behavior) and the results (outcomes) of that performance if there is to be any hope of making valid attributions between the two (Campbell, McCloy, Oppler, & Sager, 1993). This distinction becomes important in understanding the limitations of current models of school accountability to foster improved instruction. It is for this reason that I have chosen the term *outcomes-based* bureaucratic accountability.

21. The ITBS is an example of the type of commercially produced, norm-referenced, multiple-choice, timed assessment used in many jurisdictions for accountability, monitoring, and placement purposes.

22. All probation schools are required to develop a corrective action/school improvement plan and literacy plan to organize their improvement efforts. These plans are reviewed at the central office, and their implementation is monitored by the probation manager assigned to the school. Assistance comes in the form of additional resources for external support providers called external partners. If the necessary improvement in test scores is not manifest at the end of a vaguely specified number of years, school personnel may be replaced en masse (reconstitution) or individually through a more extended peer review process (reengineering). Such consequences, however, have rarely been administered.

23. The Comprehensive School Reform Demonstration (CSRD) Program, is a federal effort encouraging the adoption of research-based, whole school reform models, especially in Title I schools identified as being in need of improvement.

24. This does not include the resources allocated for remedial summer or after school classes or for practice and testing materials. See Finnigan, O'Day, and Wakelyn (2001) for a fuller discussion of the assistance program.

25. The most recent reauthorization of ESEA, the No Child Left Behind Act of 2001, tightens and extends these requirements and the consequences for continued low performance (see Note 3).

26. An example is California's Public School Accountability Act of 1999, which metes out monetary awards to all schools in the state (both high and low performers) that reach their annual improvement targets on the state's Academic Performance Index (API).

27. For varying perspectives of the impact of these accountability systems, see Grissmer, Flanagan, Kawata, and Williamson (2000), Haney (2000), Klein, Hamilton, McCaffrey, and Stecher (2000), and Koretz and Barron (1998).

28. This research was conducted by a team of researchers from the University of Wisconsin–Madison and the Consortium on Chicago School Research and was sponsored by the Spencer Foundation and the Office of Educational Research and Improvement.

29. By periodicity I mean the frequency and regularity of information on student learning generated by the system. Specificity refers to the degree of detail of the information. For example, information on student knowledge regarding particular decoding skills (like facility with beginning or ending consonants) is more specific than would be a single test score covering all aspects of decoding, let alone a single score for reading.

30. The No Child Left Behind Act of 2001 promises to substantially alter the specifics of many existing school accountability systems — for example, the nature of the assessments or the timeframe for improvement — but the general intent (to implement a system that identifies lower performing units for intervention) remains.

31. See, for example, *The Debate on Opportunity to Learn Standards: Supporting Works* (National Governors' Association, 1993) or the "Report of the National Academy of Education Panel on Standards-Based Education" (McLaughlin & Shepard, 1995).

32. See, for example, the literature on the role of professional community (e.g., McLaughlin & Talbert, 1993, 2001; Newmann & Wehlage, 1995) and on information sharing in high-performing schools (Darling-Hammond, 1996; Mohrman & Lawler, 1996).

33. This conclusion derives primarily from our observations and interviews regarding the planning process in our ten case study schools but is augmented by additional analysis of the planning documents and processes in a slightly larger and more diverse group of schools. See Gross, Wei, and O'Day (2002) for further discussion of this pattern.

34. Some exceptions exist, of course, with the more self-reflective school communities generally showing the greater gains in performance (Gross, et al., 2002).

35. See, for example, Firestone and Mayrowetz (2000), Nolen, Haladaya, and Haas (1992), and Smith and Rottenberg (1991).

36. These tendencies might be mitigated if a policy included positive incentives (rewards) for learning and for improvements in instructional practice. While some systems do include rewards, these are tied to improvements in outcomes, not practice or learning. Observers often note the need for interim indicators of organizational practice and a capacity to be included in the accountability structures, but they rarely are.

37. For a discussion of these other incentives, see, for example, Mohrman and Lawler (1996) and Darling-Hammond (1996).

38. External partners are the official external support providers approved and funded through the school probation policy (see Note 22).

39. See Campbell et al. (1993) for the importance of the distinction between performance and outcomes.

40. See also Porter and Brophy (1988).

41. The work of the National Board for Professional Teaching Standards (NBPTS), the Interstate New Teacher Assessment and Support Consortium (INTASC), and the National Council for Accreditation of Teacher Education (NCATE) are promising but still beginning efforts in this regard.

42. An example of process data in the medical field might be the number of patients seen in a day or the average length of hospital stay, indicators with which health maintenance organizations and insurance companies have become noticeably concerned in recent years.

43. The partnership between the Baltimore City Public School System (BCPSS) and the Maryland State Department of Education (MSDE) was established by Maryland State Senate Bill 795 in

1997 and is a unique arrangement in educational governance. The partnership decoupled BCPSS from control of Baltimore's city government and established a new Board of School Commissioners that was jointly appointed by the mayor and the governor. It also set in place certain steps for the new board to take in its reform efforts and provided additional monies to support implementation of those steps. For a description and evaluation of the partnership, see Westat (2001).

44. Local education funds (LEFs) are community-based organizations and coalitions centered on improving public schools and student achievement through community involvement in specific locales. The Baltimore LEF, the Fund for Educational Excellence, is partnering with BCPSS in the implementation of Achievement First, a whole-school standards-based reform effort focused on improving literacy instruction through professional development of teachers and principals. See Fund for Educational Excellence (2001) and Westat (2001).

45. Teachers, for example, receive an 11 percent supplement to their base salary and seven days of paid professional development at the beginning of the school year. See Kim (2001).

46. Other jurisdictions are also experimenting with combinations of professional and bureaucratic accountability, each of which focuses substantially on intense site-based professional development and efforts to develop professional patterns of interaction and collegiality. These include the Boston Public Schools, Community School District 2 and the Chancellor's District in New York City, and the San Diego City Schools, among others.

47. To paraphrase McLaughlin (1988), you can't mandate what matters.

48. See, for example, Linn (2001, 1997).

REFERENCES

Abelman, C., & Elmore, R. (1999). *When accountability knocks, will anyone answer?* (CPRE Research Report Series RR-42). Philadelphia: Consortium for Policy Research in Education.

Adams, J. E., & Kirst, M. (1999). New demands for educational accountability: Striving for results in an era of excellence. In J. Murphey & K. S. Louis (Eds.), *Handbook of research in educational administration* (2nd ed., pp. 463–489). San Francisco: Jossey-Bass.

Arthur, W. B. (1989). The economy and complexity. In D. L. Stein (Ed.), *Lectures in the sciences of complexity* (pp. 713–740). Redwood City, CA: Addison-Wesley.

Axelrod, R., & Cohen, M. D. (1999). *Harnessing complexity: Organizational implications of a scientific frontier.* New York: Free Press.

Bennett, A. (2001, April). *The history, politics and theory of action of the Chicago probation policy.* Paper presented at the annual meeting of the American Educational Research Association, Seattle.

Berman, P., & McLaughlin, M. (1978). *Federal programs supporting educational change: Vol. VII. Factors affecting implementation and continuation.* Santa Monica, CA: RAND.

Campbell, J. P., McCloy, R. A., Oppler, S. H., & Sager, C. E. (1993). A theory of performance. In N. Schmitt, W. C. Borman, & Associates (Eds.), *Personnel selection in organizations* (pp. 35–70). San Francisco: Jossey-Bass.

Chicago Public Schools. (2002). *Iowa test of basic skills: Citywide results over time, 1997–2002* (Report ITOT-CW-white). Chicago: Author. Available at http://research.cps. k12.il.us/resweb/pdf/itbs_over_read_a.p

Cohen, D. K. (1990). A revolution in one classroom. *Educational Evaluation and Policy Analysis, 12,* 327–345.

Cohen, D. K., & Ball, D. L. (1999). *Instruction, capacity, and improvement.* Philadelphia: Consortium for Policy Research in Education.

Cohen, D. K., & Spillane, J. P. (1993). Policy and practice: The relationship between governance and instruction. In S. H. Fuhrman (Ed.), *Designing coherent education policy: Improving the system* (pp. 35–95). San Francisco: Jossey-Bass.

Daft, R. L., & Weick, K. E. (1984). Toward a model of organizations as interpretation systems. *Academy of Management Review, 9*, 284–295.

Darling-Hammond, L. (1990). Teacher professionalism: Why and how? In A. Lieberman (Ed.), *Schools as collaborative cultures: Creating the future now* (pp. 25–50). Bristol, PA: Falmer Press.

Darling-Hammond, L. (1996). Restructuring schools for high performance. In S. Fuhrman & J. A. O'Day (Eds.), *Rewards and reform: Creating educational incentives that work* (pp. 144–192). San Francisco: Jossey-Bass.

Darling-Hammond, L., & Ascher, C. (1991). *Creating accountability in big city school systems* (Urban Diversity Series No. 102). New York: ERIC Clearinghouse on Urban Education.

DeBray, E., Parson, G., & Woodworth, K. (2001). Patterns of response in four high schools under state accountability policies in Vermont and New York. In S. Fuhrman (Ed.), *From the capitol to the classroom: Standards-based reform in the states* (pp. 170–192). Chicago: University of Chicago Press.

Elmore, R. F. (1996). Getting to scale with successful educational practices. In S. Fuhrman & J. A. O'Day (Eds.), *Rewards and reform: Creating educational incentives that work* (pp. 294–329). San Francisco: Jossey-Bass.

Elmore, R. F. (1997). *Investing in teacher learning: Staff development and instructional improvement in Community District 2*. Philadelphia: Consortium for Policy Research in Education and the National Commission on Teaching and America's Future.

Elmore, R. F. (2001, April). *Psychiatrists and light bulbs: Educational accountability and the problem of capacity*. Paper presented at the annual meeting of the American Educational Research Association, Seattle.

Elmore R. F., Abelmann, C. H., & Fuhrman, S. H. (1996). The new accountability in state education reform: From process to performance. In H. F. Ladd (Ed.), *Holding schools accountable: Performance-based reform in education* (pp. 65–98). Washington, DC: Brookings Institution.

Evans, L. E., & Wei, H. H. (2001, April). *Focusing the work of teachers and schools: The Chicago public schools probation policy*. Paper prepared for the annual meeting of the American Educational Research Association, Seattle.

Finnigan, K., O'Day, J., & Wakelyn, D. (2001). *Buddy, can you lend us a hand? The provision of external assistance to Chicago elementary schools on probation*. Chicago: Consortium on Chicago School Research.

Finnigan, K. S., & Gross, B. M. (2001, April). *Teacher motivation and the Chicago probation policy*. Paper presented at the annual meeting of the American Educational Research Association, Seattle.

Firestone, W. A., & Mayrowetz, D. (2000). Rethinking "high stakes": Lessons from the United States and England and Wales. *Teachers College Record, 102*, 724–749.

Fuhrman, S. H. (1999). *The new accountability* (CPRE Policy Brief No. RB 27). Philadelphia: Consortium on Policy Research in Education.

Goertz, M., Floden, R., & O'Day, J. (1995). *Studies of education reform: Systemic reform, volume 1. Findings and conclusions*. New Brunswick, NJ: Consortium for Policy Research in Education.

Grissmer, D., Flanagan, A., Kawata, J., & Williamson, S. (2000). *Improving student achievement: What state NAEP test scores tell us* (Report MR-924-EDU). Santa Monica, CA: RAND.

Gross, B., Wei, H., & O'Day, J. A. (2002). *Planning for improvement in Chicago schools on probation*. Unpublished report, University of Wisconsin–Madison.

Gwynne, J., & Easton, J. Q. (2001, April). *Probation, organizational capacity, and student achievement in Chicago elementary schools*. Paper presented at the annual meeting of the American Educational Research Association, Seattle.

Haney, W. (2000). The myth of the Texas miracle in education [Electronic version]. *Education Policy Analysis Archives, 8*(41). Available at http://epaa.asa.edu/epaa/v8n41/

Huber, G. P. (1991). Organizational learning: The contributing processes and the literatures. *Organizational Science, 2*, 1, 88–115.

Kaufmann, S. (1995). *At home in the universe: The search for the laws of self-organization and complexity*. New York: Oxford University Press.

Kelley, C., Odden, A, Milanowski, A., & Heneman, H. (2000). *The motivational effects of school-based performance awards* (CPRE Policy Brief No. RB-29). Philadelphia: Consortium for Policy Research in Education.

Kim, T. (2001, November 14). News in brief: Some Baltimore teachers set to receive extra pay [electronic version]. *Education Week*. Available at http://www.edweek.org/ew/newstory.cfm?slug=11briefs.h21

Klein, S. P., Hamilton, L. S., McCaffrey, D. F., & Stecher, B. M. (2000). *What do test scores in Texas tell us?* Washington, DC: RAND.

Koretz, D., & Barron, S. (1998). *The validity of gains on the Kentucky instructional results information system* (Report MR-1014-EDU). Santa Monica, CA: RAND.

Lee, V., & Smith, J. (1996). Collective responsibility for learning and its effects on gains in achievement for early secondary school students. *American Journal of Education, 104*, 103–147.

Levinthal, D. A. (1991). Organizational adaptation and environmental selection: Interrelated processes of change. *Organizational Science, 2*, 140–145.

Levitt, B., & March, J. G. (1988). Organizational learning. *Annual Review of Sociology, 14*, 319–340.

Lewin, R. (1992). *Complexity: Life at the edge of chaos*. New York: Macmillan.

Linn, R. L. (1997). Evaluating the validity of assessments: The consequences of use. *Educational Measurement: Issues and Practice, 16*, 2, 14–16.

Linn, R. L. (2001). *The design and evaluation of educational assessment and accountability systems* (CSE Technical Report). Los Angeles: University of California, Los Angeles, Center for Research on Evaluation, Standards, and Student Testing.

Little, J. W. (1990). The persistence of privacy: Autonomy and initiative in teachers' professional relations. *Teachers College Record, 91*, 509–536.

Lortie, D. C. (1975). *Schoolteacher: A sociological study*. Chicago: University of Chicago Press.

March, J. G. (1991). Exploration and exploitation in organizational learning. *Organizational Science, 2*(1), 71–87.

March, J. G. (1994). *A primer on decision making: How decisions happen*. New York: Free Press.

Marion, R. (1999). *The edge of organization: Chaos and complexity theories of formal social systems*. Thousand Oaks, CA: Sage.

McLaughlin, M. (1988) Learning from experience: Lessons from policy implementation. *Educational Evaluation and Policy Analysis, 9*, 171–178.

McLaughlin, M. W., & Shepard, L. A. (1995). *Improving education through standards-based reform: A report by the National Academy of Education Panel on Standards-Based Reform*. Stanford, CA: National Academy of Education.

McLaughlin, M. W., & Talbert, J. E. (1993). *Contexts that matter for teaching and learning*. Stanford, CA: Stanford University, School of Education, Center for Research on the Context of Teaching.

McLaughlin, M. W., & Talbert, J. E. (2001). *Professional communities and the work of high school teaching*. Chicago: University of Chicago Press.

Mohrman, S. A., & Lawler, E. E. (1996). Motivation for school reform. In S. H. Fuhrman & J. A. O'Day (Eds.), *Rewards and reform: Creating educational incentives that work* (pp. 115–143). San Francisco: Jossey-Bass.

National Governors' Association. (1993). *The debate on opportunity-to-learn standards: Supporting works*. Washington, DC: Author.

Newmann, F. M., & Wehlage, G. G. (1995) *Successful school restructuring: A report to the public and educators by the Center on Organization and Restructuring of Schools*. Madison, WI: Center on Organization and Restructuring of Schools.

Nolen, S. B., Haladyna, T. M., & Haas, N. (1992). Uses and abuses of achievement test scores. *Educational Measurement: Issues and Practice, 11*(2), 9–15.

O'Day, J. A. (1996). Incentives and school improvement. In S. Fuhrman & J. A. O'Day (Eds.), *Rewards and reform: Creating educational incentives that work* (pp. 1–16). San Francisco: Jossey-Bass.

O'Day, J., & Smith, M. S. (1993). Systemic school reform and educational opportunity. In S. H. Fuhrman (Ed.), *Designing coherent education policy: Improving the system* (pp. 250–312). San Francisco: Jossey Bass.

O'Reilly, F. E. (1996). *Educational accountability: Current practices and theories in use*. Cambridge, MA: Harvard University, Consortium for Policy Research in Education.

Porter, A., & Brophy, J. (1988). Good teaching: Insights from the work of the Institute for Research on Teaching. *Educational Leadership, 45*, 75–84.

Scott, W. R. (1998). *Organizations: Rational, natural, and open systems* (4th ed.). Upper Saddle River, NJ: Prentice Hall.

Senge, P. M. (1993). *The fifth discipline: The art and practice of the learning organization*. London: Century Business.

Simon, H. A. (1986). Theories of bounded rationality. In C. B. McGuire & R. Radner (Eds.), *Decision and organization: Volume 2* (pp. 161–176). Minneapolis: University of Minnesota Press.

Siskin, L. S. (in press). The challenge of the high schools. In S. H. Fuhrman & R. F. Elmore (Eds.), *Redesigning accountability systems*. New York: Teachers College Press.

Sitkin, S. B. (1992). Learning through failure: The strategy of small losses. *Research in Organizational Behavior, 14*, 231–266.

Smith, M. L., & Rottenberg, C. (1991). Unintended consequences of external testing in elementary schools. *Educational Measurement: Issues and Practice, 10*(4), 7–11.

Spillane, J. (2000). Cognition and policy implementation: District policy-makers and the reform of mathematics education. *Cognition and Instruction, 18*, 141–179.

Spillane, J. (2002). Local theories of teacher change: The pedagogy of district policies and programs. *Teachers College Record, 104*, 377–420.

Staw, B. M., Sanderlands, L. E., & Dutton, J. E. (1981). Threat-rigidity effects in organizational behavior: A multilevel analysis. *Administration Science Quarterly, 26*, 501–524.

Waldrop, M. M. (1992). *Complexity: The emerging science at the edge of order and chaos*. New York: Simon & Schuster.

Weatherly, R., & Lipsky, M. (1977) Street-level bureaucrats and institutional innovation: Implementing special-education reform. *Harvard Educational Review, 47*, 171–197.

Weick, K. (1976). Educational organizations as loosely coupled systems. *Administrative Science Quarterly, 21*, 1–19.

Westat. (2001). *Report on the final evaluation of the City-State Partnership*. Rockville, MD: Author.

About the Contributors

Alfredo J. Artiles is a professor in the College of Education at Arizona State University. His professional interests center on how constructions of "difference" mediate the response of educational systems to the needs of culturally and linguistically diverse students. His research examines the implications of the role of culture in learning for the construction of competence in special education placement practices and in teacher learning in urban multicultural schools. He is coeditor of *Reducing Disproportionate Representation of Culturally Diverse Students in Special and Gifted Education* (with G. Zamora-Durán, 1997). Artiles received the 2001 Early Career Award from the AERA Committee on Scholars of Color in Education.

Jim Cummins is a professor in the Department of Curriculum, Teaching, and Learning at the University of Toronto's Ontario Institute for Studies in Education. His research focuses on language and literacy development in educational contexts, with particular emphasis on the social and educational barriers that limit academic success for culturally diverse students. He is coeditor of *Lost for Words? How Technology Can Help Solve the "Literacy Crisis"* (with K. R. Brown and D. Sayers, in press) and author of *Language, Power, and Pedagogy: Bilingual Children in the Crossfire* (2000). In 1997, Cummins was awarded an Honorary Doctorate in Humane Letters from the Bank Street College of Education in New York City.

Lisa D. Delpit, executive director and eminent scholar at the Center for Urban Education and Innovation at Florida International University in Miami, is interested in improving urban education, particularly for children of color, and in the perspectives and aspirations of teachers of color. Her recent publications include *The Skin That We Speak: Thoughts on Language and Culture in the Classroom* (coedited with J. Kilgour Dowdy, 2003) and *The Real Ebonics Debate* (coedited with T. Perry, 1998). She received a MacArthur Fellowship in 1990 and the Horace Mann Humanity Award in 2003.

Pat English-Sand has been a public school inclusion coordinator and a teacher of students with significant disabilities for the past eighteen years. She is currently completing her doctorate in educational leadership at Syracuse University.

Linda May Fitzgerald is an associate professor of curriculum and instruction and a research fellow at the University of Northern Iowa's Regents' Center for Early Developmental Education. Her research is focused on constructivist education. Fitzgerald is the coauthor of "Disability, Schooling, and the Artifacts of Colonialism" in *Teachers College*

Record (with C. Kliewer, 2001), and of *Children at Home and in Day Care* (with K. Clarke-Stewart and C. Gruber, 1994).

Alan Gartner is chief of staff to the deputy mayor for policy in New York City. His areas of responsibility include the Department of Education and the City University of New York (CUNY). He has previously served as dean for research at the CUNY Graduate School and University Center, and as executive director of the Division of Special Education of the New York City Public Schools. With Dorothy Kerzner Lipsky, he is the coauthor of more than two score articles and four books. *Inclusion and School Reform: Transforming America's Schools* (1997) was cited as an "outstanding academic book" of the year by the American Library Association.

Patresa Hartman is a school psychologist with the Heartland Area Education Agency in Iowa, where she works with students in junior high and high school, and in an alternative secondary program. Her professional interests include teaching students with disabilities about their Individualized Educational Plans as a means to self-advocate.

Thomas Hehir is a professor of practice at the Harvard Graduate School of Education, where he directs the School Leadership Program. He is also a distinguished scholar at the Educational Development Center in Newton, Massachusetts. Hehir consults with a number of large school districts to help support their special education services and is an advocate for children with disabilities. He is coeditor of *Special Education at the Century's End: Evolution of Theory and Practice Since 1970* (with T. Latus, 1992). Hehir served as director of the U.S. Department of Education's Office of Special Education Programs from 1993 to 1999, playing a leading role in developing the Clinton administration's proposal for the 1997 reauthorization of the Individuals with Disabilities Education Act.

Christopher Kliewer is an associate professor of special education at the University of Northern Iowa. He teaches courses on inclusive education and conducts research on the literacy development of young children with significant disabilities. He is the author of "Literacy as Cultural Practice" in *Reading and Writing Quarterly* (2003), and *Schooling Children with Down Syndrome: Toward an Understanding of Possibility* (1998).

Dorothy Kerzner Lipsky is director and founder of the National Center on Educational Restructuring and Inclusion (NCERI) at the City University of New York's Graduate School and University Center. She has previously served as superintendent of schools in Riverhead, New York, and as chief administrator in the Division of Special Education, New York City Public Schools. With Alan Gartner, she is the coauthor of more than two score articles and four books. *Inclusion and School Reform: Transforming America's Schools* (1997) was cited as an "outstanding academic book" of the year by the American Library Association.

Jodi Meyer-Mork is currently completing a doctorate in curriculum and instruction at the University of Northern Iowa. She has previously worked as a special educator in the Cedar Falls (Iowa) Community School District. Her publications include "Walking the Labyrinth: Journey to Awareness" in *Journeys of Hope: Risking Self-Study in a Diverse World* (edited by D. Tidwell, L. M. Fitzgerald, and M. Heston, 2004).

Jennifer A. O'Day is a principal research scientist and policy analyst in the Education Program of the American Institutes for Research. She served previously as the associate director and a member of the Pew Forum on Standards-Based Reform. O'Day has carried out research and written extensively in the areas of systemic reform, educational equity, and capacity-building strategies. She has served with several national advisory groups, including most recently the Education Commission of the State's National Forum on Accountability. Her publications include *Rewards and Reform: Creating Educational Incentives That Work* (coedited with S. H. Fuhrman, 1996).

Donna Raschke is a professor of early childhood special education at the University of Northern Iowa. She coordinates the graduate education of early childhood teachers focused on inclusive schooling. Raschke's publications include "A Unified-Birth through Grade Three Early Childhood Endorsement: Challenges to the IHE Faculty Across Iowa" in *Teacher Education and Special Education* (with S. Maude, M. Brotherson, and P. Milburn, in press).

Timothy Reagan is dean of the School of Education and professor of linguistics at Roger Williams University in Bristol, Rhode Island. His areas of research include foreign language education, TESOL, applied and educational linguistics, and the linguistics of natural sign languages. He is coeditor of *Language in the 21st Century* (with H. Tonkin, 2003), and coauthor of *The Foreign Language Educator in Society: Toward a Critical Pedagogy* (with T. A. Osborn, 2002).

Thomas M. Skrtic is professor of special education and senior research scientist at the University of Kansas. His current academic interests are educational policy and leadership, democratic educational and social reform, and civic professionalism. He is coeditor of *Special Education Policy and Practice: Accountability, Instruction, and Social Challenges* (with K. Harris and J. Shriner, 2005), and editor of *Disability and Democracy: Reconstructing (Special) Education for Postmodernity* (1995).

About the Editors

Lauren I. Katzman is a consultant for the New York City Board of Education, providing research and evaluation services to support the improvement of the district's special education programs. She has done similar work in other large cities, including Washington, D.C. Katzman also provides professional development to school districts, and teaches special education courses at Brandeis University and for the Boston Teacher Residency Program. She earned her doctorate from the Harvard Graduate School of Education, where her research focused on the perspectives of students who have disabilities on their inclusion in high-stakes assessments. She served on the Board of the _Harvard Educational Review_, and also helped develop one of the first inclusive middle school programs in New York City.

Allison Gruner Gandhi is a doctoral student at the Harvard Graduate School of Education. Her research focuses on the impact inclusion has on the achievement of nondisabled children, and on the ways inclusion is defined in research, policy, and practice. Gruner also works as a consultant to school districts, providing research and evaluation services related to special education and other programs. Most of her work has been in large urban districts, including New York City and Washington, D.C. Gruner previously worked as a research analyst at the American Institutes for Research, where she conducted research and policy analysis for the U.S. Department of Education, and she served on the Board of the _Harvard Educational Review_.

Wendy S. Harbour is a doctoral student at the Harvard Graduate School of Education in the area of higher education administration and policy. Her research focuses on disability and the implementation of universal design in higher education settings. She has been a board member of the Postsecondary Education Programs Network and recently completed an international study of disability service providers for the Association on Higher Education and Disability. Harbour has worked as a disability specialist and research associate at the University of Minnesota and a project manager at CAST, Inc. She is coauthor of the sign language interpreter curriculum called "Charting the Way: A Handbook for Postsecondary Interpreters" and is editing an anthology of disabled college students' college experiences. She is currently on the Board of the _Harvard Educational Review_.

J. D. LaRock is a Presidential Fellow and doctoral student at the Harvard Graduate School of Education. He first became involved in disability issues in 1988, when his family founded My Friend's House, a neighborhood respite program in Queens, New York, for children and young adults with severe disabilities. LaRock was also a campus leader of

Best Buddies, the national organization that promotes friendships between college students and young adults with intellectual disabilities. He has served as a spokesperson for the New York City public school system, and covered K-12 and higher education as an on-air reporter for NY1, a television news channel. He has worked as the Senior Education Fellow at the U.S. Conference of Mayors in Washington, D.C., and is a current Board member of the *Harvard Educational Review.*